CITIZENSHIP, EUROPE AND CHANGE

Also by Paul Close

*FAMILY AND ECONOMY IN MODERN SOCIETY (*co-editor with R. Collins*)
*FAMILY DIVISIONS AND INEQUALITIES IN MODERN SOCIETY (*editor*)
*THE STATE AND CARING (*editor*)

**Also published by Palgrave Macmillan*

Citizenship, Europe and Change

Paul Close
*Senior Lecturer in Social Science, School of European Studies,
and Director of the Centre for European Social Research (CESR),
University of Derby*

© Paul Close 1995

All rights reserved. No reproduction, copy or transmission of this publication may be made without written permission.

No paragraph of this publication may be reproduced, copied or transmitted save with written permission or in accordance with the provisions of the Copyright, Designs and Patents Act 1988, or under the terms of any licence permitting limited copying issued by the Copyright Licensing Agency, 90 Tottenham Court Road, London W1P 9HE.

Any person who does any unauthorised act in relation to this publication may be liable to criminal prosecution and civil claims for damages.

First published 1995 by
MACMILLAN PRESS LTD
Houndmills, Basingstoke, Hampshire RG21 2XS
and London
Companies and representatives
throughout the world

ISBN 978-0-333-62831-7   ISBN 978-1-349-23780-7 (eBook)
DOI 10.1007/978-1-349-23780-7

A catalogue record for this book is available
from the British Library.

10 9 8 7 6 5 4 3 2 1
04 03 02 01 00 99 98 97 96 95

To Emiko

Contents

	List of Tables	viii
	Acknowledgements	ix
	Introduction	x
1	Towards a Framework for Analysing Modern European Citizenship	1
2	Citizenship, the State, the Nation-state and Nationality	55
3	Citizenship, Migration, Asylum and Race-ethnicity	97
4	Citizenship, Social Change and the Individual	138
5	Individualism, Citizenship and the European Union	187
6	Citizenship and the European Supra-state	231
	Notes	299
	Bibliography	316
	Index	327

List of Tables

1.1	Age of Consent to Engage in Homosexual Acts (end of June 1993)	26
1.2	Lone Parent Families in the European Community, 1992	38
5.1	Rank-order of Welfare States in Terms of Decommodification	202

Acknowledgements

The author wishes to thank the following for their valuable support during the preparation of this book: Paul Bingham, John Brennan, Dominique Davison, Bob Faithorn, Robert Hudson, Paul Stirling and Gwen Wallace.

Introduction

The issues encapsulated in the title *Citizenship, Europe and Change* have long attracted extensive popular, policy and scholastic attention. But, as the twentieth century draws to a close, they have been injected with enhanced interest by a set of major historical events that have had not only European-wide, but also world-wide ramifications. We have witnessed what is commonly celebrated as the advent of a 'new world order', marking the end of the 'Cold War', the 'collapse of communism' and the Eastern Bloc; and so the victory or vindication of the Western, liberal-democratic, capitalist way of life and way forward. A symbol and beneficiary of these events has been the progress and appeal of the *European Community and Union*, with its promise of European integration and unification, prosperity and security, and strength and resurgence – economically, socially and politically. The prospect is in place of the European Community and Union evolving as a twenty-first-century super-power *and* supra-power: as both a rival on the world stage to the United States, Japan, China or whatever; and a supra-state, marking and hastening the demise of the nation-state.

Such possibilities have far-reaching implications for all aspects, levels and corners of European society, and thus for the people of Europe. Apart from anything else, the confirmation of a European supra- (perhaps federal) state would have considerable consequences for people's everyday lives, relationships and experiences through the part it would necessarily play in shaping the status, the rights and (most important) the realisation of *citizenship*. The eventual ratification of the Maastricht Treaty has established the European Union and introduced Citizenship of the Union, and so has brought European Supra-citizenship, even though for the time being merely in a rudimentary form. The further development and impact of the European Union's own superordinate category and tier of citizenship may emerge as a focal point for people's judgements, demands and struggles with regard to the Union; as a test of the worth, stature and strength of the

Union; as a challenge for the institutions, policies and policy-makers of the Union; as a device for consolidating the Union; and furthermore as a laboratory for critically examining and further refining sociological ideas, insights and theory. The following chapters are meant to make a contribution to the task of handling the intellectual and practical problems thrown up around European citizenship *and citizens* at this pivotal moment in European history.

1 Towards a Framework for Analysing Modern European Citizenship

In this first chapter I will begin to clarify a notion of *citizenship* which seems to me to be helpful to the sociological task of studying and making sense of *modern citizenship*, especially in the context of late-twentieth-century European social change around the evolution of the European Community and Union. There will be no attempt to present a complete survey of *the concept of citizenship*.[1] Instead, references will be confined to a selection of influential and instructive notions for guidance as to a sociologically appropriate and analytically useful approach. As we will see, this exercise reveals a set of common (but not always universal) conceptual features, including:

(a) citizenship is a status and a set of rights;
(b) citizenship is a relationship;
(c) citizenship is, first of all, a relationship with the state;
(d) citizenship is basically a legal relationship;
(e) citizenship as a legal relationship provides capacities which may not be readily, fully and equally realised owing to interference from prevailing societal inequalities of condition and opportunity;
(f) citizenship is a multi-stranded relationship, being not just legal, but also political, economic, and otherwise social;
(g) citizenship, being a relationship with the state, brings people into citizenship relations with each other;
(h) citizenship relations are power relations;
(i) citizenship relations are characterised by process and change;
(j) citizenship relations occur to some extent between people within and through collectivities (and thereby between collectivities), but citizenship *per se* is always an *individual* relationship;

(k) essentially, citizenship is an *internally oriented* relationship which people as individuals have with the nation-state of which they have full formal membership by virtue of their enjoyment of the full range of citizenship rights granted, guaranteed or enforced by the state.

For me, the *individualistic* character of citizenship is of the utmost social importance and sociological significance, judged in terms of its social, economic, political, ideological and theoretical ramifications, and therefore emerges as a principal focus of attention of the ensuing discussion. An examination of citizenship as an *individual* relationship provides a convenient vehicle for elucidating further major conceptual, socially important and sociologically significant features. A striking impression to emerge from an examination of notions of citizenship – legal, sociological, popular[2] – is the way they either explicitly or implicitly assign the status of 'citizenship' specifically to people, and moreover to people as individuals, as distinct from collectivities and organisations.

For example, the United Kingdom's Commission on Citizenship, appointed by the Speaker of the House of Commons in December 1988, is, in its final *Report*, unequivocal about defining citizenship in terms of 'the status and entitlements of … individuals', and thereby of 'the rights of individuals' (Commission on Citizenship, 1990, p. xv). The Commission emphatically asserts that citizenship rights: '*are necessarily individual.* "Although a limited company or charitable foundation … can epitomise and espouse the characteristics of citizenship, neither can enjoy citizenship. Only a single human being can claim whatever it is that is citizenship"' (ibid., pp. 6–7; italics as in original).[3]

The approach to citizenship whereby the rights entailed are invariably attached to individuals rather than to collectivities or organisations of whatever kind is supported by J. P. Gardner in his summary of 'What Lawyers Mean by Citizenship' at the end of the Commission's *Report*.[4] Thus:

Citizenship is an attribute of individuals as members of a political body, but the rules which establish that body and the relationship of individuals to it are legal rules. It is therefore necessary to take account of the rules which make up the legal relationship between individuals and the State which together identify the legal attributes of citizenship. (Ibid., p. 63)

Following Gardner, from a legal perspective, citizenship is a status occupied exclusively by individuals; it is a status to which are attached legal (citizenship) rights; and it is a status through which individuals *qua individuals* sustain a legal relationship with *the state* – with the set of political institutions which lie at the core of the *nation-state*. This approach leads Gardner to clarify further the legal notion of citizenship by drawing two basic distinctions: first, between 'citizenship' and 'nationality' (ibid., pp. 64–5); and second, between 'nationality citizenship' and 'new citizenship' (ibid., pp. 63–4). These distinctions are legally, practically and sociologically important, and I will return to them shortly.

For now, I will pursue in further detail the theme and ramifications of the individualistic character of citizenship. Sociologists and other social scientists (loosely interpreted) who have written on the topic of citizenship have been inclined, like lawyers (following Gardner), to adopt an individualistic approach to the notion. Garry Wickham summarises this tendency by telling us that citizenship is 'a device ... which assumes individuality and operates through and on individuals, citizenship cannot operate through and on organisations' (Wickham, 1993, p. 2). The (any) sociological notion of citizenship is about, at least in the first instance, the status, categorisation and identity of people as individuals. It is not about, except consequentially or derivatively, the status, categorisation and identity of collectivities or organisations (groups, associations, corporations or whatever). This individualistic approach to citizenship can be illustrated with reference to a range of scholarly writings, including those with a feminist orientation. For instance, as Claire Wallace asserts, 'Citizenship is of fundamental importance to everyone because it defines an individual's legal, political and social relationship to the society of which they form part' (Wallace, 1993, p. 1).[5]

However, it is precisely the individualistic orientation of citizenship (conceptually, legalistically, ideologically, practically) which has attracted criticisms and objections from feminist writers. As Wallace puts it, the concept of citizenship[6] has been challenged by feminist writers, whose

> critique focuses on the fact that because women are dependents they are not citizens in the same way as men – they are citizens only through their husbands who claim [social welfare] benefits and pay taxes on behalf of the family. Lister (1990) argues that full social citizenship [through welfare rights, benefits and services] must recognise women's position as carers within the family in order to be universal and Summers (1991) argues that the idea has been defined in male terms – most of the rights for men were not won for women until much later. Thus, in England women could not vote until the twentieth century, married women could not own property or take jobs without their husbands' permission until the late nineteenth century and even now their access to social welfare depends in some instances upon their relationship to a man. The concept ... assumes a free, individualistic competitor, a model which women with dependents cannot meet.

> Despite the struggles for women to be accepted as equal citizens with men over the past 150 years, women are still in practice unable to participate equally with men in the economic, political and civil spheres because they are mainly responsible for children. It follows, therefore, that a welfare state commitment to providing full citizenship rights for women needs also to make some provision to see that these are attainable.   (Summers, 1991, p. 24)

> [As it stands], citizenship is a male-defined concept... (Wallace, 1993, pp. 3–4)[7]

For Wallace, the concept of citizenship, including its individualist orientation, reflects and reinforces a particular pattern of citizenship relations between men and women in modern society. This pattern, while characterised by the universal provision of citizenship rights, is marked also by an unequal distribution of (what I will refer to as) *enabling resources*, of associated distributions of power, control and independence, and consequently of the *realisation* of citizenship rights. Men's greater possession of and access to enabling resources and power bring greater independence and thereby opportunity to *realise* formally equal citizenship rights. This greater opportunity consolidates men's greater possession of and access to resources and power, and in turn brings greater influence and control over citizenship, with both its individualistic orientation and its male-oriented range and disposition of rights. The kind and allocation of rights which constitute citizenship in modern society underpins women's relative dependency (compared with men) and relational dependency (on men, in the interests of men). In other words, women's disadvantage is confirmed by the combined effect of the *male-biased content* combined with the *individualistic form* of citizenship.

Claire Wallace's definition of citizenship finds echoes in the more elaborate notion presented by Rainer Baubock:

> As a starting point I suggest the following definition: citizenship designates a political status of individuals as well as a particular quality of a political system. As a normative concept citizenship is a set of rights, exercised by individuals who hold the rights, equal for all citizens, and universally distributed within a political community, as well as a corresponding set of institutions guaranteeing these rights. (Baubock, 1991, p. 28)

Baubock tells us that the 'two most fundamental principles mentioned in the [normative] definition are egalitarianism and universalism', but adds how 'we have to recognise that some systems have embraced these principles, while severely limiting their application' (ibid., p. 29). Accordingly, Baubock urges us to distinguish between the *normative concept* of citizenship and any 'analytical definition' (ibid., pp. 29–30). Baubock's concern is to formulate an analytical definition because his focus is 'on different statuses of citizenship for different categories of individuals' (ibid., p. 29) within the *limited systems* of, what he refers to as, 'the real world communities' (ibid., p. 30).

Baubock's definition of citizenship not only underscores the individualistic orientation of the notion (approached normatively or analytically), but also confirms the social science tendency to specify citizenship as a status which qualifies individuals for a certain set of legal rights which are, at the same time, necessarily political rights. They are political rights in that they are (a) sought, acquired and realised by people within a *political community*; while (b) being granted and guaranteed or enforced by the set of political institutions which constitute the core of that political community, or the set of institutions which is otherwise referred to (by Gardner, for instance) as the state.[8] Here, the point is being touched on that citizenship brings people into political relations through the way citizenship is primarily a relationship which people have with the state. The political relations thereby established may be characterised by an unequal distribution of (political) power, independence and *individuality*, such as in the case of (following Wallace) the political relations between men and women in modern society. This political inequality then ensures the everyday, practical unequal realisation of formally equal citizenship rights. The set of political institutions with which people have citizenship relationships by virtue of the granting and guaranteeing of formally equal citizenship rights turns out to be instrumental in helping to produce and reproduce such gender inequality. The male-biased content and individualistically oriented form of citizenship is politically rooted in and politically serves the political power advantages of men within and through the state (in support of such views, see, for instance, Bornat et al., 1993; Close, 1989, 1992; Dalley, 1988; Showstack Sassoon, 1987; Ungerson, 1985; Williams, 1989).

The approaches of Baubock and Wallace, among other social scientists, are consistent with the principal features of what is widely regarded as *the classic* notion of citizenship as formulated by T. H. Marshall. For Marshall, citizenship is

> a status bestowed on all those who are full members of a community. All who possess the status are equal with respect to the rights and duties with which that status is endowed... Citizenship [accompanies] a ... community ... of free men [sic] endowed with rights and protected by common law. (Marshall, 1950, pp. 28–9 and 40–1)

Marshall argued that citizenship has three elements: the civil, the political and the social. These three distinct types of statutory right have been sequentially developed (at least in Britain) over the course of three centuries: civil rights in the eighteenth century, political rights in the nineteenth century, and social rights in the twentieth century. Each type of right emerged in conjunction with a corresponding set of political (state) institutions. Marshall clarifies:

> The civil element is composed of the rights necessary for individual freedom – liberty of the person, freedom of speech, thought and faith, the right to own property and to conclude valid contracts, and the right to justice.... The institutions most directly associated with civil rights are the courts of justice. By the political element I mean the right to participate in the exercise of political power, as a member of a body invested with political authority or as an elector of the members of such a body. The corresponding institutions are Parliament and councils of local government. By the social element I mean the whole range from the right to a modicum of economic welfare and security to the right to share to the full in the social heritage and to live the life of a civilised being according to the standards prevailing in a society. The institutions most closely connected with it are the education system and the social services. (Marshall, 1950, pp. 10–11)

However, while numerous writers covering various disciplines and perspectives support the view that citizenship is an individualistic notion, there is far from complete consensus over the issue. There appear to be some notable dissenting voices, including that of J. M. Barbalet (1988). Barbalet seems not to accept that citizenship rights are exclusively attached to individuals, but claims instead that citizenship rights can be attached to and exercised by collectivities and organisations. For Barbalet, this seems to apply to what he distinguishes as a fourth element of citizenship, that of *industrial citizenship rights*. Barbalet presents his argument in this regard in the course of examining various general features of *modern citizenship* while assessing T. H. Marshall's analysis.

Barbalet describes his book as being about citizenship in the sense of that which 'defines those who are, and who are not, members of a common society' (ibid., p. 1). Loosely speaking, citizenship in general 'can be readily described as participation in or membership of a community' (ibid., p. 2). But, Barbalet notes, the particular characteristics of citizenship vary in socially important ways across time. For instance:

> The chief difference between citizenship in the classical Greek city-state and the modern democratic national-state is the extent or scope of the political community in each. [In the former,] citizenship was the privileged status of the ruling group of the city-state. In the modern democratic state the basis of citizenship is the capacity to participate in the exercise of political power through the electoral process. Thus participation by citizens in the modern nation-state entails legal membership of a political community based on universal suffrage and therefore also membership of a civil community based on the rule of law [so that] today national citizenship extends across society. The expansion of citizenship in the modern state [or, that is, the] generalization of modern citizenship across the social structure means that all persons as citizens are equal before the law and therefore no person or group is legally privileged.　(Ibid., p. 2)[9]

What Barbalet has in mind here is the way modern society is marked by, relatively speaking, the extension of citizenship 'across the lines dividing unequal classes'. This extension legally allows 'those disadvantaged by the class system' to participate in the modern nation-state by virtue of their inclusion as members of the political community and civil community. However, this does not by itself facilitate 'the practical ability to exercise the rights or legal capacities which constitute the status of citizen'. In other words, continuing social class inequalities intervene between the possession of citizenship rights (entitlements, capacities) and the realisation of such rights, ensuring that *the disadvantaged* 'are unable to practically participate in the community of citizenship in which they have legal membership' (ibid., p. 2).

But, while Barbalet's qualification of his claim about the *generalization of modern citizenship* may be appropriate, it is by no means adequate. It is not so much that his qualification fails to cover the way not just social-class inequalities, but also sex-gender, race-ethnicity and age-generation inequalities intervene between the possession and the realisation of citizenship rights. It is more that it is inaccurate to suggest that *all persons* in the *modern nation-state* are *equal before the law* so that *no person or group is legally privileged*. In particular, the possession of citizenship status is an attained status following a process during which citizenship rights are acquired or achieved over the early part of the life-cycle on the way to adulthood. In the modern nation-state, children (and adolescents) remain unequal and underprivileged relative to adults *before the law*, and remain excluded from modern citizenship – at least in the sense of possessing the full range of citizenship rights, including those political rights which for Barbalet provide the basis of modern citizenship.

The way children are denied citizenship rights enjoyed by adults – and are therefore excluded from (full) membership of and participation in (adult) society – can be demonstrated by examining the process through which children acquire such rights as they progress towards adulthood. The process whereby children gradually acquire citizenship rights and eventually achieve citizenship can be illustrated with reference to any modern society. In Britain, for example, children begin to accumulate citizenship rights at the age of five years, when they acquire the right to see certain categories (U and PG) of films at the cinema unaccompanied; as well as the right to consume alcoholic drinks in private, such as at home. At the age of seven, children acquire citizenship rights concerned with banking: they can open and draw money from a National Savings account, and they can do the same with respect to a Trustees Savings Bank account ('Rights: Young at Heart', *Guardian*, 5 January 1993).

The way childhood is distinguished and separated from adulthood by the denial of citizenship rights is underscored by the way children are, none the less, expected and liable to meet various legal requirements and responsibilities, which are similarly accumulated during the process of attaining adulthood. That is, while children are liable to meet a gathering and more demanding range of what may be regarded as adult requirements and responsibilities, they are also denied a range (albeit a gradually decreasing one) of adult rights, including ones with considerable personal and social importance, right up to the point at which they make the final transition to adulthood. In Britain, from the age of five, children are required to be formally educated or *schooled* (perhaps at home and by their parents) in a statutorily approved fashion, hence the application of the label 'compulsory school age' (ibid.). In addition, from the same age, children are required to pay fares on public transport such as trains, buses and tubes (ibid.).

Perhaps the most important event in this regard prior to people's final attainment of adulthood in Britain – or more precisely in England and Wales – occurs at the age of ten (and in Scotland at the age of eight). From the age of ten, children 'can be convicted of a criminal offence if it is proved the young person knew what s/he was doing was wrong' (ibid.). At this age, therefore, children reach the *age of criminal responsibility*, as clarified more fully by Heather Tyrell and Grania Langdon-Down:

> Ten is the youngest age at which a child can be charged with any crime in England and Wales [eight in Scotland]. Below that age, the law considers children are not aware of the consequences of their actions. The age of criminal responsibility was set at 10 in the 1962 Children and Young Persons Act. A clause in the 1969 Act raised the age of criminality to 14, but it was never implemented... . The Home Office said that between 10 and 14, a child is presumed not to know the difference between right and wrong and is therefore incapable of committing an offence. For a child to be tried between those ages, the prosecution must prove that at the relevant time he or she knew that what they were doing was seriously wrong and not just naughty or mischievous. (Tyrell and Langdon-Down, 21 February 1993)

In more legalistically precise terms, David Barker and Colin Padfield tell us:

> There is an irrebuttable presumption that a child under ten cannot commit a crime. If a child is between ten and fourteen there is a rebuttable presumption that he [sic] cannot do so; but the prosecution can rebut this by evidence of 'mischievous discretion', i.e. that he knows that what he was doing was gravely wrong... . The criminal liability of children over fourteen is the same as for adults. (Barker and Padfield, 1992, p. 319)

Here is an illustration of how children who have reached the age of criminal responsibility, and therefore a major watershed on the way to adulthood, are none the less – in recognition of their continuing childhood – given *protection* through the provision of legal privileges, special legal rights which, as with the denial of (adult) citizenship rights, help to distinguish childhood from adulthood. The protective rights enjoyed by children represent what may be otherwise called 'compensatory rights', in that they are intended specifically to give protection to those who are regarded as having been rendered vulnerable by virtue of being denied citizenship rights:

> Not all rights and not even all legal rights are citizenship rights... Marshall (1950: 81) ... demonstrates that the provision of certain rights is precisely to compensate those who are excluded from the status of citizenship. Citizenship is a status bestowed on those who are full members of a national community, and citizenship rights, therefore, are those which derive from and facilitate participation in this 'common possession', as Marshall (1950: 92) calls it. (Barbalet, 1988, p. 18)

In the United Kingdom along with other modern societies, children enjoy special legal rights, ones which do not merely set childhood apart from adulthood, but which are designed to protect children from adulthood and adults. Such protective rights are, at the same time, compensatory rights, non-citizenship rights designed to compensate for the denial of citizenship rights. These rights serve to confirm the way children are excluded from citizenship, or, that is, full membership of a national community, perhaps in major ways, while none the less being subjected to the kind of legal liabilities, requirements and responsibilities which help characterise and distinguish adulthood.

Children enjoy various distinctive protective, compensatory, non-citizenship rights at various points within criminal and judicial proceedings. Thus, also in contrast with adults:

> Children taken into police custody must have an appropriate adult, such as a parent, guardian, social worker or lay volunteer, with them when they are being questioned to

look after the child's physical and emotional welfare. This is required under the 1984 Police and Criminal Evidence act, which includes codes of practice to safeguard the rights and civil liberties of 10 to 17-year-olds.   (Tyrell and Langdon-Down, 1993)

Even after being charged with a criminal offence, the treatment of children is somewhat (and has become increasingly) different from that of adults. As Tyrell and Langdon-Down report, 'under recent guidelines, it is usual that a child is released into the hands of social services and kept in a children's home – under security if required' (ibid.). Similarly, although children

> (i.e. persons under 14) and young persons (i.e. persons over the age of 14 and under 17 years) are as a general rule tried in a Juvenile Court by magistrates, if the case is a serious indictable offence, e.g. homicide, the child or young person will usually be committed for trial at the Crown Court. No person under 17 may be sent to Prison, however. Other institutions, e.g. Borstal, Community Homes and Detention Centres, are used for custodial treatment and punishment. (Barker and Padfield, 1992, p. 99)

When a child or a young person (a juvenile) is convicted of a serious crime

> such as murder, manslaughter, arson or rape [he or she is] dealt with under Section 53 of the 1933 Children and Young Persons Act. Part 1 governs those convicted of murder, which has a mandatory life sentence. Part 2 provides for terms of detention, up to the adult maximum, for those below the age of 17 convicted of any offence attracting an adult sentence 14 years or more, including attempted murder, manslaughter, wounding with intent, rape or arson. After their eighteenth birthday, the person would go on to a young offenders institution before being moved to an adult prison at 21.   (Tyrell and Langdon-Down, 1993)

When children are found guilty of homicide, they can be detained '"during Her Majesty's pleasure" for a specific period – including a life sentence' ('Rights: Young at Heart',

Guardian, 5 January 1993). However, children who have been convicted of murder[10] (among other serious crimes such as rape) are still protected at the point of incarceration, in recognition of their continuing childhood, by the legal privilege of not being required to serve their sentences in an adult prison, at least until they reach the age of twenty-one.

Essentially, despite legal (compensatory) privileges and protection compared with and in relation to adulthood, childhood is still characterised and distinguished by a gradual accumulation of legal liabilities, requirements and responsibilities, alongside being a stage within the life-cycle during which people are denied legal, including citizenship, rights. Some of the citizenship rights denied to children are undoubtedly more important personally and socially than others, but even the less important ones serve to confirm the highly complex, and perhaps somewhat contradictory, manner in which people progress through childhood to adulthood in modern Britain. For instance, even though a child reaches the age of criminal responsibility at ten years, he or she does not have the right to buy a pet animal before reaching the age of twelve.

Also at the age of 12, children acquire the legal right to 'be trained to participate in dangerous public entertainments subject to the grant of a local authority licence' ('Rights: Young at Heart', *Guardian*, 5 January 1993), even though it is not until a couple of years later that children begin to acquire the legal rights whereby they are eligible for paid employment. It is not until the age of thirteen that children 'can get a part-time job, [albeit with] restrictions – for example, [they] cannot work for more than two hours on a school day or a Sunday'. This is followed at the age of fourteen by the acquisition of the right, 'subject to local authority byelaws, [to] be employed on a weekday as a street trader by ... parents'. A child's fourteenth birthday also brings with it the rights to 'go into a pub, [albeit without being able to] buy or drink alcohol there', as well as to 'possess a shotgun, air gun, air rifle or ammunition'. On the other hand, from the age of fourteen, 'a boy can be convicted of rape, assault with intent to commit rape and unlawful sexual intercourse with a girl under 16'. Also in a gender-specific way, from the age of fifteen, 'a boy ... can be sent to prison to await trial'. On the other hand, from the age of fifteen, a child 'can see a category 15 film' at the cinema, and 'can open a Post Office Girobank account, [albeit with] a guarantor – someone who will be liable for [any] debts' the child may incur (ibid.).

The age of 16 brings with it a number of personally and socially important rights. At this age, people acquire the rights to leave school, and to marry with parental consent (or without in Scotland). Also, females acquire the right to consent to sexual intercourse (the *age of consent* was established at 12 years in 1275, was raised to 13 years in 1875 and then to 16 years in 1885); males are allowed to join the armed forces with parental consent; and people 'are allowed to enter or live in a brothel' (ibid.). From the same age, people are allowed to drink beer, cider or wine with a meal in a restaurant; to buy cigarettes and tobacco; to drive an invalid carriage or a moped; and to become a street trader. On the other hand, if convicted of a prisonable offence, a person 'can be given a community service order' (ibid.). From the age of seventeen, criminal charges against people are dealt with in the adult courts; people 'can hold a licence to drive most vehicles', and people 'can buy or hire any firearm or ammunition' (ibid.). It is then one year later that people gain a set of legal rights which vies with the set gained at the age of sixteen as the most important on the way to the attainment of adulthood, full membership of (adult) *society*, and citizenship. At the age of eighteen people are allowed to 'buy and drink alcohol in a bar' (ibid.); 'to serve on a jury'; 'to vote in general and local elections' (following the Representation of the People Act, 1969, when the voting age for parliamentary and local elections was reduced to eighteen years and over from twenty-one years and over); to 'make a valid will' (Barker and Padfield, 1992, p. 100); to open a bank account or Post Office Girobank account without a parent's signature; and to get married even without parental consent.

There are restrictions on property rights before people reach the age of eighteen years. As Barker and Padfield put it: 'A minor may own all kinds of personal or moveable property, but he cannot ... legally own land (Law of Property Act, 1925, s. 19)' (Barker and Padfield, 1992, p. 100). Here, the term 'a minor' is significant in that at the age of eighteen people reach 'the age of majority', becoming *an adult in the eyes of the law*. That is, 'Section 1(1) of the Family Reform Act, 1969, provides that as from 1 January 1970, a person "shall attain full age on attaining the age of eighteen instead of attaining the age of twenty-one'" (ibid., p. 99). Reaching the age of majority is of considerable personal and social importance in that it brings release from legally sanctioned parental authority and control. This marks a major step in adult–child (and especially parent–child) relations, being that point at which people become *legal adults*.

However, the line of demarcation between childhood and adulthood is by no means as clear-cut as the existence of legal adulthood may be taken to indicate. Some commentators have argued that in the United Kingdom the line has been weakened by the Children Act (passed 1989; came into force October 1992), which it is claimed has substantially reduced parental rights, authority and so power in relation to children. For instance, Gerison Lansdown[11] tells us:

> Traditionally in our society ... children are viewed as the property of their parents.... [Accordingly,] the dominating feature of childhood is that of powerlessness and lack of control over what happens to them [sic]. [Adults] perceive children as essentially irrational, irresponsible and incapable of making informed choices on matters of concern to them and to a large extent our legislation still reflects this view – the Children Act being the notable exception. (Lansdown, 1993, pp. 1–2)

The Children act has been described by Fiona Millar as

> the most important reform affecting children to have been passed for many years. The whole statute applies in England and Wales and parts of it apply in Scotland and Northern Ireland.... The new statute covers the care for, bringing up and protection of children. It deals with what may happen to children when parents separate or divorce and with the intervention of a local authority if a child has suffered or is likely to suffer significant harm. Central to the act is the belief that children, classed as boys and girls under 18, are generally best looked after in their families. [However, in] court proceedings the welfare of the child is the most important factor. The child's wishes must be given a high priority but the court will decide what is in the child's best interests. A novel feature of the Act is that children may bring proceedings on their own

behalf [such as against parents with whom they do not wish to live]. Before a child's case can proceed the court must give its permission for the application to be brought. The magistrate or judge will decide whether the child has sufficient understanding of what is involved: they will not allow frivolous applications to be made. (Millar, 1993)

The Children Act (1989) has established children's right to be consulted as to their wishes when decisions are being made about what counts as and what is conducive to their welfare and interests during certain judicial proceedings, including those concerned with parental separation and divorce. Consequently, children have been granted the right to be consulted over where and with whom – which parent – they wish to live. This right to be consulted, moreover, extends to children being allowed to seek a court's permission to initiate judicial proceedings with a view to being able to live with their own choice of parent or guardian. That is, as Lansdown tells us,

> The Children Act in England and Wales incorporates the principle ... that children's wishes [be] considered when decisions which affect them are being made. The recent cases of children applying to court for judgements about where they live and who with are positive examples of the application of this right ... to have their views heard by the judicial system. (Lansdown, 1993, p. 6)

Thus:

> Three recent so-called 'child divorce' cases have been brought by girls: a 14-year-old wanted to live with her boyfriend's parents because she did not get on with her father;[12] a girl of 15 applied to live with her grandparents rather than her mother; and an 11-year-old wished to live with her former foster parents and not with her mother because she objected to her mother's boyfriend. (Millar, 1993)

More recently, as Claire Dyer reports:

> A 13-year-old girl, thought to be the first adopted child to invoke the Children Act in an attempt to leave her parents,

will tomorrow appeal against a High Court order making her a ward of court. The case, to be heard in the Court of Appeal, highlights the conflict between wardship, under which children have few rights, and the six-month-old act, which allows young people who are deemed to be of sufficient understanding to hire a solicitor, obtain legal aid, and make a court application. [The] act's intention [is that] of giving children the right to a say in their upbringing. Wards of court cannot instruct solicitors or make applications for court orders. They are represented by the Official Solicitor, who must report the child's views to the court, but may recommend a different course of action. The teenager fell out with her adoptive parents, and was put into voluntary care by them. For the past year she has lived with foster parents, but wants to live with her natural father's parents, with whom she kept in touch after she was adopted. (Dyer, 1993)

It seems to me, however, that Lansdown's view of the implications of the Children Act for children's *power* in their relations with parents and other adults is somewhat optimistic. The *right to be consulted* granted under the Children Act is very limited in what it allows children. It is a largely inconsequential right when judged in terms of its effect on the legally constituted authority and control – the power – which adults retain in relation to and over children. Children's *right to be consulted* during certain judicial proceedings preserves (not to say confirms and consolidates) adults' legal right to make decisions about, on behalf of and for children – about what counts as and is conducive to the welfare and interests of children – whatever children's expressed opinions and wishes.

The Children Act has redistributed decision-making power with regard to children's welfare and interests not so much in a vertical direction from adults to children themselves, as in a horizontal direction, from one set of adults to another, and especially from parents to magistrates and judges. While the Children Act may mean some redistribution of legally based decision-making power within parent–child relationships, it does not mean the same within adult–child relationships. Children have not gained the legal right to make decisions about and for themselves independent of adult intervention. Adults have retained the right to make decisions about and on behalf of children. The Children Act (in merely establishing the right of children to be consulted) has not weakened, but has if anything confirmed and consolidated, the legally based power-imbalance between adults and children. To paraphrase Lansdown: *the dominating feature of childhood for children remains that of powerlessness and a lack of control over what happens to them.*

The perception of children which persists in sustaining this power imbalance – the view of children as (again to paraphrase Lansdown) *incapable of making informed, independent choices on matters of concern to them* – is not only noted by Lansdown, but also endorsed by her. Lansdown prescribes what she refers to as a 'protective model of adult relationships towards children' on the grounds that 'children are vulnerable', their 'vulnerability [being] twofold'. She distinguishes between 'inherent vulnerability' and 'structural vulnerability' (Lansdown, 1993, pp. 2–3), clarifying what she means by the former in the following manner:

> The very fact of their physical weakness, immaturity, lack of knowledge and experience renders children dependent upon adults around them... . Clearly the degree of vulnerability diminishes rapidly as they grow older and become better able to exercise responsibility themselves. (Ibid., p. 3)

It is on the grounds of their assumed *inherent vulnerability* that children are denied a range of legal rights, including the citizenship right to make decisions about and for themselves in an independent way – independent, that is, of the determining intervention of (seemingly inherently capable and responsible) adults.[13] In the United Kingdom, despite – and perhaps to some extent because of – the Children Act, childhood may still be distinguished from adulthood around the point at which people attain the *age of majority* and become *legal adults* through (a) the absence and denial of citizenship rights on the part of children, including the right of independent decision-making with regard to their own welfare; and (b) the enjoyment of citizenship rights on the part of adults, including both (i) the right of independent decision-making with regard to their own welfare, and (ii) the right of decision-making with regard to others', specifically children's, welfare.

The ideological assumption that children are inherently vulnerable, combined with children's resulting lack of citizenship rights to engage in independent decision-making, becomes the rationale for the provision and imposition of childhood-specific, compensatory, protective rights. People below the age of majority enjoy legal rights to be protected from (a) adults and adult society, as well as from (b) what is claimed by adults to be their (children's) own inherent vulnerability. Children are ostensibly protected from these things by adults – in the guise of parents, magistrates and judges, teachers, social workers, and others – in a way which underlines and compounds their exclusion from (full) membership of and participation within (adult) society. Such a protective approach serves to underscore the demarcation line between childhood and adulthood. The point at which people become *legal adults* is marked by a disjunction in people's enjoyment of citizenship rights; in people's legal rights to make decisions about themselves and others; and in people's legally sanctioned authority, control and power within and through adult–child relationships.

The protective model of children's rights, whereby the denial of citizenship rights to children is rationalised on the grounds of children's inherent vulnerability, sidelines the other type of source of children's vulnerability as identified by Lansdown, namely their 'structural vulnerability'. In practice, however, the protective approach will feed into children's structural vulnerability, which consequently may become the major feature of children's (and especially of older children's) lives and relationships, not just in the United Kingdom but in all modern European societies. In practice, as a result, children's structural vulnerability becomes the key to unravelling and making sense of their legally-based and persistent 'powerlessness' (as Lansdown calls it) in their relationships with adults. Lansdown clarifies what she means by the structural vulnerability of children in the United Kingdom as follows:

> Children are also vulnerable because of their complete lack of political and economic power and their lack of civil rights in our society. This aspect of childhood derives form historical attitudes and presumptions .... [It] is a social and political construct and not an inherent or inevitable consequence

> of childhood [in] itself. Children have, in general, no access to money, no right to vote, [no] right to express an opinion or be taken seriously, no access to the courts – except within the framework of the Children Act – [no right] to challenge decisions made on their behalf, no right to make choices about their education .... [Within] their families they have no right to physical integrity – parents are at liberty to hit them if doing so falls within the boundaries of 'reasonable chastisement' – and they have no formal voice in society at all. (Ibid., p. 3)

In whatever way the protective approach to and denial of citizens rights to children is rationalised, the outcome of the approach is to feed into children's structural vulnerability, which in turn may be interpreted as lending support to the claim that children are inherently vulnerable; are incapable of independent decision-making; are too immature for the responsibilities of exercising citizenship rights – at least those reserved for legal adulthood; and so will benefit from protective rights.

For Lansdown, however, the UK's Children Act goes further than assigning only protective rights to children. She argues that the Act represents a major step towards implementation of the United Nations Convention on the Rights of the Child, as adopted by the UN's General Assembly in 1989 and signed by 136 countries by the middle of 1993, including the United Kingdom (in December 1991). The Convention's *principles* 'can be broken down into 3 main categories – provision, protection and participation' (ibid., p. 5). Lansdown argues that the Children Act awards rights to children which are consistent with the last of these three categories:

> The participation Articles are to do with civil and political rights. They acknowledge the rights of children to a name and identity, to be consulted and to be taken account of, to physical integrity, access to information, freedom of speech and opinion, to challenge decisions made on their behalf. It is [this] set of principles which, if fully implemented, would represent a significant shift in the recognition of children as participants in society and which pose a substantial threat to the traditional boundaries between adults and children. (Ibid., p. 5)

For Lansdown, the Children Act 'incorporates [these] principles' as specified in Article 12 of the Convention, 'which states that [a] "child shall, in particular, be provided with the opportunity to be heard in any judicial and administrative procedures affecting the child"' (ibid., p. 6). But, as far as I am concerned, the notion of 'participation' being employed here is limited in terms of what seems to qualify as *participation*. The notion is relatively limited when judged with reference to the participation which adults are legally allowed within the decision-making processes concerning their own welfare as well as children's. Accordingly, it is more accurate to regard the Children Act as incorporating not so much the UN Convention's *participation principles* as its *protection principles*, which 'identify the rights of children to be safe from discrimination, physical and sexual abuse, exploitation, substance abuse, injustice and conflict' (ibid., p. 5).

Despite Lansdown's complimentary interpretation of the Children Act, she does accept that it is limited in one important respect when judged by its implications for children's participation in the decision-making process concerning their own welfare. That is, Lansdown claims that the Act is narrow in scope, given that it is confined to children's right to be consulted within judicial activities only. She complains about the Act not extending children's right to be consulted to the 'education system where there is no duty whatsoever to listen to or take seriously children's views when decisions about school choice [for instance] are being made' (ibid., pp. 6–7). Likewise, there 'is no obligation to listen to children and take account of their views written into health legislation' (ibid., p. 7); nor 'is there any requirement to take account of the views of children within the family' (ibid., p. 8). On these grounds, the UK's Children Act may be contrasted with equivalent legislation elsewhere in Europe. In Finland 'there is a requirement written into [the] equivalent of the Children Act that parents must consult with children in reaching any major decision affecting them subject to the child's age and understanding. Similar provisions exist in Germany, Sweden and Norway' (ibid., p. 8). Such a requirement on parents has attracted a distinguishing label:

> Some countries have taken up the principles of 'democratic parenting', meaning that parents should exercise their

authority in consultation with their children. Greek law says that parents should consider the children's opinions before making any decision regarding their responsibilities. In Finland parents must discuss issues with their children and take account of their opinion, wishes and feelings. ('Rights: Young at Heart', *Guardian*, 5 January 1993)

However, the question arises as to whether it is appropriate to apply the label 'democratic', with its connotations of popular control, rule or sovereignty over decision-making,[14] to a process within which parents retain the right to make decisions about children which may turn out to ignore or contradict the children's own expressed wishes.

In each European country, there will be a line of demarcation between children and legal adults, given that the latter have acquired the right to independent decision-making with regard to their own (as well as children's) welfare. This is not to ignore the way the age of majority differs between countries and is even variable within certain countries:

The most popular age for this in Europe is 18. It was 21 in England and Wales until 1969, but it then came down to 18 – since which time many other European countries have followed. In France and West Germany, for instance, the age came down from 21 to 18 in 1974, and in Italy the following year. In Greece, Ireland, Holland and Denmark the age has also been reduced to 18 – often in response to young people's demands. In Austria it is 19 and in Switzerland, 20. Scotland, where the age of majority is 18, divides under-18s into two categories: boys under 14 and girls under 12 are 'pupils', and girls from 12 to 18 and boys from 14 to 18 are 'minors' who have some rights denied to pupils. Many countries let their young people reach the age of majority earlier if they have been emancipated or released from all parental control. This might happen on marriage, such as Denmark, France, Ireland, Spain and Switzerland, or at the request of the young person and a parent or guardian. In France, a young unmarried woman with a child automatically reaches the age of majority, although she loses this if she gives the child away.   ('Rights: Young at Heart', *Guardian*, 5 January 1993)

Having reached the conclusion that there is a personally and socially important, and so sociologically significant, line of demarcation between children and legal adults, which coincides with a disjunction in the legally based distribution of authority with regard to decision-making, it needs to be recognised that nevertheless reaching the age of majority does not inevitably bring with it the attainment of full citizenship. In the United Kingdom, for instance, eighteen-year-olds are still denied a number of citizenship rights and remain, therefore, partially excluded from full (legal) membership of (adult) society. The acquisition of certain citizenship rights is reserved until the age of twenty-one. Just as it is not until the age of twenty-one that people convicted of criminal acts are liable for incarceration in places of adult detention, likewise it is not until the age of twenty-one that the final set of (adult) citizenship rights is acquired. In the United Kingdom, from the age of twenty-one, people are allowed to hold a licence to drive a large passenger vehicle; to hold a licence to sell alcohol; and to become a Member of Parliament ('Rights: Young at Heart', *Guardian*, 5 January 1993). In addition, and perhaps most important, at the age of twenty-one 'a man may consent to a "homosexual act" in private if ... his partner [is also] over 21' (ibid.). In the UK, there are no legal prohibitions on homosexual acts between females. While the current law relating to homosexuality is restrictive (in a gender-biased manner), it represents a considerable relaxation of the previous total ban on male homosexual acts:

> The Sexual Offences Act 1967, which reformed the law on homosexual sex, retained the view that it ought to be restricted more than heterosexual sex. Rather than allow homosexuals to enjoy the same sexual freedom as heterosexuals, the new law loosened the absolute ban on absolute ban on homosexual acts. They were now permissible in private between consenting men aged 21 or over, providing they were not serving in the armed forces or merchant navy. (Like previous Acts, it ignored relationships between women.) The suspicion that a man or woman is gay is sufficient grounds for dismissal from the military. Homosexual activity can be punished by up to two years in jail. It is perfectly lawful for a man and woman to flirt with

and chat up each other in public. Between men, however, this behaviour in public remains a criminal activity. It is illegal for a man to make contact with another in a public place which could be considered as making an arrangement to have sex.   (Kingston, 1993a)

The legal proscription of homosexual acts by or with any man under twenty-one and by any man, whatever his age, in a public place leads to several hundred criminal prosecutions each year: 'In 1991 there were 244 prosecutions against gays and bisexual men for consenting sex under the age laws. These led to 184 convictions and 13 jail terms' (Pilkington, 1993). Moreover, occasionally, there are vigorous attempts at enforcement, and not always by the police:

> Police yesterday confirmed that no charges will be brought against two young men who said on a radio programme that they were lovers, although one was under the age of consent for homosexuals. The decision was welcomed by gay groups but condemned by the Conservative Family Institute, which had called for the men to be prosecuted. The Crown Prosecution Service advised Devon and Cornwall police that there was insufficient evidence for a case against [the two men] aged 24 ... and ... 20. They said they were lovers on BBC [radio]. The two men are campaigning through the European Court of Human Rights for a change in the law to reduce the age of consent from 21. Dr Adrian Rogers, an Exeter GP and director of the Conservative Family Institute, asked a police officer to arrest the pair. The officer declined, and Dr Rogers reported the matter to the Crown Prosecution Service. Dr Rogers said last night that the decision was historic and that the law had fallen into disrepute.   (Campbell, 1993)

Historically, in Britain, the legal prohibition against homosexual acts first of all became tighter and more specific, before being eased:

> The first law in Britain aimed at punishing homosexuality was passed by Henry VIII in 1533, directed against certain sexual acts rather than specific people. Execution was one punishment. It was only in the last century that people have

been identified specifically as homosexuals. The term itself ... was first recorded in 1892. For centuries beforehand, homosexual acts were legislated against together with other non-procreative sexual acts. This implies that homosexuality was not, until the 19th Century, seen as a completely distinct [sexual] tendency. The death sentence for sodomy was finally abolished in England and Wales in 1861 (28 years later in Scotland). It was replaced by prison with hard labour for between 10 years and life. In 1885 all male homosexual acts, in public and in private, were made illegal. For no clear reason, the law overlooked lesbian sex. The total ban on sex between men remained in force until 1967 when the law was relaxed. It now permitted homosexual activity in private between consenting men over the age of 21. Obsenity laws, however, have continued to be used against gay men. (Kingston, 1993b)

Laws relating to homosexuality, and more precisely laws establishing whether and at what age men and women can engage in homosexual acts, show considerable variation not only historically but also cross-nationally. Thus:

Britain has the highest age of consent for homosexual men in western Europe .... With an age of consent for homosexuals of 21 compared with 16 for heterosexuals, Britain is the most discriminatory western European country outside Cyprus where homosexual acts are illegal although the European Court of Human Rights has ordered it to lift the ban. Of 19 European countries in western Europe five discriminate. Austria allows sex between consenting males at 18 (14 for heterosexuals), Finland at 18 (16), and the former West Germany at 18 (14). But the German government has announced it will introduce a unitary age of consent at 16. Fianna Fail, senior partner in the Irish government coalition, has voted to decriminalise homosexuality and place it on an equal footing at 17.[15] [There is] a more patchy picture across the former communist eastern bloc. Russia recently accepted an equal age of consent at 18 and gay men held in prison are expected to be released soon. Estonia, Latvia, Lithuania, and Ukraine have also recently lifted bans. However, six countries still forbid male homosexual acts. In Romania, both gay and lesbian sex is outlawed. (Pilkington, 1993)

At the end of the twentieth century, there is a notable variation between European countries over the law relating to homosexual acts, and in particular over the minimum age at which (if at all) it is legally permissible to engage in such acts. Accordingly, in this regard, there is a sizeable variation between European countries over when (if at all) people acquire the citizenship right involved, with the United Kingdom displaying the highest age of male acquisition (see Table 1.1).[16]

But, in any European country, people who have not reached the age at which the right to engage in homosexual acts is ac-

TABLE 1.1 Age of Consent to Engage in Homosexual Acts (end of June 1993)

	Heterosexual age of consent	Male homosexual age of consent	Female homosexual age of consent
Austria	14	18	14
Belgium*	16	16	16
Bulgaria	14	14	14
Cyprus	16	illegal	16
Czech Republic	15	15	15
Denmark	15	15	15
Finland	16	18	18
France*	15	15	15
Germany (W)	14	18	14
Germany (E)	14	14	14
Greece	15	15	15
Hungary	14	18	18
Ireland	17	17	17
Italy	16	16	16
Liechtenstein	14	20	14
Luxembourg*	16	16	16
Malta	20	20	20
Netherlands	16	16	16
Norway	16	16	16
Poland	15	15	15
Portugal	16	16	16

TABLE 1.1—*continued*

	Heterosexual age of consent	Male homosexual age of consent	Female homosexual age of consent
Slovakia	15	15	15
Spain	12	12	12
Sweden	15	15	15
Switzerland	16	16	16
Turkey	18	18	18
United Kingdom	16	21	16

SOURCE: based on tables presented in (a) Peter Kingston, 'Homosexuality: Loosening the Straitjacket', *Guardian*, 29 June 1993; and (b) Edward Pilkington, 'UK heads Europe Bias against Gays', *Guardian*, 20 August 1993**.

NOTES:
* Belgium, France and Luxembourg had total bans on male homosexuality only up until the end of the eighteenth century. France lifted its total ban in 1791, and Belgium and Luxembourg did the same in 1792. The Netherlands made the same move in 1811, and Spain did so in 1844 (Peter Kingston, 1993b).
** The second of these two articles includes the following variations on the details presented in Table 1.1: Italy – 14, 14, 14; Netherlands – 12, 12, 12; Portugal – 12, 12, 12.

quired have yet to attain full citizenship. In the particular case of the United Kingdom, those people who have reached eighteen years – the *age of majority* – and have become, therefore, legal adults, have nevertheless yet to become what might be distinguished as 'social adults' or 'full adults', ones who have acquired the full range of citizenship rights. In the United Kingdom, people become *full adults* at the age of twenty-one, when they finally acquire not only (for men) the right to engage in homosexual acts in private, but also (for both men and women) the rights which enable people to hold a licence to drive a large passenger vehicle, to hold a licence to sell alcohol, and to become a Member of Parliament. In the United Kingdom, judged with reference to the acquisition of citizenship rights, people do not attain full adulthood, full membership of (adult) society, and so *full citizenship* until the age of twenty-one. People under twenty-one are still in that stage of the life-cycle which might be referred to as 'social childhood', in that they remain legally excluded from *full* membership of and participation in (adult) society, by virtue of being denied full citizenship rights. Indeed, in so far as (following T. H. Marshall and J. M. Barbalet), citizenship is specifically equated with being *full* (legal) members of society, we might regard people under the age of twenty-one as 'non-citizens', in that while they enjoy some citizenship rights they have yet to acquire the full range of such entitlements (including some personally and socially important ones).

Childhood can be distinguished from adulthood on the grounds of children being denied (full) citizenship rights and, therefore, being excluded from that relationship with the state which I have previously labelled 'citizenship' and through which people conduct, realise and experience citizen relations. It is as citizens and through citizen relations that people (adults) enjoy and experience formal (citizenship) equality. Children, as non-citizens, experience formal inequality, through the state, with adults, even though the particulars of this formal inequality very between societies. Thus, between European societies, children may acquire the same right at different ages in the process of attaining full adulthood and full citizenship. For instance, in the case of the (citizenship) right to marry:

> Girls can marry earlier than boys in many countries. In Greece, a boy can get married at 18 but a girl at 14 – although she needs the permission of her parents or a court if she is under 18. In Austria boys must be 19 and girls 16. In France a 15-year-old girl can marry (with parental consent) whereas a boy must be 18. Irish law sets the age at 16 for both sexes, although the courts can lower this. In Scotland, young people can marry at 16. This is two years earlier than in England and Wales, unless parents give their permission for an earlier marriage. Norway has no absolute lower age limit for marriage, although parents' or a local governor's permission is needed if young people are aged under 18. Both boys and girls in Spain can marry at 14, although if under 18 they need the consent of their parents or a court,

which must hear the parents' and young people's views. ('Rights: Young at Heart', *Guardian*, 5 January 1993)

Likewise, between European societies, children may acquire the same examples of legal liabilities, requirements and responsibilities at different ages in the process of attaining full adulthood and full citizenship. Of considerable importance in this regard is the acquisition of *criminal responsibility*. As we have seen, in England and Wales, ten-year-olds are considered responsible for any crimes they commit, whereas in Scotland the age is eight (ibid.). In contrast:

> In Greece the age is as low as 7, and in Luxembourg there is no minimum age. In Germany, Norway and Italy the age of criminal responsibility is 14. In France, young offenders are criminally responsible from age 13. Those between 13 and 18 receive shorter sentences, although courts can ignore this for people over 16. Austria, Denmark and Sweden set the age at 15. Belgium has the highest age of criminal responsibility: the law presumes that offenders aged under 18 act 'without discernment', although 16- and 17-year-olds can be tried as adults for some serious crimes.   (Ibid.)

The gradual, age-related acquisition of citizenship rights, the full enjoyment of which demarcates (full, adult) citizenship, occurs along with a similarly gradual acquisition of legal (adult) liabilities, requirements and responsibilities in all modern European societies. At the same time, there are notable and significant variations between these societies in the ages at which people acquire particular rights and responsibilities, and connectedly reach particular markers on the way to the attainment of adulthood and thereby (full) citizenship.[17] The significance of these variations in the present context is that formal inequality between adults (citizens) and children (non-citizens) throughout Europe is accompanied by formal inequality among children themselves – between, that is, children from different European countries.

In turn, of course, the particular inequalities so far addressed are compounded by the occurrence of yet further, crucial inequalities among children both within and between countries: those *inequalities of opportunity* among children for realising their *formal* citizenship rights *informally*, within their everyday lives. Such inequalities are a reflection and consequence of the unequal distribution among children of what I will call 'enabling resources'. Enabling resources are all those financial and other material possessions which allow people to transpose their formal citizenship rights into informal, everyday or 'real' citizenship.[18] Alongside children's relative (compared with adults) lack of citizenship rights, resulting in their relative (formal) exclusion from membership of and participation in society, is an unequal distribution of enabling resources *among* them, bringing unequal opportunities for exercising the formal citizenship rights they do enjoy. While a set of children may equally enjoy a particular range of citizenship rights – during the process of attaining (full) citizenship and adulthood – which afford equal degrees of *formal* inclusion in (adult) society, the same children may none the less have unequal possession of (or access to) enabling resources and thereby unequal opportunity for *actual* inclusion in (adult) society.

It is well recognised among social researchers, commentators and policy-makers that some people's levels of enabling resources are low enough to mean that (whatever their formal citizenship rights) they are unable to avoid 'social exclusion' – unable, in other words, to prevent themselves from being deprived of full membership of and participation in (adult) society. It is on the grounds of such inadequate levels of enabling resources that the people involved are sometimes categorised as 'poor'.

It is commonplace to remark that there is no universal consensus over how to approach the issue of the conceptualisation, definition and measurement of 'poverty'. But, this conceptual issue is important because of the determining part it plays in establishing patterns and trends of *poverty*, and in arriving at policies designed to reduce poverty. Helpfully, certain approaches have gained more widespread acceptability than others. In particular, the relative perspective has achieved almost a taken-for-granted status among social scientists and policy-makers, especially as a result of the influential writings of Peter Townsend. Townsend has outlined what has been described as his 'famous' conceptualisation of poverty (Holman, 1993) in the following way:

Individuals, families and groups in the population can be said to be in poverty when they lack the resources to obtain the types of diet, participate in the activities and have the living conditions and amenities which are customary, or at least widely encouraged or approved, in the societies to which they belong. Their resources are so seriously below those commanded by the average individual or family that they are, in effect, excluded from ordinary living patterns, customs and activities. (Townsend, 1979, p. 31)

While Townsend's *relative* notion of poverty is presented as preferable to what he has distinguished as 'the absolute' approach (ibid., pp. 32–9) it itself has not gone unchallenged. For instance, Paul Corrigan has criticised Townsend for focusing on the distributional side of social inequality, stratification and deprivation in defining and analysing poverty to the neglect of the relational side, wherein lie inherent social divisions between, for instance, the exploited and the exploiters; the powerless and the powerful; the excluded and the included (Corrigan, 1978).

Strong echoes of Townsend's relative approach to the conceptualisation, study and understanding of poverty are to be found in a December 1984 statement by the European Community's Council of Ministers. Here, the poor are defined as 'persons whose resources (material, cultural and social) are so limited as to exclude them from the minimum acceptable way of life in the Member State in which they live' (quoted in Commission of the European Communities, *Background Report: The European Poverty Programme*, August 1991, p. 1). On the basis of this approach, the European Commission has come up with evidence that in Europe there is considerable overall, widespread and increasing poverty, which at the same time is variable in its extent. The Commission has arrived at figures using the following operational definition of poverty: 'the poverty threshold is 50% of the average disposable income per head in the country in question' (ibid., p. 1). The Commission has recognised, however, the somewhat arbitrary character of this particular threshold:

Different definitions and calculation methods produce varying figures for poverty. E.g. if the poverty threshold is taken as

40% of disposable income per head, the number of low-income persons is reduced by almost half. Equally, using a European average instead of the national average income per head produces considerable variation in figures. (Ibid., p. 2)

The arbitrary character of the commission's *average income* definition is underlined by the way the Statistical Office of the European Communities (Eurostat) has adopted a somewhat different operational definition:

Equivalent mean national expenditure is an indicator which may be used to measure relative poverty in different countries. Poverty is defined as having less than 50% of the equivalent mean national expenditure of one's country, e.g. less than 50% of Denmark's ECU 6721 in 1985 or less than Portugal's ECU 2618 (at constant 1980 prices). (Eurostat, 1992, p. 78)

While either the *average income* or the *average expenditure* approach may be taken as a guide to overall and national patterns and trends in the amounts and rates of poverty within the European Community, the Commission seems to have come around to favouring the latter. We are told by David Brindle that a European Commission 'spokesman said expenditure was regarded as a more reliable measure than income because experience showed that not all income was declared in surveys' (Brindle, April 1991). The Commission has, then, presented figures 'based on family budget surveys', which show 'that between 1975 and 1985, the number of persons [in poverty] in the Community increased from 44 million to 50 million' (Commission of the European Communities, *Background Report: The European Poverty Programme*, 1991, p. 1). But, such blanket figures hide cross-national variations as revealed by Eurostat:

The highest totals are those of France (10.3 million in 1980) and the United Kingdom (10.3 million in 1985). The proportion of poor individuals in the total population varies widely from one country to another: from 5.9% in Belgium (1985) to 32.7% in Portugal. It is around 20% in Ireland, Spain, Greece and the United Kingdom, around 15% in France and Italy, and around 10% in the Netherlands, Germany and

Denmark. Between 1980 and 1985 the proportion of the poor in the total population increased substantially in the United Kingdom, rising from 14.6% to 18.2%; in France, on the other hand, it fell from 19.1% to 15.7% and in Belgium from 7.1% to 5.9%. Denmark has 1.6% of the Community's population, but only 0.8% of its poor; Belgium 3.2% of the population but only 1.2% of the poor. The United Kingdom, on the other hand, with 17.6% of the Community's population, has 20.7% of its poor, whilst Portugal has 3.2% of the population and 6.7% of the poor. (Eurostat, 1992, pp. 78–9)

Eurostat's findings have been more thoroughly examined by David Brindle with particular reference to the United Kingdom, but in comparative perspective, as follows:

More people are living in relative poverty in the United Kingdom than in any other European Community country, according to a European Community report.[19] One in five of all EC residents defined by the commission [sic] as poor[20] lives in the UK .... Measured by family group, the findings are even more stark. Almost one in four of all EC households is defined as poor in the UK. The report ... also suggests that the UK's record has worsened dramatically while the EC as a whole has kept the growth of poverty at bay. Between 1980 and 1985, the number of relatively poor people in the EC remained broadly stable, but in the UK, they grew by a quarter. The number of poor households grew by a third .... According to the ... figures, 49 million EC residents were living in poverty in 1980 and 50 million in 1985. Of these, 8.2 million in 1980 and 10.3 million (18.2 per cent) in 1985 were in the UK, representing 2.8 million and 3.8 million households respectively. This ... means that ... the UK moves to the 5th poorest state .... Similarly by household, the UK moves ... to the 2nd poorest. In absolute numbers, however, the UK has the most poor people. Between 1980 and 1985, when the ... poverty figures fell in Belgium, Greece, Spain and France, and remained constant in Denmark and the former West Germany, those for the UK rose by 25.5 per cent for people and 35 per cent for households. By 1985 the UK accounted for 23.5% per cent of all EC households living below their respective national poverty lines. (David Brindle, April 1991)

The Commission has attempted to unravel and account for the trends in and prospects for the overall amount and rate of poverty by pinpointing what are sometimes referred to as the *immediate causes*. In the first place, the Commission has mentioned how between 1975 and 1985 'poverty among the elderly decreased although the total population of elderly showed a sharp increase during the same period' (Commission of the European Communities, Background Report, 1991, p. 2). The decline in poverty among the elderly, and therefore due to the *immediate cause* of *old age*, was offset, however, by increases within other sections of the population. Thus:

> The rise in unemployment, particularly long-term unemployment, is the main [immediate] cause of poverty in the Community. This has been caused [in turn] by economic recession in the late [1970s] and early [1980s], [along with] industrial restructuring. Additionally, structural underemployment has long been a problem in poor rural regions. Between 1975 and 1985 in the Community of 10, unemployment rose from 3.7% to 9.5% of the workforce. Economic restructuring has led to 'new poverty' in the form of relatively qualified young people being made redundant from apparently secure jobs and finding [it] subsequently hard to adjust to managing on a low income. There are also those who are in temporary employment, workers taking early retirement on reduced pensions, nomads, migrant country-dwellers, the homeless and women who are not taken into account in the official unemployment statistics. Gaps in social protection systems of Member States mean that a significant number of those people counted as unemployed do not receive unemployment benefit or social assistance. Social assistance that is available does not always provide sufficient income to avoid poverty. (Ibid., p. 2)

However, the Commission offers a hopeful assessment of the prospects for the overall trend in the extent of poverty in view of the way there appeared to be a levelling off during the early part of the 1980s. After pointing out that between 1975 and 1985 the number of people in poverty in the Community increased from 44 million to 50 million, the Commission notes that in the second half of this period – between 1980 and 1985

– there was a 'stabilisation of poverty' (ibid., p. 1). The Commission has interpreted this development as part of a longer term trend whereby 'it can be assumed that levels of poverty have fallen slightly since 1985 given that unemployment is down a little, and some countries have improved their social protection systems' (ibid., p. 1).

In retrospect, this prognosis has turned out to be over optimistic given that, following a dip in the *official* unemployment rate between 1985 and 1992, the figure has since risen sharply to reach around 11 per cent 'of those of working age' by 1993 (Almond, September 1993). The considerable rise in the unemployment rate for the European Community overall has been accompanied by similar but varying upsurges across all Member States. Towards the end of 1993, Larry Elliot reported: 'Britain's seasonally adjusted jobless rate of 10.4 per cent compares with 21.1 per cent in Spain, 16.7 per cent in Ireland, 11.5 per cent in France, 6.9 per cent in the United States, 5.9 per cent in Germany, 2.5 per cent in Japan and an EC average of 10.6 per cent' (Elliot, September 1993). Furthermore, there is considerable agreement that the rise in the figures is set to continue. As Lucy Walker tells us, 'the number of jobless in the EC is forecast to rise from 17.4 million to more than 20 million by 1995' (Walker, October 1993). In response, Walker adds:

> At a conference in Brussels, the EC's Social Affairs Commissioner, Padraig Flynn, is to urge industry, diplomats and researchers to contribute ideas on how to reduce non-wage labour costs – which average 30 per cent of EC employers' wage bills .... EC officials believe social security charges could be lowered by shifting the burden of taxation to other factors of production. (Ibid.)

However, even though such modifications may have some impact on the increasing unemployment rate, first of all the possibility arises that they will run counter to the firm tendency within the European Community to otherwise extend and strengthen the *non-wage* remuneration and social protection enjoyed by employees – as reflected in, for example, the provisions of the *Community Charter for the Fundamental Social Rights of Workers* (adopted in November 1980); the subsequent *social chapter* of the Maastricht Treaty; and the decision of a meeting of the Council of Ministers in Luxembourg on 12 October 1993 to 'limit the hours worked by adolescents aged between 15 and 17' (Carvel, October 1993). Second, the impact could be little more than a slight dent given that (as the European Commission's directorate for social affairs estimates) 'halving the unemployment rate would require the creation of 24 million new jobs in the Community'. And third, while the modifications may shift some people from unemployment into employment, they could do so by likewise moving the *social composition and balance* of the poor in the same direction.

With regard to the latter consideration, already – while there may well be good grounds for the Commission's claim that (the rise in) unemployment rooted in the economic recession in the main 'cause' of poverty – the poor are far from exclusively unemployed. In the United Kingdom, for instance:

> The number of working people earning below the Council of Europe's decency threshold has increased by nearly 1 million since the Conservatives came to power. In 1991 more than 4.7 million people who worked full-time were paid less than the threshold, compared with 3.9 million in 1979. The threshold is set at 68 per cent of average gross weekly earnings for full-time employees and was £60 in 1979 and £190 last year. Department of Employment figures ... show a near doubling of the proportion of men earning less than the threshold .... Government figures show that the South-east has the lowest proportion of low-paid workers, the North the highest of low-paid women and Wales the highest of low-paid men. Although the proportion of women below the threshold fell in all but two regions, the overall proportion of women below it (53.9 per cent) still far exceeds that for men (21.3 per cent).   (Weston, August 1992)

The gender imbalance among low-paid employees is largely explicable (at least in the first instance) in terms of women's gender-specific family ties,[21] and as such brings to mind certain additional factors which have been identified to help account for the increase in the extent of poverty, factors which also have *family connections*. Thus, the Commission claims that 'Economic and social changes have brought into existence new poverty factors such as the increase in single parent families and a corresponding growth in dependency upon social assistance' (Background Report, 1991, p. 2). In Great Britain, for instance, the proportion of the population living in *lone parent with dependent children* households rose between 1961 and 1991 from 2.5 per cent to 10.0 per cent (*Social Trends 23*, 1993, p. 28), with over 90 per cent of such households being headed by a lone mother. Moreover, in the particular case of *families with dependent children*,[22] the percentage that are *lone parent families* more than doubled between 1971 and 1991, rising from 8 per cent to 18 per cent, 'reflecting the rise in both divorce and births outside marriage' (ibid., p. 29).

These rises were accompanied by a similar trend in the proportion of dependent children living in such families. That is, the percentage of all dependent children living in *lone parent families* more than doubled from 1972, to reach 18 per cent by 1991 (ibid., p. 28), again *reflecting the rise in both divorce and birth outside marriage*. On the latter, the number of births occurring outside marriage has 'increased dramatically' since 1960. For instance, during the 1980s, the proportion of births taking place outside marriage more than doubled to reach 'three in ten of all births in 1991' (ibid., p. 32). But, while the rise in the rate of births outside marriage has been considerable in the UK, rises in some other European countries have been even greater:

> The United Kingdom is not the only country where births outside marriage are rising. All countries ... have seen ... increases. Despite the high figure in the United Kingdom, [it] still lag[s] behind Denmark, France and Sweden. There are some staggering differences between countries – one in two births in Sweden are outside marriage, but only one in fifty in Greece.   (Ibid., p. 33)

Such European-wide trends have then fed into two accompanying developments. First, there is evidence of a general increase in the 'percentage of single parent families as a proportion of all families' (Nereth and Reid, November 1993), as reflected in the data in Table 1.2:

TABLE 1.2 *Lone Parent Families in the European Community, 1992*

Country	Percentage of single parent families as a proportion of all families
UK	19
Denmark	15
Germany	13
France	11
Luxembourg	10
Netherlands	10
Portugal	10
Ireland	9
Belgium	9
Spain	6
Italy	6
Greece	5
EC average	10
Poland	5
Norway	10

SOURCE: Pelle Nereth and Julie Reid, 'Mothers Pay Price of Being Single', *The European*, 15–25 November 1993.

Nereth and Reid add:

> On average, European single mothers are twice as likely to be living in poverty as the average household. They are also twice as poor as single fathers, where poverty is defined as [having] half or less of the national average income. (Ibid.)

Second, therefore, the European-wide upsurge in the numbers and proportions of births occurring outside of marriage will – as signalled by the European Commission – feed into a parallel development in the numbers and proportions of children who are in poverty across the Community. In Britain, for instance, it has been estimated that 'one in four children live below the breadline' (*The European,* June 1993). While this is an exceptionally high estimate, even lower ones indicate a considerable rise in the proportion of children in poverty. John Carvel provides an overview of recent *Unicef* findings with particular reference to Britain:

> Britain has slipped in world league tables of children's health and welfare because of the Government's cutbacks in the welfare state, Unicef, the United Nations Children's charity, said [in a report published[23]] yesterday. The English-speaking world as a whole has done relatively badly because of espousal of laissez-faire policies by Britain, the United States, Canada and Australia, according to Unicef .... Child poverty is the starkest measure of Britain's relatively poor performance, with a rise of 40 per cent during the 1980s in families living below a poverty line taken as 40 per cent of national disposable income. The US is shown to have more than 20 per cent of its children below this poverty line. Britain, Canada and Australia each have about 10 per cent. Sylvia Hewlett, author of a companion Unicef report on child neglect in rich nations, said the data reflected the Anglo-American world's market-driven policies which had 'privatised child-rearing at a point where families were so very fragile they could not pick up the slack'. (Carvel, September 1993)

According to Unicef, in contrast with the decline in the 'condition of children' in 'English-speaking countries', in 'Western Europe the condition of children has consistently improved' (ibid.). None the less, as Carvel goes on to tell us, this has not prevented the European Commission from showing concern about the overall patterns and trends in poverty along with a strong interest in tackling what it sees as a major problem for the European Community:

> The European Commission yesterday proposed a doubling of its anti-poverty programme in response to evidence of growing a problem for the 52 million people in the community it estimates are having to live [in poverty]. Padraig Flynn, the social affairs commissioner, said these people – who make up 15 per cent of the Community's population – are facing 'unacceptable and rising levels of poverty and exclusion ....' If member states agree, the commission will

allocate about £100 million for the [poverty] programme, which would run from July [1994] until December 1999. This compared with £45 million for the current programme, which has run since 1989.   (Ibid.)

The Commission's poverty programmes reflect its long-standing interest in tackling poverty, which at the same time it has ever more emphatically equated with 'social exclusion'. The First Poverty Programme ran from 1975 to 1980; the Second Programme from 1985 to 1989; and the Third Programme from 1989 to 1994 (Commission of the European Communities, *Background Report*, 1991, p. 1). The increasing concern of the Commission about poverty is perhaps reflected in the rising budget allocation given to its poverty programmes. The Second Programme attracted an eventual (on being extended to Spain and Portugal) budget allocation of 29 million ecus, being used to fund 91 'Action-research Projects' (ibid., p. 3).[24] But the Third Programme:

has a much larger budget than the Second Programme: 5 [million] ecus. Furthermore the Third Programme has moved away from the action-research phase of 'Poverty 2', to a phase of selective development. A much smaller number of projects are targeted for funding: 39 in total across the Community. Of these 39 projects: 27 are large-scale 'model actions' based on local initiative and the principle of partnership; 12 are 'innovatory initiatives' that deal with social exclusion on behalf of a particular population group or problem area.   (Ibid., p. 5)

In the UK, three 'Model Actions' are being funded, including the Liverpool Toxteth Pilot Project, where 'the emphasis is on coordinated and integrated action for economic, physical and social regeneration' (ibid., p. 5). In addition, there is 'one UK Innovatory Initiative being funded', the Single Parent Action Network in Bristol, which 'aims to support the setting up and autonomy of single-parent, multi-racial groups in deprived situations' (ibid., p. 5).

The Commission's use of the phrase 'social exclusion' in relation to the aims of the Third Programme follows its use of the same notion in summing up the 'experience gained from

"Poverty 2"' (ibid., p. 3). That is, the Second Programme led the Commission to equate tackling poverty specifically with 'the fight against social exclusion' (ibid., p. 4); and to viewing a successful programme as making a 'contribution to social solidarity in Europe' (ibid., p. 4). Towards this end, the Commission proposed a 'course of action', which included the 'stimulation and coordination of ideas, experience and practices in the fight against exclusion'; and the 'development of initiatives to help fight exclusion in the context of Community policies' (ibid., p. 4). The latter includes, for instance, the 'Community Charter for the Fundamental Social Rights of Workers: a programme of action [which] was adopted by the EC in November 1989'. More accurately:

> At the meeting of the European Council in Strasbourg on 8 and 9 December 1989, the Heads of State or Government of the European Community Member States, with the exception of the United Kingdom, adopted the Community Charter of Fundamental Social Rights for Workers. The signatories intend the Charter to be at once a solemn statement of progress already made in the social field and a preparation for new advances – so that the same importance may be given to the social dimension of the Community as to its economic aspects, in the construction of the [single] market of 1992. (Commission of the European Communities, *European File: the Community Charter of Fundamental Social Rights for Workers*, Luxembourg: Office for Official Publications of the European Communities, May 1990, p. 2)

In addition to what became known as the *social charter*, the Commission also had in mind a 'number of legal initiatives to assist in anti-exclusion policies', including those behind the 'action programmes to benefit vulnerable groups such as women or the disabled' (Commission of the European Communities, *Background Report*, 1991, pp. 4–5).

The European Commission, along with the other institutions and bodies of the European Community, has come around to firmly favouring and notion of 'social exclusion' in order to signify what above all else characterises and distinguishes 'poverty':

> Social exclusion is another word for the poor, or those living on the margins of society such as the long-term unemployed, immigrants, single parent families, drug addicts and the elderly living on low incomes. The term is now truly part of EC social jargon along with *cohesion* and *solidarity*. It represents the Community's attempts to tackle outstanding social problems as an integral part of the social dimension of the internal market. So far, EC action has been limited to financing studies and pilot projects under the 55m ECU poverty action programme, topped up with small grants from the regional and social funds. The Commission is now proposing to extend the scope of the regional and social funds to include combating social exclusion as a priority objective for training programmes and thus entitled to a far larger slice of the cake. Parliament wants funding to concentrate on the most extreme cases. The UK government, on the other hand, is so far resisting this proposal, whereas the Commission sees it as the first step towards an expanded role in helping the Community's 50 million poor, as agreed under [a] paragraph in the protocol on the Social Chapter to the Maastricht Treaty which, of course, the British government insists will not apply to Britain. (*Europe Parliament News*, June 1993, p. 3)

As the *poverty problem* has become ever greater, the Community has increasingly embraced the term 'social exclusion' in preference to alternative notions, even including that of 'poverty' itself. As reported in the middle of 1993:

> The forgotten one in seven living below the breadline in the EC are being brought into the spotlight this week in a major conference on poverty. Four hundred ministers and officials are meeting in Copenhagen in an effort to solve what is fast becoming a crisis in the Community, and to discuss a programme which will direct funds towards Europe's neediest citizens. The swelling number of poor – what the Commission terms 'the socially excluded' – has now reached 'unacceptably high level', say Commissioner for Social Affairs Padraig Flynn. (*The European*, 'Focus on Forgotten who Live in Poverty', 3–6 June 1993)

Birna Helgadottir expands:

according to Padraig Flynn [there is] a crisis so huge that it goes beyond the ability of member states to cope individually. 'the Community cannot accept the continued rise of poverty and social exclusion.' The Commission rejects the term 'underclass', and is even unhappy about 'poverty', preferring the more politically correct terms of 'social exclusion' and 'marginalised persons'. '"Underclass" is used by some experts in the US and Britain, but it is a much debated term,' says Flynn. 'We don't like to refer to people in terms of class. Also the concept of poverty is generally understood to refer exclusively to income and resources, but there are other ways of being poor than just being short of cash. You can be excluded because of loneliness, housing conditions, your state of health and being long-term unemployed. The number of people who are not considered to have a role in society is growing.' (Helgadottir, *The European*, June 1993)

As if to confirm the Commission's conceptual preference, Padraig Flynn goes on to label the Community's planned Fourth Poverty Programme as the 'social exclusion' programme (ibid.). However, Flynn's comments serve to draw our attention to an important analytical issue, that of the conceptual relationships between such terms as 'poverty', 'the poor', 'social exclusion' and 'the underclass'. In this context, Lynne Berry attempts to throw light on the meaning and implications of the notion of 'underclass':

Social stability seems in danger as poverty effects more than 53 million people in Europe. With almost a quarter of the European population apparently unconstrained by obligations of work, family and community, the search is on for something or someone to blame. Britain has decided it is the underclass. France, Germany, Italy, the Netherlands, Greece and the institutions of the EC choose instead to describe people living outside the rules of society as the marginalised and excluded. The difference is important because one analysis points the finger at members of the underclass. The other does not allow us to absolve ourselves or the politicians from our responsibilities. (Berry, *The European*, June 1993)

Lynne Berry argues that the notion of the 'underclass' is more popular and 'powerful in America than in Europe', which explains why Britain has found some appeal in it: 'As always, Britain looks both ways.' Within the USA and Britain, the 'idea of the underclass acts as a symbol for a range of worries', such as the 'increasing cost of welfare budgets [and] worries about creating a dependency culture'. In this sense, claims Berry, there 'is certainly no such thing as a European underclass, though each country has its own group of disenfranchised people'. For instance

> In Britain they are people without jobs, families without fathers, young men turning to crime and violence, the victims and sometimes the perpetrators of racial abuse. In France they are the North African workers and their families who scrape together a semi-legal life, the unemployed and the unsupported. In Germany they were drinkers and drug-takers, the homeless and the guest workers; now the marginalised are migrants from the whole of eastern Europe. They are the outsiders we fear and to who we deny citizenship. In France there are *les exclus*, and social policy focuses on the dangers of exclusion from society, on the revitalisation of 'degraded neighbourhoods'. Social action projects in the inner cities deal with people damaged by the economic crisis. *Les précaires* are offered family support, as part of training for citizenship.   (Berry, ibid.)

Berry argues that in contrast to France, where social policy is designed to help the socially marginalised and excluded to realise their citizenship, in 'Britain, citizenship has been individualised and has become a form of self-reliance. We have tried to tackle the underclass by an emphasis on the individual and the family.' This interpretation is consistent with John Carvel's representation, mentioned earlier, of the adoption by the English-speaking world of *laissez-faire* or *market-driven* policies, with the result that the *health and welfare* of children in Britain, for example, has *slipped in world league tables*. In Britain, in line with the New Right social and economic policies of the Conservative government which came into office in 1979, people's social marginalisation and exclusion or, instead, realisation of citizenship, is seen as a matter for individual and family responsibility and effort. Attempts by way of social policy to assist with the expansion and realisation of citizenship, if anything, undermine this responsibility and effort by creating a 'dependency culture'. The latter encourages *welfare dependency* by discouraging (especially economic) independence, individuality and initiative, and is the hallmark of the underclass. Berry's journalistic representation of the meaning and implications of 'the underclass' is consistent with Rosemary Crompton's assessment of the notion from a sociological perspective (Crompton, 1993, pp. 157–62).[25] Crompton clarifies the way John Rex (Rex and Tomlinson, 1979) has used the term 'the underclass' in his account of 'the marginalisation of the immigrant community' (Crompton, 1993, p. 156):

> Rex argues that the immigrant population (and its children) has been excluded from the 'welfare-state deal' struggled for by the British working class, and thus also from the benefits of social citizenship. As a consequence, Rex suggests that minorities of immigrant origin may be described as an 'underclass'. His use of the term 'underclass', it should be stressed, differs from its more usual use to describe groups who have failed altogether to become economically self-supporting.[26] This use of the term, however, has become highly contentious, particularly in the light of right-wing arguments that the effect of the development of social citizenship and the welfare-state deal has been to create an 'underclass' in advanced industrial societies. (Ibid., pp. 156–7)

Rex applies the term 'underclass' to what he sees as a section of society which is excluded from social citizenship, 'understood as rights to welfare' (ibid., p. 157). This contrasts with the right-wing application of the same term to that section of society which, far from being excluded from social citizenship, extensively and even *excessively* actually realises such citizenship. For right-wing theorists, the underclass exercises social rights to welfare benefits and services to the point of 'welfare dependency'. Thus, the underclass is primarily characterised by a 'culture of dependency,[27] which is encouraged by the expansion of social citizenship and which, in turn, encourages (self-)marginalisation and exclusion by way of a *failure to be economically self-supporting* and a failure to realise their other (civil, political) citizenship rights.

Accordingly, Crompton mentions those right-wing claims that

> collective provisions have actually had the effect of undermining individual capacities. Thus state provision for the economically disadvantaged is argued, by some right-wing theorists, to be making an active contribution to the problem it is trying to solve, through the creation of 'welfare dependency' and thus the development of an underclass. (Ibid., p. 157)

Right-wing theorists, therefore, can be counted among those 'neo-liberal critics' who have argued that 'the provision of social citizenship through collectivistic welfare-state provisions has served to undermine the individual freedoms enshrined within civil and political rights' (ibid., p. 157). This has occurred both for those who, through taxation, help finance such provisions and for those who are in receipt of them. With the former in mind, 'libertarian critics of welfare-state provision have argued that *compulsory* redistribution of income should be kept to a minimum, and that individuals should be free to determine the nature and extent of their own welfare provision' (ibid., p. 157). The same critics go on to argue in favour of a '"minimalist" system of provision' in the interests also of the freedom, independence, individuality and *initiative* of the recipients (or potential recipients) of welfare-state provisions. A minimal provision is seen as conducive to personal responsibility and self-reliance; as encouraging people to be economically self-supporting by way of, in particular, paid employment; and thereby as facilitating the realisation of *civil and political citizenship rights*. Personal freedom, independence and individuality is not so much fostered by the provision and expansion of social citizenship, as undermined by it – and this effect applies throughout society, to rich and poor alike. Welfare state provisions encourage welfare dependency, a 'culture of dependency', an underclass, and so a socially (self-)excluded section of society.

For example, P. Saunders (Saunders, 1987) has argued that in Britain and similar societies there is a 'major faultline' between 'a majority of people who can service their key consumption requirements through the market and a minority who remain reliant on an increasingly inadequate and alienative form of direct state provision' (ibid., ch. 3 – quoted in Crompton, 1993, p. 158). Charles Murray has argued along the same lines about the 1960s' 'Great Society' welfare reforms in the United States:

> The first effect of the new rules [increasing welfare provisions] was to make it more profitable for the poor to behave in the short term ways that were destructive in the long term. The second effect was to subsidize irretrievable mistakes. We tried to provide more for the poor and produced more poor instead. (Murray, 1984, p. 9 – quoted in Crompton, 1993, p. 158)

Moreover, Murray argues, the same reforms created an *underclass*, which is composed of 'particular groups of the poor – unmarried single mothers, labour-force drop-outs, and those engaged in criminal activities' (Crompton, 1993, p. 159). At the same time, however, Murray gives the notion analytically important cultural connotations. For Murray, 'the poor develop a moral stance which effectively removes the will to effort and further deepens the cycle of poverty' (ibid., p. 160). The underclass is characterised by distinctive moral or cultural traits which, in effect, keep its members in poverty in what amounts to a process of *self-exclusion*.[28]

As a result, some writers (see for instance Dean, 1991) 'have argued that the term has been developed not in order to describe an objective phenomenon but, rather, as a stigmatising label which effectively "blames the victims" for their misfortunes' (Crompton, 1993, p. 158). It is on such grounds that Melanie Phillips finds the term objectionable:

> The term has unpleasant connotations. It means that there is a group of people whose position in society is so low they are not even members of the very lowest social class. As a result, they are not the same as the rest of us, [being] not properly civilised that thus not entitled to the same individual respect and civic rights. It lends itself to the political philosophy of blaming the victim. Moreover, because the term has been appropriated by rightwing American writer

Charles Murray, who has used it to attack the culture of dependency and by extension those who are dependent on state benefits, there are many political analysts in [Britain] who refuse to accept that there is such a phenomenon as an underclass at all. This is unfortunate because it means that they don't [sic] address the fact that there are groups of people who are not merely poor but who are prevented from participating fully in society.   (Phillips, March 1992)

Despite this, the term has been applied to Britain, by both Murray himself and other notables. Turning his attention to Britain, in a *Sunday Times* article in 1989, Murray described himself as 'a visitor from a plague area come to see whether the disease was spreading' (Murray, November 1989 – quoted in Lister, 1987, p. 25 [29]). Murray was not disappointed, and the British underclass he found is (according to the *Sunday Times* editorial on Murray's claims):

Characterised by drugs, casual violence, petty crime, illegitimate children, homelessness, work avoidance and contempt for conventional values. The underclass spawns illegitimate children without a care for tomorrow and feeds on a crime rate which rivals the United States in property offences. (*Sunday Times*, 26 November 1989)

In a similar vein, Ralf Dahrendorf has described the 'underclass' as 'a cancer which eats away at the textures of societies', and has argued that its development is 'critical for the moral hygiene of British society' (Dahrendorf, June 1987). For Dahrendorf, being in the underclass – which he estimates makes up no more than 5 per cent of the British population[30] – means being 'socially excluded', and as such its existence casts doubt on the social contract itself. It means that citizenship has become an exclusive rather than an inclusive status. Some are full citizens, some are not' (ibid.). What Dahrendorf seems to have in mind is that, although the (adult) members of the underclass share equally in the universal provision of citizenship rights, their material conditions and *moral* characteristics undermine their potential for realising such rights, and this in turn presents a threat to all sections of society.

The right-wing solution from the United States is, together with minimalising welfare provisions and social rights, to introduce a 'work obligation' on those who remain recipients. For instance, Lawrence Mead has argued that 'the enforcement of obligations – in particular, work obligations – is "as much a badge of citizenship as rights" [Mead, 1986, p. 229]' (Lister, 1987, p. 8). Mead elaborates:

> For recipients, work must be viewed, not as an expression of self-interest, but as an obligation owed to society. At the same time, to fulfil this obligation would permit the poor a kind of freedom that benefits alone never can. An effective welfare [sic] must include the recipients in the common obligations of citizens, rather than exclude them. To require the dependent to function in minimal ways, onerous as it seems, is essential to banish the worse bondage of unequal citizenship. Given the evenhanded nature of citizenship, only those who bear obligations can truly appropriate their rights. (Mead, 1986, p. 257 – quoted in Lister, 1987, p. 8)

Such an argument has been taken seriously by the United States' federal government, which has introduced the social policy known as 'workfare'. The involves an obligation to take on some paid employment or some training for paid employment as a condition of receiving social welfare benefits (Lister, 1987, p. 8).

Approaches to citizenship where not only rights but also responsibilities, obligations and duties are specified as defining features have found echoes in the views of writers and policy-makers elsewhere. T. H. Marshall maintained that 'if citizenship is invoked in the defence of rights, the corresponding duties of citizenship cannot be ignored' (Marshall, 1952, p. 70). Likewise, towards the end of 1988, the UK government minister John Moore told the Conservative Party Annual Conference that the purpose of the government's social policies was that of

> correcting the balance of the citizenship equation. In a free society the equation that has 'rights' on one side must have 'responsibilities' on the other. For more than a quarter of a century public focus has been on the citizen's 'rights' and it is now past time to redress the balance. (Quoted in Lister, 1987, p. 7)

While the UK government has shown some interest in the possibility of introducing something along the lines of the United States' workfare programme, it has managed so far to resist the temptation.[31] Instead, the UK government has come up with the notion of 'the "active citizen", an individual who gives money and time to serve the community. This paragon has been invented in response to the argument that the free market, as promoted by Thatcher's government, is hard and uncaring' (Rogaly, October 1988 – quoted in Lister, p. 14).

Ruth Lister points out that the promotion of 'active citizenship' was assumed by the British government's Home Secretary, Douglas Hurd, in 'an attempt to engender social cohesion in the face of growing concern about hooliganism and other forms of anti-social behaviour; to counter the damaging assertion by the Prime Minister [Margaret Thatcher] that "there is no such thing as society." [Margaret Thatcher interview in *Woman's Own*, 31 October 1987]' (Lister, 1987, p. 14). Douglas Hurd has argued that 'the idea of active citizenship is a necessary complement to that of the enterprise culture. Public service may once have been the duty of the elite, but today it is the responsibility of all who have the time or money to spare' (Hurd, *Independent*, September 1989 – quoted in Lister, 1987, p. 14).

Therefore, as Ruth Lister adds, 'charitable giving and voluntary service are the two key components of active citizenship. The third element is the denigration of taxation as a means of discharging the obligations of citizenship' (ibid., pp. 14–15). However, the result is that, despite Douglas Hurd's 'concern that the duty of public service should not be confined to the elite, his notion of active citizenship is inherently inegalitarian' (ibid., p. 15). Active citizenship through public service – and so the contribution to, participation in and membership of society it implies – can be more fully pursued, achieved and enjoyed by the better off, privileged, advantaged:

> lurking behind the active citizen is the successful, self-reliant, enterprising citizen, alias the consuming,[32] property-owning citizen. The unsuccessful and unenterprising are thereby excluded from the ranks of citizens. ... Thus, in the

name of social cohesion, the Conservative's eulogy to the active citizen merely serves to underline the divisions that exist in society. (Lister, 1987, pp. 15–16)

The promotion of citizenship responsibilities, obligations and duties – and thereby of people *making a contribution to society* – both in return for citizenship rights and as necessary for participation in and membership of society *in its fullest sense*, serves to emphasise certain important social division. It establishes social divisions which are unequal in terms of social inclusion–exclusion by way of *making a contribution to society*. It thereby accentuates the occurrence of social divisions which are unequally placed within underlying distributions of enabling resources; which have unequal opportunities for transposing *formal citizenship rights* into *real citizenship activities*; and which consequently have quantitatively and qualitatively unequal experiences of *actual* participation in and membership of modern society. The promotion of the principle of citizenship responsibilities, obligations and duties serves to highlight the way in which the universal provision of citizenship rights by itself far from ensures equality of social inclusion. Instead, considerable inequalities among people in terms of *social inclusion–exclusion* are not only left in place, but also consolidated and augmented by the underlying and sustained unequal distribution of enabling resources.

In the following summary, Lister touches on the possibility of the unequal distribution of enabling resources being sustained in part by the way the promotion of the principle of *citizenship contribution* – or of *active citizenship* – ideologically (not to say ironically or even contradictorily) obscures more fundamental issues and determining factors:[33]

Citizenship has been redefined on the Right using the language of obligation and responsibility. [For instance, there is] the work obligation imposed upon the poor as a means of combating 'dependency culture'. In practice, this tends to operate as an obligation to take low-paid, unpleasant jobs, thereby reinforcing existing labour market relations. [But,] the new model citizen is also the active citizen.

Charitable giving and voluntary activity are now the hallmarks of good citizenship. In this way, obligation is shifted from the regulated public arena of tax-funded benefits and services to the uncertain private arena of good works, and the beneficiaries of a decade of redistributive policies to the better-off are made to feel good. In [effect] the emphasis on the obligations of citizenship serves to obscure and reinforce the inequalities of power, resources and status that an earlier emphasis on the rights of citizenship sought to combat.   (Lister, 1987, pp. 20–1)

Citizens are those people who have acquired full citizenship rights – the full range of legal rights necessary for full membership of (for full inclusion within) society. But, such rights by themselves are insufficient for *real citizenship*. Citizens are divided between those who are able to realise citizenship rights and those who are unable; between those who *really* enjoy and experience full inclusion, participation and membership and those who do not; between those who have sufficient enabling resources to allow them to be included as full members of society and those who have insufficient; between those who enjoy the *power* to be *real citizens* and those who do not. The unequal distribution of power among citizens is then reinforced by that power which, in turn, comes from being *real citizens* – that is, from being one of those citizens who enjoys the advantages of being fully *socially included.*

Those citizens whose enabling resources are insufficient to allow them to realise their citizenship through inclusion as full members of society may be regarded as 'poor'.[34] The 'underclass' – as regularly conceptualised and identified – may be regarded as a sub-section of *the poor*. The poor in general suffer social exclusion, and the underclass in particular do so specifically by virtue of their labour market non-participation or marginalisation. At the same time, the underclass's social exclusion is (frequently interpreted as) *self-exclusion* by way of their *excessive* use (or *abuse*) of social citizenship rights, or of their social welfare dependency. In such an approach to the relationship between 'the poor' and 'the underclass' there are, of course, shades of Seebohm Rowntree's distinction between the 'deserving poor' and the 'undeserving poor'.[35]

At the same time, however, by equating 'poverty' with 'social exclusion' – taking as a guide Townsend's proposal that poverty occurs when people suffer *exclusion from ordinary living patterns, customs and activities* – our attention is drawn to the way people can be socially excluded as a result (to recall Padraig Flynn's argument) not just of limited *income and other material resources*, but also of *non-monetary* factors, as the European Commission points out:

> Non-monetary aspects of poverty include such areas as: educational aspects (e.g. literacy), poor health, restricted access to health services, poor accommodation and homelessness. Increased numbers of people with rent arrears in Member States led to greater numbers of people being threatened with eviction towards the middle of the 1980s. Chain reactions can lead to an accumulation of handicaps. (European Commission, *Background Report: The European Poverty Programme*, August 1991, p. 2)

What I wish to add to the list of factors which thread through and augment poverty in the sense of social exclusion is that of *limited or restricted citizenship rights*. Whatever people possess or have access to in the form of *enabling resources*, they can be socially excluded, and therefore in poverty, by virtue of their inadequate citizenship rights, judged with reference to what is required to permit full membership of and inclusion within modern society. This approach lends itself to the conclusion that children – all children – in modern societies suffer (relative) *poverty* due to the way they are denied full (adult) citizenship rights. Whatever their access to enabling resources (such as those of their parents), all children may be counted as *poor* by virtue of being denied full citizenship rights and therefore of being legally excluded from (full) membership of and participation in (adult) society. Although, at the same time, the further possibility arises of some children having access to enabling resources which are, in any case, *inadequate* when judged in terms of those resources which combined with full citizenship rights are required in order to permit full membership of and inclusion within modern society.

But, of course, it is not only children who suffer poverty in the sense of relative social exclusion due to restricted citizenship rights. Armed with the framework outlined over the course of this chapter, we can proceed to examined how and why certain sections of the *adult* population of modern society, with particular reference to western Europe, are similarly deprived.

2 Citizenship, the State, the Nation-state and Nationality

If, as J. M. Barbalet suggests, citizenship defines, or distinguishes between, those who are and those who are not members of *a common community or society*, it follows, as Barbalet goes on to say, that citizenship 'can be characterized as both a status and a set of rights', where (guided by Marshall) civil, political and social rights make up the separate elements of specifically modern citizenship (Barbalet, 1988, p. 15). Barbalet suggests that, in whichever society or epoch they are possessed, 'rights in general ... are [socially] important' and sociologically 'significant because they attach a particular capacity to persons by virtue of a legal or conventional status' (ibid., pp. 15–16). That is, 'rights provide a minimum of social capacities and entitlements [in that] the violation of a right is sufficient justification for the use of force in correcting the situation' (ibid., p. 17). Barbalet argues that rights

> provide persons with capacities or capabilities and opportunities and ... they can do so with a measure of security. This is because ... their contravention will be subject to sanction. This characterization raises a number of questions, especially [about] the relationship between rights and the distribution of social resources, power and interests.   (Ibid., p. 17)

A distinctive feature of specifically citizenship rights is that they are 'legally constituted rights' (ibid., p. 16), and as such 'are defined and enforced by public authorities' (ibid., p. 16). This gives citizenship rights – as distinct from merely non-legal or simply conventional rights – extra political importance, *social value*, and thereby sociological significance. At the same time, however, not all legal rights are identical, or equal, in the capacities and opportunities they provide. The capacities and opportunities provided by a particular citizenship right will depend upon its type. Thus, some rights, such as 'welfare rights' automatically entitle people to actually possess 'a minimum level of material well-being', and thereby 'provide access ... to opportunities [and] conditions' (ibid., p. 17).[1] The capacities and opportunities provided by these social rights[2] can be contrasted with those provided by such civil rights as property rights. Thus:

> 'A property right', [as] Marshall (1950, p. 88) remarks, 'is not a right to possess property, but a right to acquire it, if you can, and to protect it, if you can get it'. Thus paupers and millionaires possess the same capacities through property rights without the distribution of property being in the least degree affected.   (Barbalet, 1988, p. 17)

A property right provides a capacity, but its realisation in the actual possession of property is not guaranteed by the right itself. The realisation of the right or capacity to acquire property is dependent upon extraneous, intervening factors, which amount to 'abilities of one sort or another, or other means through which opportunities are taken' – these means being 'unevenly distributed through a population' (ibid., p. 17). These intervening factors amount to the current and prior conditions on the basis of which people try to realise their citizenship rights, entitlement and capacities, and which affect their ability and opportunity of so doing. Such conditions include the property already possessed. In so far as this is unequally distributed among citizens, it may well remain so, unaffected – and even sustained – by the *equally* distributed property right. As Barbalet neatly summarises:

> Citizenship is a manifestly political enterprise, yet ... the political dimension is insufficient for a proper understanding of it. The issue of who can practise [or realize] citizenship and on what terms is not only a matter of the rights entailed in it. It is also a matter of the non-political capacities of citizens which derive from the social resources they command and to which they have access. A political system of equal citizenship is in reality less than equal if it is part of a society divided by unequal conditions.   (Ibid., p. 1)

An important type of social resource, and one which, following the terminology of the previous chapter, is an important example of *enabling resources*, is property. 'Property' is perhaps more accurately referred to as *property rights* or *ownership rights*. Property rights determine relationships between things (as property) and their owners.[3] As pointed out by Barker and Padfield:

> Ownership has been described as 'the entirety of the powers of use and disposal allowed by the law' (Pollock: *First Book of Jurisprudence*). The owner of a thing has an aggregate of rights, namely (i) the right of enjoyment, (ii) the right of destruction, and (iii) the right of disposition, subject to the rights of others. (Barker and Padfield, 1992, p. 260)

Things in themselves are not property, are not owned by anyone or anything else (a corporation or whatever). What makes things property are (legally granted, guaranteed or enforced) property or ownership rights in, over and through them.[4] Any piece of property (any property right) is, in effect, a social relationship. It is, in the first instance, a legal relationship. But, furthermore, property is a social relationship among actual and prospective (no matter how remotely prospective) property owners: that is, the possessors of property rights. Property is a social relationship characterised by power and control in relation to (in and over) a thing; as well as (through that thing) in relation to (over) other people. The latter means that property is a social relationship which necessarily entails a distribution of social power. The more property possessed by someone or something (for example, a corporation) the more social power he, she or it enjoys, although property rights vary in the types and degree of social power they bring.

Property is markedly unequally distributed within modern societies, albeit more so in some rather than others. In comparison with most European societies, property in the United Kingdom, for instance, is not only more unequally distributed than most, it has also become yet more unequal over the last decade or so. This can be illustrated with reference to evidence on patterns and trends in various types of property, including the two basic types: (a) wealth (a stock or store of property); and (b) income (a flow of or promised property).

Andrew Glyn (Glyn, 1992) has examined the trend in income distribution in the United Kingdom during the 1980s, and has compared this with the trends in other European countries. In the UK during the 1980s, the 'spending power' of those people at the top of the 'income spectrum' was 'boosted in a number of ways':

> High earnings rose relatively fast: in 1981 highly paid (top tenth) non-manual workers earned just over three times as much as low paid (bottom tenth) manual workers: by 1989 the ratio was four to one. High interest rates and booming dividends pushed unearned income (and capital gains on shares) up twice as fast as income from employment between 1979 and 1989, of most benefit to the best off. Most notoriously, tax cuts and benefit changes between 1979 and 1991 left the real incomes of three quarters of households more or less unaffected on average, while they raised the average income of the best-off 10 per cent by more than £90 per week. The worsening relative position of those at the other end of the income distribution resulted from falling relative pay of the lowest paid, from rising numbers of dependents on state benefits and from the linking of state benefits to prices rather than earnings. Between 1979 and 1987 the number of people in families receiving less than half the average income more than doubled to 10.5 million. In [sum,] the poorest tenth of the population were worse off, after allowing for inflation, than in 1979, while the richest 1 per cent saw their real incomes rise by 72.4 per cent.   (Ibid.)

According to Ruth Kelly, the ever-widening income gap in the United Kingdom under the impact of Conservative governments' New Right inspired taxation and redistribution policies was maintained and exacerbated between 1989 and 1991:

> Government policy has widened the gap between rich and poor .... Data from the Central Statistical Office [show] that, before government intervention, the poorest fifth of society earned 2 per cent of total income – unchanged from 1989. But if the impact of taxes and benefits is taken into account, the relative income of the poorest fifth of house-

holds fell sharply from 6.9 per cent of the total in 1989 to 6.6 per cent. At the same time, the figures [show] the wealthiest segments of society increasing their advantage. The post-tax income of the richest fifth increased from 43 per cent in 1989 to 44 per cent – continuing the trend of the previous decade.   (Kelly, May 1993)

Indeed, other sources suggest that the same inegalitarian trend has a far longer history than this. Michael White and Keith Harper (White and Harper, July 1993), for instance, refer to evidence which suggests that 'nearly two-thirds of the population has an income below the family average of £250 a week and ... extremes of income are wider than at any time since 1886'.[5]

Andrew Glyn addresses the question of how the patterns and trends in income inequality in the United Kingdom during the 1980s compares with developments elsewhere in Europe. He brings together information for the period 1979 to 1991 which 'shows the ranking of the UK for a number of indicators of changes in economic inequality: the lower the ranking, the more inegalitarian the trend'. He reports that on 'each of these inequality indicators the UK comes at or near the bottom (biggest increase in inequality)' (Glyn, 1992). For instance, the

> excess of the rise in unearned income is greater than the average for Europe .... Poverty, when measured in a comparable way, appears to have risen more in the UK than elsewhere other than Ireland. Top tax rates have been cut more in the UK than anywhere else, and this has contributed to the UK showing the largest rise in the share of the top income groups.   (Ibid.)

Glyn comes to the conclusion that the period of Conservative government in Britain has been an increase in income inequality which 'seems larger than in almost any other European country'. The New Right's justification being 'that by increasing incentives, it will improve economic performance. What a convenient theory, as J. K. Galbraith has remarked, that economic efficiency required making the rich richer (e.g. tax cuts) and the poor poorer (e.g. benefit cuts)' (ibid.).

Whereas Glyn focuses on income patterns and trends by accounting for these in terms of the impact of *fiscal factors*, David Brindle (Brindle, January 1992) links the same features to patterns and trends in the distribution of wealth in the UK using figures from *Social Trends 22* (*Social Trends 22*, 1992). To begin with Brindle mentions that in 1988 the top 20 per cent of post-tax income recipients enjoyed between them 44 per cent of such income, whereas in 1979 the figure had been only 37 per cent. Brindle then points out that much of the income received by the top income recipients takes the form of investment income, or (to use Glyn's term) *unearned income*. This form of income amounted to 8 per cent of all personal income in 1989. It comes from, for instance, company share ownership. In 1991, about 25 per cent of all adults owned some company shares (as, therefore, privately owned company shares). However, these adults held between them only 20 per cent of the total national stock of company shares – the other 80 per cent being held by institutions (as, therefore, institutionally owned company shares). Company shares generate investment income or unearned income by virtue of representing ownership and control of what are variously referred to as 'productive property', 'productive wealth', 'productive resources', 'the means of production' and 'capital'.

Chris Pond elaborates on the patterns and trends in the distribution of overall wealth:

> in 1985, the top one per cent of the adult population owned more than a fifth of net personal wealth – three times as much as the poorer half of the population ... one per cent of the population represents just 400 000 people [out of about 57.5 million]. The top five per cent (about two million people) own almost 40 per cent of the total personal wealth, and the top ten per cent own more than half ... [The] distribution of wealth was little different in the 1980s to that which existed 60 years before ... [Over this] sixty year period ... the share of the top one per cent [declined] by an average of 0.7 per cent a year .... The statistics ... seem to give credence to the notion of a self-perpetuating upper class [of] rich. ... [The] declining fortunes of the wealthiest were contained within fairly narrow limits. While the top one per cent saw their share diminish, the rest of

the top five per cent retained almost as big a share of personal wealth in 1985 as they did in 1923 (20 per cent compared with 21 per cent 60 years earlier). The rest of the top ten per cent own twice as much wealth now as they did sixty years ago [14 per cent compared with 7.1 per cent]. This would seem to suggest that what we have witnessed over this period is not so much the redistribution of wealth, as the reordering of affairs among the richest families. Largely as a means of avoiding estate duty, the wealthy have been encouraged to disperse their wealth amongst members of their families, most members of which remained within the top ten per cent of wealth holders. [Moreover, there was] a remarkable symmetry about wealth inequalities in the 1980s: while ten per cent of the population [owned] more than half the nation's wealth, half the population [owned] less than ten per cent. (Pond, 1989a, pp. 68–9)

Transfers of wealth both within and between generations as well as both before and at death have helped the rich as a section of society or social class (the 'upper class', according to Pond) to effectively avoid the full impact of regressive taxation; to retain and boost their wealth; to maintain their position within the social class system; and to consolidate the social class system around a stubbornly very unequal distribution of wealth. Thus, in support of Pond's argument, Harbury and Hitchins (Harbury and Hitchins, February 1980), after carrying out a detailed examination of the patterns and trends in the inheritance of wealth between generations, assert that 'without question, the firmest conclusion to emerge from this study is that inheritance is the major determinant of wealth inequality' (quoted in Pond, 1989a, p. 71). Since the early 1980s, the process of inter-generational wealth transfers has continued unabated, perhaps at a gathering pace:

The value of property passed down from generation to generation is set to quadruple to £25 billion a year over the next two decades .... Over the past decade, the number of [inherited houses] has risen from 88,000 in 1981 to 128,000 in 1991, and its total value has spiralled from £2.2 billion to £8.5 billion over the same period. [By] 2011 [the number of inherited houses will have risen] to 235,000 ... worth £35.8

billion. In 1991 there were almost 260,000 beneficiaries (excluding spouses) who received an average of £30,000 of housing inheritance. By 2011 almost half a million people will inherit property worth an average of £75,000. (Goodway, July 1993)

One factor underlying this development has been the way, as Chris Pond tells us:

> home ownership has spread rapidly since the 1950s, encouraged by the Conservative governments' policy of the 'right to buy' for council tenants: between 1979 and 1987 the proportion of households [sic] who were owner-occupiers increased from 56 per cent to 64 per cent. This is reflected in the importance of owner-occupied housing in overall wealth holdings: in 1970 'homes' represented 27 per cent of all personal wealth ... rising to 37 per cent by 1984 .... This reflected not only the extension of home ownership, but also the increase in the real value of property. (Pond, 1989a, p. 71)

At the same time, as Pond stresses, it is 'important to distinguish between different types of wealth in making an assessment of their importance in determining economic and political power, as well as assessing the effect of property ownership on lifestyles' (ibid., p. 72). That is:

> Popular wealth, in the form of owner-occupied housing, pensions and insurance policies confers on the owners greater security and control over their lives. The ownership of land or company shares and partnerships, by contrast, means not only an enhanced standard of living, but also control over the lives of others. Halsey [Halsey, January 1978] has identified a distinction between 'property for power by which [is meant] property which carries control over the lives of other people, and property for use – posessions that free a man [sic] from other people's control .... A tiny minority has monopolised wealth, and an even tinier minority has monopolised property for power'. (Pond, 1989a, p. 72)

This distinction between two types of wealth in terms of the kind and degree of power each brings is important when assessing the implications of patterns and trends in wealth (and income) for people's lives and relationships; for power and control within and through the social class system; and for (combined with the process of transferring and inheriting wealth) the perpetuation of the social class system around persistently high unequal distributions of property (and in particular of *productive property* or *property for power*), and so social – including economic and political – power and control. As Pond tells us:

> despite the extension of popular wealth, the ownership of power-conferring assets remains concentrated in the hands of a very few. Just one per cent of the population owns nearly two-thirds of the private land in Britain, while five per cent own almost 90 per cent and ... ownership of land is becoming increasingly concentrated among the rich. While the richest one per cent own only 5 per cent of residential buildings, their portfolios include one sixth of all privately owned buildings. The richest one per cent also own two thirds of unlisted company securities and foreign securities, almost half the listed company securities, and a third of the trade assests and shares in partnerships. The rich are not particularly interested in the ownership of assets which confer comfort and security but not very much power. Thus, the top one per cent own only 5 per cent of the value of privately owned residential buildings, only 8 per cent of cash and bank deposits, only 6 per cent of insurance policies, and only 0.2 per cent of superannuation benefits. (Pond, 1989a, p. 74)

The *upper class* help to maintain their privilege, power and control within the social class system by favouring ownership of productive resources, and so what Halsey distinguishes as *property for power* not just over their own lives but also over other people's lives. Hence, they way in which much of the considerable increase in the *value of property passed down from generation to generation,* as reported by Nick Goodway, is finding its way into (re-) investments in such property:

> Inherited wealth is becoming an increasingly important part of the flow into financial investments such as shares, unit trusts and building societies. On the most recent statistics almost eight out of ten inherited houses are sold and some 46 per cent of the resulting cash finds its way into investments. (Goodway, July 1993)

Ownership of land, company shares and other productive property brings to the owners investment returns in the form of unearned income, which feeds into not only the upper class's lifestyle, standard of living and security, but also their further ownership of such property, with the result that

> the wealth that confers social and political power – land, shares and company securities – remains heavily concentrated in the hands of a few. All these provide their owners with an ability to control not only their own lives, but the lives of others as well. (Pond, 1989b, p. 197)

Hence, one consequence of 'the prosperity generated towards the end of the 1980s ... was the enhancement of the wealth of ... the rich who ... managed to retain and reinforce their status as an upper class continuing to wield significant economic, social and political power' (Pond, 1989a, p. 76). While Pond argues that the upper class's hold over social, economic and political power is based on their ownership of *productive wealth* rather than *popular wealth*, such as owner-occupied housing, he adds a word of caution is this regard:

> We should be careful [about] assuming that assets which we may define as components of 'popular wealth' confer no power, no matter what form their ownership takes. The ownership of housing property, for instance, has always provided large landlords with a substantial degree of influence. It is when the purpose of ownership moves from that of profit to that of use that the nature of the assets themselves changes, and the link between ownership and control is broken. In the case of many forms of popular wealth, power and control have been separated from ownership, through financial institutions. (Pond, 1989a, p. 74)

However, for myself, Pond's qualification about the power conferred by *housing property* does not go far enough. While housing property as a component of popular wealth may not bring quite the same kind or degree of power and control to the owners involved as is attached either to housing property as a component of institutional holdings (*property for profits*) or to productive wealth (*property for power*), it is nevertheless a major source of both personal power and social (covering economic and political) power. It is precisely because housing property and various other occasional elements of popular wealth bring some personal and social power that such property has considerable *popular* appeal in Britain and modern societies in general, and not only by virtue of the fact that it can be (and is perhaps increasingly) exchanged on the housing market for returns to be (re-) invested in productive wealth. Moreover, it is precisely because of what underlies, establishes and secures the personal and social power attached to popular wealth that housing property, for instance, is itself sometimes the target of investment by institutions and, what is more, shows up as a component of productive wealth. Housing property is often an element of the productive wealth of *productive enterprises*, including small – perhaps family – businesses, such as retail outlets.

The main point here is that whether housing property is a component of productive wealth, institutional wealth or popular wealth, in each case it confers on its owners personal and social power, albeit to some extent of differing types and degrees. Housing property does this because of the underlying legal framework which establishes and secures for the owners of housing property personal and social power by virtue of the framework's constituent property rights and property laws, which establish housing *as* property in the first place, whatever its form or forms (including not only those of popular wealth, institutional wealth and productive wealth, but also that of *socialised wealth*). In Britain and similar societies, there is a framework of laws and legal rights which establishes and secures housing *as* property; housing property forms; housing property rights; and accordingly housing – even in its popular form – as a source of, sometimes considerable, personal and social power. Because housing property in the form of popular wealth is very unequally distributed within Britain and other

European societies, it contributes to a very unequal distribution of personal and social power at the *popular* level: among, that is, *the people*, including those who are citizens. This unequal distribution of personal and social power then intervenes between the possession of citizenship rights, including the *civil* citizenship right to own (or, following T. H. Marshall, to acquire) property, such as housing property in its various forms.

This argument is consistent with the point made earlier that *an important type of enabling resource is property – or, more precisely, property rights or ownership rights*. Following Barker and Padfield, a property right defines a relationship between a thing (as 'property') and its owner, who has thereby in relation to that thing the right of enjoyment, the right of destruction, and the right of disposition, subject to the rights of others (Barker and Padfield, 1992, p. 260). Consequently, any piece of property (any property right) is, in effect, a social relationship, whatever piece it is and whatever form it takes. It is by virtue of being in the first instance a legal relationship that property is a social relationship among people as actual and prospective property owners – the possessors of property rights. Moreover, any piece or form of property – such as housing in the form of popular wealth – is necessarily a social relationship characterised by power and control in relation to a thing; as well as (through that thing) in relation to other people. The latter means that property is a social relationship which necessarily entails a distribution of social power. The more property possessed by someone or something the more social power he, she or it enjoys, even though property rights vary in the type and degree of social power they bring.

Popular wealth is very unequally distributed within modern societies, such as Britain, where it appears to have become even more so under the New Right economic and social policies of Conservative governments since 1979. Because of the legally granted and guaranteed rights – and thereby personal and social power – attached to such property, it follows that there is markedly unequal distribution of enabling resources which, by virtue of mediating between the provision of formal citizenship rights and the informal, everyday realisation and experience of such rights, ensures that the latter is also very unequally distributed. The formal citizenship rights affected include the civil citizenship right to own – or more accurately to acquire – property. The everyday personal and social power and control which property (the ownership of property; property rights) brings, including popular wealth, entails the *power* to transpose the possession of the formal civil citizenship right to acquire property into the informal, everyday realisation and experience of actually owning property, attached to which is (various types and degrees of) personal and social power. Hence, what might be referred to as 'the property-owning cycle', with its implications for *real citizenship*, begins again.

Here, a legal distinction with important sociological implications is being drawn upon. It is the distinction between (a) the civil citizenship right to own or acquire property, a right which will be possessed by people whether or not and to what extent it has been realised in the actual ownership of property; and (b) the property rights which are attached to the actual ownership of property and which, therefore, can be exercised only by actual owners. The issue then arises of the empirical, practical, everyday link between (a) and (b), and the discussion so far suggests that, for instance, although legally the civil right is necessary for the actual ownership of property, practically it is not sufficient. A person's realisation of the civil citizenship right to own property is dependent upon his or her enabling resources, and therefore upon his or her previous record of realising the civil citizenship right by actually owning property. The outcome is that among people, including citizens, in Britain and other European societies there are in practice very unequal distributions of rights, power and control over the total stock of popular wealth; and that these inequalities are self-perpetuating despite – and perhaps because of – the equal, universal provision among people (or at least among full citizens or adults) of the civil citizenship right to own or acquire property.

Of course, in addition, not all people share equally in the so-called *universal* provision of the civil, citizenship right to own or acquire property. As we have noted, children (or minors) in Britain do not share equally in this right. We might recall that in Britain *a minor may own all kinds of personal or moveable property, but he or she cannot own land* (Barker and Padfield, 1992, p. 100). This distinction coincides with the way, under English law, property is divided into two classes: (a) real property (that is, freehold interest in land); and (b) chattels – where 'chattels real' refers to leaseholds in land; and 'chattels personal' covers both (i) 'choses in possession' (physical, material or corporeal things); and (ii) 'choses in action' (non-physical or non-tangible things), including debts, patents, copyrights, trademarks, stocks and shares, registered designs, insurance moneys, and cheques (ibid., pp. 263–4).

Similarly, until the end of the nineteenth century, women – or more precisely, married women – were denied the civil citizenship right to (independently) own property:

> The fact that most of the nation's wealth is concentrated in the hands of a few means that the vast majority of women and men are deprived of their rights; but women are doubly deprived. At no level of society do they have equal rights with men. At the beginning of the nineteenth century, women had virtually no rights at all. They were the chattels of their fathers and husbands. They were bought and sold in marriage. They could not vote. They could not sign contracts. When married they could not own property. They had no rights over their children and no control over their own bodies. Their husbands could rape and beat them without fear of legal reprisals. When they were not confined to the home, they were forced by growing industrialisation to join the lowest levels of the labour force. (Coote and Gill, 1988, p. 16)

However, coming back to the present, not only have women gained legal, property and citizenship rights, but so have children. Moreover, as we have noted, where children are still denied citizenship rights, they have increasingly acquired compensatory, or protective, rights. That is, we might recall how, following Barbalet, we can distinguish the broad category of citizenship rights from other categories of legal rights. While citizenship is a status attached to which there are citizenship rights, *not all rights and not even all legal rights are citizenship rights* (Barbalet, 1988, p. 18). Indeed, as Barbalet tells us, *the provision of certain rights is intended to compensate people who are excluded from the status of citizenship*, where the latter 'is a status bestowed on those who are full members of a national community' (ibid., p. 18).

Here, perhaps significantly, Barbalet identifies citizens not merely as those who are members of a 'national community', but as those who are *full members*. While this is not the approach of all writers (see for instance Rainer Baubock, October 1991, pp. 27–48), as I have indicated already, it seems to me that there is a sociologically useful distinction to be drawn between the mere possession of (some) citizenship rights and the acquisition of the full range of citizenship rights, and that it is therefore apposite to employ the label 'citizen' in a way which pinpoints and highlights this distinction. Citizens are those who, having attained the full range of citizenship rights, are (in the legal of formal sense) full members of a 'national community'.[6] Those who have not gained full (or any) citizenship rights within a *national community* are not 'citizens' – they are instead 'non-citizens'.

However, children are not the only example of non-citizens in modern national communities. Furthermore, children are not alone in illustrating the way legal rights may be granted in order to compensate (and protect) people in view of their lack of (full) citizenship.[7] The further example to which I wish to turn is that of 'aliens' (or foreigners or foreign nationals). Aliens within a national community may well enjoy some citizenship rights, and thereby a degree of membership, but they will not enjoy the full range of citizenship rights and so the status of *being a citizen*. The gap is then partly bridged by the provision of legal (but non-citizenship) rights: that is, of *aliens rights*. In this way, there is a degree of overlap between the legal rights, treatment and experience of aliens and of children within modern *national communities*, including those of the European Community.[8]

Foreign, or *third country*, nationals make up a substantial proportion of the European Community's estimated 345 million total population (Eurostat, 1992, p. 107). As reported by Rory Watson in October 1993:

> last weekend [thirty-two] European countries unanimously insisted on the protection and respect of the national minorities within their boundaries .... The commitment [from] the first ever Council of Europe Summit is the most visible sign to date of efforts to defuse ethnic and racial tensions .... British Labour MEP Glyn Ford, author of the European Parliament's report on racism and xenophobia, explained:

'We want all European residents, not just European citizens, to have the same rights as everyone else. There are some 12 to 14 million third country nationals in the Community – what I call the EC's 13th state. Minority rights within the Community are crucial. (Watson, October 1993)

Glyn Ford's estimate suggests that over a five-year period there had been a huge increase in the number and proportion of foreign nationals in the EC. According to Eurostat's *A Social Portrait of Europe* (1991, pp. 18–19), in 1988, 7.9 million of the 324 million inhabitants of the European Community, or 2.5 per cent of the total population, were nationals from non-Community countries. A further 4.9 million were nationals from Community countries not living in their 'country of origin'. Almost 80 per cent of the extra-Community foreigners were living in three countries: the Federal Republic of Germany (3.2 million); France (2.1 million); and the United Kingdom (1.0 million); 74 per cent of 'Community foreigners' were living in these three Member States. In the Federal Republic of Germany and France, foreigners accounted for 7.3 per cent and 6.6 per cent of the total population respectively, with most foreigners in the FRG coming from non-Community countries; 43 per cent of 'extra-Community' foreigners came from European countries not members of the EC, especially from Turkey and (what was then) Yugoslavia; and 28 per cent came from Africa, mainly from the Maghreb countries, Algeria, Morocco and Tunisia.

Within the European Community, foreign nationals are subject to restrictions which distinguish them from – and disadvantage them in relation to – Member State nationals. Whatever their age, they are denied various citizenship rights. In the case of the United Kingdom, legally defined *aliens* 'are subject to certain restrictions concerning entry into the [country] and employment after entry' (Barker and Padfield, 1992, p. 89). Legally, according to Barker and Padfield:

All persons other than Commonwealth citizens,[9] British protected persons and citizens of the Republic of Ireland are aliens. The following general restrictions apply to an alien: (i) he [sic] may not vote at local or Parliamentary elections; (ii) he may not become a Member of Parliament; (iii) he may not work in the United Kingdom unless specifically permitted; (iv) he must register with the police and notify changes of address to them; (v) he is liable to deportation if he engages in crime.[10]   (Ibid., pp. 90–1)

While aliens do not enjoy the right to engage in paid employment in the United Kingdom, they often gain permission to have jobs. According to Eurostat's *A Social Portrait of Europe* (1991, pp. 56–7), in 1988 there were over 820 000 legally employed foreign nationals in the UK, 422 000 of whom were non-Community nationals. These figures compare with 1 557 000 and 1 073 000 respectively for the Federal Republic of Germany (FRG) and 1 130 000 and 561 000 respectively for France. Proportionately, in 1988, of all legally registered employees in the UK, 2.6 per cent were non-Community foreign nationals and 1.6 per cent were Community foreign nationals. These figures compare with 5.0 per cent and 2.7 per cent respectively for the FRG and 3.3 per cent and 3.1 per cent respectively for France.

Moreover, while aliens in the United Kingdom are deprived of certain pivotal – and most notably civil and political – citizenship rights, entitlements and capacities, they do share a range of other legal rights with United Kingdom citizens. Thus, according to J. P. Gardner:

> Aliens are entitled to avail of certain rights, which can be broadly classed as 'social and economic rights', while resident in the U.K. These rights include the right to treatment under the National Health Service, supplementary welfare benefit and social security. A local education authority is under a duty to bestow on persons who are 'ordinarily resident in the area of the authority' awards in respect of attendance on certain educational courses. None of these provisions is restricted to British citizens or Commonwealth citizens per se although obviously it must be presumed that in order to take up residence and avail of them most aliens will have complied with any applicable immigration requirements.   (Gardner, 1990, pp. 68–9)

None the less, the rights of aliens fall short of the rights of citizens in socially important ways – in ways which reduce their social capacities and social power relative to and in relation to citizens. Consequently, there is a range of specific compensatory rights incorporated into the UK's legal system – rights which originate in international law and conventions and which are therefore variously labelled as 'universal rights' or 'human rights'. In this context, Gardner (ibid., p. 65) refers to the *Universal Declaration of Human Rights* prepared by the United Nations in 1948 as 'the first major document to recognise [the] limits' on 'the way a State could act towards its own nationals' as well as individuals in general. Gardner explains that whereas 'traditionally States and not individuals were legal persons in international law, the atrocities of the thirties and forties led to the recognition of certain limitations and controls on the way in which the State could act towards its own nationals' (Gardner, p. 65), as well as individuals in general. That is, 'the impact of' the Universal Declaration of Human Rights, 'and its progeny, is usually seen in the importance of giving individuals a status in international law, ... undermining the assumption that the regulation of the relationship between the State and individuals is [merely] concerned with the relationship between the State and its [own] citizens' (ibid., p. 65).

Gardner points out that the rights specified by the Universal Declaration have been 'concretized' by the UN Covenants on Civil and Political Rights, as well as by the European Convention on Human Rights and Social Charter (Gardner, 1990, pp. 65–6). He argues that the rights involved are specifically 'human rights because they must be granted to all, without distinction on national or any other ground' (ibid., p. 66). The particular legal character of these rights lies in the way they 'emphasise, not who is defined as belonging to the political entity which is the State in such a way as to be given the right to participate, but what each individual may expect from the State, whatever the individual's degree of involvement with it' (ibid., p. 66). It is as a result of this legal specificity that human rights are 'importantly different' form the rights which Gardner labels as 'nationality citizenship rights' (ibid., p. 66). Gardner comes to the conclusion that such rights 'may be described as constituting new citizenship' (ibid., p. 66).[11]

The State, the Nation-state and Nationality 73

Gardner asserts that since the Second World War, the United Kingdom for instance has 'moved away from the nationality citizenship model' in the direction of the *new citizenship model* (ibid., p. 68). New citizenship rights

> affect a number of very important relationships between the individual (as opposed to the [nationality] citizen) and the State. In the first place they protect civil and political rights including the prohibition of certain ill-treatment, the control of detention and the protection of privacy, free speech, religion, assembly and fair trial, to name but a few examples. In addition they protect social and economic rights and claims including property rights, education, employment and benefits. (Ibid., p. 66)

New citizenship, like national citizenship, is about *individual* rights and relationships, as opposed to (at least in the first instance) collective rights and relationships. But, unlike national citizenship rights, new citizenship rights determine an individual's relationship to 'the State' in the special and novel sense of *any* 'State', whichever (if any) nation-state, national community or national political community the individual belongs to by virtue of his or her nationality, national citizenship or national citizenship rights – what might be referred to as, in other words, his or her 'membership state'. The United Nations' Universal Declaration of Human Rights includes the following examples of such human or universal rights: everyone has the right to freedom of movement and residence within the borders of each state (Article 13); everyone has the right to leave any country, including his [sic] own, and to return to his country (Article 13); everyone has the right to a nationality (Article 15); everyone has the right to work, to free choice of employment, to just and favourable conditions of work, to protection against unemployment (Article 23); everyone, without discrimination, has the right to equal pay for equal work (Article 23).[12]

The United Nations' Universal Declaration of Human Rights (proclaimed by the United Nations' General Assembly on 10 December 1948) was used to draw up the list of human rights contained within the Council of Europe's Convention for the Protection of Human Rights and Fundamental Freedoms, first signed on 4 November 1950 in Rome by the governments of all the then member countries of the Council of Europe. The Council of Europe had been set up a short time earlier, in 1949, to help secure 'greater unity between its Members', on the assumption that 'one of the methods by which that aim is to be pursued is the maintenance and further realisation of Human Rights and Fundamental Freedoms' (Commission on Citizenship, Appendix B, 1990, p. 55). Maurice Roche has portrayed the Council of Europe (CE) as follows:

> a human and social rights grouping ... which consists of 23 West European democracies, including the EC states, signatories to the European Declaration of Human Rights (Helsinki 1950) and the European Social Charter (1961). Its main institutions are the European Court of Human Rights, the European Commission of Human Rights and the CE's Parliamentary Assembly of representatives of member states' national parliaments .... It offers a court of appeal and redress ... to defend the human rights of the weak (e.g. prisoners, mental patients and immigrants) and to control the power of nation-state authorities. (Roche, 1992, pp. 195–6)[13]

The Council of Europe's headquarters are in Strasbourg, along with its Court – the European Court of Human Rights – which adjudicates on alleged breaches of the European Convention on Human Rights by individuals and their legal representatives.[14]

According to Malcolm Dean (December 1992), in order to become a member of the Council of Europe, a country's government is required to incorporate the European Convention on Human Rights into its legal system and provide its 'citizens with the right of individual petition' to the European Court of Human Rights. Furthermore, joining members are required to put their signatures to the subsequent European Social Charter. The European Social Charter is a declaration by the members of the Council of Europe that, having 'agreed to secure to their populations the civil and political rights and freedoms' (Commission on Citizenship, 1990, pp. 61–2) specified in the 1950 Convention, they will 'make every effort in common to improve the standard of living and to promote the social well-being of both their urban and rural populations by means of appropriate institutions and actions'. Moreover, the Charter's signatories accept that 'the enjoyment of social rights should be secured without discrimination on grounds of race, colour, sex, religion, political opinion, national extraction or social origin'. To these ends, the Charter contains such 'rights and principles' as: 'Everyone shall have the opportunity to earn his [sic] living in an occupation freely entered upon'; 'Children and young persons have the right to a special protection against the physical and moral hazards to which they are exposed'; 'Anyone without adequate resources has the right to social and medical assistance'; 'Everyone has the right to benefit from social welfare services'; 'The family as a fundamental unit of society has the right to appropriate social, legal and economic protection to ensure its full development'; and 'Mothers and children, irrespective of marital status and family relations, have the right to appropriate social and economic protection.'

The Council of Europe was created with the signing on 5 May 1949 of the Statute of the Council of Europe, which came into force on 3 August, when the first session of the Consultative Assembly of the Council of Europe took place. The original signatories to the Statute were Belgium, Denmark, France, Ireland, Italy, the Netherlands, Norway, Sweden and the United Kingdom. However, these original ten were quickly followed in 1949 by Greece and Turkey (Archer, 1990, p. 43), and by the end of the 1980s the following countries had also become members: Iceland (1950), West Germany (1951), Austria (1956), Cyprus (1961), Switzerland (1962), Malta (1965), Portugal (1976), Spain (1977), Liechtenstein (1978), Finland (1988), and San Marino (1988). At the end of the 1980s, the 23 full members of the Council of Europe were complemented by four countries (from what was then the *Eastern Bloc*) which had either 'associate membership' or 'special guest status': Yugoslavia, Poland, Czechoslovakia and the USSR. Since then, of course, there have been major political and economic changes in eastern and central Europe centred on *the collapse of Communism* and the fragmentation of several nation states, including Yugoslavia, Czechoslovakia and the USSR. These developments have led to Bulgaria, the Czech Republic, Hungary, Poland, Slovakia, the former Yugoslav federal republic of Slovenia, along with the Baltic states of Estonia and Lithuania becoming full members. John Palmer then reported at the beginning of October 1993, 'Romania – despite doubts about its human rights record – will join in the next few days. Applications for membership are being considered from Latvia, Albania, Russia, Ukraine, Croatia, Byelorus and Moldova' (Palmer, October 1993).

By the autumn of 1993, the Council of Europe's membership had risen to thirty-two countries following the admission of Romania (Watson, October 1993), all of which were represented by government ministers at the Council's Summit in Vienna at the beginning of October. At this meeting, all thirty-two member states, according to Rory Watson, 'insisted on the protection and respect of the many national minorities within their boundaries', there being '75 potential flashpoints involving national minorities [which] have been identified in Europe, Turkey and the former Soviet Union'. But, despite this common declaration, the treatment of one particular ethnic minority within Romania lay behind the way the 'recent decision by the Council of Europe to grant Romania membership has been met with dismay by the country's 1.8 million Hungarians' (Marrett and Bond, October 1993). Marrett and Bond claim that for 'many years', the Hungarian minority 'have met with unfair treatment. The international rights organisation Helsinki Watch recently said that Hungarians in Romania have been "increasingly subjected to a series of abusive policies" through local officials'.

It is because of such *abuses* that, following Rory Watson, there 'has been a growing clamour to incorporate the protection of [minorities] into the existing European Convention on Human Rights'. Watson argues that these rights, 'clearly set out, and rigorously enforced by independent judges in Strasbourg, have proved to be the backbone of civil liberties in western and, increasingly, in central and eastern Europe. Few governments have escaped the judges' condemnation and not been forced to change some item of legislation.' Watson touches on the example of how Council of Europe officials have 'given advice to Latvia in framing its citizenship legislation', or more precisely (following Gardner's terminology) its national citizenship legislation. The case of Latvia and the other Baltic states is instructive with regard to the relationship between national citizenship and new citizenship within the context of late-twentieth-century European social, economic and political frameworks, processes and change.

The two Baltic states of Estonia and Lithuania were admitted to the Council of Europe on 14 May 1993 to coincide with the end of Britain's turn to hold the presidency of the Council. Their entry followed an uncertain period during which their applications to join were controversial and closely scrutinised because of the way their governments were treating their ethnic minority populations, and especially the *ethnic Russians* who had been left behind when they were constituent republics of the USSR. All three Baltic states declared independence in 1990, and it was 'the failure of the August 1991 Moscow coup and [subsequent] dissolution of the USSR which set the seal on independence' (Duplain, July 1993).[15] Malcolm Dean (Dean, December 1992), reporting at the end of 1992 when the Baltic states were in the process of applying for membership, tells us that each had 'had an inspection by a Strasbourg team' because all three had 'introduced a variety of laws to deprive Russian residents of their citizenship and their right to vote, own property, or work for the government'. More precisely, 'Latvia's new law denies citizenship to people who have not been resident for at least 16 years, Lithuania sets 10 years, but Estonia only three.' As a result of these new laws, almost '50 per cent of Latvia's population is now "foreign" (Russian, Ukrainian or Belorussian) as is 40 per cent of Estonia's. Only in Lithuania is the proportion much lower'. The new laws evoked strong condemnation from the similarly newly emergent Russian Federation. The two most northerly Baltic states of Estonia and Latvia became the main targets of Russian criticism, anger and threats, As Christine Verity (Verity, June 1993) points out:

> Unlike Lithuania, with its small Russian minority and liberal [national] citizenship law, [Estonia and Latvia] face almost daily denunciations from Moscow for denying full voting rights to their large Russian minorities – in Latvia's case one-third of the voting-age population. Russian troop withdrawals are bogged down by accusations of human rights

abuse against Latvia's Russian population. The fact that Latvia has not allowed the vote to people who have come to the republic since its incorporation into Stalin's empire in 1940 has caused particular offence to Moscow. Western governments have been more understanding of Latvia's position: Latvia faced a chilling period of deportations and persecution under Stalin, who also imported hundreds of thousands of migrant workers to change the ethnic balance of the country once and for all. Now, with nearly half the country's population of Russian origin, many Latvians want to secure their position by carefully regulating the citizenship rights of the postwar colonisers in their newly-liberated state. The Russian minority feel disadvantaged by not having citizenship. Most of the local Russians voted with the Latvians for independence in 1990. They interpret as a kick in the teeth the refusal to let the half-million of them who do not meet citizenship requirements vote in the recent parliamentary elections [which took place on 6 June 1993]. They are the group in society most likely to lose their jobs when economic reform bites. They have to put up with bureaucratic hassle, and delays in registration for citizenship.

In Estonia, the new laws attracted both external and internal protests. As reported in the *Guardian* towards the end of June 1993 (*Guardian*, 24 June 1993):

Russia said yesterday it would retaliate politically and economically against Estonia for passing an aliens law which it sees as a discriminatory law against ethnic Russians. Vitaly Churkin, Russia's deputy foreign minister, said: 'Russia has warned Estonia against discriminatory measures. Now that the law has been passed, the foreign ministry is working on a complex set of measures to influence Estonia which will include political, economic and other steps.' The law obliges non-Estonians to apply for citizenship or obtain a residence permit within two years. Those who do not will have to leave Estonia. It also limits the rights of former Soviet army officers and their families to apply for citizenship or residence permits. Mr Churkin said that Moscow's measures could affect trade relations with Estonia and the withdrawal of former Soviet troops.

This external pressure on Estonia was accompanied by internal demands from the Russian and other *non-Estonian* ethnic minorities. As reported in *The European* (*The European*, 24–7 June 1993):

> Half a million ethnic Russians in Estonia, most of whom have lived in the country for decades, were classified by the Estonian parliament as 'foreigners', prompting thousands of local Russians to march in protest. The ethnic Russians, Byelorussians and Ukrainians who form 40 per cent of Estonia's 1.6 million population now have to apply for residence permits every five years. The law is the latest of many passed by the Estonian parliament which Russia says discriminates against the Russian ethnic minority living in Estonia. Few of the new arrivals bothered to learn Estonian, one of Europe's most difficult and least spoken languages, which is one reason why they are denied citizenship.

In addition to the external Russian and internal ethnic-Russian pressure against its new laws, the Estonian government was mindful of its aspiration to become a member of the Council of Europe. There had been signs already that this consideration had led the Baltic states to limit their actions against ethnic Russians: 'Russians who are refused citizenship will not be expelled [because it] would be a clear breach under article three of the [Council of Europe's 1950] convention, which prevents the persecution of minorities'; as well as of 'article four of protocol four [which] prevents collective expulsions' (Dean, December 1992). At the same time, however, the new laws, requirements and restrictions might still have had the (indirect) result of persuading ethnic Russians to leave. As Malcolm Dean puts it: 'the [Strasbourg] court will want to examine whether the restrictions are an implicit expulsion by denying people the chance to work, a home and a vote' (ibid.). Apparently, the findings of the Court's investigation were favourable enough for the Council of Europe to admit Estonia and Lithuania as its thirtieth and thirty-first members in the middle of May 1993. However, this event did not bring an end to the pressure on the Baltic states to ease back on their new laws, including what emerged as effective pressure from the Council of Europe. As reported by the *Guardian* early in July 1993:

> Estonia's aliens law, which provoked a crisis with Russia, does not meet European legal standards, the Council of Europe said yesterday. A five-member panel appointed by the council at the request of the Estonian president, Lennart Meri, called for the law to be revised. The legislation which was passed last week, governs the status of about 38 per cent of the Baltic republic's 1.6 million population, mainly ethnic Russians. It gives local Russians two years to seek citizenship, apply for a residence permit or leave the country. Moscow reacted to the law by threatening economic sanctions and imposing a temporary gas embargo against Estonia, which won independence from the Soviet Union in 1991. 'The experts' first opinion highlights a number of deficiencies in the law and inconsistencies with the norms of European law', the Council of Europe said. The experts said the law gave the authorities too much discretionary power and contained vague language which was open to abuse. (*Guardian*, 7 July 1993)

This decision led to an alteration in the legislation, but only after a confrontation between Estonia's head of state and parliament:

> The Estonian president, Lennart Meri, has refused to sign a law which sparked a row over the rights of the Baltic state's Russian minority. He has returned it to parliament to be reconsidered. A presidential spokesman said Mr Meri decided to return the 'law on aliens' to parliament 'after thorough consultations in Estonia and with international experts'. (*Guardian*, 8 July 1993)

A few days later, on 12 July 1993, the president felt able to change his mind about signing:

> Estonia's president, Lennart Meri, yesterday signed a revised version of a controversial law classifying most Russians in the state as foreigners. 'This law is now in accordance with European legal principles,' Mr Meri said. The law, which has been heavily criticised, went back in an amended form to

parliament last week after the president bowed to international pressure and refused to sign the original version. (*Guardian*, 13 July 1993)

What this Baltic states example illustrates is the distinction between, following Gardner, *national citizenship* and *new citizenship*, and the way the former can be shaped by and may incorporate the latter. It illustrates also how – using Rainer Baubock's terminology (Baubock, 1991; see ch. 1) – a hierarchy of sub-national political communities within an overarching national political community which are defined, separated and unequal in terms of national citizenship rights can be shaped not only by internal political struggles (such as between ethnic groupings), but also by external political relations and pressures. In this particular example, the external pressures were what may be referred to as *extra*-national ones, covering both *inter*-national pressure (especially from Russia) and *supra*-national pressure (especially from the Council of Europe).[16] The extra-national pressure, as we have seen, entailed a combination of the deployment and threat of political (including military) and economic sanctions from Russia and disapproval from the Council of Europe, from which Estonia could have been expelled for failing to bring its laws, regulations and requirements relating to national citizenship rights in line with the Council's 1950 Convention.

However, the Baltic states example follows a long sequence of cases where member states have bowed to pressure from the Council of Europe, often with the help of Court action. For instance, as Malcolm Dean (Dean, December 1992) reports, 'aliens' rights have become more firmly established by a Belgian case in which a delinquent Moroccan, who had lived in Belgium with his mother since the age of two, was due to be deported back to North Africa at the age of 20 when the deportation was stopped by Strasbourg'. Earlier, the British government was brought before the Court in the 1960s 'under article three of the convention, which prevents the persecution of minorities'. That is, 'Britain was taken to Strasbourg for its 1968 Act which withdrew automatic residency rights from East African Asians. Britain was found in breach of article three through its "inhuman and degrading treatment" of the intended immigrants' (ibid.).

This example of Britain contravening the 1950 Convention is by no means isolated. Malcolm Dean (Dean, May 1993) tells us that the 'European Court has found Britain in breach of the convention in more than 30 landmark rulings, requiring the government to extend individual rights'. Moreover, according to David Rose (Rose, May 1993), Britain has 'the worst record of any of the signatories to the Human Rights Convention, with nearly 50 adverse decisions in the Strasbourg court. Decisions in Strasbourg have forced Britain in make important concessions in the fields of free speech and prisoners' rights.' Or, as John Palmer adds, in 'recent years the British government has been found at fault in a series of Northern Ireland human rights cases, as well as in appeals against corporal punishment in schools' (Palmer, October 1993).

The total number of cases being brought to the Court has been increasing, and it seems likely to continue to do so even more rapidly. Malcolm Dean (Dean, May 1993) tells us that 'Over 5,500 individuals petitioned Strasbourg last year, and officials estimate this could rise to 15,000 by the year 2000'; and with 'the increase in member states from eastern Europe the backlog [of petitions] is getting worse'. Although John Palmer presents us with somewhat different statistics, his sense of foreboding is similar:

> Last year, out of 1,861 applications to the court, only 189 were 'admissable'. [Nevertheless,] 'At present it can take five or six years before there is a definitive ruling in some cases,' Catherine Lalumière, secretary-general of the Council of Europe, said. 'It is vital to speed up the process, not least because we foresee a big increase in appeals brought to the court as more and more countries in central and eastern Europe are admitted as full members.' (Palmer, October 1993)

According to David Rose (May 1993), the 'reform favoured by the majority of the Convention signatories is to replace the present two-tier system with a single layer court, which would, unlike the present arrangement, sit permanently. The court, which now has judges from each of [the] signatory nations sitting in every case, would also get smaller. But earlier this month, Britain supported only by Ireland, Italy and Denmark, blocked this proposal.' Malcolm Dean tells us that 'Britain brought its six-month presidency of the Council of Europe to a close in Strasbourg yesterday, having succeeded in further delaying the reform of the European Court of Human Rights. Almost all member states now support the idea of a single court to replace the existing complex arrangements, but Britain, having originally opposed any change, said at yesterday's meeting of ministers that it wants to change to a two-tier system, necessitating further negotiations' (Dean, May 1993).

Eventually, however, Britain came around to giving its agreement in time for the Council Summit in Vienna in October 1993. As a result:

> The European Court of Human Rights is to be expanded and its legal proceedings speeded up, in anticipation of a huge wave of appeals from countries in central and eastern Europe. Under proposals to be put before the heads of government of the Council of Europe, human rights cases will be sent directly to the court, bypassing initial vetting by individual governments. The council summit is also expected to abolish the Commission on Human Rights. The commission, consisting of lawyers from the council members, has until now acted as a preliminary filter restricting the number of cases referred to the court. (Palmer, October 1993)

The claim has been made that Britain had an ulterior motive in delaying the reforms given, in particular, the way they would allow petitioners to bypass governments and go directly to the Court:

> The [British] government is secretly trying to undermine the European Court of Human Rights, blocking reforms urgently needed to avoid the system collapsing. 'It looks as if the British Government's strategy is to let the system collapse at the seams to prevent further embarrassment,' a senior Strasbourg source said last night. 'This business smells very bad.' (Rose, May 1993)

The embarrassment referred to presumably arises out of Britain having, following Rose, *the worst record of any of the signatories to the Human Rights Convention*, especially because in 'recent years the British government has been found at fault in a series of Northern Ireland human rights cases' (Palmer, October 1993). However, not all judgements concerning Northern Ireland have gone against the British government. For instance, in 1993, the Court gave its verdict in a case where it was claimed that Britain had contravened Article 5(3) of the 1950 Convention, which states that everyone 'who is arrested or detained shall be brought promptly before a judge or other officer authorised by law to exercise judicial power and shall be entitled to trial within a reasonable time or to release pending trial'. This is the case of *Brannigan and McBride v. the United Kingdom*, the Court presenting its judgement on 26 May 1993. As David Sharrock summarises:

> The court said that the situation in Northern Ireland justified an exemption for Britain from a requirement under the Human Rights Convention to bring suspects to court promptly. Peter Brannigan, aged 29, from Downpatrick, and 42-year-old Partrick McBride, from Belfast, were arrested in January 1989. Mr Brannigan was held for more than six days and Mr McBride, more than four. The act allows police to detain a suspect for up to 48 hours. This can then be extended by five days with the approval of the Home Secretary. But the Human Rights Convention requires that anyone arrested or detained 'shall be brought promptly before a judge and shall be entitled to trial within a reasonable time'. The European Court [had] found Britain guilty of violating the convention in December 1988 after a similar case. The Government then invoked an exemption under another convention provision [Article 15(1)]. This states that in time of war or 'other public emergency threatening the life of the nation', a government can be exempted from its obligations 'to the extent strictly required by the exigencies of the situation'. (Sharrock, May 1993)

Greater detail about the case and the judgement has been provided by Shiranikha Herbert (Herbert, May 1993):

> UK legislation which allows terrorist suspects to be detained for several days without being brought before a judge was

declared by the European Court of Human Rights to be an appropriate measure taken in a public emergency. Therefore such detention is not a violation of the UK's obligations under the European Convention for the Protection of Human Rights and Fundamental Freedoms. In January 1989 Peter Brannigan and Patrick McBride were arrested and interrogated in Northern Ireland under the Prevention of Terrorism (Temporary Provisions) Act 1984 which permits the arrest without warrant of those suspected of terrorist activity. The Home Secretary granted extensions of their detention. They complained of violations of article 5(3) of the Human Rights Convention which states everyone arrested and detained 'shall be brought promptly before a judge'. The UK government relied on article 15 which states that 'in time of war or other public emergency threatening the life of the nation [a state] may take measures derogating from its obligations' under the convention 'to the extent strictly required by the exigencies of the situation'. The court said that national authorities were in a better position than international judges to determine whether the life of the nation was threatened by a public emergency and, if so, how far it was necessary to go to overcome the emergency. Nevertheless the court had to rule on whether the state had gone beyond the extent strictly required by the exigencies of the crisis. In the light of the material before it on the extent and impact of terrorist violence in the UK, the court considered there was no doubt such an emergency existed. The Government had responsibility for establishing a balance between combating terrorism and respecting individual rights. In Northern Ireland, where the judiciary was vulnerable, public confidence in the independence of the judiciary was a matter to which the Government attached great importance. In the circumstances, the Government had not exceeded the margin in deciding against judicial control. The court held by 22 votes to four that the UK's derogation from the convention was valid.

In response to the Court's judgement, as Sharrock (Sharrock, May 1993) reports, the 'Belfast based Committee on the Administration of Justice said it would continue its campaign against' the Prevention of Terrorism Act. However, for the time being, the Act continues to be used by the British government. Thus, in July 1993, David Sharrock reported the case of John Matthews, the 22-year-old 'who was flown back to Northern Ireland from England in handcuffs last week after two and a half months in prison':

> Although charges against Mr Matthews were dropped, the Home Secretary, Michael Howard, signed an exclusion order against him, in effect exiling him to his native Derry, because he said he had information which implicated him in terrorism. This week, Mr Matthews met 40-year-old [Danny] McBrearty [who] was made the subject of an exclusion order banning him from Great Britain in circumstances which closely resemble the Matthews case. It is not difficult to believe him when he says he lives in fear; it is etched on his face. In October 1989, while working on a London building site, he was arrested and held for seven days under the Prevention of Terrorism Act, at the end of which he was charged with possessing explosives. Three months later, after numerous remand hearings at which magistrates were told there was compelling forensic evidence against him, the charge was dropped. Mr McBrearty was about to leave Lambeth magistrates' court a free man in January 1990 when he was rearrested, taken to Paddington Green police station and held over night while awaiting the exclusion order. This January [1993] he watched the post anxiously. Days before the three-year order was due to expire another one arrived, for another three years. In total, 81 exclusion orders were in force at the end of [1992], fewer than in any year since 1982.   (Sharrock, July 1993)

On the face of it, such exclusion orders may be viewed as being contrary to Article 5(1) of the Council of Europe's 1950 Convention, according to which 'Everyone has the right to liberty.' Perhaps more straightforwardly, they are inconsistent with the United Nations' Universal Declaration of Human Rights, Article 13(1) of which stipulates that *everyone has the right to freedom of movement and residence within the borders of each state*; and Article 13(2) of which stipulates that *everyone has the right to leave any country, including his [sic] own, and to return to his country*. Such possibilities aside, it has been claimed that the exclusion order against Danny Matthews contravenes yet another extra-national agreement to which the British government is a signatory – that of the European Community's *Single European Act*. The Single European Act (SEA) was signed by all the Member States of the European Community in February 1986, and it 'entered into force on 1 July 1987' (Swann, 1992, p. 16). The SEA has *Treaty status* in that 'First, and foremost, there are provisions amending the EEC Treaty, [including] Article 8A EEC (now Article 7A EC), containing a definition of the internal market and setting the deadline of December 31 1992' for its full implementation (Shaw, 1993, p. 37). As Swann tells us, the SEA specifies that '"the internal market shall comprise an area without internal frontiers". Moreover, this area without frontier controls [is] to apply across the board, to goods, services, persons and capital. The [European] Commission was of the view that in the short term, checks and controls were to be relaxed and rationalised, though in the long term they were destined to go' (ibid., p. 18).[17] It is because of the way the *treaty provisions* of the SEA stipulate that within the internal market there is to be *free movement of people*, that the Matthews case was taken to the Commission.

As John Carvel reports:

> The European Commission promised yesterday to investigate whether the Government's exclusion order on John Matthews was a breach of EC rules on the free movement of citizens. Raniero Vanni D'Archirafi, the commissioner responsible for the internal market, said he would take up the case following an appeal in the European Parliament from John Hume, leader of the Social Democratic and Labour Party and one Northern Ireland's three MEPs. 'Mr Hume asked how it was possible for a man to leave court without a stain on his character and be subjected to limits on his freedom of movement which were in conflict with the principles of the EC Single Market. His officials said last night that it was very unlikely the commission would take action against the Government pursuing what British ministers consider to be a domestic matter involving alleged terrorism. But Mr Hume's intervention succeeded in raising the

issue of how British citizens can be confined to one part of the United Kingdom when all EC citizens are supposed to be allowed to pass unimpeded throughout the community. The exclusion order was described by Kevin McNamara, Labour's Northern Ireland spokesman, as a form of 'internal exile which even the Russians did away with'. A Government spokesman in Brussels said that the Matthews case was an internal UK affair. 'We are talking about movement within a country rather than movement between the countries of the EC,' he said. 'This is a matter of internal security and the Single European Act preserves member states' discretion to take whatever measures they consider necessary' he said.   (Carvel, July 1993)

This interpretation of the SEA has received support from elsewhere. As Dennis Swann points out:

> The SEA calls for the complete free movement of persons – a matter about which there has been, and no doubt will continue to be, considerable controversy. Mrs Thatcher [when British prime minister] has been forthright on this subject. In her famous, to some infamous, speech in Bruges in 1988 she declared 'it is a matter of plain common sense that we cannot totally abolish frontier controls if we are also to protect our citizens from crime and stop the movement of drugs, or terrorists, and of illegal immigrants' [Margaret Thatcher, 1988, p. 7]. The UK argued that though the SEA envisaged easier passage for nationals of member states, it did not intend this to apply to nationals of third countries; therefore it could maintain border controls if only to control third country nationals. This may be a convenient piece of logic chopping, but nevertheless there is no doubt that the SEA did provide support for UK resistance since one of the declarations at the end of the act guarantees that nothing in it shall prevent states taking such measures as they consider necessary to control third country immigrants, terrorism, crime, drug-trafficking and illicit trade in art and antiques.   (Swann, 1992, pp. 18–19)

Apart from the progress of the Matthews case being of interest in itself, it is, in combination and comparison with other cases, instructive with regard to the distinction and relationship between national citizenship and new citizenship; to the political frameworks within which this relationship develops both in particular cases and in general, and so historically; to the political relationships, political communities, political bodies (such as national governments and extra-national institutions) and political interests which characterise these frameworks and developments; and to the part played by the relative *power* of the political communities, interest groups and bodies in the frameworks and developments, and thereby in determining the parts played by national citizenship and new citizenship in the everyday lives of the people of the United Kingdom and the rest of Europe.

The cases demonstrate how national and sub-national political communities, interest groups and bodies which are engaged in struggles, clashes and conflicts over national citizenship can be drawn into extra-national political frameworks which are founded on extra-national agreements (conventions, treaties) and supported by extra-national institutional arrangements concerning the administration of new citizenship. When national governments are charged with not only the tasks of granting and guaranteeing or enforcing national citizenship rights, but also the tasks of interpreting, implementing and incorporating new citizenship rights, people (individuals, collectivities, interest groups, sub-national political communities) may complain about their performance, challenge their decisions, and take them to the extra-national agencies (including the United Nations' International Court of Justice; the Council of Europe's Court of Human Rights; and the European Community's Court of Justice) which are in turn charged with the tasks of judging such cases, and of trying to ensure compliance (by national governments) and consistency (between national citizenship and new citizenship).

However, a further point has to be made about the processes through which national citizenship rights and new citizenship rights are arrived at and altered; through which new citizenship is interpreted, implemented and incorporated; through which the struggles, clashes and conflicts over the latter proceed and are settled; and through which extra-national agencies become involved, intervene and make decision. The point is that these processes take place within political frameworks which are characterised by diverse, perhaps irreconcilable, political interests which are pursued by political communities within the context of unequal distributions of political power, influence and control. The issue emerges, therefore, of the way such patterns of diversity and inequality affect the processes (in particular cases and in general), and whether the results include inconsistencies and contradictions between national citizenship and new citizenship, between cases, over time, between national communities, between sub-national communities, and so on.

The comparative details and outcomes of the Matthews case, the Brannigan and McBride case, the Romania case, and the Estonia case, among others, bring to mind the issue of the part played, in these particular cases and in general, by the interests and power of the national governments involved in relation to (a) sub-national political communities; (b) other national governments; and (c) the extra-national bodies and agencies charged with administering extra-national agreements and new citizenship rights. Thus, the Estonian government was strongly and successfully put under pressure by the Russian government and the Council of Europe to alter its national citizenship laws, regulations and requirements so as to bring them into line with the Council of Europe's 1950 Convention. In contrast, the British government was not put under the same level of pressure when the Court of Human Rights recognised that in the Brannigan and McBride case it had similarly failed to comply with the provisions of the convention. The Court resorted to Article 15(1) of the convention, and claimed that the British government had legitimately derogated – or deviated from – the convention given the prevailing national circumstances, emergency and interest. This is despite the fact that the Court had, as was noted by David Sharrock, *found Britain guilty of violating the convention in December 1988 after a similar case.* Here, whereas the Court failed to excuse the British government's deviation with reference to Article 15(1), the British government itself did so in support of its rejection of the Court's finding.

The cases mentioned bring to mind the issue of the part played in the Court of Human Rights' deliberations and decisions by the Court's own relative power and comparative interests in relation to national governments, political communities, interest groups, and so on. The possibilities arise, for instance, of the Court coming to decisions guided by its own interests (in securing the Council of Europe and its institutions) and by its own power and control relative to national governments' power and control, both in general and in particular; of the Court, given its own comparative interests and relative power, arriving at decisions which suit the interests of national governments rather than sub-national political communities, interest groups and individuals; and of the Court making decisions which correspond with the interests of some national governments more than others.

Of course, the issue of the relative power and control of the Court of Human Rights, the Council of Europe, national governments, sub-national political communities, individuals and so on, is about the balance of *sovereignty* within Europe over decision-making with regard to, for instance, citizenship. As such, the issue has itself generated concern, clashes and conflict among a similar array of interested parties in view of the implications for citizenship of what appears to be a drift within Europe towards ever-greater *political union*, especially by way of the European Community, perhaps to the point of *political federation* and therefore a 'United States of Europe' (see Ernest Wistrich, 1989, 1994). Certainly, the passage of the Maastricht Treaty, which finally came into force on 1 November 1993, reflects the general character of what might be referred to as *the struggle over sovereignty* within the European Community, including the common tendency for the struggle to bring no more than temporary delays in what appears to be an irresistible march towards stronger and tighter *European Union*.

This is perhaps reflected in the way in which, in celebration of the coming into force of the Maastricht Treaty, or more accurately of *The Treaty on European Union*, John Palmer has written:

> From midnight yesterday the Common Market was finally buried, the European Community faded into Hallowe'en's shadows and the European Union proudly awaited the first light of a new day. 'For legal purposes the European Community continues a sort of half-life within the European Union. Under the [Maastricht] treaty, the 12[18] will continue

to do certain important things as a "Community". But overall, and certainly in areas such as foreign, security and eventually defence policy, they will be deciding as the "Union",' one EC constitutional lawyer explained yesterday. 'It is all to do with the fact that the treaty sets out different decision-making "pillars", as they are known. Some are an extension of the old Community powers and some are specific to the new Union.' (Palmer, November 1993)

However, it has been otherwise claimed that

> The first thing to be said is that the EC is not dead. Maastricht specifically states: 'The Union shall be founded on the European Communities, supplemented by the policies and forms of co-operation established by this treaty'. As Noreen Burrows, professor of European Law at Glasgow University explained last week: 'Only the European Community, under article 215 of the treaty has legal personality.' This means that it is only the EC which can sign international treaties and trade arrangements with third countries. The 25,000 full-time European officials are employed by the EC, not the Union. (Walker, November 1993)

In other words, these officials are employed by one of what are identified as the three *decision-making pillars* of the emergent European Union, and more specifically by the central pillar:

> The supranational EC is the core of the new Union, buttressed on either side by two inter-governmental pillars. One will deal with common foreign and security policy, the other with co-operation on justice and home affairs. That structure is collectively known as the European Union. Decisions taken by the EC on a range of issues are subject to the rule of law and may be challenged or enforced by the European Court of Justice in Luxembourg. Being outside the formal EC framework, no such recourse is available for action carried out under the other two pillars. The various Community institutions – Council of Ministers, Commission, Parliament, Court of Auditors and Court of Justice – are EC bodies with clearly defined roles laid down in law.

Apart from the Council, consisting of government ministers, their position in the Union is less clear-cut. The powers of the two courts do not extend to the Union and the status of both the Commission and Parliament are considerably reduced – largely to a consultative level. The British government has opted-out of the Social Chapter – covering social security, labour relations and trade union agreements – which is the basis for social policy among the remaining 11 members of the EC. Britain has also reserved its position on whether to join the final stage of the EC's programme for economic and monetary union (EMU), including the single currency. Under Maastricht, EMU will be achieved by 1999 at the latest.   (Lucy Walker, ibid.)

Edward Pilkington has suggested that while 1 November 1993 'may come to be remembered as the dawn of a new era' for Europe, most 'people in Britain remained blissfully unaware of the day's significance, as the date when the Maastricht treaty finally dragged itself wheezing across the finishing line. It was the day when the British citizen was transformed into a new, elevated being: the Citizen of Europe, or COE' (Pilkington, November 1993). Pilkington asks 'what this brave new world of supranationals might look like', and answers:

The bulk of the treaty's provisions are so rarefied as to be hardly noticeable to the individual. They include greater collaboration over such matters as education, health, culture, foreign policy and crime. The most immediate change for the COE next door is that citizens of the 12 member states are now entitled to vote in each other's elections, provided they fulfil local criteria. That means that Britons living abroad will be able to vote in local and European elections, and stand for election.   (Ibid.)

However, the Maastrict provisions on the voting rights of the new Citizens of the Union are not universally applicable. As Lucy Walker explains:

The exception will be tiny Luxembourg, where a cluster of EC institutions and a long-established Portuguese community give it the highest proportion of EC immigrants of any

Community country. Here, residents will have to wait five years to stand or vote for the European Parliament and ten years for local elections. (Walker, November 1993)

Luxembourg is the only exception because of its small population size, but there is a clause in the Maastricht Treaty that would allow other Member States to opt out of the general provision. This is clarified by Vitali Vitaliev in the following way:

> Luxembourg, which besides the smallest state, is also Europe's 'largest' immigrant nation. Proportionately, that is. Almost 30 per cent of the country's 400,000-strong population are foreign nationals, and more than one-third of those are Portuguese. It has become a cliche to refer to Luxembourg as the melting pot of Europe. And yet all foreign nationals living in Luxembourg are still denied one basic [citizenship] right – the right to elect and be elected. Only 'a Luxembourger, man or woman', says the constitution, enjoys that right. Why don't the Portuguese take Luxembourg citizenship, which any foreigner can do after ten years of residence? [The answer partly lies in the fact that] Portugal doesn't recognise double citizenship. That's why less than one per cent of the Portuguese in Luxembourg volunteer to become citizens of the Grand Duchy, which means loss of their Portuguese nationality. [Maastricht] gives every EC national the right to vote in the European elections, no matter in which EC state he lives. But for countries with a foreign population above 20 per cent, there is a derogation clause. [The] only EC country with more than 20 per cent of foreigners is Luxembourg. (Vitaliev, November 1993)

The issue arises of whether in this case there is evidence of an *ethnically-sensitive, perhaps biased*, opt-out clause in the Maastricht Treaty provisions on the rights of the Citizens of the Union. Certainly, there is evidence of how Citizens of the Union may in practice exercise – and even may be required to exercise in an ethnically laden manner – one supra-national citizenship right at the expense of another. Thus, according to Article 8a(1) of the Treaty of European Union: 'Every citizen of the Union shall have the right to move and reside freely within the territory of the Member States, subject to the limitations and conditions laid down in this Treaty and by the measures adopted to give it effect.' This provision is, of course, consistent with the purpose of the Single European Act, which describes the single or internal market as 'an area without internal frontiers in which free movement of goods, persons, services and capital is ensured' (UK Office of the European Parliament, 1989, p. 3). But, it is not wholly consistent with the Maastricht Treaty's derogation clause with regard to the pan-EC electoral rights of Citizens of the Union.

The issues of the particulars of the Maastricht Treaty's provisions on Citizenship of the Union and the ethnically-biased ramifications of the European Community and Union's treaties and acts are of obvious importance to the task of analysing and understanding the part played by citizenship within Europe – including within the everyday, immediate lives, relationships and experiences of the people of Europe – and therefore recur as major threads running through the ensuing chapters.

Certainly the further, underlying issue of the trend in the balance, distribution and *re*-distribution of sovereignty within Europe in favour of extra-national arrangements, organisations and institutions is more germane in the case of the European Community and Union than it is in the case of the Council of Europe. This is due, in the first place, to differences in the type of founding agreements involved, given that the Council of Europe is based upon its 1949 Statute, 1950 Convention and 1961 Charter; whereas the European Community and Union is rooted in its original 1950s Treaties as amended by the SEA and in the Maastricht Treaty. It is the European Community and Union's treaties rather than the Council of Europe's *weaker* types of founding agreements[19] which bring super-ordinate and binding laws, rights, requirements and responsibilities accompanied by supporting, supranational administrative arrangements. Thus, the Matthews case is likely to have more far-reaching consequences than the Brannigan and McBride case within and through the relationship between 'European new citizenship' and UK national citizenship. A major focus of the remaining chapters is specifically that of the implications of the evolution of the

European Community and Union for European citizenship. In this regard, the relevance of the trend within the European Community and Union towards ever-greater supra-national sovereignty is explored in much more detail in the final chapter. In the next chapter, however, I will turn to elucidating a couple of other fundamental features of the relationship between national citizenship and new citizenship within Europe.

3 Citizenship, Migration, Asylum and Race-ethnicity

Earlier, we noted how in the Brannigan and McBride case the Court had to *rule on whether the state had gone beyond the extent strictly required by the exigencies of the Northern Ireland crisis* when the British government applied its Prevention of Terrorism Act. The Court decided that the emergency which existed in Northern Ireland justified the British government's derogation of the 1950 Convention. The Court argued that the British government *had a responsibility for establishing a balance between combating terrorism and respecting individual rights,* and the emergency in Northern Ireland warranted the way in which the latter had been sacrificed in pursuing the former and, thereby, the national community interests.

Perhaps what the Court's opinion in this case serves to confirm is that *in the final analysis* the balance is firmly tipped in favour of the interests of the national community (and therefore those members and sections of the national community whose interests coincide most with it) against the interests of the individual, even within liberal democracies with their ideological emphasis on individual rights and freedoms in relation to and through the state. Certainly what the Court's opinion confirms is the way in which new citizenship corresponds with national citizenship in being about individual rights rather than collective rights. Both national citizenship and new citizenship establish in the first place the relationships of individuals rather than collectivities with *the state* (that which grants and guarantees or enforces the rights involved), even though national citizenship does so in relation to an individual's particular 'membership state' and new citizenship does so in relation to all states (whatever the individual's involvement, as Gardner puts it) which are bound by the necessary extra-national agreements. In this way, both national citizenship and new citizenship reflect and reinforce the ideological emphasis, in liberal democracies, on the individual and individualism as distinct from collectivities – at least certain collectivities (e.g. trade unions) rather than others (e.g nation-states).

The point about the *individualistic* character (albeit with collectivistic ramifications) of the Council of Europe's founding agreements has been registered by Malcolm Dean (Dean, December 1992) in the following way: 'Strasbourg has been a place associated with establishing individual rather than collective rights, [even though] the individual cases have frequently produced protection for groups', such as ethnic minorities in the Baltic countries. However, while both national citizenship and new citizenship are individualistic in character, the two types of citizenship differ in another socially important and sociologically significant respect. This difference follows from Gardner's distinction between 'citizenship' and 'nationality' on legalistic grounds, and concerns the point that while all the 'national citizens' of a particular nation-state are 'nationals', not all 'nationals' are 'citizens'.

Gardner's notion of 'nationality citizenship' invites an examination of what is meant by 'nationality' and of how this status may be distinguished from that of 'citizenship'. For Gardner, 'nationality' and 'citizenship' are legally distinct concepts which none the less overlap as 'nationality citizenship' (Gardner, 1990, p. 63), or as what I prefer to call 'national citizenship'. The legal distinction between nationality and citizenship hinges upon Gardner's prior clarification of (a) the notion of 'State',[1] or perhaps more accurately of his notion of 'nation state'; (b) the legal relationships between nation-states and people; and (c) by way of these relationships, the empirical, practical or substantial relationships between nation-states. Thus

> The legal analysis of citizenship derives in part from the notion of a State [sic] in international law. A State in international law is a territory, subject to an authority which is recognised by other States as competent in respect of that territory and the people living there. An attribute of a State, an aspect of its sovereignty, is therefore its ability to confer nationality on its population, a nationality which derives its legitimacy from its acceptance by other nation states. It

follows that States represent and protect the interests of their nationals vis-à-vis other States. (Ibid., p. 64)

Gardner's legal definition of *State*, or *nation-state*, resembles Max Weber's sociological definition of 'the state' as 'an organization which successfully upholds a claim to binding rule-making over a territory, by virtue of commanding a monopoly of the legitimate use of force' (Mann, 1983, p. 373). In other words, following Weber, the 'state is sovereign, or the supreme power, within its territory, and by definition the ultimate authority for all law, i.e. binding rules supported by coercive sanction' (Dunleavy and O'Leary, 1987, p. 2).[2] For Gardner, nation-states derive their existence, legitimacy, authority and sovereignty through their relationships with, and more precisely from their acceptance by, other nation-states. Their legitimacy means that, apart from anything else, they have the capacity to confer on people the status of 'national'. Nationality is a relationship which an individual has with a nation-state by virtue of having been recognised as a national by that nation-state while, at the same time, such recognition has been accepted and legitimated by other nation-states. Because nationality is a relationship which depends upon *inter*-national recognition and entails nation-states representing people *inter*nationally, it is a relationship which brings nation-states into a network of *inter*-national (external, and so *extra*-national) relations.[3]

The concepts of 'nationality' and 'national' (along with such antonyms as 'alien' or 'foreign') rest on the prior existence of nation-states and of a network of external relations among nation-states: they refer to a relationship–identity–status nexus which exists only and wholly within such a network. The concept of 'national' refers to a status which is occupied by people within the network of external relationships among nation-states. Nationality involves a person in an external relationship with a nation-state which recognises him or her as its national, and moreover in an external relationship which depends upon him or her having relationships with other nation-states (that is, those which do not recognise him or her as their national). Nationality is an external relationship which a person has with any nation-state which legitimately recognises him or her as its national and which accordingly represents him or her – acts on his or her behalf – in relation to other (legitimating) nation-states.

The point is otherwise presented by Gardner as follows:

> Nationality is the external manifestation of the relationship between individuals and the State to which they belong. When they travel abroad they do so with the authority of a passport issued by the State of which they are a national and in the event of difficulty, it is the State of which they are a national which may seek to defend their interests. (Ibid., p. 64)

The status of *national* provides a means by which, following Gardner, an individual's identity, rights and duties within the network of external relations among nation-states (of *inter* national relations) are established and recognisable. Its importance both to people and to nation-states is acknowledged in Article 15 of the United Nations' Universal Declaration of Human Rights (1948), which asserts that *everyone has the right to a nationality,* and that *no one shall be arbitrarily deprived of his* [sic] *nationality nor denied the right to change his nationality.*[4] These provisions do not mean, however, that in practice an individual's wish to change his or her nationality in a particular direction, or for that matter to retain his or her current nationality, will necessarily be successful, as the following British case illustrates:

> A High Court judge yesterday ordered the deportation of a mother of four young children to Pakistan ... Naheed Ejaz, aged 28, whose children have lived in Britain all their lives said ... she had been 'quite prepared for the worst'. The court declared her an illegal immigrant because her husband Arshad Iqbal had deceived authorities to obtain British nationality. He was deported two years ago. [The] Home Secretary, Kenneth Baker, had had no choice last year when he declared that her naturalisation as a British citizen was a nullity because of her husband's deception. ... Mrs Ejaz ... became a British citizen in 1990. (Simmons, July 1993)

In Gardner's terms, Naheed Ejaz was being deprived of her British nationality along with her associated national citizenship.[5]

The status of *national* becomes redundant for people in their relationships with the nation-state which accepts them as nationals when these relationships become removed from the network of external relations among nation-states. At this point, an individual's relationship with a nation-state which accepts him or her as a national becomes an internal relationship, and it is this internal relationship to which the category of 'citizenship' refers. While nationality is a status which establishes (the operation of) an individual's external relationship with the nation-state which accepts him or her as a national, citizenship is a status through which individuals have internal relationships with nation-states. Gardner makes the point as follows:

> Citizenship is usually regarded as the reflection of [the] relationship [between people and a nation state which accepts as its nationals] within the boundaries of the State concerned. It described the relationship of nationals to their own State when they are within that State. Its functional attributes are to describe matters such as who may vote and stand for election in States who allow democratic activity and ... to regulate ... other acts which nationals may do which non-nationals either may never do, or may not do as of right. These activities include owning property, holding certain offices, taking certain jobs and enjoying many economic benefits. This legal relationship, where the enjoyment of various ... rights as a citizen depends upon nationality, is described [here] as 'nationality citizenship'. (Gardner, 1990, p. 64)

Nationality, being an identity which plays a part within the network of external relations between nation-states, is of interest and importance within international relations. Accordingly, this particular identity can be contrasted with citizenship, which is an internal relationship with a nation-state. That is:

> traditionally, a State is sovereign and uncontrollable in international law in the way it treats its own nationals. These are matters which are often thought to fall within the 'reserved domain' of domestic jurisdiction. However, it is

also thought that the extent of the reserved domain may vary as international law develops. (Ibid., p. 64)

Despite the convention which underpins the *reserved domain*, whereby in principle a nation-state can treat its own nationals and national citizens within its own territorial borders in a way which goes unchecked by other nation-states, in practice international attention, scrutiny, criticism, interference and control are common, and following Gardner will become even more so. In this regard, we can recall the Russian government's successful attempt in 1993 (although with the supranational support of the Council of Europe) to intimidate the Estonian government into changing its regulations and requirements concerning Estonian nationality and national citizenship. The Russian government decided to *retaliate politically and economically against Estonia for passing its alien law which it saw as discriminatory in relation to ethnic Russians* (*Guardian*, 24 June 1993). In effect, as we have noted, the Estonian government was *forced* to ease the stringency of its regulations and requirements by bringing them into line with the Council of Europe's 1950 Convention.

In another case during 1993, Britain attacked the way the People's Republic of China was treating many of its nationals and national citizens:

> China has been urged, in a highly critical report commissioned by [Prime Minister] John Major, to transform its attitude to human rights. The report talks of 'harrowing accounts of brutality and violence', and calls for an amnesty of political prisoners. It also asks Beijing to abolish regulations under which more than a million Chinese are detained without trial every year. The report deplores China's policy of widespread capital punishment and the practice of publicly parading those on their way to execution ... But conservatives in the Chinese Communist Party, who say that foreign countries have no right to criticise their human rights record, will consider the report provocative. The report expresses concern about detention without charge, torture in Chinese jails, and delayed access to lawyers. It notes that there is no presumption of innocence in Chinese law, contrary to the Universal Declaration of Human Rights. (Gittings, June 1993)

Here, Britain, in criticising China, is able to find support in citing the provisions in the United Nations' Universal Declaration of Human Rights. It is the increasing availability of such extra-national agreements which appears to lie behind Gardner's expectation of a withering of the reserved domain with regard to nation-states' treatment of their nationals and national citizens, and of an associated increase in the part played by new citizenship – at the expense of wholly national citizenship – in the everyday lives of the people of Europe and elsewhere.

However, I wish to make the point, in view of the details of the Estonia case for instance, that certain types of interference in an attacks on the reserved are more likely to succeed than others. The chances of nation-states interfering in and reducing one another's reserved domain by appealing to such extra-national agreements as the UN's Universal Declaration of Human Rights are likely to be slim, unless backed by the use or threat of sanctions or force which comes from the occurence of accompanying international power imbalances (such as between Russia and Estonia) or supra-national arrangements, such as the Council of Europe and perhaps even more so the European Union. Otherwise, nation-states may simply resort to mutual, equally weighty criticism supported by rhetorical references to the same extra-national agreements and codes. Thus, China might counter Britain's attempt to encroach on its reserved domain by in return criticising Britain's *brutal* treatment of *its* nationals and national citizens in the Matthews case, the Brannigan and McBride case and others, given that in such cases people have been treated as *guilty without trial* and have been subjected to *internal exile* in contravention of several new citizenship provisions contained in, for instance, the Universal Declaration of Human Rights. After all, Article 9 of the Declaration asserts that *no one shall be subjected to arbitrary arrest, detention or exile*; Article 10 asserts that *everyone is entitled in full equality to a fair and public hearing by an independent and impartial tribunal, in the determination of his rights and obligations and of any criminal charge against him;* Article 11 asserts that *everyone charged with a penal offence has the right to be presumed innocent until proved guilty according to law in a public trial at which he has had all the guarantees necessary for his defence*; Article 13 asserts that *everyone has the right to freedom of movement and residence within the borders of each state*, and that *Everyone has the right to leave any country, including his own, and to return to his country.*

The chances for the Council of Europe or for any other supra-national organisation, such as the European Union, of effectively encroaching on the reserved domain of its member states will depend on its treaty-based supra-national power and control in relation to such states by way of its decision-making sovereignty. It will depend also on its institutional arrangements for monitoring, safeguarding, guaranteeing and enforcing its new citizenship codes, and therefore on its capacity for preventing its member states from becoming deviant, or alternatively for bringing its miscreant member states back into line. However, in so far as the European Union, say, is effective in encroaching on the reserved domain of its member states, the possibility emerges of regarding its citizenship provisions as representing not just new citizenship, but also *supra-citizenship*. This possibility, and its implications for the progress of citizenship within Europe, is examined in detail and critically later.[6]

For now, having distinguished between the legal statuses, categories and identities of 'national' and 'citizen' – and accordingly defined the further category of 'national citizen' – I wish to underline the distinction by making (or more accurately returning to) the point that not all the nationals of a particular nation-state will necessarily be national citizens of that nation-state. Large sections of the populations of modern European nation-states enjoy the status of being nationals without being national citizens. That is, there are many nationals of modern (eastern, central, and western) European nation-states who can be regarded as non-citizens (their status as new citizens or *supra-citizens* aside)[7] on both legal or technical grounds and sociologically pertinent and useful grounds. These grounds become clear by refining the notion of 'citizenship' through further examination of its relationship with 'nationality'. David Barker and Colin Padfield provide an account of United Kingdom law concerning nationality and citizenship in which they tell us that by 'a person's nationality we mean his [sic] status as a citizen or member of a particular [nation] state to which he owes allegiance' (Barker and Padfield, 1992, p. 88). However, this statement is ambiguous. On the one hand, it can be taken to mean that, as far as Barker and Padfield are concerned, the legal statuses of 'citizen' and 'national' are synonymous and interchangeable. On the other hand, the statement could be taken to imply that the category of 'nationals' is composed of two sub-categories: 'citizens' and 'others', where the latter are individuals who are nationals but not citizens. None the less, in each case, all nationals (whether citizens or not) are characterised and distinguished by Barker and Padfield as *owing allegiance to a particular nation-state*, by virtue of which they are 'subject to certain duties' (ibid., p. 88) in relation to that nation-state. For Barker and Padfield, above all else a nation-state's nationals are *the subjects* of that nation-state. For example, the United Kingdom's nationals 'owe allegiance to the crown in the form of the Sovereign. The origins of this relationship are historical and derive from medieval obligations' (ibid., p. 67).

This approach to nationality, whereby first and foremost it is about people's statutory duties and allegiance, is reflected in the was Barker and Padfield attempt to clarify the legal distinction between the notions of 'nationality' and 'domicile':

> Domicle is a concept distinct from nationality. Thus a person may be a British subject and yet be domiciled, for example, in France. The concept of domicile, under English law, involves two elements: (i) actual residence; and (ii) *animus manendi*, i.e. the intention to remain in that place or country. Where these two elements co-exist a person is said to have a domicile in that country. Whereas nationality implies a political relation existing between a person and the state to which he owes allegiance, domicile determines important civil rights and obligations. (Ibid., p. 91)

Being a national entails being *a subject*, showing *allegiance* and performing *duties*; not being a national, but being merely domiciled, brings or leaves a distinct set of rights and duties. At the same time, however, being a national brings not only duties. While in the first place being a national brings duties, it consequently brings rights. In effect, nationals, as the subjects of a nation-state, are obliged to give their allegiance and to carry out their duties as one side of an *exchange* arrangement. In return, nationals enjoy rights granted by the nation-state of which they are nationals, where (following Barker and Padfield) these rights include above everything else the right to *protection*:

> Apart from stateless persons everyone is the subject of some state to which he owes political allegiance and loyalty, for which he may be called upon to fight, pay taxes and support, and from which he may expect protection.   (Ibid., p. 88)

Nationality may be distinguished and defined in terms of – and so the status of being a 'national' may be conditional upon – being a *loyal subject*, which in exchange brings the right of protection. It follows, in view of the earlier discussion, that this right will be manifestation of the external relationships which people have with the nation-states of which they are nationals and will be exercised within the network of external relations among nation-states.

However, although an individual's nationality is the external relationship which he or she has with a particular nation-state, the status can have legal implications and practical consequences for his or her internal relationship with that nation-state. Nationality, as well as bringing the right to protection within the network of external relations among nation-states, may bring additional internal rights, entitlements, capacities and opportunities, perhaps including the opportunity to be a national citizen, and thereby the yet further rights and duties entailed. That is, nationality may be a preliminary to, and even a pre-requisite for, the acquisition of citizenship. If so, it follows that all the citizens of a particular nation-state will necessarily be nationals. But the converse does not follow. It does not follow that all nationals will necessarily be citizens. While the status of being a national may bring with it preliminary eligibility for the status of citizen, the final achievement of citizenship may depend upon nationals satisfying further, supplementary or intermediate qualifying requirements.

Being a national in relation to a nation-state does not mean that an individual will automatically or eventually acquire the status of national citizenship. Whether a national is (allowed to be) a citizen may depend on him or her meeting certain further eligibility criteria and requirements, actual operational examples of which include ones concerned with domicility, birth and descent as well as with race-ethnicity, social class, sex-gender and age-generation. The operation of such intervening factors in determining the acquisition of national citizenship[8] can be illustrated with reference to the enjoyment of the rights which Gardner has labelled as 'functional attributes' of this status (ibid., p. 64). Gardner's list includes rights which distinguish between those who can and those who cannot vote in elections, stand for election, hold certain offices, own property, take certain jobs, enjoy certain economic benefits (ibid., p. 64), and be resident in and enter the territory of a particular nation-state (ibid., p. 66).

In the case of the United Kingdom, some nationals are denied the right to vote in parliamentary and other elections on the grounds of their domicile. Prior to the Representation of the People Act (1985) no nationals who were deemed to be resident abroad could vote. As a result of the 1985 Act, this strict rule has been modified. Under this Act, Padfield and Byrne inform us that 'British citizens resident abroad may vote (for up to five years after departure)' (Padfield and Byrne, 1987, p. 29). In other words, despite or because of the Act, many UK nationals – those who have been resident abroad for more than five years – remain barred from voting. This restriction on voting in effect divides nationals into two distinct categories, and moreover does so in a socially important manner. Accordingly, the possibility arises of employing separate legal and sociological labels in recognition of, and as a way of highlighting, the distinction and its importance. Whereas Padfield and Byrne seem prepared to employ the label 'citizens' to cover both those nationals who can vote and those who cannot, the possibility arises of reserving the label and notion of 'citizen' for the former only. Indeed, the possibility arises of going even further and reserving the label and notion of 'citizen' for only those nationals who enjoy the full range of citizenship rights.

There are several approaches to drawing a line between nationals who are citizens and nationals who are not. First, it may be decided that 'citizens' and 'nationals' are identical; second, it may be decided that citizens are those nationals who have gained the minimum of citizenship rights; third, it may be decided that citizens are those nationals who have gained some other level or levels of citizenship rights short of the maximum; fourth, it may be decided that citizens are those nationals who have gained the full quota of citizenship rights. Adopting the fourth approach to the demarcation of citizens from other nationals is, as previously indicated, consistent with Barbalet's view (following Marshall). For Barbalet (Barbalet, 1988):

> Citizenship is a status bestowed on those who are full members of a national community, and citizenship rights, therefore, are those which derive from and facilitate participation in this 'common possession', as Marshall (1950: 92) calls it.   (Barbalet, 1988, p. 18)

This approach, moreover, helps obviate the problem of (a) using the labels 'national' and 'citizen' synonymously, and so in effect making one of them redundant; or (b) trying to decide where else to draw the line between nationals and citizens given the former's enjoyment of different sets and levels of citizenship rights, followed by trying to decide whether differing levels of citizenship rights should still be recognised and highlighted with the use of appropriate distinguishing labels; or (c) using the labels of 'national' and 'citizen' so loosely, variously and inconsistently that their sociological value is reduced or lost.

Gardner may be signalling his unease about applying the label 'citizen' to all nationals, and especially those who are denied the full range of citizenship rights, when he tells us that 'the right of residence, which is often regarded as an attribute of nationality citizenship, has increasingly not been enjoyed by a significant group of individuals whose nationality status depends upon, or is regulated by, the British Nationality Act 1981' (Gardner, 1990, p. 68). Gardner may be reluctant to use the label 'citizen' to describe those people who enjoy UK nationality status while being denied the national citizenship right to be resident in the UK. The Act of Parliament whereby these nationals are denied the right of residence in the UK was specifically designed to discriminate among nationals on the grounds of descent, birth and residence. In addition, however, what the Act does – whether intentionally or otherwise – is to discriminate on the grounds of race-ethnicity. As Gardner tells us:

In the case of the United Kingdom the British Nationality Act 1981 defines a British citizen and certain other statutes, such as the Representation of the People Act 1983, refer back to this definition in conferring the right to vote or stand for election, or other enabling provisions. (Ibid., p. 65)

As Gardner points out, the first codification of the law on nationality and citizenship was the British Nationality and Status of Aliens Act 1914 (ibid., p. 65). Gardner adds:

The 1914 British Nationality and Status of Aliens Act and subsequent legislation adhered to the traditional methods of acquisition of citizenship through birth, by descent and by naturalisation. However, the first two of these methods, known as *jus soli* and *jus sanguinis* respectively have been modified by the 1981 British Nationality Act. (Ibid., p. 67)

The 1981 Act, with slight amendments, established what continues to apply during the 1990s as the statutory definition of United Kingdom nationality and national citizenship, and subsequently 'certain other statutes, such as the Representation of the People Act 1983, refer back to this definition in conferring the right to vote or stand for election, or other enabling provisions' (ibid., p. 65). Prior to the 1981 Act, British nationality was defined under the British Nationality Act of 1948. As Padfield and Byrne tell us:

The British Nationality Act, 1948, as amended [prior to the 1981 Act], divided 'British subjects' into two classes: (a) Citizens of the independent nations of the British Commonwealth. Into this class fall citizens of Canada, Australia, New Zealand, India, Pakistan, Sri Lanka, Ghana, Nigeria and the other twenty independent Commonwealth countries. These persons are known as 'Commonwealth citizens'; (b) Citizens of the United Kingdom and Colonies. This [class] of citizenship could be acquired by way of birth or descent, naturalisation, registration, marriage or incorporation of territory. However, the British Nationality Act, 1981, introduced a number of fundamental changes in the law of citizenship (as from 1983). Consequently, there are now three [classes] of citizenship: (a) British Citizenship ... i.e. those who are citizens of the UK and Colonies who have the right of abode in the UK; (b) Citizenship of the British Dependent Territories ... i.e. those citizens of the UK and Colonies by birth, naturalisation or registration in a Dependent Territory (these include Hong Kong, Gibraltar, the Falkland Islands, St Christopher and Nevis and St Helena); (c) British Overseas Citizenship ... i.e. those UK and Colonies Citizens who, on 1 January 1983, did not fall into (a) or (b) above. Each status brings with it a different set of rights and entitlements, especially concerning entry to the U.K. (Padfield and Byrne, 1987, p. 280)[9]

Essentially, the 1981 Act narrowed the range, types and numbers of people who enjoy the rights of automatic entry into and residence within the United Kingdom. It did this by refining the range of UK nationals who have these rights, so that just one of three classes or categories of UK national was left to enjoy them. It entailed a tightening of the requirements and criteria for determining which people have these rights by, more specifically, distinguishing and discriminating among UK nationals in such a way as to create two categories with rights which variously fall short of the full range of national citizenship rights. More precisely, the outcome was that two of the three categories of UK nationals do not enjoy those *basic* national citizenship rights – of entry and abode – on which many other national citizenship rights depend. The rights of entry and abode have become confined to that category of UK nationals designated as British Citizens. In particular, in determining British Citizenship, the requirements with regard to people's residence, birth and descent have become tighter and more restrictive. The effect – whether intended or not – has been to narrow the range of people, including UK nationals, who enjoy the rights of entry and abode in a way which is skewed in terms of *race-ethnicity*. For instance, the 1981 Act reduced the number of residents of the British Dependent Territory of Hong Kong who have the right of entry and abode, something which conveniently slimmed the prospective flow of migrants from Hong Kong to the UK in the face of the dependency being handed over to the People's Republic of China in 1997. However, the effect was to especially reduce the number of ethnic Chinese residents of Hong Kong who have the rights of automatic entry and abode. As compensation, the UK government set up a quota system to allow a selection of Hong Kong residents who are UK nationals of the British Dependent Territory category to take up UK residence with the possibility of promotion to the status of British Citizenship and thereby, in turn, of (full) national citizenship.[10]

Only those UK nationals who qualify for the category of British Citizenship are left with the rights of entry and abode, and this category can be achieved under the 1981 Act in several ways: (i) by birth within the United Kingdom to a parent who is a British Citizen or who is settled in the United Kingdom, or who becomes a British Citizen or becomes settled in the United Kingdom; (ii) by adoption under an order made by any court in the United Kingdom authorising the adoption of a minor who is not a British Citizen; (iii) by descent – that is, being born outside the United Kingdom but to a parent who is a British Citizen by birth, adoption, registration or naturalisation (but not by descent); (iv) by registration – that is, any minor may apply for British Citizenship, which is granted at the Home Secretary's discretion (persons who are British Dependent Territories Citizens, or British Overseas Citizens or British Subjects or British Protected Persons[11] may apply after satisfying periods of residence in the United Kingdom. There is a special entitlement for British Dependent Citizens who are nationals of the United Kingdom for the purposes of the European Community, which in practice means Gibraltarians); (v) by naturalisation – that is, any person may apply to the Secretary of State for a certificate of naturalisation (the conditions of grant – which is at the discretion of the Home Secretary – are that the applicant must be of full age and capacity, of good character, have sufficient knowledge of the English language, the Welsh language or the Scottish Gaelic language, and have satisfied residence requirements and intend that the United Kingdom will be their home or their principal home); (vi) by marriage – that is, an alien woman who immediately before commencement of the Act was the wife of a Citizen of the United Kingdom and Colonies may acquire British Citizenship if she chooses to do so by registration as in (iii) above within five years provided the marriage subsists (Barker and Padfield, 1992, pp. 89–90).[12]

Of course, the requirements which regulate nationality vary not only over time within the United Kingdom; they also vary considerably between nation-states, including between the Member States of the European Community and Union. There are variations in the way birth, descent and residence are used to determine present nationality, and connectedly in the way the same requirements among others are taken into account in granting nationality through, for instance, the process of naturalisation. The variations which occurred at the start of the 1990s have been summarised as follows:

> Broadly, countries opt for one of two principles: *jus soli* (birthplace) or *jus sanguinis* (blood). In France, citizenship depends largely on the first, in Germany on the second. This can affect how fast immigrants become part of their new society. Most French-born children of foreigners become citizens. Only a few German born ones do. Few EC countries automatically treat as citizens anyone born within their borders. Ireland is an exception. In France and Spain at least one parent has to have been born there. Denmark, Britain and Italy let foreigners' children become citizens if they live there for a period of years. People not born in an EC country can generally get citizenship in one if they live there long enough (five years in Britain and France, for example, ten years in Spain and Germany). Marrying a citizen can shorten the wait. Britain, France, Ireland and Italy allow dual citizenship. Germany and Denmark make people drop the old one when becoming Germans or Danish.[13] When a Turk gives up his or her citizenship, he or she forfeits rural property rights in Turkey. This is [one] reason so few Turks in Germany become German .... Other EC countries show ancestral, colonial or neighbourly preference. Britain has a rule of 'patriality' under which a (typically white) Commonwealth citizen with at least one parent born in the United Kingdom can enter the country to work before claiming citizenship. Spain gives citizenship after just two years' residency to people from its former colonies (and to Sephardic Jews wherever they are from). Denmark lowers its residency requirement from seven years to two for Nordic applicants. EC countries as a rule (Spain and Ireland are exceptions) require foreigners seeking natural-

isation to speak the language of the nation they are joining. Good character references and a job are also often required. Naturalisation is dear in some countries, free in others. ('Citizenship: What is a European?', *The Economist*, 17 August 1991)

The requirement on foreigners (aliens, non-nationals) who are seeking naturalisation to speak the language of the nation-state of which they wish to become nationals, brings to mind the *Estonian case*. Here, however, a language requirement was introduced with the intention, not so much of restricting the range of foreigners who would be eligible for naturalisation, as of depriving a range of people of their recent statuses of being 'nationals' and 'national citizens', in response to the way they were seen (by the Estonian government) to have become *ethnically alien*.

But this perhaps unusual case aside, ethnically-oriented or ethnically-biased criteria appear to be widely used across Europe for deciding on, first of all, people's eligibility for particular national citizenship rights. As we have seen, this applies within the European Union, and even to the implementation and provisions of the Maastricht Treaty with regard to the electoral rights of Citizens of the Union. The Treaty contains a derogation clause which permits Luxembourg to preclude foreign nationals, including those from other Member States, from voting and standing in European Parliament elections. This opt-out given to Luxembourg is in response to the estimated *almost 30 per cent of the country's population who are foreign nationals*, and is indicative of a general European Union concern about the implications and impact of an *ethnic balance* within a Member State which may be reaching (what might be referred to as) socially and politically *sensitive* proportions.

Secondly, ethnically-biased criteria are widely used across Europe for deciding who can become a 'national', and thereby a 'national citizen', through naturalisation. For instance, language requirements commonly contribute to the ethnic sifting process by which those suitable for naturalisation are identified. Here, of course, I am using the term 'national' where *The Economist* article on 'What is a European?' uses the term 'citizen'. *The Economist* employs the term 'citizenship' when clearly it means 'nationality', in the sense of the status whereby people have external relationships with those nation-states which accept them as nationals. In my terms, in contrast, 'citizenship' is that status where people enjoy the full (adult) list of citizenship rights within, and so sustain an internal relationship with (entailing full legal membership of), the same nation-state.

Claire Wallace similarly uses the two terms in an overlapping, ambiguous and confusing manner (Wallace, 1993). That is, Wallace uses the term 'citizenship' to cover both the internal relationship and the external relationship which an individual has with his or her nation-state, even though she alludes to the conceptual, legal and sociological differences involved. Wallace tells us:

> Although Marshall never mentioned this, it is evident that citizenship is tied explicitly or implicitly to the nation state. This is very clear in countries other than Britain [for example] where one key dimension of citizenship is the obligation to do national service – for men to fight and even to die for the state which claims them as citizens. (Ibid., p. 6)

Here, Wallace is referring to the features of (in my terms) 'nationality' given that she is concerned specifically with people's external relationships with their membership states, but what she says would have been clearer and sharper if she had used the term 'nationality' instead of 'citizenship'. The benefits of distinguishing between citizenship and nationality become even more apparent when Wallace goes on to suggest:

> we need to distinguish two meanings of citizenship: *Buergerschaft*, that is the rights and obligations of a citizen within the state in the Marshallian sense ... and *Staatsangehoerigkeit*, formal citizenship or the right to belong to a state .... . There then arises the problem of who is eligible to become a citizen .... . This second sense of citizenship is defined in different ways by different states as well. In most countries this is determined by *jus soli* or *jus sanguinis*, the right [by] birth or the right by parentage and then other criteria would include factors such as length of residence. However, in some countries, such as Germany ...,

ethnic descent is the determining factor, so that people who have lived there for many years may have few rights of citizenship, whereas those who have never lived there but have some claims to be ethnically German ... instantly have full citizenship rights. (Ibid., pp. 6–7)

Instead of recommending *two meanings of citizenship*, Wallace might have adopted just one meaning for the sake of analysis, clarity and consistency. She might have used the term to refer to that relationship which an individual has *within* his or her membership state, with the state – given that the term 'nationality' is available for distinguishing what she obviously recognises as the same individual's external relationship (which occasionally entails, for instance, *the obligation to do national service*). Wallace makes the point that some European nation-states – those that rely most on the principle of *jus sanguinis* – have rules and requirements for deciding on nationality which are more ethnically-biased compared with those that rely most on the principle of *jus soli*. At the same time, Wallace claims, there is a variation among European nation-states in their degree of concern with the issue of externally-oriented nationality (or 'formal citizenship in [the] second sense') at the expense of the issue of internally-oriented national citizenship – a variation which, in turn, is linked 'systemically' to a variation among them in their degree of concern with ethnic issues, divisions and pressures. Accordingly, there is a tendency for nation-states to focus more on the issue of nationality the closer they are to the eastern side of Europe, due to an underlying tendency for nation-states to have greater *ethnic problems* the closer they are to this side. Here, Wallace draws on and endorses the analysis of Ernest Gellner (Gellner, 1992, pp. 285–93),[14] who has delineated 'a number of time-zones of Europe in the construction of nation-states' (Wallace, 1993, p. 7). She argues:

On the Atlantic sea coast, modernisation helped bring about culturally homogeneous nation states, ones based on 'forgetting' rather than the recognition of ethnic identity. The stable and mature democracies in these countries bolstered by a long period of post-war economic growth mean that [national] citizenship in the sense of social welfare has been an important post-war preoccupation; other [national citizenship] rights are taken more or less for granted. In the second time-zone moving eastward, the later unification of states such as Germany and Italy during the late nineteenth century was facilitated by an established high culture. In Germany substantive citizenship, or *Buergerschaft* [or in my terms, 'national citizenship'], was self-consciously used as a form of social and system integration in the newly constructed state. Again, the long period of post-war economic growth and political stability facilitated the establishment of [national] citizenship, even in societies which had previously been dominated by totalitarian dictatorships. However, in the third time-zone, moving further eastward, there were a 'patchwork of folk cultures and cultural diversities, separating social strata as well as distinguishing adjoining territories' ([Gellner, 1992] p. 291). This made the creation of national states more 'arduous' and 'brutal' because political and cultural identity had to be created at the same time. Furthermore, being states where there had been no opportunity to establish a stable democracy, but rather where democracy and nation states had been crushed by foreign empires, there are only fragile and insecure nation states. These are now further de-stabilised, as in the inter-war period, by economic recession. In the fourth time-zone the creation of a new empire served to swallow some of the nation states in the third time-zone, but it is this empire which is now disintegrating. In this region the creation of nation states can depend crucially upon ethnic identity and we are currently witnessing some new definitions of this. In Latvia, for example, people are required to take a language test and have been resident for at least 16 years to be eligible for citizenship [or, in my terms, national status] if they are not that half of the population which are 'ethnic Latvians', and this effectively excludes many of the resident Russians. In the Czech Republic, resident Slovaks are being forced to choose a nationality in the newly divided state and in the former Jugoslavia, states are being ethnically constructed though more brutal means. Under these circumstances citizenship [or nationality] is a very important aspect of political identity and citizenship in Marshall's sense [that is, national citizenship] is of lesser importance.   (Wallace, 1993, p. 7)

The more easterly time-zones within Europe are characterised by emergent and fragile nation-states within a fluid, uncertain and threatening extra-national framework; by weak nation-states pervaded and pressured by a web of internal and external ethnic divisions, cleavages and conflicts; and by an associated emphasis on externally-oriented nationalism,[15] national identity and nationality, rather than internally-oriented (national) citizenship. In contrast, the more settled and secure – economically, politically and ethnically – westerly time-zones are characterised by long-standing, well-established nation-states, and an associated concern with the issue of internally-oriented (national) citizenship rather than externally-oriented nationality. Essentially, the relative absence of *ethnic problems* means that the (external) issues of national identity and national boundaries are less problematic for the more westerly European nation-states, allowing them to focus on (internal) issues concerning national citizenship.

However, such a broadly drawn picture needs to be viewed with some caution in the light of what we are invited to believe, by a host of other writers, are various complicating social, ethnic and political details and tendencies. To begin with, some writers have detected a decline in, and even the demise of, the nation-state within Europe and more widely. For instance, Alvin Toffler and Heidi Toffler have argued:

> nations, as such, are becoming less important. Powerful transnational businesses are creating information networks that 'bypass the nation-state framework,' in the words of Riccardo Petrella, director of science and technology forecasting for the European Community. Regions are also growing in power. Mr Petrella continues: 'By the middle of the next century, such nation-states as Germany, Italy, the United States or Japan will no longer be the relevant socio-economic entities and the ultimate political configuration. Instead, areas like Orange County, California; Osaka, Japan; the Lyon region of France, or Germany's Ruhrgebiete will acquire predominant socio-economic status. The real decision-making powers of the future ... will be transnational companies in alliance with city-regional governments.' Another type of unit is also growing in world importance: thousands of transnational organisations – Greenpeace, for

example – are springing up like mushrooms in order to form a new 'civil society'. Add to these components of the new global system world religions like Roman Catholicism and Islam, plus fast-multiplying media networks like CNN that cross (and blur) borders, and it is clear that the world system built around neatly defined nation-states is being replaced by a kind of global computer, with thousands of diverse components plugged into a three level motherboard. (Toffler and Toffler, November 1993)

According to this, there is a process under way in which Europe, along with the rest of the world, is returning to the pre-modern (or mediaeval) social, economic and political pattern where nation-states had yet to emerge (see Giddens, 1986, pp. 152–5). At the same time, however, *the new global system* which has emerged towards the end of the twentieth century is characterised by a novel feature: extensive, ubiquitous *transnational* arrangements, organisations, and so on. The result is that nation-states are being squeezed between the combined impact of, on the one hand, a sub-national regional thrust and, on the other hand, a supra-national (to some extent global) thrust. The same tendency has been not only noted but also welcomed by Roy Hattersley, the former deputy leader of Britain's Labour Party:

> The nation state is outdated. It is too large to allow the sensitive and representative administration of health, education and welfare. It is too small to withstand the power of multinational companies and international currency speculators. The future lies with devolution and federalism. (Hattersley, November 1993)

Here, Roy Hattersley is alluding to an aspect of the *transnational* arm of the squeeze on the nation-state which Toffler and Toffler fail to specify: that of the drive towards supra-national social, economic and political formations as exemplified by the European Community and Union, as well as by the Association of South East Asian Nations (Asean) and the nascent North American Free Trade Agreement (Nafta), for instance. The same theme has been pursued by Christopher Bryant (Bryant, 1991, pp. 189–207) from the starting assumption about the

Community that 'changes within and between the Council of Ministers, the European Commission and the European Parliament in the direction of greater supranationalism do seem likely' (ibid., p. 203). From this standpoint, Bryant criticises writers, most notably Anthony Giddens (Giddens, 1985), for attempting to analyse European developments around the Community while 'only [thinking] in terms of traditional national and multi-national states' (Bryant, 1991, p. 203):

> It is not easy to fit the 1992 [Single European Act] project into [Giddens's] theory of nation-states in the global state system. He allows for just three kinds of organisations 'that stand beyond the boundaries of states, perhaps appropriating capacities previously held by states – intergovernmental agencies; cartels, economic unions and transnational corporations; and military alliances – and treats the Common Market [sic] as a hybrid which combines elements of the first and second ([Giddens, 1985] p. 282). He argues that the transfer of sovereignty from the nation-states which compose it has been largely confined to economic matters, and in any case has been part of 'a two-way exchange, since member states have gained certain forms of autonomy that would otherwise have been forfeited in international trading relations in other parts of the world' [ibid., p. 283]. The European Community would only become of major consequence to the global state system if at some point it became a super-power, but 'short of some major world conflict it is difficult to see this as more than a relatively remote possibility' (ibid.). (Bryant, 1991, p. 203)

Bryant complains that Giddens's 'theory is insensitive to the possibilities the European Community now presents'; that Giddens is 'unprepared for a Community which turns out to be more than an intergovernmental organisation and less than a super-state' (ibid., p. 203). Bryant argues that the Community is a 'novel formation', and if 'it were also to deal directly with regional and local governments in the member countries, as seems possible, it would further expose the inadequacy of [Giddens's] theory of nation-states in the global state system. (German Länder already have their own representation in Brussels.)' (ibid., p. 203).

While Bryant finds fault with Giddens's approach, he recommends that of P. Schmitter (Schmitter, 1990),[16] who argues that *the process of European integration* 'must be explicitly treated as a new form of political domination, capable of evolving into one of several end-states'. Bryant tells us that in order to 'grasp what these may be we have to conceptualise alternatives to the state and the market; "somewhere between sovereign units each with an unambiguous monopoly of violence ... and diffuse networks based on multiple voluntary exchanges", there is the possibility of novel forms of order which should not be treated as "just way-stations on the route to becoming a state or a market"'(Bryant, 1991, p. 204). For Bryant, following Schmitter, the European Community is progressing as a supra-national organisation without doing so in the direction of a *supra-national state*, or, that is, without doing so around a supra-state (as distinct from a *super-state* within *the global state system*).[17] As far as both Schmitter and Bryant are concerned, the Community will not be 'a state, "at least not in the strict sense of the term"' (ibid., p. 204).

Now, the issue of whether or not the Community (and now Union) is developing as a supra-state has direct implications for citizenship – including for national citizenship, new citizenship, supra-national citizenship, citizenship of the Union – and these will be explored later.[18] For the time being, I will focus on the indirect or incidental implications of the same issue by way of nationality, national identity, nationalism and *race-ethnicity*. This theme is implied by Bryant Turner (Turner, 1990, pp. 189–217) in his comments on the combined impact of sub-national and supra-national trends on 'citizenship':

> While the notion of citizenship continues to provide a normative basis for the defence of the welfare state, certain crucial changes in the organisation of global systems have rendered some aspects of the notion of citizenship redundant and obsolete. The contemporary world is structured by two contradictory processes. On the one hand, there are powerful pressures towards regional autonomy and localism and, on the other, there is a stronger notion of globalism and global political responsibilities. The concept of citizenship is therefore still in a process of change and development. We do not possess the conceptual apparatus to

express the idea of global membership, and in this context a specifically national identity appears anachronistic. Indeed the uncertainty of the global context may produce strong political reactions asserting the normative authority of the local and the national over the global and international [Robertson and Lechner, 1985; Robertson, 1987].[19] (Turner, 1990, pp. 211-12)

Here, Turner does not refer to the European Community (or anything else) to indicate in a more concrete manner what he has in mind by the 'global and international' political process which is putting pressure on 'the national' in conjunction with the (*contradictory*[20]) 'local and regional' process. However, Turner appears to be alluding to (he could have been much more explicit and precise) a distinction between 'citizenship' and 'nationality' which resembles the way I have contrasted the notions in terms of the internal-orientation of the former with the external-orientation of the latter. Whereas citizenship is about internal relationships and membership, nationality is about external relationships between the individual and the nation-state, and thereby between nation-states. The drive towards international and global arrangements has implications for 'citizenship' at least, according to Turner, at the conceptual level. However, from this point Turner's argument would have benefited from the use of a more explicitly, clearly and consistently drawn distinction between what he means by 'citizenship' and 'nationality'. A more careful conceptual approach might have led Turner to the conclusion that the drive towards *international and global arrangements* is conducive to the development of new, supra-national and even global *citizenship*, while being portentous – at least for Turner in the first instance – vis-à-vis nation-states and nationality. The threat to nation-states and nationality is compounded by the pressure stemming from the local and regional thrust, although at this point Turner introduces a twist in the tale. That is, what Turner sees as 'the uncertainty of the global context' may feed into a resurgence of localism, regionalism and nationalism, and thereby a countervailing re-assertion of the nation-state and nationality against, perhaps hindering, the international and global tendency. In the end, it is difficult to be sure after all where the 'stronger' (to use Turner's description) process and pressures lie and what (theoretically) is the most likely outcome. Turner appears prepared for all (including what he conceptualises as contradictory) eventualities. His analysis and prognosis might have been more certain and convincing with the help of clearer and more consistent conceptualisation, in particular with regard to the distinction and relationship between 'citizenship' and 'nationality'.

However, the conceptual confusion aside, Turner touches on (he could have provided more elucidatory detail and support) the important issue of the empirical links between the supra-national tendency, nationality and citizenship, and does so in a way which brings to mind the further issue of the empirical link between these matters and that of race-ethnicity. Whereas Turner does not elaborate on what he has in mind by 'the uncertainty of the global context', we can speculate on his behalf about the possibility that owing to the supra-national tendency and consequential threat to and weakening of nation-states and national identities, there is a resurgence not only of regionalism and localism but also of associated (what can be referred to as) 'ethnicism' and racism. Whereas nation-states, national identity and nationality have helped to screen out or suppress the sub-national and cross-national web of localism and regionalism linked to ethnic and racial identities, divisions and *dangers*, the supra-national tendency helps generate the kind of *ethnic uncertainty* which for Gellner helps explain the relative emphasis on nationality in eastern Europe compared with the emphasis on (national) citizenship in western Europe. If so, we might expect the supra-national tendency affecting western Europe, primarily by way of the evolution of the European Community and Union, to feed into a re-assertion of national identity and nationality, perhaps infused by considerations, concerns and fears centred on ethnicity and race, and perhaps at the expense of (national) citizenship. There is evidence which can be interpreted so as to suggest that in this way the rights, experience and *quality* of citizenship across western Europe have suffered, albeit within some nation-states more than others and for some ethnic groupings rather than others.

The changes in the rules, requirements and rights surrounding nationality contained in the United Kingdom's 1981 British Nationality Act may be seen as reflecting the greater focus on and concern with nationality-linked-to-ethnicity issues across western Europe. Certainly the effect of this Act has been to reduce not only the overall numbers of people who have made successful applications for United Kingdom naturalisation, but also the proportions of successful applicants who come from what are euphemistically referred to as the 'New Commonwealth countries' of Africa, Asia and the Caribbean:

> The number of successful applicants for United Kingdom [nationality] fell by 28 per cent last year to 42,200, according to Home Office figures. This is the lowest level for at least 10 years. The fall of 16,400 compared with 1991 is partly due to the final implementation of the 1981 British Nationality Act which sharply restricted those entitled to claim British [nationality]. The 36,000 new applications received last year suggests that the 1981 Act will have a permanent effect in reducing immigration. The Home Office said that people from New Commonwealth countries including India, Pakistan, and Bangladesh accounted for only half the number granted British [nationality] compared with four-fifths in 1989 when immigration in the 1980s peaked at 117,000. The other large groups were 1,658 from Iran, 1,526 from Vietnam, 1,315 from South Africa, 1,122 from Canada and 1,039 from the Philippines. A further 48,700 people were granted British [nationality] in Hong Kong last year under legislation in preparation for the handover to China in 1997. The Home Office said the number of outstanding applications for British citizenship stood at around 50,000 at the end of last year with the number of refusals remaining at 9,000. (Travis, June 1993)

However, the increased concern in western Europe with the nationality–ethnicity nexus is even more evident elsewhere. In France, for instance, where, we might recall, nationality depends largely on the principle of *jus soli* (birthplace), in contrast with Germany, where it depends largely on the principle of *jus sanguinis* (blood), there have been recent moves to tighten up considerably the naturalisation rules and requirements in an obviously ethnically-biased manner. Thus, as reported by Andrew Bell:

The French national assembly yesterday began debating a change in the law which would restrict the right to acquire French nationality of children born in France to foreign parents. The move is part of a government campaign to restrict the entry of immigrants and to crack down on illegal foreign residents. Opponents of the reform say it is the first attack on the fundamental principle of the right to [nationality] in the country of birth since the wartime Vichy government persecuted foreigners and Jews. Under the current nationality code, children born in France to foreign parents have an automatic right to French [nationality] at 18, provided they have been resident in the country for the previous five years. With the proposed reform, the automatic right would be lost. Instead, children would have to apply for [nationality] between the age [sic] of 16 and 21, with the possibility that the application would be refused. According to the wording of the new code, they would be 'foreign presumed French' until then. The change was decided by a commission in 1988, but until now no government has chosen to take it up. The present government, however, made the tightening of control over French nationality one of its election pledges. Its tougher stance on nationality and immigration was one of the issues which contributed to its overwhelming victory. The French public remains sensitive to the immigration issue, and 12.5 per cent of the electorate voted for Jean-Marie Le Pen's National Front in the first round in March … . The nationality change would be largely symbolic, as it would probably only affect around 25,000 people a year, and applications for nationality would only be refused to a tiny percentage.[21] In the words of the prime minister, Edouard Balladur, however, it would ensure that 'those who wish to be French must clearly make a choice to that effect' … . There is wide consensus within the government on the changes, but there is far less on measures planned by the interior minister, Charles Pasqua, to restrict immigration and expel illegal immigrants. The social affairs minister, Simone Veil, is known to oppose some of Mr Pasqua's proposals. She has expressed particular concern about giving police the right to carry out random identity checks.   (Bell, May 1993)

Simone Veil's misgivings were widely shared, including by the French Human Rights League and, crucially, by France's constitutional council or court,[22] which had the task of vetting the laws and the enabling measures passed by the parliamentary assembly. As Henry Meyer tells us:

> Eight radical proposals in the French government's new immigration legislation were blocked by the constitutional court [or council] last week, citing human and constitutional rights. Two of the three laws have been passed by the council. On July 20 [1993] it ratified the *Réforme du Code de la Nationalité*, removing the automatic acquisition of French nationality at age 18 by the children of immigrants. On August 15, it passed *Loi sur les Contrôles d'Identité*, although with some reservations. This permits police to stop people at random to check their papers and allows customs controls within 20km of all airports, railway stations and ports. The most controversial changes, however, were to be incorporated into *Loi Relatif à la Maîtrise des Migrations et Conditions d'Entrée, D'Accueil et de Séjour des Étrangers en France* (Law on the Control of Immigration and Conditions of Entry, Reception and Residence of Foreigners in France). On Friday the constitutional council threw out or altered eight of its articles. One of these forbade any immigrant expelled from France to return for at least a year and another excluded students from arrangements to reunite immigrant families in France. The newly divorced or separated wishing to bring intended [*fiancés* and *fiancées*] to France would face a two-year wait, and mayors would have to power to refuse to marry persons they believed were intent on a marriage of convenience (*mariage blanc*) in order to get French citizenship for one of the partners. France would not have been able to give sanctuary to an asylum-seeker turned down by another EC country. The council also spoke out against the dangers of random identity checks and moves to deprive some immigrants or asylum-seekers of social security benefits. (Meyer, August 1993)

In response to the council's rulings, the interior minister, Charles Pasqua, claimed that, none the less, 'the central philosophy of his anti-immigration policy – which includes 43 other measures which the council approved – was still intact' (Webster, 16 August 1993). In particular, despite the widespread misgivings, criticisms and objections, the law on *identity controls* reflecting the concern of the French government and electorate about nationality, immigration and race-ethnicity was passed. As Paul Webster reports:

> Police powers to demand proof of identity at random without any justification came into force in France for the first time yesterday [12 August 1993] despite warnings from the opposition and lawyers that they are open to abuse. The laws, approved by parliament last month, will be used to combat illegal immigration ... . Any one unable to show identity papers, which must be carried at all times in France, can be held for up to four hours in a police station until proof of identity is provided.   (Webster, 8 August 1993)

So, the decision to tighten up the rules and requirements on the granting of nationality in an ethnically-biased fashion was consistent with the election pledges on which the right-wing government of Édouard Balladur was installed as a result of the general election in March 1993;[23] it was supported by *public opinion*; it was approved by the parliamentary assembly; and it was (with some reluctance) ratified by the constitutional council. At the same time, the increased restrictions on legal immigration through naturalisation was accompanied by an associated clamp-down on illegal immigration by way of, as Andrew Gumbel explains:

> tough new ... laws [that] entitle police to make identity checks virtually at random, to carry out expulsions without consulting the judiciary, and to take a tough line on foreigners wishing to marry or bring their families to France. Charles Pasqua, the hardline interior minister, says the new rules will weed out illegal immigrants but should pose no threat to foreigners with a legal right to be in France. Opponents of the measures see only the rise of racial hatred and infringement of human rights. (Gumbel, October 1993)

Despite the assurance by Charles Pasqua, the new laws permitting random identity checks mean that not only illegal immigrants, but also legal immigrants, legal foreign residents, legal foreign visitors and, moreover, French nationals and national citizens can and will be stopped, checked, questioned and perhaps detained by the police, who in the process may well operate in ethnically and racially biased, not to say motivated ways. As Gumbel reports:

> 'In a few weeks we have seen practices develop, sometimes in advance of the law being introduced, which are terrifying in their arbitrary brutality,' said Michel Tubiana, secretary-general of the French Human Rights League. 'Foreigners have entered a zone where the law is no more than a mirage.' The league has collected examples of foreigners being held in custody for simple driving offences. In some cases even French citizens – usually non-white – have had difficulty persuading the police of the validity of their identity paper.   (Ibid.)

The right-wing concern in France with ethnic and racial matters (identity, influx, balance) lay behind the government's focus on externally-oriented nationality and led to changes in the rules and requirements on naturalisation, and did so in an ethnically and racially biased and more restrictive direction. But, in addition, the same concern has had consequences for internally-oriented citizenship: it has resulted in French citizens being subjected to random police checks, albeit again in an ethnically and racially skewed manner. In effect, there has been a curtailment of those rights that are, or would have been, enjoyed by either people with French nationality (and perhaps national citizenship) or people with Citizenship of the Union which permit or guarantee *freedom of movement*. In this context, we can recall Article 8a of the Maastricht Treaty, according to which *every citizen of the Union shall have the right to move and reside freely within the territory of the Member States*. But, as a result of the more assiduous attempts to root out illegal immigration in France, there is a chance of visiting British *Citizens of the Union* being stopped and interrogated by the police; and, moreover, there is a greater chance of visiting black British *Citizens of the Union*, compared with white ones, experiencing the everyday hindrances that the tightening of both the nationality and the citizenship regulations, requirements and rights has brought. A further source of potential difficulty for black British *Citizens of the Union* on the streets of France stems from the fact that in the United Kingdom there is no requirement to carry 'identity documents'.

Interestingly, and perhaps ironically, it is the provisions of another major Community agreement, that of the 1986 Single European Act, which have fed into – by being used to rationalise – a Community-wide tightening up of the rules and requirements on nationality, immigration and asylum, in conjunction with a clamp-down on illegal immigration and an associated reduction of citizenship rights and diminution in *citizenship experience*. That is, the aim of the SEA is to establish *the internal market* as 'an area without internal frontiers in which the free movement of goods, persons, services and capital is ensured' (United Kingdom Office of the European Parliament, 1989, p. 3). Consequently, as summarised in a European Commission pamphlet designed to inform and reassure the 'ordinary people' of the European Community (Commission of the European Communities, March 1993, p. 1):

> The removal of internal frontiers within the Community is being matched by a corresponding strengthening of controls at the EC's external frontiers. These are aimed at preventing terrorists, drug smugglers and other criminals as well as illegal immigrants from entering the Community. In addition, spot identity checks will still be possible inside the territory of the Member States. Community countries have drawn up a common list of States whose nationals will need visas to enter the Community. In addition, the conditions of granting asylum to political refugees will be tightened to make it more difficult for so-called 'economic' migrants to settle in the EC. National police forces will cooperate through a new body called Europol.   (Ibid., p. 8)

With a view to tightening up the pertinent rules, regulations and procedures, the issue of asylum, political refugees and *economic migrants* was addressed by a meeting of European Community *immigration ministers* in Copenhagen at the beginning of June 1993. The meeting, as John Carvel reports, was presented with evidence of a dramatic change in the profile of people seeking asylum in the European Community. Since refugee numbers started to surge in the late 1980s, ministers ... have been justifying increasingly restrictive measures by arguing they could no longer afford to remain liberal in the age of the jumbo jet. Unlike 'traditional refugees' ... , the new wave of asylum seekers came by air [and] were accused of being economic migrants seeking a better lifestyle and evading normal immigration controls. Latest figures from the United Nations High Commissioner for Refugees show, however, that the EC's asylum problem is now predominantly European in origin. (Carvel, June 1993)

In 1992, 64 per cent (or 356 720) of the 556 947 people who arrived at immigration control in EC states and declared themselves to be refugees in need of sanctuary from persecution were from Europe, and most of these were from Bulgaria, Romania and what had been Yugoslavia. This represents a considerable increase on the figure for 1991, when only 44 per cent of the lower number of 420 150 were from Europe.[24] The number of asylum seekers arriving in the EC from eastern Europe almost doubled from 186 659 in 1991 to 356 720 in 1992, and 'it was this influx which was responsible for the rise in total applications' (ibid.). The number arriving from elsewhere declined slightly.

The inflow of asylum-seekers is highly concentrated in Germany. In 1992, Germany received 437 996, or 79 per cent, of all the applications for asylum made within the EC. Almost 75 per cent of the applications for asylum made within Germany were from people arriving from eastern Europe. As many as 56 per cent of all Community asylum applications made during 1992 were from east Europeans in Germany. The figures for all other Member States are considerably lower than those for Germany. For instance, in 1992, France was the next-most-popular destination for asylum-seekers, receiving 26 825 applications. The United Kingdom was not far behind France with a figure of 24 610; followed by Belgium and the Netherlands, each of which had just over 17 000; Denmark, almost 14 000; Spain, about 12 500; and finally Italy, Greece, Luxembourg and Portugal with about 6 000 between them.

However, the trend in the composition of asylum-seekers applying to Germany has been echoed more generally. Thus, in 1991, the United Kingdom received 1 625 asylum applications from eastern Europeans – 'less than 4 per cent of a total that was dominated by Africans and Asians' (ibid.). But, in 1992, the number of applications from eastern Europeans rose to 8620 – '35 per cent of the total and more than the influx from any other contintent' (ibid.). During 1992, eastern European refugees also made up the largest proportion of asylum applicants to Belgium, Denmark, Greece, Italy and Luxembourg. Carvel points out that the 'evidence of the first three months of [1993] suggests that the numbers are still increasing. Provisional figures show 118,064 applications, mostly from Romania, former Yugoslavia and Bulgaria – an increase of more than 20 per cent on the same period in 1992' (ibid.).

As Carvel goes on to explain, the trend in the profile of the asylum-seekers within the EC is due in part, but only in part, to the political changes, upheavals and conflicts throughout eastern Europe:

> The trend [is] not only the by-product of conflict in Bosnia and ethnic tensions in other former Communist states; it suggests that measures agreed at previous meetings of EC immigration ministers are making it increasingly difficult for inter-continental refugees to reach European airports. Hefty fines on airlines bringing in passengers without proper passports and visas, coupled with 'technical assistance' for immigration departments in the main refugee-exporting countries, are keeping out genuine refugees as well as bogus ones .... Today's meeting is expected to make the moat of Fortress Europe a little deeper by agreeing procedures for classifying most parts of the world safe enough for asylum seekers to be sent back to without long hearings on their cases. But none of this solves the problem of what to do about the thousands streaming across the German frontier from the east.   (Ibid.)

The meeting on 1 July 1993 proceeded, as Carvel anticipated, to 'make the moat deeper', including for eastern Europeans, as Carvel himself subsequently reported:

European Community ministers yesterday agreed to crack down on illegal immigrants and limit the rights of specially vulnerable Bosnian internees and rape victims who have been given temporary sanctuary in the West to be reunited with members of their families. In Copenhagen, the EC ministers pressed ahead with an agenda to strengthen the walls of 'Fortress Europe' without any concessions to the latest atrocities in Bosnia and within the community's own borders.... The ministers published their first report about levels of persecution in different parts of the world. The information, based on reports from embassies, will be used to reject asylum seekers who claim to have been tortured in areas which the officials deem safe.   (Carvel, July 1993)

This collective tightening of the asylum laws and procedures by the EC Member States was, according to Melanie Phillips, to a large extent at the instigation of the French government:

In France, new immigration laws have removed the previous automatic link between residence and citizenship. The Interior Minister, Charles Pasqua, ... feels sufficiently confident brazenly to express in public virulently racist attitudes. His declared intention is to reduce immigration to zero.[25] This attitude is now infecting the community of nations. The June meeting of the Trevi group in Copenhagen adopted various French initiatives to help set the Community on a similar path. These include the proposal that expulsions should embrace not only those who have breached entry conditions but any foreign settlers who may have employed them, or rented them accommodation or otherwise helped them.   (Phillips, August 1993)

While the French state may have responded to the *ethnic problem* in a relatively extreme fashion, both in the way it has altered its externally-oriented nationality regulations and requirements and in the way it has diminished internally-oriented citizenship rights and experience, its approach is none the less representative of a more general western European tendency, in part due to France's own lead in shaping the collective approach of the European Community. Melanie Phillips summarises:

Since the 1970s, when Britain turned against its immigrants it had once so assiduously courted to service economic expansion, a succession of immigration laws has progressively closed the gates against them and eroded their rights ... . Throwing people out of the country has become far more common since the passage of the 1988 Immigration Act. That removed the right of full appeal against deportation from immigrants who have been living [in Britain] for less than seven years. ...This is [consistent with] the way in which Britain and the other EC member states have formed themselves into an exclusive club which is devising ever-more ruthless rules to bar from membership those poor or black people it is happy to exploit. Poor black people are used to the dirty jobs, while at the same time they are progressively excluded from their rights of citizenship. This naturally produces an illegal underclass upon which regular raids are mounted amid cries of outrage from those who benefit mightily from their (unlawful) labours. The United Kingdom had hardly been a backward conscript in Fortress Europe. On the contrary, it has taken the lead in pushing for even more draconian measures against immigrants ... . And now this British obsession is helping to fuel–and is being fuelled by–rampant European xenophobia. In secret meetings conducted under the aegis of the Trevi Group of European Interior Ministers, policies are drafted to curb immigrants' rights with no opportunity for national parliaments to discuss their implications or for the public to express its view. Human rights are going down the Eurodrain with no questions asked.... Developments in Germany and France are particularly odious. Germany has overturned its constitutional right to asylum, its one claim to a liberal attitude towards foreigners, refusing to connect the burgeoning racist violence in the country with the fact that it has created a class of *unter-menschen*, immigrant workers who are excluded down the generations from rights of citizenship because nationality laws are based on blood rather than residence (an odious criterion to which British nationality law now subscribes). (Ibid.)

Under Germany's 1949 constitution, any foreigner was able to seek asylum and remain in the country for the period –

months or years – it would take for the application to be processed and evaluated. But this provision was removed in May 1993,[26] as Anna Tomforde tells us:

> Germany's parliament yesterday ... tightened the country's asylum laws in a move that critics say will help create a 'fortress Europe' against a growing tide of migration from countries stricken by poverty and war. ...The 521–132 vote to dispose of the guaranteed right of all foreigners to seek asylum came after 13 hours of heated debate that mirrored the tumult outside the parliament.... . After approval tomorrow in the upper house, the measure will become law on July 1. Officials said the law, which would turn back most refugees at Germany's borders would protect those threatened with political repression while keeping out the economic migrants. (Tomforde, May 1993)

Shortly afterwards, the British government had its *Asylum and Immigration Appeals Act 1993* passed by Parliament, as reported by Alan Travis:

> The Asylum Act, which come into force today [26 July 1993], will increase the number of asylum seekers who find themselves on an international merry-go-round, shunted from airport to airport as governments pass the buck, claims Amnesty International. It says ... that Britain already summarily expels dozens of asylum seekers because they have not travelled here directly from the country where they claim to be in fear of their lives. Refugees fleeing persecution are expected to seek asylum in the first 'safe' country they reach. Amnesty [objects to] the new 'fast track' procedures in the act [whereas a] Home Office spokesman said the legislation was designed ... 'to speed things up where there is a justifiable reason to dismiss their case'. (Travis, July 1993)

Consistent with the collective approach among the EC Member States to asylum seeking and granting, as reported by Paul Webster (Webster, 26 August 1993), during August in response to the constitutional council's 'ruling [which] would have made it possible for an asylum applicant rejected by one

EC country to make a new demand in France', the French government was 'preparing to rush through measures to restrict political asylum'. Although the prime minister, Edouard Balladur, 'gave assurances of his attachment to human rights, he was "extraordinarily determined" to respect the wishes of the ring-wing electorate in the March general election which endorsed moves to restrict foreigners'.

At the same time, the tightening of asylum legislation and requirements together with the increased vigilance over illegal immigration is far from confined to the European Union. The Swedish government, for instance, has taken similar steps, as Greg McIvor reports:

> More than 400 mainly Russian Jews face deportation from Sweden under toughened asylum laws .... Traditionally one of Europe's more generous refugee havens, Sweden has introduced restrictions after an influx of about 150,000 asylum seekers, mainly from the former Yugoslavia, in two years. (McIvor, November 1993)

The hardening of Sweden's treatment of asylum-seekers has been atributed by Greg Mcivor to the 'rightwing New Democratic party, which holds the balance of power in the *Riksdag* (parliament)' (McIvor, July 1993). The New Democratic Party's leaders put pressure on the *centre-right government* to adopt 'repatriation incentives for immigrants and tougher admission'. As in France, however, there is evidence that this right-wing approach is consistent with 'rising public disaffection':

> a substantial influx of refugees to Sweden in the past two years has inflamed passions. Some have always branded foreigners *svartskallar* (black heads) but prejudice, once beneath the surface, is now more overt. In the past 18 months, 100,000 people have arrived from former Yugoslavia alone and costs this year for asylum-seekers have soared to 12 billion krona (£1 billion), prompting a widespread feeling that the burden is too heavy. Resentment focuses on what is perceived as over-generous welfare provision for refugees. Subsistence allowances have been pruned by 10 per cent this year .... The centre-right government

has responded ... by ordering a more restrictive interpretation of the Geneva Convention on refugees. Four years ago, 80 per cent of asylum applicants were successful, now only half that number are allowed to stay. (Ibid.)

Asylum-seekers across western Europe – within the European Union and beyond (although Sweden along with Norway, Finland and Austria are preparing to join the EU) – have felt the sharp edge of the general, and to an important extent the collective, strengthening of *Fortress Europe*, perhaps in the manner graphically portrayed in May 1993 by David Gow:

Fortress Europe will increasingly look like this: a sealed, makeshift transit area beyond the main terminals where the fate of bewildered asylum-seekers and refugees from the Third World is swiftly decided before they are flown back home. (Gow, May 1993)

As we have seen, this aspect of *Fortress Europe* will be a feature of the outer-rim defences where would-be legal immigrants – by way of asylum, residence and naturalisation – are repulsed. This line of defence will be backed by an inner-rim entailing the control, detection and ejection of those who have slipped through to become illegal immigrants. This is most strikingly, and perhaps ominously, exemplified by the legal and procedural changes introduced in France. However, the construction of such an edifice will bring – albeit incidentally, even unintentionally – greater impediments and restrictions for people outside the *target populations*. At both lines of defence, the *genuine traveller* may well suffer. At the outer-rim, more and more non-nationals – including more and more that would previously have been allowed through and in – will be turned down and away; and at the inner-rim, the rights and experience of nationals and citizens (national, Union) will be impaired. Moreover, at each line, the changes introduced will have an impact on travellers of all kinds, which will none the less vary according to race-ethnicity. Essentially, non-white travellers, both within and across national boundaries, will suffer most, both quantitatively and qualitatively, irrespective of their nationality, national citizenship and nation-state.

In the light of this, a somewhat modified version of Gellner's nationality–citizenship model as applied to western Europe is invited. First of all, towards the end of the twentieth century, western Europe as well as eastern Europe has its attention focused on nationality and national identity. This focus throughout Europe is fuelled by a common concern with ethnic issues, pressures and (perceived) *threats*, albeit with differing details. In eastern Europe, the *ethnic problem* is rooted in the weakness of nation-states within an unsettled web of sub-national and international (indigenous) ethnic divisions, cleavages and alliances. In western Europe, the *ethnic problem* is centred on the issue of inward migration, including increasingly from eastern Europe, of people who are (at least viewed as being) ethnically and racially non-indigenous and thereby problematic.

But second, in western Europe, because of the particulars of the *ethnic problem*, the focus on externally-oriented nationality has consequences for internally-oriented citizenship. This follows because, apart from anything else, having nationality status is a pre-requisite for the attainment of citizenship status. The ethnically-biased tightening of the rules and requirements on immigration, asylum and naturalisation will feed into the process of citizenship (national, Union) acquisition, and will do so in an ethnically-skewed manner. At the same time, however, the ethnically-biased strengthening of the outer-defences of western *Fortress Europe* against would-be legal immigrants is matched by a similar shoring of the inner-defences against illegal immigrants. In this way, citizenship rights (as distinct from citizenship acquisition) are curtailed and the quality of citizenship experiences is diminished, again in an ethnically-weighted manner.

Third, therefore, within western Europe there has been something of a re-assertion of nationality against the supra-national tendency by way of, in particular, the progress of the European Community and Union. The development of the European Community and Union entails threats to the nation-state, nationality and national identity through, for instance, the provisions of the Maastricht Treaty and the Single European Act. The former introduced the supra-national status of Citizenship of the Union, entailing rights of unhindered movement for all the nationals of all the Member States across and within all national boundaries; while the latter has the aim of creating a supra-national internal single market encouraging in a similar way the unhindered movement of nationals engaged in economic and related activities. But, in response, there are signs of a *reactionary* re-assertion of nationality, national identity and even nationalism against supranationalism, as reflected in for instance the reluctance on the part of large sections of the Danish, British, French and even German populations to endorse the Maastricht Treaty. This is consistent with Bryan Turner's analysis, according to which global uncertainty will encourage a resurgence of localism, regionalism and nationalism. At the same time, however, in western Europe, this process is infused by one particular mediating and precipitating factor: the *ethnic problem*, which for people, parties and governments (individually and collectively through the European Community and Union) is linked to inward migration, asylum and naturalisation. The resulting irony–even contradiction–is that the *ethnic problem* not only shapes the approach to externally-oriented nationality, but also is allowed to undermine internally-oriented citizenship, contrary to the progress which has been made in this area over the last three centuries, and continues to be made or promised by the European Community and Union. In the end, in so far as citizenship is not only internally-oriented but also individually-oriented, it is the individual in his or her everyday life, activities and experiences who suffers.

4 Citizenship, Social Change and the Individual

In the second chapter I made the distinction, following Gardner (Gardner, 1990, pp. 63–6) between 'national citizenship rights' and 'new citizenship rights', where the latter are *specifically human rights because they must be granted to all, without distinction on national or any other ground* (ibid., p. 66). The human rights involved are those to be found in such international agreements as the United Nations' Universal Declaration of Human Rights (1948) and the European Convention on Human Rights (1950). Whereas national citizenship rights determine a person's (internally-oriented) relationship with a particular 'state', namely that 'state' of the nation-state which is his or her particular membership state, new citizenship rights determine a person's relationship with 'the state' in general, that is, with any 'state' irrespective of his or her particular membership state.[1]

However, despite this distinction, both national citizenship rights and new citizenship rights have one socially important and sociologically significant feature in common: *new citizenship, like national citizenship, is about individual rights and relationships, as opposed to (at least in the first instance) collective rights and relationships.* This chapter addresses the social (empirical) and sociological (theoretical) links between this common feature and the socio-historical context within which citizenship has developed.

The sociological significance of the individualistic character of citizenship rights, whether of the 'national' type or of the 'new' (human rights) type, lies in the way such rights fit in with and flow from a particular set of *intellectual* traditions, as summarised in the case of human rights by Norberto Bobbio:

> It is a mark of our era that the three main trends of modern political thought – liberalism, socialism and socio-christianity – have all converged around human rights without clash-

Social Change and the Individual 139

ing .... Chronologically, the liberal view of the right to freedom came first. Social rights – in the form of a public education system and the provision of work [sic] – were first mentioned at the beginning of the French Constitution of 1791 and made their entry into modern constitutional history on the broader scale with the Weimar Constitution. As for socio-christianity, there was a turning point with Pope Leo XIII and the encyclical *Rerum novarium* of 1891, which stressed the right of freedom of association, which belongs to the liberal tradition. (Bobbio, March 1992)

For Bobbio, the way in which 'the three main ideological trends of our time have come together in certain basic human rights' is exemplified in the UN's Declaration of Universal Human Rights, Article 3 of which states that 'Every individual has the right to life, freedom and security'; and in the 'European Charter on Human Rights', Article 1 of which recognises 'the right to life, but is limited to the defence of the individual from intentional killing, in other words, the defence of life that is in full swing, not life about to begin or end' (ibid.). But what Bobbio does not mention is the major sociologically pertinent point that the three intellectual, or ideological, traditions which have converged in the provision of human (new citizenship) rights are specifically *Western* traditions. They are better described as *the three main trends of Western political thought*, which reflect therefore specifically Western cultural traditions with their distinctive emphases, such as on 'the right to freedom' and especially on the right to freedom of *the individual.* Accordingly, it is a specifically Western set of rights which have been enshrined in the UN's Declaration as human and *universal* rights.

The geo-political and cultural specificity – not to say bias – of the UN's Declaration, most notably in its emphasis on *individual rights*, emerged at the United Nations Conference on Human Rights held in Vienna in the middle of 1993. According to Liesl Graz, while 'the conference's most important result will probably be its re-affirmation of the principle that basic human rights should apply to all people everywhere', the conference was none the less marred by 'deep divisions'. Whereas the 'West insisted the rights of the individual were universal; a group of Arab and Asian countries emphasised collective rights and "cultural specificity"' (Graz, June 1993). The somewhat ambivalent outcome of the conference is summarised in the following way by Ian Traynor:

> The conference secured progress on various contentious issues by strongly attacking violence against women, endorsing rights of indigenous people and children, and reaffirming that rights are universal despite Arab and Asian attempts to stress factors of culture, religion and tradition. (Traynor, June 1993)

While the conference ended by supporting a range of human and universal rights, the cultural split generated by the Western emphasis on the individualistic character of such rights showed up in the way non-Western delegates failed to support the supra-national arrangements which Western countries had proposed to help ensure the everyday application, operation and enjoyment of such rights:

> the ... conference [ended] after a bruising battle over whether new United Nations agencies should be created and empowered to enforce observance of rights worldwide. [The result was that] the most important part of the [final] declaration..., the action plan that was to detail specific mechanisms, resources, and institutions for monitoring, promoting and enforcing human rights, was left vague.   (Ibid.)

Non-Western representatives at the conference showed resistance against the imposition of universal human rights, which they saw as culturally weighted in favour of the West's individualistic approach to such rights. In effect, the conference interfered with the progress of the globalisation of new citizenship in response to the latter's individualistic character; to that characteristic which new citizenship shares with national citizenship; to that feature which characterises citizenship in general, of whatever type; and therefore to that feature whereby citizenship of whatever type can be distinctively located – geo-politically, historically, culturally – in the West.

At the beginning of the first chapter, I proposed that 'essentially, citizenship is an *internally oriented* relationship which people as individuals have with the nation-state of which they have full formal membership by virtue of their enjoyment of the full range of citizenship rights granted, guaranteed or enforced by the state'. I suggested that 'citizenship *per se* is always an *individual* relationship', even though 'citizenship relations occur to some extent between people within and through collectivities (and thereby between collectivities)'. This last point may be underscored by adding that *citizenship rights are always individual rights even though they may be exercised on behalf of individuals by collectivities*; and even though, perhaps connectedly, they may have been gained through the activities of collectivities (such as political parties, trade unions, and pressure groups). The point is about, in essence, the relationship between individuals and collectivities by way of the individualistic character of citizenship, and it will be examined in some detail in this chapter.

Also in chapter one, I mentioned that the individualistic view of citizenship is consistent with T. H. Marshall's approach. For Marshall, citizenship is a status attached to which is a set of legal rights that bring full (formal) membership of (to use Baubock's phrase) a national community. In effect, citizens are 'free men' whose freedom is 'protected by common law' (Marshall, 1950, pp. 28–9 and 40–1; quoted in Commission on Citizenship, 1990, pp. 4–5). Marshall identified three types of citizenship rights which emerged and developed in turn over the course of three centuries, at least in Britain. Civil rights, which are 'necessary for individual freedom', emerged in the eighteenth century; political rights to 'participate in the exercise of political power' emerged in the nineteenth century; and the twentieth century is marked by the expansion of social rights – those rights which give access to the kind of 'welfare and security' for which the 'education system and the social services' have been established (Marshall, 1950, pp. 10–11; quoted in Commission on Citizenship, 1990, p. 5). Following Marshall, *each type of citizenship right emerged and developed in conjunction with a corresponding set of political (state) institutions.*

One recent writer on citizenship whose approach has been shaped by Marshall's is J. M. Barbalet. In chapter one, I mentioned how, for Barbalet, modern citizenship (as opposed to *classical city-state* citizenship) is distinctive in that its *basis is the capacity to participate in the exercise of political power through the electoral process*. For Barbalet, participation in the exercise of political power through political citizenship rights is the basis for the further enjoyment, extension and expansion of citizenship rights – including the extension of such rights to the working class during the nineteenth century and their expansion into social rights during the twentieth century. The result is that, in the 'modern state', what Barbalet refers to as *national citizenship* 'extends across society', most notably to such previously excluded sections of society as the working class (ibid., p. 2) and (we might add) women – even though the extension, as we have noted, has a lower age limit at the line of demarcation between adults and children; and has occurred in conjunction with the persistence of a highly unequal distribution of *enabling resources*, whereby formal citizenship rights are transposed into informal, everyday citizenship experience in a highly disparate fashion.

These qualifications aside, participation in the exercise of political power by way of *legal membership of a political community based on universal suffrage* (ibid., p. 2) is consistent with Barbalet's use of the label 'democratic national-state' (ibid., p. 2) to describe the modern societies involved. However, what I wish to suggest is that an alternative label is 'liberal democracy', reminding us of the way not only new citizenship (or human) rights, but also national citizenship rights, given their individualist character, fit in with and flow from distinctively Western intellectual traditions, including *liberalism*, with its emphasis on individual freedom, rights and opportunities. As Patrick Dunleavy and Brendan O'Leary tell us:

> The 'liberal' component of liberal democracy derives from liberalism – a pre-democratic political ideology which asserts that there should be as much individual freedom in any society as is compatible with the freedom of others. Liberalism is an individualist creed, which mushroomed in the seventeenth and eighteenth centuries .... Traditionally, liberals have wanted freedom from the state, demanding that some individual freedoms, or rights, should be protected both from the state and from majority decisions .... Most current Western political systems thus represent the democratization of liberalism. Put more formally, liberal democracy is a system of representative government by majority rule in which some individual rights are nonetheless

protected from interference by the state and cannot be restricted even by an electoral majority. (Dunleavy and O'Leary, 1987, pp. 4–6)

Dunleavy and O'Leary expand on the 'democracy' component of 'liberal democracy':

> The concept of 'democracy' is best understood through its Greek roots: *demos*, meaning the 'citizen body', and *cracy*, meaning 'the rule of'. Originally democracy meant the rule of the citizen body as opposed to the rule of the aristocracy or the monarchy. [In a modern] liberal democracy citizens rule at one remove from executive decision-making. The citizen body is sovereign mostly in name, exercising its sovereignty only while rulers of the state are being elected. [That is,] the mass of citizens do not participate directly in policy-making or administration. Under liberal democracy the citizens' representatives make laws and develop policies, instructing full-time state employees, loosely described as bureaucrats, to implement them. (Ibid., pp. 4–5)[2]

Here, Dunleavy and O'Leary are making a point about the operation of liberal democracies, by way of the participation of citizens within the prevailing political processes, which qualifies and complements Barbalet's argument that political citizenship rights in particular provide the basis for the enjoyment, extension and expansion of citizenship rights in general. It may well be that political rights have considerable personal and social importance along the lines suggested by Barbalet, given the political power they bring and the *individuality* they permit and promote. However, Dunleavy and O'Leary remind us that citizens exercise their political rights in relation to decision, policy and law-making only indirectly, through their elected representatives (as distinct from delegates); that citizens' participation in the exercise of political power and thereby in the conduct of political processes is highly conditional and very limited; that when citizens participate in political processes through the exercise of their political rights, they do so within a system of political power which is far from reducible to (the power brought by) such rights; that the system of political power within modern liberal democracies is hierarchical and dependent upon a broad and complex range of 'non-democratic' factors rooted in, for instance, social class and property, sex-gender and patriarchy, race and ethnicity, and age and generation. The exercise by citizens of their political rights within the processes leading to the enjoyment, extension and expansion – or the gaining and granting – of further citizenship rights takes place within a system of political power which is unequally distributed; which is conditioned by extraneous distributions and sources of power; and which is characterised by struggle, resistance and conflict. Returning to Barbalet's argument, the somewhat non-democratic, hierarchical and conflictual features of the political processes within modern liberal democracies need to be taken into account in analysing and making sense of the (vertical) extension of citizenship to the working class (women and so on) during the nineteenth and twentieth centuries, along with the associated (horizontal) expansion of citizenship rights from the civil, through the political, and to the social over the same period.

Accordingly, I will proceed with an examination of the issue of, as Barbalet himself puts it, 'the role of the contest of interests, of struggle, compromise and containment, in the extension of citizenship rights to previously excluded groups, and especially the working class' (Barbalet, 1988, p. 30); and of the way this is represented in the work of T. H. Marshall and of more recent writers, most notably Anthony Giddens. David Held tells us that for Giddens, Marshall

> understood the unfolding of citizenship rights from the eighteenth to the twentieth century as a process supported and buttressed by 'the beneficent hand of the state'. In Giddens's analysis, Marshall seriously underestimated the way 'citizenship rights have been achieved in substantial degree through struggle' [Giddens, 1982, p. 171]. (Held, 1989, p. 166)

However, in response, Held attacks Giddens for a misplaced criticism, given that as far as Held is concerned Marshall does grant conflict a central place in the process by which rights are gained and granted (ibid., p. 170). Held argues that for Marshall:

the chief factor ... underpinning the development of rights was, in fact, struggle – struggle against hierarchy in its traditional feudal form, struggle against inequality in the market place and struggle against social injustice perpetuated by social institutions. Rights had to be fought for, and when they were won they had to be protected .... When Marshall discussed citizenship and class, and when he described the relationship between the two as one of 'warfare', he was addressing himself explicitly to some of the major social movements which have shaped the contemporary world.   (Ibid., p. 167)

Other writers have interpreted Marshall's analysis in a way which lends support to Held's criticism of Giddens. These writers include B. S. Turner (Turner, 1986, p. 60), S. M. Lipset (Lipset, 1973, p. xx), and A. H. Halsey (Halsey, 1984, p. 11). Halsey, for example, specifically and categorically rejects Giddens's interpretation:

Giddens' criticism cannot be fully sustained when ... Marshall describes class and citizenship as principles or social forces which have been 'at war in the twentieth century' and this conflict of principles 'springs from the very roots of the social order'.... Marshall saw conflict ... as a permanent and indeed desirable feature of a dynamic society. (Halsey, 1984, p. 11; quoted in Barbalet, 1988, p. 30)

On the other side, however, Giddens receives support in his criticism of Marshall from Barbalet, who claims that the 'consensus of intepretation' of Marshall's work as giving a central dynamic place to *social conflict* is misleading:

Marshall [1973, p. 92] does say that the growth of citizenship is stimulated 'by struggle to win those rights'. But [the] struggle which Marshall refers to here is not necessarily social struggle, between groups or classes or people, but principally struggle against established ways of doing things. Elsewhere ... Marshall [1950, pp. 84, 122] refers to conflict ... [in the sense of] conflict between opposing principles of citizenship, on the one hand, and class or capitalist society, on the other .... Marshall's discussion of conflict here does not point to social struggle and certainly not social violence, for these latter refer to a particular type of relationship between social actors. The conflict which Marshall refers to is between sets of institutions or the parts of a social system, as opposed to the actors within it [see Lockwood, 1964][3]. Giddens [1979, p. 131][4] has shown ... that the term 'conflict' properly refers only to struggle between actors or groups expressed as actual social practices, whereas the term contradiction would be used to refer to the disjunction of structural principles of system organization. Marshall's conflict is more contradiction than struggle. (Barbalet, 1988, pp. 30–1)

Marshall's mention of a *conflict of principles* between 'the equality of status in citizenship' and 'the inequality of class in market society', is a reference to a structural *contradiction*, rather than to, as such, social conflict (ibid., p. 31). For Marshall, the development of citizenship is 'through the opposition and contradiction between the principles of citizenship and class' (ibid., p. 31), rather than through social conflict between social classes, for instance. For Marshall, 'the relationships between social groups caught up in this process [are characterised more by] bargaining and reconciliation ... than social conflict and struggle or violence' (ibid., p. 31).

Given this distinction, I wish to argue that the pivotal issue in the study, analysis and understanding of the development of modern citizenship is precisely the relationship between social conflict, on the one hand, and *structural* contradictions, on the other, by way of the process through which citizenship rights are granted, acquired and realised, while taking into account the mediating influence of such *social and structural* threads as social class, race-ethnicity, sex-gender and age-generation, along with such *ideational* factors as culture and ideology (as exemplified in, to recall Bobbio's list, liberalism, socialism and socio-christianity). For Giddens, as for Marshall and Barbalet, class conflict in particular has provided the impetus and direction for the emergence and continuing development of citizenship. As Held points out, for Giddens, the struggle for citizenship has taken 'a variety of forms' (held, 1989, p. 171), but 'the most enduring and important' has been class conflict: first, the class conflict of 'the bourgeoisie against the remnants of feudal privilege'; and second, the class conflict of the working class against 'the bourgeoisie's hold on the chief levers of power'. These conflicts 'shaped two massive institutional changes, respectively'. The first of these changes was the gradual separation of 'the state from the economy': it 'was the establishment of civil and political rights by the bourgeoisie which first and foremost helped free the economy, and more generally civil society, from the direct political interference of the state'. The separation of the state from the economy 'remoulded both sets of institutions' (ibid., p. 171). As Giddens himself adds, these new citizenship rights

> should not be seen as being created 'outside' the sphere of the state, but as part and parcel of the emergence of the 'public domain', separated from 'privately' organised economic activity. Civil rights thus have been, from the early phases of capitalist development, bound up with the very definition of what counts as 'political'. Civil and political citizenship rights developed together and remain, thereafter, open to a range of divergent interpretations which may directly affect the distribution of power. (Giddens, 1985, p. 207; quoted in Held, 1989, p. 171)

David Held argues that the development of what he labels 'polyarchy' (or 'rule by the many') – otherwise known in its Western form as 'liberal democracy' – can be 'understood against this background' (Held, 1989, p. 171). For Held:

> The new 'public' domain became concerned in principle with protecting the space for citizens to pursue their activities unimpeded by illegitimate state action and with ensuring the responsiveness of government to the preferences of its citizens considered as political equals.[5] The 'public' and 'private' spheres were formed through interrelated processes. (Held, 1989, p. 171)

This reminds us, of course, of the way Dunleavy and O'Leary have summed up 'liberal democracy' as a *system of representative government by majority rule in which some individual rights are nonetheless protected from interference by the state* (Dunleavy and O'Leary, 1987, pp. 5–6). As Dunleavy and

O'Leary stress, liberalism is 'an individualist creed' (ibid., p.5), so that under liberal democracy the state is purportedly the political apparatus by which democracy (rule by the majority) operates alongside and in a balanced way with the principle that *there should be as much individual freedom as is compatible with the freedom of others* (ibid., p. 5).Hence, the historical emergence and consolidation of liberal democracy occurred along with the establishment of 'civil society' and 'civil rights', which are specifically 'individualistic': *civil rights* are attached to individuals in order to permit and promote the capacity for ('free') individual *human action*. As Barbalet puts it:

> Civil rights include not only property rights and the right of contract but also the rights to the freedom of thought and speech, religious practice, and of assembly and association. They are in principle unified as civil rights in so far as each is a right permissive of human action. But they are more than this. In his 'Reflections on Power', Marshall [1969, p.141] says that 'civil rights though vested in individuals, are used to create groups, associations, corporations and movements of every kind'. In this sense, Marshall [1969, p. 142] continues, civil rights are 'a form of power'. (Barbalet, 1988, p. 19)

Thus, Marshall emphasises the part played by civil rights in the development of 'the working-class movement and its political and industrial opposition to capitalism' (Barbalet, 1988, p. 19). Given this, Barbalet tells us that, nevertheless, 'individual rights are paramount in civil citizenship, and any collective action can only be justified as an expression of civil rights if the right of the individual in them is preserved' (ibid., p. 26). Civil citizenship rights are always individualistic in character; their emergence marks the advent of modern citizenship in general; and, for Marshall, they 'were indispensable to a competitive market economy' (Marshall, 1950, p. 87 – quoted in Barbalet, 1988, p. 8) in that, as Barbalet goes on to explain, 'civil rights bestow on those who have them the capacity to enter market exchanges as independent and self-sufficient agents' (Barbalet, 1988, p. 8). That is, civil rights were conducive, and even essential, to the operation and progress of 'a competitive market economy' (Barbalet, 1988, p. 21) because they gave each person 'the power to engage as an independent unit in the economic struggle' (Marshall, 1950, p. 87 – quoted in Barbalet, 1988, p. 21). Coincidentally, following Giddens, such individualistic civil rights were encouraged by the principles of liberal democracy – by that intellectual or ideological tradition which lay behind the separation of 'the state' from 'civil society', centred on the economy, or, that is, behind the separation of 'the public' and 'the private'.

This argument, however, invites a point of terminological and conceptual clarification. Giddens's dichotomy between 'the public' and 'the private' does not correspond with that which is frequently proposed (and sometimes criticised) in the literature on family life and gender relationships, such as in E. Gamarnikow's *The Public and the Private* (Gamarnikow, 1983).[6] The public–private distinction in the title of Gamarnikow's book is between the private sphere of social life centred on the family, and the public sphere encompassing both the state and the economy. Giddens uses the term 'the private' to designate what is otherwise referred to as 'civil society': that area of social life centred on the economy, at least when the latter is separated from (is 'privatised' in relation to) the state, as it is under capitalism. Giddens then distinguishes the private or civil domain of modern, capitalist society from the public domain of the state. Hence, Giddens's notions (following Marshall) of 'civil citizenship' and 'civil rights' apply to what, for him, is the *private* 'domain of organised economic activity', that domain which, with the emergence of capitalism, was separated from the public domain of the state. This is consistent with the original Hegelian specification of 'civil society' as summarised by Michael Mann:

> Hegel described civil society as part of Ethical Life, which was made up of three elements, the family, civil society and the state. Civil society was the intermediate phase between the close-knit, immediate dependency of the family bond, and the universal interest and perspective of the state. It referred to the sphere of social life where individuals pursue their own self-interest within universally recognised bounds. The protection of private property, the recognition of the public authority of the law and the police, together with other necessary provisions for the safety of individuals were

preconditions for this pursuit of self-interest. Civil society encompassed both economic and legal institutions, and arose from a system of human physical and social needs. It thus entailed a bond of 'unity through necessity' between interdependent individuals, 'a system of complete interdependence, wherein the livelihood, happiness and legal status of one man is interwoven with the livelihood, happiness and rights of all' ... transcended the egoism of civil society, rising above the realm of the individual's particular interests through the universal protection of the common good. Marx criticised Hegel's conception of civil society [on the grounds that] Hegel derived his scheme from the particular bourgeois social and economic order of his day and failed to realize that the .... institutions of civil society were instruments for the domination of one class over another and the tools for the particular interests competing in civil society. (Mann, 1983, p. 45)

Following Marshall, such *civil institutions* include those associated with the exercise of the 'civil element' of citizenship (see Roche, 1992, p. 19; Barbalet, 1988, p. 6), or, that is, of those 'rights necessary for individual freedom – liberty of the person, freedom of speech, thought and faith, the right to own property and to conclude valid contracts, and the right to justice. ... [Where] the institutions most directly associated with civil rights are the courts of justice' (Roche, 1992, p. 19). For Giddens, in line with Marx's criticism of Hegel, civil rights and institutions do represent an arena within capitalist society within which the dominant class has pursued its interests, including that of sustaining its domination. At the same time, the civil domain is (like the public domain) one in which the policies and practices of those who dominate and govern have not been just passively accepted, but have been, instead, contested by the dominated and governed within a struggle over civil citizenship rights. Class conflict took place within the emergent private domain, during the process of its separation from the state, between the old (extant but declining) dominant class, or the feudal land-owning aristocracy, and the newly dominant class, or the capitalist bourgeoisie. Having been separated, the class conflict, which has provided the dynamic behind the changing form and content of the civil domain under capitalism, has occurred largely between the bourgeoisie and the working class. The latter initially struggled to acquire civil rights, which it then used as a foundation for the further (vertical) extension and (horizontal) expansion of complementary citizenship rights, including yet further civil ones.

For Giddens, one particular set of civil rights, gradually forged through class struggle, can be distinguished as 'economic civil rights', which Held tells us are to be equated with what Marshall refers to as 'industrial citizenship' (Held, 1989, p. 168). According to Giddens the 'institutional centre or locale where [such] rights are championed and fought over' (ibid., p. 169) is the 'work-place', and such rights include those which permit people to form and join trade unions. Marshall paid attention to the way trade unions have played a part in the development of working-class citizenship, arguing that trade unionism, and 'the collective bargaining with employers it permits' (Barbalet, 1988, p. 9), became the means by which 'the economic and social status of organized workers was raised'. For Marshall, 'the collective exercise of rights by members of the working class in creating and using trade unionism' (Barbalet, 1988, p. 9) established 'the claim that they, as citizens, were entitled to certain social rights' (Marshall, 1950, p. 94 – quoted in Barbalet, 1988, p. 9). However, while Giddens and Marshall both recognise that trade unions have played a major part in the extension and expansion of citizenship rights, Giddens's assumptions and emphasis with regard to the details involved are somewhat different from Marshall's. Giddens stresses how:

> 'economic civil rights' ... had to be fought for by working-class and trade-union activists. The right to form a trade union was not gracefully conceded, but was achieved and sustained only through bitter conflicts. The same applies to the extension of the activities of trade unions in their attempt to secure regularised bargaining and the right to strike. (Held, 1989, p. 168)

The point being that in order to gain citizenship, 'groups previously excluded from its scope have had to struggle against the resistance of those who have opposed the extension'

(Barbalet, 1988, p. 32). For Giddens, in other words, the struggle over the extension and expansion of citizenship rights has been, in a sense, two-way and mutual. The demands of *the excluded* over citizenship rights have been resisted by those who, helped by being *included*, have had the power to grant or withhold such rights. The excluded's demands may be met if the included and powerful perceive that it is in their interests to accede or acquiesce. As Barbalet puts it:

> struggle is important in the advancement of citizenship, but significantly because it disposes the dominant class and the state to accommodation and conciliation, if it is to their advantage to be so disposed. If the extension of democratic citizenship is not in the interests of the powerful then struggle is as likely to lead to repression as to the gaining of rights; indeed, more likely. Thus the interests of the dominant class (and the state) are as important as lower-class struggle for an understanding of the rise and extension of modern citizenship. (Ibid., p, 36)

Essentially, therefore, following Giddens, 'government expedience and not only class struggle can extend citizenship rights' (Giddens, 1982, p. 171; quoted in Barbalet, 1988, p. 36). Barbalet concurs with this interpretation, and stresses its general applicability:

> The rise of modern democratic citizenship has occurred in a number of different historical, societal and institutional contexts. The significance of capitalist development and especially the capitalist class structure for the expansion of citizenship is not confined to those societies which arose out of the collapse of feudalism, but extends to all societies in which democratic citizenship has a real presence. The attainment of citizenship through struggle, and especially class struggle, reflects not only the impact of lower-class demands but also dominant class requirements for security. (Barbalet, 1988, p. 43)

In the particular case of feudal society giving way to capitalist society from the end of the sixteenth century, the emergence and extension of modern citizenship is viewed by

Giddens as integral to the general progress of modern democracy, while at the same time being understandable in terms of the powerful serving their interests and security. The interests and security of the powerful were served through the expansion of the state – state sovereignty and the state's 'apparatus of government' – in conjunction with the replacement of social control through coercion with social control through a combination of co-operative social relations and 'the state's capacity for surveillance; that is, the collection and storing of information about members of society, and the related ability to supervise subject populations' (Giddens, 1981, pp. 169ff.; quoted in Held, 1989, p. 170). Held summarises:

> As the state's sovereign authority expanded progressively and its administrative centres became more powerful, the state's dependence on force as a direct medium of rule was slowly reduced. For the increase in administrative power *via* surveillance increased the state's dependence on co-operative forms of social relations; it was no longer possible for the modern state to manage its affairs and sustain its offices and activities by force alone. Accordingly, greater reciprocity was created between the governors and the governed, and the more reciprocity was involved, the more opportunities were generated for subordinate groups to influence their rulers. Giddens refers to this 'two-way' expansion of power as 'the dialectic of control' [Giddens, 1985, pp. 201ff.]. (Held, 1989, p. 170)

This is the 'context' within which, Giddens claims, the 'struggle for rights' occurred and, therefore, 'can be understood'. As a concomitant to the 'expansion of state sovereignty' (or authority), the progressive development took place of 'the identity of subjects' (of the governed) as 'political subjects', or, that is, 'as citizens'. Giddens argues that 'the expansion of state sovereignty means that those subject to it are in some sense – initially vague, but growing more and more definite and precise – aware of their membership in a political community and of the rights and obligations such membership confers' (Giddens, 1985, p. 210). Essentially, for Giddens, the development of citizenship, understood as 'membership of an overall political community', is 'intimately bound up with the novel (administrative) ordering of political power and the "politicization" of social relations and day-to-day activities which follows in its wake' (Held, 1989, p. 170). The outcome is that in modern society:

> each category of citizenship right should be understood as an arena of contestation or conflict, each linked to a distinctive type of regulatory power or surveillance, where the surveillance is both necessary to the power of superordinate groups and an axis around which subordinate groups can seek to reclaim control over their lives.[7] (Ibid., pp. 168–9)

For Giddens, the civil domain (other than the area of 'economic civil' rights, which, as we have noted, are *championed and fought over* in the *work-place*) is characterised by conflict over the extension of civil rights centred on the institution of the *law court* and under the regulatory control and surveillance of *policing* (ibid., p. 169). Giddens writes:

> Civil rights are intrinsically linked to the modes of surveillance involved in the policing activities of the state. Surveillance in this context consists of the apparatus of judicial and punitive organizations in terms of which 'deviant' conduct is controlled. ... [As with other kinds of rights,] civil rights have their own particular locale. That is to say, there is an institutionalised setting in which the claimed universality of rights can be vindicated – the law court. The law court is the prototypical court of appeal in which the range of liberties included under 'civil rights' can be defended and advanced.   (Giddens, 1985, pp. 205–6; quoted in Held, 1989, p. 169)

As already mentioned, for Giddens, that class conflict entailing the working class's challenge to the bourgeoisie's hold on the *chief levers of power* shaped two *massive institutional changes* (ibid., p. 171). Following the extension of the franchise to the working class, the second of these changes was marked by the successful struggle by the working class, from the late nineteenth century, for the expansion of citizenship rights into the area of social rights.[8] This particular area of struggle resulted in 'the welfare order – the modern welfare interventionist state' (ibid., p. 171). But, Giddens argues, social rights are not merely an expanded version of civil and political rights: 'they are in part the creation of an attempt to ameliorate the worst consequences of the worker-citizen's lack of formal control of his or her activities in the work-place' (ibid., p. 171), the institutional locale for struggle over 'economic civil' rights.

At this point, we might turn (or return) to what emerges in Giddens's analysis as a pivotal conceptual distinction and, thereby, modification of Marshall's approach. Despite the way Held equates Giddens's 'civil economic' rights with Marshall's 'industrial' rights, Giddens specifically criticises Marshall's three-fold classification of citizenship rights, objecting in particular to Marshall's view of civil rights as a unitary or homogeneous type. Held summarises Giddens's argument as follows:

> He emphasizes that the civil rights of individual freedom and equality before the law were fought for and achieved in large part by an emergent bourgeoisie. These rights helped consolidate industrial capitalism and the modern representative state. As such, they are to be distinguished from what Giddens calls 'economic civil' rights. This latter group of rights had to be fought for by working-class and trade union activists. The right to form trade unions was not gracefully conceded, but was achieved and sustained only through bitter conflicts. The same applies to the extension of the activities of unions in their attempt to secure regularized bargaining and the right to strike. All this implies that there is 'something awry in lumping together such phenomena with civil rights in general' [Giddens, 1982, p. 127]. If individual civil rights tended to confirm the dominance of capital, economic civil rights tended to threaten the functioning of the capitalist market. (Held, 1989, p. 168)

Held (ibid., p. 175) attempts to cut through the terminological and typological differences by suggesting that the broad range of citizenship rights which Marshall subsumes under the headings 'civil', 'political' and 'social', and which Giddens refines as 'civil', 'economic civil', 'political' and 'social', pertain to four separate areas which are preferably distinguished using the labels 'civil', 'economic', 'political', and 'social' (ibid., p. 175). For Held, economic rights are what Giddens refers to as 'economic civil' rights (and what Marshall refers to as 'industrial' rights), and they cover those citizenship rights which

> have been won by the labour movement over time and which create the possibility of greater control for employees over the work-place. Removing this category from civil rights distinguishes usefully those rights which are concerned with the liberty of the individual in general from those rights which seek to recover elements of control over the work-place, and which have been at the centre of conflicts between labour and capital since the earliest phases of the Industrial Revolution. (Ibid., p. 175)

Now, aside from the issue of the category of civil rights and the character of its relationship with the category of economic (or industrial) rights, Held claims that the categories of political rights and social (or 'welfare') rights can be treated, guided by both Marshall and Giddens, as unproblematic (ibid., p. 175). On the other hand, however, Marshall and Giddens are jointly criticised by Held for none the less restricting the number of categories by failing to take account of what he sees as the full spread of citizenship rights:

> there are other categories which neither Marshall nor Giddens develops, linked to a variety of domains where, broadly speaking (non-class specific) social movements have sought to re-form power centres according to their own goals and objectives. Among these is the area of struggle for reproductive rights – at the very heart of the women's movement. Reproductive rights are the very basis of the possibility of effective participation of women in both civil society and the polity. (Ibid., p. 175)[9]

For Held, such reproductive rights include those whereby the state and various 'political agencies' become responsible for 'the medical and social facilities' and for 'the material conditions' which 'help to make the choice to have a child a genuinely free one and, thereby, ensure a crucial condition for women if they are to be "free and equal"' (ibid., pp. 175–6).

Perhaps the rights which Held has in mind under the heading of 'reproductive rights' include those which would be furthered by the British government's reported 'Plan to widen choice of birth':

> Plans for radical changes in maternity care aimed at giving mothers' wishes priority will be announced in a government report on Thursday. Recommendations designed to give pregnant women more say over where and how they give birth are likely to lead to a significant increase in home deliveries.... The report has been drawn up by a review group ... set up after criticism of maternity services by the Commons select committee on health, which described childbirth as often an 'over-medicalised' and degrading experience and found no evidence that hospital deliveries were safe. At present 96 per cent of babies are born in hospital. (*Guardian*, August 1993)[10]

However, if these changes were to have the effect of enhancing the kind of rights which Held regards as reproductive rights, then it is difficult to see how such rights can be regarded as anything other than 'civil rights'. Of course, both Marshall and Giddens have shown considerable interest in civil rights, even though they have failed to single out reproductive rights for special attention, their main focus being on social class conflict rather than sex-gender struggles. For me, it is not surprising that Giddens does not treat reproductive rights as an extra or separate category of citizenship rights. For me also, while reproductive rights (in so far as there are any such things) are to be counted as civil rights, the grounds variously presented by Held, Giddens and Marshall for treating 'economic rights' (Held), or 'economic civil rights' (Giddens), or 'industrial rights' (Marshall) as a distinct type of right seem reasonable.[11] Certainly, this approach has received the support of J. M. Barbalet, who, moreover, goes on to present a picture of 'industrial rights' (as he prefers to call them) which suggests not only that they constitute a separate category of rights alongside the civil, political and social categories, but also that they constitute an ontologically distinct variety of rights on the basis of one particular characteristic. As we will see, I wish to argue that this claim is misplaced.

For Barbalet, Giddens's conclusion 'about the independent status of industrial rights in modern citizenship is entirely acceptable' (Barbalet, 1988, p. 23). Barbalet agrees with Giddens's objection to Marshall's treatment of industrial rights – 'the rights of employees to form trade unions, to collectively bargain and to strike' – as civil rights (ibid., p. 22). Barbalet notes how Marshall viewed the nineteenth-century emergence of 'collective bargaining as a strengthening of civil rights rather than the creation of a new right' (Barbalet, 1988, p. 23), and so viewed trade union involvement and activity as the collective deployment by members of the working class of their civil rights to 'assert basic claims to the elements of social justice' (Marshall, 1950, pp. 93–4), or, that is, to expand citizenship into the area of social rights. But, Barbalet explains, Marshall not only fails to view industrial rights as a separate category of citizenship rights, he also fails even to count industrial rights 'as an authentic component of citizenship along with civil, political and social rights' (Barbalet, 1988, p. 22). As far as Marshall is concerned

> trade unionism has 'created a secondary system of industrial citizenship parallel with and supplementary to the system of political citizenship'. Here is Marshall's argument about industrial citizenship: it is a secondary system of citizenship, based on the institution of trade unionism, which is responsible for collective bargaining as a means ... of laying claim to certain basic rights of social justice. (Ibid., p. 24)

Barbalet, however, contradicts Marshall by asserting that 'trade unions do not exercise collective civil rights, but rights of a different kind' (ibid., p. 24). Trade unions exercise rights which are neither secondary nor of the civil category. Instead, they exercise *collective* industrial citizenship rights. But the particular phrasing here is significant. Barbalet's choice of the phrase *collective rights* signifies a yet further fundamental difference between his approach and Marshall's to citizenship rights. Whereas, for Marshall (as well as for a range of other writers, as we saw in chapter one), all citizenship rights are *individualistic* in character, for Barbalet this is not quite the case. Barbalet argues that, in contrast with social rights:

Social Change and the Individual 159

Industrial rights are not individualistic, obligatory or consumption-oriented, but the rights of individuals permitting (and perhaps enabling) their collective action and organization. The institutional bases of industrial rights are trade unions and similar associations of employees. Industrial citizenship is a status limiting the commodification of persons in employment and therefore includes the right to influence the terms of employment, the conditions of work or the level of pay, and is therefore also the right to develop and sustain the independent means of achieving these things through the organization of combinations or unions. (Ibid., p. 26)

Turning to a comparison between industrial rights and civil rights, what they have in common, and in fact share with all citizenship rights, is 'a permissive quality and an enabling capacity' (ibid., p. 26). On the other hand, whereas 'Individual rights are paramount in civil citizenship, and any collective action can only be justified as an expression of civil rights if the right of the individual in them is preserved', such 'conditions do not necessarily obtain in the case of industrial rights' (ibid., p. 26). Barbalet clarifies what he has in mind in the following way:

Trade unions can only function properly if the rights of their individual members are subordinated to the rights of the collectivity, and in their operations they [trade unions] frequently infringe the rights of property and contract by preventing manufacture and trade through strike action ....Thus the exercise of industrial rights may be injurious to the civil rights of individual workers, possibly including trade unionists, and employers alike .... Industrial rights are not only distinct from civil rights but in their application may be opposed.   (Ibid., p. 26)

Here, however, we might note that for Barbalet, any opposition between industrial rights and civil rights will not be unique: civil rights may be opposed not only by industrial rights, but also by social rights. That is, Barbalet argues elsewhere, that the 'different rights which are components of modern citizenship are not cut from the same cloth, and, under certain circumstances, serious tensions may develop between them', something that 'can be demonstrated by a comparison of civil and social rights' (ibid., p. 19). As we have already noted, Barbalet summarises by pointing out that civil rights include those which permit and promote the *freedoms of thought and speech, religious practice, and of assembly and association*; their unifying characteristic being that *each is a right to permissive action* (ibid., p. 19). Given this, circumstances arise when civil rights and social rights 'find themselves in antagonism' (ibid., p. 20). Primarily, the clash in this particular case is due to the way the exercise and enjoyment of civil (permissive) rights is constrained by the imposition of those taxes which are required to allow the state to grant and guarantee social rights by way of the provision of social (welfare) benefits and services. Barbalet puts it as follows:

> The constraint exercised by social rights against the state is direct and imposes costs on the state and therefore taxes on citizens. There is therefore a structural budgetary basis for a potential threat to social rights .... During periods of economic decline there may arise a contradiction between the need for the maintenance of the institutional basis of social rights through taxation and the requirements of capital accumulation. At such times a pressure against social rights may take the form of a reassertion of civil rights, not simply as property rights ... but as an independent source of economic action and power. Marshall's [1950, p. 87] comment that civil rights were essential to a competitive market economy because they gave each person 'the power to engage as an independent unit in the economic struggle' is followed by his observation that for this reason civil rights 'made it possible to deny social protection on the ground that [a person] was equipped with the means to protect himself'. Recent developments in advanced capitalist societies have given these notions new voice. (Barbalet, 1988, pp. 20–1)

Here, Barbalet is alluding to how, especially since the 1960s, combined economic and political developments, entailing especially the ascendancy of the New Right, have been behind a trimming of social welfare provisions and thereby a curtailment of social rights, purportedly to the advantage of both tax payers and *welfare recipients*. These developments are interpreted by Barbalet as evidence that, under capitalism, 'different component rights of modern citizenship are [not] equally guaranteed by the state' (ibid., p. 21). Barbalet elaborates as follows:

> the threat to social rights from civil rights ... is ultimately a class threat. While citizenship rights can be exercised by all who possess them, they in fact tend to serve members of different classes differently. Marshall was well aware that civil and social rights each have a clear class bias in their principles and operation. But he failed to seriously consider ... the propensity of the state to defend different elements of citizenship unequally. Certain civil rights are central to the foundation of capitalist economies and their operation. For these reasons they have the potential to undermine social rights. (Ibid., p. 21)

It is because, for the New Right, the exercise of social rights impedes the operation of the market, against the requirements of capitalism, that the state may, and has recently, curtailed such rights. This is against the interests of the working class, but in the interests of the middle class, given that it brings a boost to taxpayers and their civil rights, not to mention social-class inequality around the distribution of property, or material possessions, or (what I have referred to as) 'enabling resources'. In so far as the state is inclined to pursue policies and practices which suit the requirements of capitalism, it will tend to defend civil rights against the *antagonism* from social rights, and therefore may reverse the expansion of citizenship rights into the area of the social rights, especially during periods of actual or perceived economic difficulties or decline. That is, the development of citizenship is not inevitably progressive and accumulative, essentially because it is shaped through a process of mutual, two-way struggle, conflict and resistance between social classes centred on the state, which mediates in a committed and biased fashion within a hierarchical system of power and control. As Barbalet tells us:

> there is the idea that the exercise of citizenship rights can never be guaranteed and is often precarious. Recent trends

in advanced capitalist societies have led Anthony Giddens [1982, p. 177], for instance, to argue that Marshall's evolutionary account of the development of citizenship ignores the fact that we 'cannot suppose ... that the battle for civil and political rights has been won'. In a complementary vein Bryan Turner [1986, p. 64] has emphasised the 'contingent' nature of the process through which citizenship develops, and cautioned that such a development has 'no necessary historical logic or unfolding process'. (Barbalet, 1988, p. 29)

We might note here that the criticism from Giddens of Marshall, apparently shared by Barbalet, is not accepted by all writers, including David Held:

[An] area of criticism voiced by Giddens concerns Marshall's treatment of the expansion of citizenship rights as a purely 'one-way phenomenon' [Giddens, 1982, p. 173]. Marshall is criticised for regarding the development of citizenship as an 'irreversible process'.... However, [the criticism] in general seems misplaced. For instance, Marshall documented the way in which primitive forms of social rights ... existed prior to the eighteenth century and yet pratically vanished in the latter half of the eighteenth century and the early nineteenth century. He argued that their revival began with the development of public elementary education, but that this process of revival itself had by no means a stable history, and depended on the particular strength of the various movements supporting reform. (Held, 1989, pp. 167–8)

The reference by Held to the ups and downs of specifically social rights brings to mind that Giddens might have acknowledged how *we cannot suppose that the battle, not just for civil and political rights, but also – and perhaps especially – for social rights has been won,* in view of the way such rights undermine civil rights and thereby pose a threat to the progress of capitalism. At the same time, again following Barbalet, the potential antagonism which characterises the relationship between civil rights and social rights is repeated in the case of the relationship between civil rights and industrial rights, presumably raising the possibility of the latter also being unstable and reversible. To echo the proposal made above about social rights, this time with respect to industrial rights: in so far as the state is inclined to pursue policies and practices which suit the requirements of capitalism, it will tend to defend civil rights against the *antagonism* from industrial rights, and therefore may reverse the expansion of citizenship rights into the area of industrial rights, especially during periods of actual or perceived economic difficulties or decline. The development of specifically industrial citizenship rights is not inevitably progressive: it is shaped through a process of two-way struggle, conflict and resistance between social classes centred on the state, which mediates in a committed and biased fashion within a hierarchical system of power and control which favours civil rights and, therefore, the middle class. Hence, it would seem, the example whereby the Thatcher governments from 1979 tackled, and effectively tempered, trade union power in the United Kingdom.[12]

While civil rights are in prospectively antagonistic relationships with both social rights and industrial rights, with the possibility in each case of civil rights being defended by the state at the expense of the other category, and therefore of the working class, there remains something distinctive about the relationship between civil rights and industrial rights by virtue of a unique characteristic of the latter, at least according to Barbalet. This characteristic takes us back to the significance and meaning of Barbalet's proposal (against Marshall) that trade unions exercise *collective* industrial citizenship rights, at which point, however, a problem arises. There is a problem over the precise meaning of Barbalet's proposal – a problem over how to interpret Barbalet's ambiguous phrasing. Barbalet's proposal can be taken to mean either (a) that trade unions exercise industrial citizenship rights attached to individuals, but being collectivities do so collectively; or (b) that trade unions exercise industrial citizenship rights attached to themselves *qua* collectivities.

Further and closer reading of Barbalet fails to finally clear up the issue. For Barbalet, while industrial rights are legally attached to individuals, they are not *individualistic*, they are legal rights *permitting (and perhaps enabling)* individuals to engage in *collective action and organisation*, especially in the form of trade union action and organisation. Trade unions, thereby, exercise *collective industrial citizenship rights*. Indeed, trade unions *can only function properly if the rights of their individual members are subordinated to the rights of the collectivity* – to trade union rights. However, what such an approach to industrial citizenship rights raises is a range of questions about what precisely is being proposed and implied. Primarily, are we to take it that for Barbalet there is (always and necessarily) a disjunction between the legal possession and the practical exercise of industrial citizenship rights, with individuals being the possessors and trade unions being the exercisers? It certainly seems that, for Barbalet, even though individuals legally possess industrial citizenship rights, they none the less do not and cannot exercise such rights individually, and so, individualistically. It is difficult to avoid the conclusion that, for Barbalet, industrial citizenship rights can only be exercised collectively, and so, collectivistically, by way of their complete and categorical subsumption to the collective rights, decisions and actions of trade unions. But if this is so, does it not follow that, in practice, industrial citizenship rights are not only exercised by, but also attached to, trade unions and so to *collectivities*; that industrial citizenship rights are only nominally attached to individuals, being in effect transferred to collectivities in the form of trade unions – trade unions being dependent upon and legally entitled to this process taking place?

It seems that for Barbalet, at least by implication, industrial rights are unique, not only in *not* being individualistic, but also in being in practice (*de facto*, if not *de jure*) attached to collectivities. However, on both counts, we should treat this view of industrial rights with considerable caution. The proposal that industrial citizenship rights are not individualistic, but are instead always and necessarily collectivistic, not only makes them unique among citizenship rights; it also runs counter to generic notions of 'rights', including that indicated by Barbalet himself.

In his more explicit statements, Barbalet tells us that industrial rights are *legally* (the emphasis being 'legally') attached to *the individual*. Thus, for Barbalet, industrial rights are 'the rights of employees to form trade unions, to collectively bargain and to strike' (Barbalet, 1988, p. 22). Here, Barbalet is indicating that industrial rights are the same as all other citizenship rights in being legal entitlements attached to individuals, albeit individuals of a particular type, namely 'employees'.[13] But, given this, and taking into account what Barbalet among other writers has otherwise said about *rights in general*, the conclusion beckons that industrial rights are, *in the final analysis*, the same as all citizenship rights, not only in being attached to individuals, but also in providing individuals with the potential for individualistic decisions and actions, including ones which are taken not merely independently of, but also *against*, collectivities.

Barbalet tells us that 'rights ... attach a particular capacity to persons by virtue of a legal or conventional status' (ibid., pp. 15–16); that 'rights provide a minimum of social capacities and entitlements' (ibid., p. 17); and that 'rights provide persons with capacities or capabilities and opportunities' (ibid., p. 17). If, as seems to be the case for Barbalet, industrial rights are legally attached to individuals as employees, then being rights they will provide *persons* of this type[14] with entitlements, capacities and opportunities. Such an approach to what rights in general and industrial rights in particular bring to *the individual* is consistent with what David Held has said about rights in the form of *citizenship rights*, guided by the writings of Marshall and Giddens:

> The type of rights which are central to the Marshall–Giddens discussion [of citizenship] can be defined as legitimate spheres of independent action (or inaction). Accordingly, the study of rights can be thought of as the study of domains in which citizens have sought to pursue their own activities within the constraints of the community .... The autonomy of the citizen can be represented by that bundle of rights which individuals can enjoy as a result of their status as 'free and equal' members of society. (Held, 1989, pp. 174–5)

For Held – and, following Held, for Marshall and Giddens – citizenship rights in general provide legal entitlements to independent, autonomous and 'free' action, or *inaction*, at least within the *constraints of the community*. If industrial rights are 'rights' in this sense, they will entitle individuals to choices and decisions over actions and *inactions* which will necessarily express individuality, including in relation to (perhaps within and through) collectivities. Rights provide individuals with legal entitlements to decision-making and choices with regard to alternatives; industrial rights, if they are 'rights', provide individuals with opportunities to make decisions in relation to such matters as trade union membership, participation and action, strike action, and so on; industrial rights, if they are 'rights', allow individuals to choose to join a trade union or not, to engage in strike action or not, and so on; and, therefore, in so far as industrial rights are 'rights', they will necessarily permit individuals to express through their choices and decisions their individuality. An industrial right which does not permit choices and individuality – given what Held, Marshall, Giddens and Barbalet mean by 'right' – is not, as such, a 'right'.

An industrial right which does not permit the individual to whom it is legally attached the opportunity to choose not to exercise it – to choose, that is, inaction – is not a 'right'. An industrial right to join a trade union, for instance, is a 'right' only in so far as it legally entitles the individual to whom it is attached the alternative choices of either to join a trade union or not to join. The option of not joining a trade union has to be permissible and possible. If alternatives are not legally and practically available, then the so-called 'right' does not bring an opportunity for 'free', independent decision-making over action or inaction, and accordingly is not, as such, a 'right'. If the industrial right to join a trade union is accompanied by the legal entitlement not to join, then it will be a 'right'; and as well as being legally attached to 'the individual', it will allow individuals to express their individuality – to be individualistic.

If an individual is required, compelled or constrained to join a trade union, and therefore is not free to decide not to join, then it would be inconsistent with notions of 'right' to claim that the individual enjoys the 'right', as such, to join a trade union. It would be more appropriate to claim that the individual has an obligation or a duty to join, and therefore has the converse of a 'right'. The enjoyment of a legal right by someone or something (such as a trade union) depends upon the existence of a legal obligation or duty on other individuals or things whereby that right can be met and realised. Thus, as Barbalet acknowledges, citizenship rights 'may be better called duties of the state to its members' (Barbalet, 1988, p. 18). If an individual has an obligation or a duty to join a trade union, then instead of that individual having an 'industrial right' in relation to trade unions, the latter have an 'industrial right' in relation to that individual.[15]

An 'industrial right' which is, consistently speaking, a 'right' brings opportunities entailing alternative courses and choices of action, and so permits individuality. Individuals may express their individuality by deciding to exercise their industrial right to join a trade union, for instance, in a negative direction, by not joining a trade union. But, a crucial point here with regard to the uniqueness or otherwise of industrial rights – or, that is, with regard to Barbalet's argument that industrial rights are 'collective rights' – is that such individuals, none the less, do not thereby lose the right involved. Individuals who have the right to join a trade union have and retain that right whether they decide to exercise it affirmatively or not. To put it another way, the industrial right to join a trade union is enjoyed and exercised not only by individuals (employees according to Barbalet) who have joined trade unions, but also by individuals who have not joined. Individuals who have the right to join a trade union, but who have not exercised this right affirmatively by actually becoming a member, not only continue to enjoy the right, but also are nevertheless exercising it, albeit either 'inactively' or negatively. The point here is not so much the banal one that the industrial right to join a trade union must be enjoyed by individuals who have not (yet) joined, otherwise there would be no one to join. The point is more that industrial rights are not only legally attached to individuals; they are also, in practice, exercised by many (and perhaps at some stage by all) individuals outside and independently of (even against) collectivities, in particular, trade unions. Quite simply, individuals with industrial rights do not have to be members of collectivities – do not have to subordinate their *individual* industrial rights to collective rights, decisions and actions – in order for such rights to be exercised. Individuals can and do exercise their industrial rights outside of collectivities; they can and do exercise such rights individually and individualistically. Essentially, industrial citizenship rights are like all other citizenship rights in being attached to and exercised by individuals; in being individualistic; in permitting and enabling individuality; in reflecting the individualism which finds emphasis within, underpins and helps drive modern, Western liberal democracies.

The individual and individualistic character of industrial citizenship rights, along with all other categories of citizenship rights, is rooted in the legal codes, apparatuses and mechanisms of modern, Western societies. The law determines directly and indirectly that citizenship rights are attached to individuals and permit individuals to exercise their citizenship rights individualistically. It is conceivable for a writer to propose a non-legalistic definition of citizenship, but Barbalet conforms with the common, or standard, tendency to adopt a legalistic notion. Thus, Barbalet argues that citizenship rights are 'legally constituted rights' (ibid., pp. 15–16). However, if this is so, then the conclusion that industrial citizenship rights are not just attached to individuals, but also permit and facilitate 'individuality', is supported by an examination of the law surrounding the relationship between citizenship, individuals, collectivities and trade unions. The way in which the law deals specifically with trade unions in the United Kingdom, for instance, receives some acknowledgement from Barbalet in a criticism of Marshall. Barbalet tells us that for Marshall (1950, pp. 93–4):

> trade unions exercised the civil rights of their individual members collectively. He adds, though, that this is entirely anomalous, for civil rights, Marshall [1950, p. 93] says, 'were in origin intensely individual'. With the more recent development of incorporation, though, collectivities are 'enabled to act legally as individuals'. The difficulty, however, is that trade unionism has developed and functions by avoiding incorporation. Trade unions, Marshall [1950, pp. 93–4] says, can 'exercise vital civil rights collectively on behalf of their members without formal collective responsibility, while the individual responsibility of the workers in relation to contract is largely unenforceable.' The absence of the correlative civil duties should have alerted Marshall to the fact that trade unions do not exercise collective civil rights. (Barbalet, 1988, pp. 23–4)[16]

However, while this criticism by Barbalet of Marshall is well-founded as far as it goes, Barbalet himself fails to recognise

Social Change and the Individual

that, within United Kingdom law, trade unions not only do not exercise collective civil citizenship rights; they also do not exercise collective *citizenship* rights of any kind. This point is confirmed by David Barker and Colin Padfield, who begin by telling us: 'All human beings are "persons" under England law. One of the most important concepts of English law is that all persons within the realm, including aliens, have rights and are subject to certain duties' (Barker and Padfield, 1992, p. 88). But, in addition to human beings, there is 'a different kind of person, the corporation, which is an artificial or juristic person, created by law, with a legal personality distinct from the individual persons who control the corporation' (ibid., p. 88). Barker and Padfield otherwise refer to human beings as 'natural persons' (ibid., p. 100), to distinguish them from 'artificial or juristic persons called corporations'. They explain that a 'corporation is a legal entity, or artificial person, with a distinctive name, perpetual succession and a common seal' (ibid., p. 100); and that the 'essential feature of a corporation is that it has a legal personality distinct from that of its members or those who control it' (ibid., p. 100). But Barker and Padfield add the crucial point for present purposes that a trade union is *not* a corporation, but an example of another type of legal entity. That is, a trade union is an 'unincorporated association' (ibid., p. 105):

> As the name implies, these associations of people differ from corporations in that they (the associations) do not have a distinct legal personality separate from the members themselves. Common examples include societies and clubs .... Trade unions and partnerships are also unincorporated. The law regards these groups as a collection of persons bearing individual responsibility for the associations' actions. So, where an official of an association ... makes a contract for the purchase of goods for the common use of the group, the official is personally liable on such contract either alone or jointly with the committee which authorized it. (Ibid. p. 105)

Just as a trade union or similar 'unincorporated association' cannot have a distinct legal personality separate from its individual members, and so cannot have (as an association or collectivity) distinct legal responsibilities or duties separate from its individual members, so it cannot have distinct (collective) legal rights separate from its members. This sets it apart from a corporation. On the other hand, an unincorporated association and a corporation are none the less alike in one important respect as far as legal rights are concerned. Although a corporation has a legal personality, rights and responsibilities in the same way as individuals, unlike individuals, but like unincorporated associations (such as trade unions), a corporation cannot have citizenship rights. As the Commission on Citizenship asserts about citizenship rights, such 'Rights are necessarily individual. "Although a limited company or charitable foundation [or trade union] can epitomise and espouse the characteristics of citizenship, neither can enjoy citizenship. Only a single human being can claim whatever it is that is citizenship"' (Commission on Citizenship, 1990, pp. 6–7).

Citizenship rights, of whatever type (civil, political, social, industrial), as legal rights, are non-transferable from individuals to collectivities, and they cannot be lost unless they are legally withdrawn. They cannot be lost simply because, for instance, they are not being (for the time being) exercised affirmatively. If they are not lost, then by virtue of being 'rights' they continue to be not only attached to the individual, but also a source of 'individuality', albeit in a highly contingent fashion due to the conditions (material, cognitive, organisational) within and through which individuals enjoy and exercise them. It may be that when individuals choose to exercise their industrial rights by joining trade unions, they will be (organisationally) required to subordinate these, among other citizenship rights, to the collectivity – to collective rights, decisions and actions. However, first of all, this requirement may help account for why many individuals opt not to join trade unions. These individuals will none the less retain their industrial rights – their right to join a trade union, their right to strike, and so on – and will do so along with their unsubordiated and undiminished citizenship rights and associated individuality. But, in any case, even when individuals join trade unions they will not be required to completely subordinate their citizenship rights (including their industrial ones) nor, therefore, to forfeit *their* associated individuality. The latter is the potential individuals have for expressing themselves somewhat independently – not just by opting in or out of trade unions or trade union action, but also by making decisions about a huge array of other work-place and trade union alternatives for action or inaction.

Barbalet has otherwise recognised that individuals can hold citizenship rights which they may not exercise fully and even may not exercise at all. Thus, as we have previously noted,[17] in Western market-capitalist societies, civil citizenship rights include a range of rights 'to acquire' property, as distinct from, as such, rights 'to possess' property (Barbalet, 1988, p. 117). In such societies, both the rich and the poor have the right to acquire property, but the rich are able (enabled by virtue of their riches) to exercise and realise this entitlement far more than the poor, the result being the perpetuation of highly unequal distributions of material or enabling resources. The same distinction pertains in the cases of political rights and social rights. In liberal-democratic societies, adults have the political right to vote and stand for election. But not all adults will avail themselves of these rights. Likewise, in *social welfare* societies, many of the people who enjoy social rights to state-provided social services and benefits will not make full use of their entitlements.

At the beginning of his book, Barbalet points out that 'a system of equal citizenship is in reality less than equal if it is part of a society divided by unequal conditions' (ibid., p. 1). Within modern Western societies, these unequal conditions include not only a material dimension, but also a *cognitive* one and perhaps an *organizational* one. The unequal distributions of material or enabling resources, of knowledge and understanding, and of organisational arrangements within modern, Western societies will intervene between the formally equal distribution of citizenship rights and the realisation of these rights in such a way as to ensure that the latter is also distributed (quantitatively and qualitatively) unequally. This applies to the whole range of citizenship rights, including industrial citizenship ones. In the case of industrial rights, their realisation will depend upon, for instance, the availability, provision and suitability of organisational arrangements in the form of trade unions. It may be that a particular individual who is inclined to exercise his or her industrial right to join a trade union in an affirmative way will be unable to do so because of the non-availability of a suitable trade union. None the less, he or she will still possess the industrial right involved. At the same time, the same conclusion applies where an individual decides against joining an available trade union on political, religious, philosophical or other ideological grounds. The individual will retain the industrial right to join a trade union while exercising it negatively; and moreover will be thereby expressing his or her individuality, perhaps outstandingly so, given various social, political and economic pressures to conform by exercising the right affirmatively.

In sum, industrial rights, as with all the other categories of citizenship rights in modern Western, market-capitalist, liberal-democratic, social welfare societies, are not only legally attached to individuals; they also facilitate individuality, albeit in highly contingent, variable and unequal ways. Industrial rights, being legally universal (at least, following Barbalet, among employees), facilitate individuality whether or not the individuals to whom they are attached are members of trade unions; whether they are members of the working class or the middle class; and so on. Moreover, this conclusion – reached by way of a legalistic approach to citizenship rights – finds strong echoes and support in at least two other sources: first, in the evidence and interpretations which emerge from empirical studies on people's actual, everyday activities and orientations in relation to the work-place and to trade unions; and second, in recent theoretical machinations concerning the overall character and development of modern (perhaps postmodern), Western societies. For instance, as long ago as the 1960s, Goldthorpe, Lockwood, Bechhofer and Platt argued, on the basis of their evidence on 'the affluent worker in the class structure', that a 'convergence' was under way between 'the traditional "collectivism" of manual wage earners and the traditional "individualism" of nonmanual employees ... [which] had a twin focus':[18]

> First, on the acceptance of collective trade union action as a means of economic protection and advancement; and second, on an acceptance of the individual conjugal family and its fortunes as a central, life interest. 'Instrumental collectivism' and 'family centredness' [are] thus proposed as the major points of increasing similarity in the socio-

political perspectives or life-styles of manual and nonmanual strata. (Goldthorpe et al., 1969, p. 27)

The instrumental-collectivism orientation to, and participation within, trade unions on the part of individuals from both the manual working class and the non-manual middle class entails treating and tolerating trade unions as a (mercenary) means to an end – an end which is 'overwhelmingly economic' (ibid., p. 27). This reflects the way the principal life focus, interest and concern of individuals both of the manual working class and of the non-manual middle class is 'the family', and accordingly the economic support, protection and advancement of their particular families. It readily follows that individuals of whatever social class regard trade unions as mechanisms (and tolerate them as successful mechanisms) through which they are able to exercise their citizenship rights – especially but not solely their industrial citizenship rights – in the interests of their families. It is due to the way the principal life focus of individuals is firmly located outside of trade unions, employment and the work-place, that individuals become strongly inclined to exercise their industrial citizenship rights with 'individuality' – individualistically – albeit by way of their membership of collectivities such as trade unions. Individuals as employees, of whatever social class, are individualistic in their orientation to and use of employment, the work-place and trade unions; their orientation is firmly rooted in and strongly encouraged by their non-work, family-centred interests and concerns; and their expressions of individuality through employment, the work-place and trade unions are facilitated by the legally based individual and individualistic character of citizenship rights, including industrial ones.[19]

Of course, the empirical findings and interpretation presented by John Goldthorpe and his associates have been extensively criticised, including by, for instance, John Westergaard (Westergaard, 1970). However, these criticisms fail to dent the conclusion concerning the legally-based individual, and individualistic character of citizenship rights, as manifested within and through the social class system, paid employment, the work-place and trade unions (see Rosemary Crompton, 1993, including ch. 6 on 'Citizenship and Entitlements'; and Gordon Marshall et al., 1988).

The conclusion is merely confirmed by those studies which have come up with evidence that people do not only treat paid employment in an instrumental fashion, but also seek and find *individuality* within it. Thus, according to Robert Lane:

> Studies of well-being [in advanced economies] show that the things that contribute most to a sense of well-being cannot be bought, such as a good family life, friendship, work satisfaction, and satisfaction with one's leisure. There is little relation between these things and people's incomes. [For instance,] according to a recent study at the University of Michigan, when people were asked what activities they enjoyed most, they ranked their actual work activities higher than anything except playing with their children and talking to friends – and much higher than watching TV. Above a rather low level of skill and discretion, work itself is a major source of life satisfaction and not just the pain for which income is the compensating pleasure. Of all the sources of well-being, a satisfying family life is the most important and this form of satisfaction does not vary with income except at the bottom: poverty is associated with family misery. Because satisfaction with the work one does is central to a sense of well-being ... because work enjoyment and work learning depend on the use of skill and self-direction, firms converting routine jobs to jobs where workers can use their own discretion should be rewarded by government. (Lane, August 1993)[20]

Here, people's individualistic orientation to paid employment and the work-place is being recognised and championed. Such an orientation is facilitated by industrial along with all other categories of citizenship rights in modern, Western societies. The individual and individualistic character of citizenship rights is consistent with the philosophy and principles of 'liberal democracy', and it suits certain requirements of 'market capitalism'. Here the point is being alluded to that the general, individual and individualistic character of citizenship rights may not wholly suit the requirements of market capitalism, especially in so far as these include *social control or containment* needs. It might be added that equally the same characteristic may not wholly suit the requirements of the trade union movement, on similar grounds. Given this characteristic, we might expect the New Right to adopt an ambivalent stance (at least) with regard to industrial citizenship rights, as with regard to social citizenship rights. On the other hand, and somewhat contradictorily, the same characteristic appears to reflect what may be taken to be the predominant features of late-twentieth-century societal patterns and trends – features for which the New Right is the torch bearer and may in large part be responsible.

Citizenship rights permit and promote individuality through opportunities for decision-making and the provision of choices. Citizenship rights present individuals with opportunities to express and realise themselves – or, that is, their *selves*: to express, explore, and establish their *self-identities*. It is because, or in so far as, citizenship rights facilitate individuality through expressions of *self* and explorations of *self-identity*, that citizenship rights are sought, valued, protected and struggled for within the kind of conflictual political framework which has been variously portrayed by Marshall, Giddens and Barbalet among others.

A lack of opportunities for individuals to express their individuality, to realise themselves, and to explore their self-identities at, in or through paid employment and the work-place, will lie behind political demands and pressures for the expansion of industrial citizenship rights. The purpose will be to increase opportunities for choice, individuality, self-expression and self-realisation not just within the immediate social context, but also beyond, especially within 'the family' (see Close, 1985). Any expansion of industrial citizenship rights will feed into opportunities for choice, individuality, self-expression and self-realisation within not just the public arena of paid employment, but also the private sphere of family and personal life. It will do this partly by way of its consequences for paid-employment remuneration, and subsequently the market in wage goods and services; and partly by way of its consequences for an employee's psychological, mental and emotional well-being, given its feed-on effects within the private sphere (see Harris, 1983).

The promotion by and through citizenship rights of individuality is consistent with the claims of a recent spate of theoretical writings on the general character and development of late-twentieth-century Western societies. A range of often highly influential writers has proposed the advent of a stage in the history of human societies which is marked above all else by a huge, and perhaps overwhelming, expansion of opportunities for choice, decision-making and individuality – for self-expression, self-realisation and more (see below). For some writers, this development has been accompanied by a commensurate increase in individual responsibility, risk, uncertainty and anxiety; and connectedly by a deepening of the individual's vulnerability to manipulation, exploitation and control, especially through the market in wage goods and services.

According to Anthony Giddens (Giddens, 1991), for instance, under the transformations of late-twentieth-century 'modernity', individuality has been pushed into a new phase. Instead of individuality being just about self-expression and self-realisation, it is about reflexive self-development. Under the circumstances of modernity, individuals have become pro-active *subjects*, or agents, engaged in 'reflexive' action upon themselves – upon their *selves*. Individuals are reflexively engaged in shaping and re-shaping, forming and re-forming, constructing and re-constructing themselves; their selves; their self-identities. As a result, individuals have been presented with novel difficulties. As summed up by Alan Warde, Giddens 'analyses the difficulties faced by individuals in sustaining self-identities in late modernity. For Giddens, self-identity is "the self as reflexively understood by the individual in terms of his or her biography" [Giddens, 1991, p. 244]' (Warde, 1993, p. 3). The difficulties involved in sustaining self-identities reflect the distinguishing features of late-twentieth-century modernity.

The transformations of modernity have entailed the release of the individual and his or her self-identity from the social constraints, constructions and certainties of traditional society, institutions and ideas; and so have entailed a considerable increase in social and individual flexibility and diversity, but along with a concomitant increase in individual uncertainty, insecurity and sense of threat (see Irwin, 1993). Society is afflicted by 'the loss of Enlightenment confidence in the "rational society"', which 'leaves us uncertain as to the personal and institutional basis on which local and global threats should be evaluated' (Irwin, ibid., p. 338). Today, *the self* is

Social Change and the Individual 177

constantly challenged in that modernity 'confronts the individual with a complex diversity of choices and, because it is non-foundational, at the same time offers little help as to which options to be selected' (Giddens, 1991, p. 80).

Giddens (ibid., ch. 6) discusses the issues of self-identity and of anxiety through the way the individual is challenged by a series of 'dilemmas of the self', in particular over 'authority versus uncertainty' and 'unification versus fragmentation' (Irwin, 1993, p. 339). He examines the way the individual is challenged in his or her everyday social life and relationships, which under the transformations of modernity have become fragile. Thus, he 'considers the costs and benefits of "pure relationships"', a reference to 'the supposedly "free floating" character of modern relationships' (ibid., p. 338). In this context, while Giddens (1991, ch. 1) examines the major personal challenges of modernity for self-identity brought by 'divorce and the problems of "finding oneself" which such "fateful" moments reveal' (Irwin, 1993, p. 338), he focuses on the difficulties of sustaining a self-identity during the individual's more regular, routine participation in the commodity market.

The individual confronts and meets the challenge of sustaining self-identity under the circumstances and difficulties of modernity in a reflexive way with the help of *lifestyle*. For the individual, everyday life has been transformed by the patterns of modernity, and this has important consequences for the individual's sense of self – 'which has to be "reflexively made" against the wider social backdrop of doubt and diversity. Concepts such as lifestyle, trust and intimacy take on new significance as we struggle for meaning and a sense of identity' (ibid., p. 338). As Alan Irwin summarises, Giddens argues that:

> Self-identity emerges as an active and reflexive project – even those who choose to live in a 'traditional' fashion cannot but be aware of the existence of various life options. Modernity shapes even our sense of body and encourages feelings of shame and self-insufficiency. [The] 'trajectory of the self' where life-planning and life-style become central. (Ibid., p. 338)

Indeed, a major consequence of modernity for individuals 'is the primacy' in their everyday lives of lifestyle, which 'can be defined as a more or less integrated set of practices which an individual embraces, not only because such practices fulfil utilitarian needs, but because they give material form to a particular narrative of self-identity' (Giddens, 1991, p. 81). Under modernity, lifestyles are open to modification by way of individual reflexivity:

> Each of the small decisions a person makes everyday – what to wear, what to eat, how to conduct himself at work, whom to meet with later in the evening – contributes to such routines. All such choices (as well as larger and more consequential ones) are decisions not only about how to act but who to be. The more post-traditional the settings in which an individual moves, the more lifestyle concerns the very core of self-identity, its making and remaking. (Giddens, 1991, p. 81)

Giddens accepts that not all choices are (equally) open to everyone. He notes that:

> Overall lifestyle patterns, of course, are less diverse than the plurality of choices available in day-to-day and even in longer-term strategic decisions. A lifestyle involves a cluster of habits and orientations, and hence has a certain unity – important to a continuing sense of ontological security – that connects options in a more or less ordered pattern. Someone who is committed to a given lifestyle would necessarily see various options as 'out of character' with it, as would others with whom she was in interaction. Moreover, the selection or creation of lifestyles is influenced by group pressures and the visibility of role models, as well as by socio-economic circumstances. (Giddens, 1991, p. 82)

Giddens's passing recognition of the way variations in socio-economic circumstances, such as those associated with social-class divisions, help ensure variations in people's lifestyles is, of course, consistent with the point emphasised by numerous writers on citizenship in late-twentieth-century, Western societies: that highly unequal distributions of what I have called *enabling resources* intervene between the formal enjoyment of citizenship rights and the informal, everyday realisation and experience of such rights. This intervention, following Giddens, will show up as social-class related variations in lifestyle. However, for Giddens, what is distinctive about modernity is the exceptional degree to which *the individual* has been released or 'freed' from contextual (structural; ideational) conditions and constraints rooted in, for instance, social class. The result is the unconstrained individual, set adrift in *free-floating* ('pure') relationships; and consequently, considerable individual and lifestyle flexibility and diversity – lifestyles constructed and re-constructed by the unconstrained, reflexive individual, rather than (pre-)determined by social class or whatever. Accordingly, lifestyles have become not only the means, but also the *highly problematic means*, by which the individual handles and survives modernity, with its exceptional and unprecedented emphasis on individuality.

Giddens examines factors which help to make the attempts by all individuals to sustain self-identities highly problematic, including those factors which operate through the commodity market and so through consumption. He observes that 'consumption [is] a foremost instance of choice' (Warde, 1993, p. 5), and explores how, under the conditions of modernity, more specifically, 'commodification influences the project of the self and the establishing of lifestyles' (Giddens, 1991, p. 197). Given that a commodity is an item (good; service) which is exchanged on the market for payment prior to consumption, then the process of commodification undermines tradition and feeds into the process of individualisation. Under modernity, Giddens argues, 'Market-governed freedom of individual choice becomes an enveloping framework of individual self-expression' (Giddens, 1991, p. 197). But, helped by the persuasive pressures of commodity advertising:

> To a greater or lesser degree, the project of the self becomes translated into one of the possession of desired goods and the pursuit of artificially framed styles of life .... The consumption of ever-novel goods becomes in some part a substitute for the genuine development of self. (Giddens, 1991, p. 198)

The result is a society characterised by mass consumption and a tendency towards standardisation among individuals manifesting manipulated, somewhat artificial and persistently anxious selves. On the other hand, however, the tendency towards standardisation does not go unchallenged. It is met by some resistance, in which individuals respond pro-actively, creatively and re-creatively through, for instance, combining the items of mass consumption in individualistic ways (see Warde, 1993, p. 5). In effect, under modernity, on the one hand there is 'standardisation taking over from differentiation', but on the other hand there is individuality entailing degrees of individual resistance and re-creation favouring the restoration of diversity (see Warde, 1993, p. 5). Alan Warde[21] sums up Giddens's approach:

> Giddens offers a highly individualistic, cognitive and decisionistic model of the self. His world is peopled by very self-directing persons in serious pursuit of the coherent narrative of self .... He treats consumption as [one] arena of choice, and extrapolates from that to make it into one of the areas of uncertainty in modern life. (Warde, 1993, p. 5)

In this world, we can imagine a process of political struggle over citizenship rights – a struggle which, while being far from uni-directional as far as the extension and expansion of such rights is concerned, will be largely progressive in accordance with the general characteristics and tendencies of modernity. There will be an inclination towards the vertical (social class) extension and horizontal (categorical) expansion of citizenship rights in accordance with the way, or in so far as, such rights permit and promote individuality, self-expression and self-realisation (by way of reflexivity). At the same time, there will be a clash of views and interests over the relative merits of the different categories of citizenship rights in this regard. New Right policies may be seen as consistent with (as being a reflection and reinforcement of) modernity as portrayed by Giddens, but biased on the side of strengthening civil citizenship rights at the expense of both social and industrial citizenship rights. An issue which arises here is whether this particular bias, perhaps through its special affinity with the general features and tendencies of modernity, foreshadows the long-term outcome of the political struggle over citizenship rights whereby there will be an ever-greater clawback of social rights. Another issue, however, arises out of the way New Right economic and social policies support the reinforcement of capitalism along with the entrenchment of the specifically capitalist social class system. The issue here is whether such policies lend themselves to the persistence of those contextual, 'socio-economic' conditions which will constrain 'the individual' – albeit variously, unevenly and unequally – in a manner which undermines the general features and tendencies of modernity. Here, we may note the argument that it is not just the working class which is constrained by the conditions of capitalism – as distinct from the conditions of modernity – but also the capitalist class, or bourgeoisie, in that it is subjected to the (alienating) limitations of the demands and pressures of capital accumulation.

For Giddens, it would seem, modernity has acquired its own dynamic, or *head of steam*, outpacing and overcoming any counter or contradictory tendencies associated with capitalism, the interests and power of the capitalist class, and the policies of the New Right in favour of unbridled individuality, especially that centred on consumption. However, as Alan Warde points out about Giddens's argument concerning consumption activities:

> it is not an enormously threatening set of activities. Generally, consumption is positive, useful and constructive (though not inherently pleasurable), except in so far as commodification standardises and an 'artificiality' substitutes for 'the genuine development of self'. (Warde, 1993, p. 5)

While 'modernity' has delivered a society which is a 'risk society' (Irwin, 1993, p. 338), none the less, as Alan Warde (Warde, 1993, p. 5) remarks, 'Consumption is less inherently a risky process for Giddens, because biographies can be rewritten and because consumption is just one part of the procedure for creating and stabilising a self.' It is a less risky process, that is, than the one assumed by another writer on the general characteristics of late-twentieth-century society, namely Ulrich Beck (Beck, 1992). Giddens's analysis overlaps with Beck's; themes which attract the attention of Giddens are furthered by Beck. Thus, Beck argues that in what he refers to as 'risk society' there is 'a tendency towards an intensification of the process of individualisation' (Warde, 1993, p. 2), entailing increased reflexivity on the part of individuals. This development has three stages or dimensions:

> disembedding, removal from historically prescribed social forms and commitments in the sense of traditional contexts of dominance and support ...; the loss of traditional security with respect to practical knowledge, faith and guiding norms (the 'disenchantment dimension'); and re-embedding, a new type of social commitment (the 'control' or 're-integration dimension'). (Beck, 1992, p. 128)

Re-embedding is where the 'individual himself or herself becomes the reproduction unit for the social in the lifeworld'. Individuals 'become the agents of their own livelihood mediated by the market' (ibid., p. 130). In a similar way to Giddens, Beck argues that people's biographies are becoming reflexive (ibid., p. 131) because 'class differences and family connections' are receding in social importance:

> people ... within the same 'class', can or even must choose between different lifestyles, subcultures, social ties and identities. From knowing one's 'class' position one can no longer determine one's personal outlook, relations, family position, social and political ideas or identity. (ibid., p. 131)

For Beck, the individual and his or her self-identity have been – even more than Giddens allows – loosened from traditional ties and determinants. However, this does not mean that he or she has been wholly 'freed' from all constraints. The process of self-identity formation is marked by contradictory tendencies – a *societalising* one, and another which entails *individual autonomisation* (Warde, 1993, p. 3):

> The individual is ... removed from traditional commitments and support relationships, but exchanges them for the constraints of existence in the labor [sic] market and as a consumer, with the standardisations and controls they contain. The place of traditional ties and social forms (social class,

nuclear family) is taken by secondary agencies and institutions, which stamp the biography of the individual and make that person dependent upon fashions, social policy, economic cycles and markets, contrary to the image of individual control which establishes itself in consciousness. (Beck, 1992, p. 131)

The intensification of individualisation has two major components. First, 'Individualization means market dependency in all dimensions of living' (ibid., p. 132). Second, people become personally responsible for their biographies. Decision-making is called for; biographies become self-reflexive. The current epoch witnesses a shift from a 'standard' to an 'elective' biography:

> One even has to choose one's social identity and group membership, in this way managing one's own self, changing its image. In the individualized society, risks do not just increase quantitatively; qualitatively new types of personal risks arise, the risk of the chosen and changed personal identity. (Ibid., p. 136)

In *risk society*, the quantitative and qualitative increase in personal risks reflects the extent to which the individual is required to make ever-more and never-ending individualised decisions in managing self, image and identity. The decisions entail risks in the sense that there is the chance, and moreover the perceived chance, of making the wrong decisions, due to the way in which the individual is freed from traditional guidelines, influences and constraints. As a result, accompanying the individual's decision-making activities, there is the ever-present possibility of him or her assuming the blame 'for failures in image-management' (Warde, 1993, p. 3).

We can speculate on the implications of Beck's *risk society*, with its particular contradictory (societalising against individualising) tendencies and personal repercussions, for citizenship. In attempting to reflexively manage and secure self, image and identity, the highly *individualised* individual will be presented with, and will look to, non-traditional, 'secondary' sources, such as *citizenship*. The individual will look to the state, and thereby to the defence, extension and expansion of citizenship rights, including – and perhaps especially – social and industrial ones. *Risk society* encourages the individual, freed from traditional and reliable sources of identity, to exert demands and engage in struggles within the political framework for a pattern of citizenship rights, security and identity which will, however, both (a) fail in practice to reduce the everyday existence and experience of risk and anxiety; and (b) in any case, be resisted by those political and economic factions which favour civil rights at the expense of social and industrial rights; capitalist hegemony; and the prevailing capitalist social class system. At the same time, for Beck as for Giddens, the social class system has been diminished in its social and personal salience, judged in terms of its conditioning and constraining influences on identity, the individual and individuality. This helps to account for the emergent pre-eminence of the consumer market, decisions and dependency ('in all dimensions of living') for individualised, identity-seeking, reflexive individuals; and for why – whatever unfolds with regard to citizenship rights – risk will be persistent, pervasive and pernicious.

If Beck's consumption-dominated *risk society* is more risk-ridden and anxiety-generating than Giddens's 'modernity', for Zygmunt Bauman the same late-twentieth-century society provides its own consumer-based palliatives (Bauman, 1988 – see also, Bauman, 1990; 1991). As Alan Warde tells us, Bauman:

> teases out the implications of the fact that responsibility is entailed in the notion of choice. One is responsible for one's decisions. Moreover, one can make the wrong decision. As in all situations where real decisions are made, there is the possibility of anxiety being provoked. Consumer choice is not exempt ... being 'responsible for choices' may be stressful. With the historical decline of traditional ties, individuality emerges as a problem .... Bauman conceives the predicament of individuality as a problem of self-identity: modernity, and post-modernity, are seen to demand that individuals construct their own selves .... In this context, one of Bauman's ... insights is his stress on the individual responsibility incurred by consumer choice. The authority that accrues to the individual consumer by the very situation of being able to choose may often generate

anxiety .... He argues that markets offer freedom of an unprecedented kind for the majority of the population. They thereby entail that people acquire responsibilities for the creation of self. Potential anxiety is averted because the market also offers an expertise to allay anxiety: 'the same market which offers freedom offers also certainty' [1988, p. 61]. Services are offered for this purpose ... [In particular,] advertising ploys reassure people that 'choices are right and rational' [1988, p. 65]. The negative aspects of [consumer market] arrangements are ... that a substantial minority of the population are excluded for lack of resources and [thereby] pose a major problem of social control. (Warde, 1993, pp. 5–6)

What might the implications for citizenship rights be? Well, we can speculate that those who lack the kind of resources which enable people to take advantage of the way 'consumption offers security to individuals by confirming their self-image' (ibid., p. 6) will press for an increase in such resources; and that they will do this through the defence, extension, expansion and exercise of citizenship rights, perhaps especially social and industrial ones. What is more, in their campaign, they may well achieve some success, because, and in so far as, they pose a *problem of social control* for those who have influence over the procedure whereby citizenship rights are granted, guaranteed or enforced. Accordingly, through the political framework within which the struggle over citizenship rights takes place, the 'excluded' will seek to become (more) 'included' with the help of enhanced citizenship rights and enabling resources; and will enjoy the prospect and experience of some success against those who prioritise the kind and degree (social class mediated, uneven and unequal) of individuality which flows from and feeds into untrammelled market capitalism.

Giddens, Beck and Bauman all support the view that the individual's 'biography is a reflexive project and that ... consumption [is] critical to identity formation' (Warde, 1993, p. 1). Beyond this, as Warde summarises:

What these accounts have in common is the following. They agree that consumption matters ... because it seriously affects self-identity. ... It is increasingly being instanced as the principal means of ensuring the survival of the self, a particular kind of self, that which expresses its integrity through parading its 'identity'. Consumer choice is deeply implicated in the process of [the] creation of a reflexive self, constructing a narrative of self, or electing oneself to a shared form of identification. Hence, consumption is a risky business, since inappropriate selections may seriously impair personal ontological security. It is especially risky because consumers have almost entirely free choice. Hence they can make mistakes. This is particularly threatening because guidelines or imperatives that have, until recently, governed consumption have been eroded as the process of individualization has gathered further momentum.   (Warde, 1993, pp. 6–7)

Within the late-twentieth-century society portrayed by Giddens, Beck and Bauman, perhaps precisely because consumption has become *critical* to identity formation, individuals will seek, demand and defend citizenship rights both as a way of variously expressing and furthering their individuality[22] and as a way, at the same time, of dealing with the identity problems, risks and anxieties which the process of individualisation has brought, and for which consumption and the consumption market by themselves fail to provide the answer.[23]

5 Individualism, Citizenship and the European Union

> Is the European Community a Catholic conspiracy against Britain? Recently, Peregrine Worsthorne ... fired a Parthian shot on behalf of Ian Paisley: individualist, Protestant, Anglo-Saxon capitalism was rightly to be seen as opposing 'communitarian,' crypto-socialist Catholicism, which is intent on undoing the good work of Thatcherism in a European super-state [sic]. (Boyle, October 1991)

So begins a *Guardian* article written a few months before the December 1991 European Council meeting held at Maastricht which resulted in the Treaty on European Union, signed in February 1993, and finally ratified on 1 November 1993. The article takes a wry look at the implications of the development of the European Community for 'individualism' along with 'capitalism'. After summarising the politically right-wing view of Peregrine Worsthorne, Nicholas Boyle refers, for balance, to 'the other end of the intellectual spectrum', where, in the journal *National Interest,* James Kurth has suggested that it is 'wrong to think that liberal capitalism [is] now triumphant world-wide: on the contrary, a Europe dominated by German Christian Democracy, and so by Catholic social teaching, would provide a regional competitor, on the world scale, for both capitalist America and for Japan'. Boyle explains:

> For over 10 years we had to put up with Mrs Thatcher – and others – telling us that she was the champion of individualists, who know there is no such thing as society, against the morale-sapping, omnicompetent State. Yet the antithesis of individualism and the State was never convincing. (Ibid.)

In the first place, claims Boyle, 'there has never been such a thing as a pure individualist'. But, apart from this:

such terms as 'corporatism' and 'the nanny state', obscure a most important distinction. There are two different kinds of collective, social existence in which we are all involved. First, there are the local corporate associations, public or private, which lay claim to only part of their members' lives, time, activity, money and loyalty – churches, trade unions, political parties, local government bodies, schools, charities, individual industries and commercial firms. Secondly, there is the central government which claims through legislation, and monetary and fiscal policy, to control all these subsidiary associations and ... all aspects of all subjects' lives. The difference between these two kinds of public life is the difference between civil society and the state. The assault of 'individualist' Thatcherism has been almost exclusively directed at civil society, while the power of the central state has much increased. [None the less,] Protestantism is an individualist religion. Particularly in its original Lutheran form, it has a tendency to treat human beings as isolated souls seeking spiritual salvation in independence from one another and alone with their divine judge. Such a belief may well have practical political consequences.... . It may once have been true that Protestantism assisted the rise of capitalism. But the Treaty of Rome set up a largely Catholic community which knocked the Protestant economies into a cocked hat and had them suing for entry within years. The careful adjustment between central control and open competition, achieved through a consensual politician system based on proportional representation, was more in tune with the complexities of modern social and economic life than the illusory antithesis of ideological 'individualism'. Mr Worsthorne and Mr Paisley are right: good Catholics are likely to be good Europeans – opposed to the would-be absolute powers claimed by national governments. They are likely to be good liberals, good democrats, even good Christian Democrats. They are also in future likely to be rich.   (Ibid.)

The questions which arise and to which this chapter will pay attention include: is the European Community (and now Union) inclined towards – perhaps under the influence, guidance and leadership of Catholicism, Christian Democracy and Germany – 'collectivistic' (if not 'socialistic') ideology, policies and legislation; towards a prominent and pervasive centralised state apparatus; and, in particular, towards a comprehensive 'welfare state' arrangement, whereby, through the provision of social benefits, services and rights, 'individualism' is undermined? Is 'welfarism', in particular of the kind to which the Community tends to subscribe, a threat to individualism and capitalism? How far does the Community adopt a 'collectivistic' and 'welfarist' approach to policies, legislation, and therefore citizenship?

As we have already discussed, the New Right assumes that the state's provision of social rights by way of 'the welfare state' does clash with *individualism* and does pose a threat to *capitalism*. However, this view can be contrasted with that of Gill Jones and Claire Wallace (1992) in their assessment of *youth, family and citizenship* in Britain. Jones and Wallace tell us how during the twentieth century, especially during the 1960s, there has been a general tendency for 'the social security net [to be] widened to include more and more people '(ibid., p. 57), and in particular *young people*. Most importantly, 'National Assistance was replaced in 1966 by Supplementary Benefit, for which the minimum age of entitlement was 16... . In 1972 the school-leaving age was raised to 16 – at last corresponding with the age of entitlement to benefits' (ibid., p. 57). Therefore, until the 1980s

> young people's position within social security systems, whilst fragile, was becoming increasingly 'individualized': they were increasingly acknowledged as individuals. [However, the] changes introduced in the 1980s ... represent a regressive step away from individualization by extending dependence in youth. They also parallel other state interventions in education, training and the labour market.   (Ibid., p. 68)

The event which brought about this reversal was the return in 1979 of a Conservative government, 'influenced by the politics of the "New Right". It was pledged to cut welfare spending, strengthen the family and root out the so-called "dependency culture", which it claimed had developed with the expansion of the welfare state' (ibid., p. 58). Jones and Wallace summarise the Conservative government's New Right programme in the following way:

Social security was to become more selective and targeted at the most needy. These policies were put into practice, following a review of social security, in the 1986 and 1988 Social Security Acts. Young people were singled out in this legislation for benefit cuts, and their entitlements for some benefits were withdrawn altogether.... There was a gradual erosion of young people's entitlements to benefits throughout the 1980s but the major reforms took place as a result of the Social Security legislation which came into force in 1988 following the Fowler review of Social Security in 1985. Under this legislation ... entitlement to Supplementary Benefit (renamed Income Support) was withdrawn from 16- and 17-year-olds on the assumption they would be provided with places on training schemes. The changes were designed to ensure that young people would return to their families for support ... However, it assumed that parents were indeed there to support them. (Ibid., pp. 60–2)

The upshot of the 1980s Conservative governments' policies, legislation and social rights changes was that the 'age of entitlement to social citizenship [was raised to] 18' (ibid., p. 68), and that the consequences for the individuality of people below this line was far from what was purportedly intended.

For Jones and Wallace, the extension of social benefits, services and rights, rather than encouraging young people's dependency, has the opposite effect. The extension releases young people from dependency upon their families and parents, thereby enhancing their individuality. Accordingly, pruning young people's social rights plunges them back into dependency, and curtails their individuality. Jones and Wallace argue that this is precisely what took place during the 1980s under the Thatcher governments. Essentially, the 'changes introduced in the 1980s therefore represent a regressive step away from individualization' (ibid., p. 68). For the New Right, state-granted and guaranteed social rights to young people (and to anyone else) encourages dependency on such rights, and so on the state; fosters young people's dependency in general; feeds into a 'dependency culture' – *a shared way of life and frame of mind*, whereby dependency on others is preferred and prescribed. Young people are encouraged to look to others for support; to rely and depend upon others; to lack independence, self-reliance, responsibility and enterprise. Young people's responsibility for themselves and their families is weakened; the family is threatened, along with the economy, capitalism and society.

It is of interest to note at this point, however, that one particular New Right scholar, Ferdinand Mount, has argued specifically against interpreting the state–family relationship as a simple, uni-directional one in which the state is active and the family passive; in which the state determines and the family is determined; in which the state, its programmes, policies and practices necessarily undermine the family and individualism (Mount, 1982). Instead, the family has resisted, survived and fought back. That is, Mount:

> argues that the western family has shown remarkable tenacity, surviving in the face of attempts by Church and state to subordinate it to 'higher' aims than those of people's earthly aspirations and search for a social form for 'the procreation and protection of children and the mutual help and affection of the couple' (ibid., p. 255). The family, he argues stands for privacy and individualism against the Christian and statist view that 'we are all members one of another'. His position involves the anti-statist conception of liberty associated with neo-liberalism. (McIntosh, 1984, p. 211)

Mount, as a neo-liberal or New Right commentator on the state–family–individualism relationship, is consistent in treating the state as a threat to individualism, but is distinctive in stressing that, together with the family, individualism has steadfastly withstood the withering pressure of the twentieth-century welfare state. Essentially, for Mount, individualism has flourished because, in the first place, the family has done so; individualism has been protected by the persistent and resilient family. In a sense, Mount's approach stands in between the usual perspective of the New Right and the argument of Jones and Wallace, for whom the state, through the extension of social rights to young people, manages to penetrate the family; to facilitate young people's independence; and thereby to boost individuality. Against Jones and Wallace, the usual New Right view is that any reduction in young people's dependence on the family which is successfully brought about through the extension of social rights will entail, in effect, a transfer of this dependence, with its associated demands, onto the state. The New Right prescription has been neatly summarised in the Report of the Commision on Citizenship:

> Rights include social rights. [But,] supporters of the classical liberal perspective reject the concept of social rights because it undermines the market and the open society within which it is possible for individuals with differing ends and purposes to live together. (*Commision on Citizenship*, 1990, p. 7)

Those who subscribe to the neo-liberal or New Right perspective are not against all state intervention. None the less, their preference in this regard can be sharply contrasted with the kind of alternative approach advocated by Jones and Wallace, as indicated by Patrick Dunleavy and Brendan O'Leary's point that:

> some contemporary ideologies make a sharp distinction between different spheres of state intervention. The first concerns the state's role in providing a legal framework for society, ensuring that law and order prevail, protecting the national territory from external aggression, and upholding certain traditional moral values. The second sphere of state activity concerns intervention in the economic system, to regulate or manage production directly, to remove some or all the bundle of property rights normally conveyed by private ownership, to redistribute income, and to provide goods or services on a basis distinct from the market principle.... 'New right' political movements in the USA and Western Europe[1] are strongly in favour of more intervention in the first sphere of state activity (for example, by spending more on defence, or by taking a dogmatic stance on moral issues) while simultaneously proposing to 'roll back the state' in the fields of social welfare and economic management. Some forms of democratic socialism adopt a reverse position, favouring the liberalization of moral issues and a lower profile for the state in the first sphere but an extension of government activities in the second. (Dunleavy and O'Leary, 1987, pp. 7–8)

Here, of course, we might recall the distinctions between the state and 'civil society' and between the public and private spheres of modern social life, and the analytical relevance of these distinctions to the tasks of categorising and understanding the personal and social significance of different citizenship rights (along with the distinction between citizenship and nationality) in modern, Western, liberal-democratic, capitalist, welfare societies. It is, then, what Dunleavy and O'Leary distinguish as the 'democratic socialist' view of the relationship between the state and civil society, and thereby of citizenship – with its emphasis on the extension and expansion within civil society of social citizenship – with which Peregrine Worsthorne has identified the European Community, inspired, it would seem, by (as Nicolas Boyle puts it) 'crypto-socialist Catholicism'. However, first of all, as Dunleavy and O'Leary go on to point out, the available range of analytical and prescriptive approaches to the arrangement and balance between the state and civil society is much more complex than the simple dichotomy between 'democratic socialist' and 'neo-liberal' implies, in that, apart from anything else, 'modern liberal thought is increasingly bifurcating between the new right and the neo-pluralist viewpoints' (ibid., p. 9):

> any theory of the state can be expressed so as to paint three different pictures of the state in contemporary liberal democracies. The first image is that of the passive cipher state, which simply delivers whatever the dominant groups in society demand. The state is a nonentity or pawn. All five approaches, pluralism, the new right, elite theory, Marxism and neo-pluralism, have their own version of a cipher state image – although they ... differ greatly about which outside group controls the government. Pluralists see citizens as in control; the new right find this control defective; elite theorists distinguish a ruling elite, and Marxists an economically based ruling class; and neo-pluralists think citizens' preferences are followed even though they do not exert direct control over decision-makers. The second image is that of a partisan state, which primarily pursues the goals of state officials while conciliating some other interests in society whose co-operation is required. For pluralists the partisan state is a broker; for the new right it is a wasteful machine

out of control; for elitist theorists it is a dominant state sector elite; and for Marxists it is a specialised apparatus which can act independently when the class struggle is left evenly balanced. Only the neo-pluralist approach does not have a clear-cut partisan image of the state. The third image is that of a guardian state, which can re-weight the balance of forces in society according to a longer term or general interest. [Different] theories see the guardian state as oriented towards different objectives: for pluralists government pursues substantive social justice and political stability; for the new right it optimizes a restricted conception of ... social welfare; in elite theory the state fosters the national interest as defined by dominant corporatist groups; in Marxism it advances the (distorted) needs of all classes within capitalism; and for neo-pluralists public policy follows fragmented professions' image of social needs.   (Ibid., pp. 11–12)

The variety of analytical, prescriptive and practised models of the state, with particular reference to the issue of 'social welfare', is pursued by Peter Taylor-Gooby in his examination of 'welfare state regimes' (Taylor-Gooby, 1991b). Taylor-Gooby outlines 'current patterns of welfare provision', paying particular attention to what he sees as the 'disillusion with the traditional model' (ibid., p. 93). While Taylor-Gooby is not explicit on the matter, by 'traditional model' he may be taken to mean what has been called elsewhere the 'dominant paradigm' (Roche, 1992). For Maurice Roche, first of all, '"Social citizenship" refers to those rights and duties of citizenship concerned with the welfare of people as citizens, taking "welfare" in a broad sense to include such things as work, education, health and quality of life' (ibid., p. 3).[2] Roche then argues that there is a 'dominant paradigm' of 'postwar Western social citizenship', which 'stresses social rights and the need to construct major state policies and institutions of welfare', and that this paradigm 'underpins both American liberal social policy and European social democracy' (ibid., p. 6). Roche clarifies the dominant paradigm of social citizenship by telling us that it

> strongly emphasizes the legitimacy of social rights and their need to be serviced by the state. These rights are typically taken to include a range of minimum conditions and ser-

Individualism and the European Union   195

vices in education, health, housing, income, employment, consumption, and so on. It is assumed that they are claimable against a state organized to service them, a 'welfare state' together with that part of the modern state's organisation necessary for the management and development of the national economic base.   (Ibid., pp. 11–12)

But, Roche claims, this dominant paradigm, and the 'ideal of social citizenship' it represents, has been severely challenged towards the end of the twentieth century; 'social change is driving ... social citizenship beyond both the nation state and the welfare state, that is beyond the two spheres which up until now have been the principal institutional arenas of the dominant paradigm of social citizenship' (ibid., p. 8). What Roche has in mind by the assertion that social citizenship is being driven beyond the nation state is indicated by his reference to

> the development of post-national politics, economics and citizenship through the case [in particular] of the EC and contemporary trends towards European economic (and possibly political) integration in the 1990s. New social rights of European citizenship are currently being developed in the EC Social Charter [for instance].   (Ibid., p. 8)

What Roche has in mind by his proposal that social citizenship is being driven beyond the welfare state is reflected in his claim that the dominant paradigm 'has been battered by New Right ideology and by forces of economic change in Western society since the mid-1970s' (ibid., p. 13). It is with this particular development that Peter Taylor-Gooby is concerned in his discussion of the 'disillusion with the traditional model'. Taylor-Gooby pays no attention to the possibility of social citizenship being removed from the 'institutional arena' of the nation-state by the development of such supra-national arrangements as the European Community and Union (although this is something to which I will return), and instead concentrates on the way the disillusion has come about partly because of the gathering 'tendency of theorists to advocate pluralist, decentralised, mixed economy and civil society-based solutions to problems' (Taylor-Gooby, 1991b, p. 93).[3] This has undermined the traditional model of 'welfare citizenship' with the help of certain other developments, especially 'government response to economic pressures, [and] the likelihood that changes in demography, employment and popular expectations will increase demands on the state' (ibid., p. 93). Not unconnectedly, Taylor-Gooby argues, 'traditional notions of welfare citizenship have been challenged because they fail to take into account the wide variety of paths which different systems have pursued in their development' (ibid., p. 93). This, of course, takes us back to Dunleavy and O'Leary's 'pictures of the state'; and in this regard Taylor-Gooby draws our attention especially to what has become the much quoted and highly influential 'categorisation of welfare states' proffered by Gösta Esping-Andersen (1990), although Taylor-Gooby acknowledges that 'similar models are developed by a number of writers' (see, for instance, W. Korpi, 1983; R. Mishra, 1990).

Esping-Andersen adopts an analytical approach to 'the relation between state policy and the public and private spheres of social life' (Taylor-Gooby, 1991b, p. 93) which

> uses the extent of decommodification in relation to formal wage-labour to distinguish the ideal types of liberal, social democratic and conservative/corporatist regimes. State intervention is limited in the liberal model, extensive in the social democratic model and substantial but directed at maintaining the stratification order of the market in the conservative model. (Ibid., p. 93)

By decommodification, Esping-Andersen means 'the extent to which state welfare liberates people from the operation of market forces' (ibid., p. 96); or as Esping-Andersen himself puts it: 'De-commodification occurs when a service is rendered as a matter of right, and when a person can maintain a livelihood without reliance on the market' (Esping-Andersen, 1990, pp. 21–2). In other words, what Esping-Andersen has in mind is the degree to which 'the introduction of modern social rights implies a loosening of the pure commodity status' specifically of people (ibid., p. 21), a status which people have acquired under capitalism:

> In pre-capitalist societies, few workers were properly commodities in the sense that their survival was contingent

upon the sale of their [labour] power. It is as markets [under capitalism] become universal and hegemonic that the welfare of individuals comes to depend entirely on the cash nexus. Stripping society of the institutional layers that guaranteed social reproduction outside the [labour] contract meant that people were commodified.   (Ibid., p. 21)

The subsequent introduction of social rights, and so of state welfare regimes, variously check and reverse the progress of commodification in the sense specified by Esping-Andersen:

a reconceptualization of ... the salient characteristics of welfare states [centred on the] extension of social rights [entails viewing] social rights in terms of their capacity for 'de-commodification'. The outstanding criterion for social rights must be the degree to which they permit people to make their living standards independent of pure market forces. It is in this sense that social rights diminish citizens' status as 'commodities'.   (Ibid., p. 3)

Taylor-Gooby points out that Esping-Andersen's 'analysis applies to formal employment' (Taylor-Gooby, 1991b, p. 97), but argues that it can be modified to cater for 'unwaged carework, with which much social welfare is concerned' (ibid., p. 97). That is, the particulars of 'uncommodified care work in the home' may help to distinguish the three categories of welfare state regime, given their association with, for instance, differences in 'the position of women in the formal labour market', along with 'different struggles ... in response to current pressures on the welfare state' (ibid., p. 93).[4] Although we might note here that Esping-Andersen does acknowledge this issue (see, for instance, Esping-Andersen, 1990, pp. 26–8) in a manner which is consistent with his view that the 'essential criteria for defining welfare states have to do with the quality of social rights, social stratification, and the relationship between the state, market, and family' (ibid., p. 29). Taylor-Gooby argues:

In liberal regimes, equal opportunities have been pursued through law rather than direct state intervention.... In social democracy a substantial state sector provides both opportunities for women's advancement in employment and socialized care facilities that make this possible.... Under conservative/corporatism ... women's opportunities to enter paid employment have been relatively limited. (Ibid., p. 93)

Each category of welfare state regime has a distinct division of care-work which coincides with what Taylor-Gooby describes as the private–public axis:

The social democratic regime goes furthest in the socialization of care through the expansion of the welfare state.... Conservative/corporatist regimes tend to define care as largely the province of women, and locate it in the informal sector, outside the realm of welfare citizenship. The liberal regime increasingly commodifies care-work, so that inequalities in this sphere increasingly reflect the pattern of inequalities in the market. (Ibid., p. 97)

This variation between welfare state regimes takes us back to the issue of the gender-biased thread running through citizenship. We might recall how, for Claire Wallace (1993), the universal provision of formal citizenship rights to men and women does not translate into everyday, informal gender equality of citizenship experience. Apart from the intervening influence of the unequal distribution of enabling resources between men and women, there is the accompanying (and empirically connected) distribution of restraining and restrictive 'unwaged care-work', or domestic labour, responsibilities to take into account. However, it is precisely this latter distribution that those social citizenship rights which reflect the socialisation (the 'uncommodification' within the welfare state as opposed to within 'the home') of *care-work* will differentially and unevenly affect (mitigate if not diminish) within the three categories of welfare state regime. In social democratic regimes, considerable socialisation of care-work will be to the relative advantage of women as citizens; in conservative–corporatist regimes, the comparative absence of care-work socialisation will be to the disadvantage of women as citizens, albeit in uneven, occupationally-linked ways; in liberal regimes, comparatively meagre and even diminishing socialisation and social rights with respect to care-work will be to the relative disadvantage of women as citizens. At the same time, however, the disadvantages to female citizens will vary in all welfare state regimes, but especially in conservative–corporatist and, perhaps above all, in liberal ones, by social class.

While Esping-Andersen, in defining and distinguishing welfare state regimes, focuses on the type and degree of decommodification specifically, or narrowly, of people – or more precisely of people's labour power[5] – his theme of capitalist-market commodification versus welfare-state decommodification is a reminder of the 'social theories' of Anthony Giddens, Ulrich Beck and Zygmunt Bauman (Warde, 1993, p. 1), a common feature of these being

> the notion that, today, people define themselves through the messages they transmit to others through the goods and practices that they possess and display. They manipulate or manage appearances and thereby create and sustain a 'self-identity'. In a world where there are an increasing number of commodities available to act as props in this process, identity becomes more and more a matter of the personal selection of self-image. Increasingly, individuals are obliged to choose their identities.   (Ibid., p. 2)

According to these theorists, late-twentieth-century Western societies are developing in the direction of increasing and more inclusive commodification, and therefore in a direction which is diametrically opposed to the (albeit narrow, people, anthropocentric) welfare-state decommodification which for Esping-Andersen is the defining feature of all welfare regimes. For these theorists, there is supposedly a general shift in the direction of commodification, this being consistent with the neo-liberal or New Right onslaught on the welfare state and social rights. At the same time (as touched on towards the end of the previous chapter), the individuality of comprehensively individualised and commodified Western societies would entail the kind of personal pressures, problems and *pain* which could inspire something of a contrary inclination towards the retention or revival of expansive decommodification, and in particular of welfare-state decommodification. There may be considerable appeal in citizenship, and so in the defence, extension and expansion of citizenship rights, and perhaps especially social (together with industrial) ones. Citizenship in general (as a status and identity) may gather considerable appeal in societies characterised by a ubiquitous, ever-increasing and perhaps overwhelming individualised reflexive struggle with regard to self-image due to its symbolic (identity; membership; security) connotations. This aside, however, social (and industrial) rights in particular may be especially appealing because of their straightforward practical worth in relation to benefits and services, *enabling resources*, the commodity market in wage goods and services, and so on. In other words, social citizenship rights may be especially appealing in late-twentieth-century Western societies because of their value, following Esping-Andersen, in facilitating welfare-state (people) decommodification; which in turn would seem to have major implications for people's individuality. This follows from Esping-Andersen's point that the process of decommodification means that 'social assistance or insurance ... emancipate individuals from market dependence' (Esping-Andersen, 1990, p. 22). Here, of course, there are echoes of the argument presented by Jones and Wallace that social citizenship rights promote the individuality of young people by enhancing their independence from family and parents. We can imagine Jones and Wallace asserting something similar to the following from Esping-Andersen, about 'the young person' instead of 'the worker', and 'the parent' instead of 'the employer': 'De-commodification strengthens the worker and weakens the absolute authority of the employer' (ibid., p. 22). Furthermore, referring back to Taylor-Gooby's attempt at modifying Esping-Andersen's analysis by covering the issue of 'care-work', we can imagine reading 'the wife' instead of 'the worker', and 'the husband' instead of 'the employer'.[6]

At the same time, Esping-Andersen inform us that:

> De-commodified rights are differentially developed in contemporary welfare states. In social-assistance dominated welfare states, rights are not so much attached to work performance (as they are in conservative–corporatist 'social insurance' regimes) as to demonstrable need. Needs tests and typically meagre benefits, however, serve to curtail the decommodifying effect. Thus in nations where the model is

Individualism and the European Union 201

dominant (mainly in Anglo-Saxon countries), the result is actually to strengthen the market since all but those who fail in the market will be encouraged to contract private-sector welfare. A second dominant model espouses compulsory state social insurance with fairly strong entitlements. But again, this may not automatically secure substantial de-commodification, since this hinges very much on the fabric of eligibility and benefit rules. Germany was the pioneer of social insurance, but over most of the century can hardly be said to have brought about much in the way of de-commodification throught its social [programmes]. Benefits have depended almost entirely on contributions, and thus on work and employment. In other words, it is not the mere presence of a social right, but the corresponding rules and preconditions, which dictate the extent to which welfare [programmes] offer genuine alternatives to market dependence. The third dominant model of welfare, namely the Beveridge-type citizens' benefit ... offers basic, equal benefit to all, irrespective of prior earnings, contributions, or performance. It may indeed be more solidaristic, but not necessarily de-commodifying, since only rarely have such schemes been able to offer benefits of such a standard that they provide recipients with a genuine option to working. (Ibid., pp. 22–3)

Nevertheless, this latter model is 'the most decommodifying' (ibid., p. 22), and accordingly has been behind some concrete examples of welfare state regimes manifesting relatively high levels of decommodification. Esping-Andersen tells us, 'the Scandinavian welfare states tend to be the most de-commodifying; the Anglo-Saxon the least' (ibid., p. 23), judged in terms of *de-commodification scores* for eighteen national welfare-state regimes (see Table 5.1), which allow us to

distinguish three groups of countries: the Anglo-Saxon 'new' nations are all clustered at the bottom of our index; the Scandinavian countries at the top. In between these extremes, we find the continental European countries, some of which (especially Belgium and the Netherlands) fall close to the Nordic.... And the clusters bring together the countries which, a priori, we expected would look similar in terms of our welfare-state regime arguments. We would anticipate a very low level of decommodification in the nations with a history dominated by liberalism... . And in the 'high decommodification' cluster we find the social democratically dominated welfare states, exactly as we would have expected. Finally, the continental European countries, with their powerful catholic and etatist influence, tend to occupy the middle ground – prepared to extend a considerable modicum of rights outside the market, but nonetheless with a stronger accent on social control than is the case with social democracy.   (Ibid., p. 51)

TABLE 5.1   *Rank-order of Welfare States in Terms of Decommodification(*)*

Australia
United States
New Zealand
Canada
Ireland
United Kingdom

Italy
Japan
France
Germany
Finland
Switzerland

Austria
Belgium
Netherlands
Denmark
Norway
Sweden

SOURCE: Based on Table 2.2 in Esping-Andersen, 1992, p. 52.
*NOTE: The higher the placing, the less the decommodification.

Here, Esping-Andersen is suggesting that, if anything, the Catholicism of the *continental European countries* has meant an affinity with the conservative–corporatist (authoritarian) model of social welfare rather than, as (according to Nicholas Boyle) Peregrine Worsthorne and Ian Paisley would have us believe, some more 'communitarian' or 'socialist' model, and in particular the social-democratic one.

As pointed out by Taylor-Gooby, what Esping-Andersen does is to distinguish between three 'ideal type' of welfare state regime (or 'welfare citizenship regime') models, so that 'different national systems in practice combine elements of all three', even though one model 'is usually dominant and may be used to characterize the pattern of [actual] welfare citizenship in each country' (Taylor-Gooby, 1991b, p. 96). Thus:

> In one cluster [of countries] we find the 'liberal' welfare state, in which means-tested assistance, modest universal transfers, or modest social-insurance plans predominate. Benefits cater mainly to a clientele of low-income, usually working-class, state dependents. In this model, the progress of social reform has been severely circumscribed by traditional, liberal work-ethic norms.... Entitlement rules are ... strict and often associated with stigma; benefits are typically modest. In turn, the state encourages the market, either passively – by guaranteeing only a minimum – or actively – by subsidizing private welfare schemes. The consequences of this type of regime minimizes de-commodification-effects [and] effectively contains [restricts] social rights.... A second regime-type clusters nations such as Austria, France, Germany, and Italy.... In these conservative and strongly 'corporatist' welfare states, the liberal obsession with market efficiency and commodification was never pre-eminent and, as such, the granting of social rights was hardly ever a seriously contested issue. What predominated was the preservation of status differentials; rights, therefore, were attached to class and status. ... [The] corporatist regimes are ... typically shaped by the church and so strongly committed to the preservation of traditional family-hood. Social insurance typically excludes non-working wives, and family benefits encourage motherhood.... The third ... regime-cluster is

composed of those countries in which the principles of universalism and de-commodification of social rights were extended also to the middle classes. We may call it the 'social democratic' regime-type since, in these nations, social democracy was clearly the dominant force behind social reform [and] translates into a mix of highly de-commodifying and universalistic [programmes]. This model crowds out the market, and consequently constructs an essentially universal solidarity in favour of the welfare state. All benefit; all are dependent; and all will presumably feel obliged to pay. [This] model is a peculiar fusion of liberalism and socialism.   (Esping-Andersen, 1990, pp. 26–8)

The social-democratic model is dominant in Sweden and other Scandinavian countries (see Ann-Magritt Jensen, 1989), and its incorporation of 'socialism' helps to account for the way it is the target for attack and resistance by those writers and policy-makers who are committed singularly to 'liberalism', and so to the defence, preservation and promotion of the liberal model of welfare citizenship is what Esping-Andersen classifies as the Anglo-Saxon nations. At the same time, however, as Esping-Andersen emphasises, 'we must recognize that there is no single pure case' (Esping-Andersen, p. 28), or, that is, no actual national welfare state system which fully and only meets all the features which distinguish any one ideal-type model. Notably, 'European conservative regimes have incorporated both liberal and social democratic impulses. Over the decades, they have become less corporativist and less authoritarian' (ibid., p. 29).

Taylor-Gooby develops the point that although the 'conclusion of [Esping-Andersen's] argument is that welfare citizenship in capitalist countries is developing along at least three trajectories' (Taylor-Gooby, 1991b, p. 97), none the less, occasionally there is an 'anomalous case', such as the United Kingdom, where 'elements of social democratic universalism co-exist in unstable combinations with the Anglo-Saxon tradition of selectivity and class-divided provision' (ibid., p. 96). Taylor-Gooby refers to the further anomalous case of Japan (see Friedman et al., 1987, p. 244; and Komatsu, 1992); as well as to 'cases of uneven development', such as those found among 'the Mediterranean Rim countries' and to the 'post-command economies of East and Central Europe' (Jeffries, 1993), whose welfare systems 'for the present remain open' (Taylor-Gooby, 1991b, p. 97).

As I have mentioned, Taylor-Gooby pays no attention (of the kind invited by Maurice Roche) to the implications of the evolution of the European Community and Union as a supra-national arrangement for 'national systems' (ibid., p. 96) of social welfare and rights. Taylor-Gooby certainly does not attempt to classify the European Community itself, in recognition of what Roche reports is the *new social rights of European citizenship currently being developed in the EC* (Roche, 1992, p. 8), in terms of Esping-Andersen's scheme or any other.[7] Nor, for that matter, does Roche, even though he is 'mainly concerned with social citizenship and thus with the welfare state and social policy in [his] book' (ibid., p. 12); focuses on how in 'Western Europe the increasing economic, legal and political integration of the European Community is beginning to challenge national sovereignty and citizenship' (ibid., p. 1); and devotes a chapter (as well as various passages) to the topic of 'reinventing social citizenship: post-nationalism and new social rights in Europe' (ibid., pp. 191–221).

I wish to propose that the European Community and Union, in so far as it is emerging as a *welfare citizenship regime* (Taylor-Gooby, 1991b, p. 96), is in the process of doing so as a 'hybrid', a term which Taylor-Gooby uses to otherwise describe the United Kingdom's *anomalous* national system (ibid., p. 97). Of course, this is not to say that the EU's supra-national system is necessarily combining elements of the ideal-type welfare state models in a manner which identically mirrors the UK's (or any other) national system. Given the supra-national, and moreover the novel supra-national, constitution of the European Community, it is reasonable to assume that the emergent welfare system represents a unique combination of elements, and so a unique hybrid; is embarked upon an unprecedented trajectory; and is even indicative of a fresh welfare state category and ideal-type. As in the case of the United Kingdom, the liberal model of welfare-state regimes, rights and citizenship is likely to play a prominent part in directing the EU's system; as is the social democratic model. At the same time, however, the balance between the liberal and social democratic models may well be tipped somewhat more towards the latter in the EU than in the UK; than fits in with the UK's current national trajectory; than suits UK Conservative governments, including the post-Thatcher ones; or than is prescribed by the neo-liberal or New Right perspective on welfare-state regimes, rights and citizenship. If so, we might expect the EU's welfare system to be at odds with – to *contradict* – the UK's, at least more so than most other Member States' systems (guided by Esping-Andersen's decommodification scores and clusters), and at least for the time being.

But furthermore, we might assume that the *continental-European* conservative–corporatist model will play a more prominent part in the EU's welfare citizenship system than it does in the UK's. At this point, however, a conceptual matter might be addressed and kept in mind when interpreting empirical evidence on the EU's system. Both Esping-Andersen and Taylor-Gooby use the label 'social rights' to cover certain rights which are intimately linked to – if not quite themselves – 'industrial rights' as defined (and distinguished from 'social rights') by J. M. Barbalet (in line with Anthony Giddens and T. H. Marshall). In the conservative–corporatist 'welfare citizenship' model, the state helps preserve social class differentials by supporting occupationally-linked social insurance schemes of social rights, benefits and services. While such rights may not be 'industrial rights', they none the less act – because of their sectoral (occupational; industrial) association with and practical dependency upon industrial rights – as a bridge between social rights and industrial rights. Even if social-insurance rights do not quite invite us to collapse the categories of industrial and social citizenship rights into one, they perhaps warrant the adoption of some inclusive label. Perhaps the label 'welfare rights' is appropriate. Certainly, this conclusion is indicated by Esping-Andersen's and Taylor-Gooby's use of the label 'welfare', and would seem to be consistent with the way this term is used in popular or journalistic reporting on matters relating to the European Union's welfare-state regime of citizenship rights, benefits and services.

John Carvel (Carvel, November 1993) outlines the European Commission's – otherwise described as Jacques Delors's[8] – White Paper on *Competitiveness, Growth and Employment*, which was published on 8 November 1993. The White Paper focuses on the 'twin crises of unemployment and dwindling competi-

Individualism and the European Union

tiveness against the economies of the Pacific rim' (ibid.). Thus, as reported by Leonard Doyle:

> The EU jobless rate is now 10.4 per cent, or 18 million and expected to reach 20 million by the end of 1994 and continue rising. Still locked in recession, the EU's economy is shrinking by 0.5 per cent as governments pursue anti-inflation policies at the cost of falling output and rising unemployment. (Doyle, November 1993)

Doyle notes the comparative international weakness of the EU's economic performance, which he accounts for in terms of

> the lack of flexibility built into the European labour market by generous protections negotiated between unions and employers. The Organisation of Economic Cooperation and Development blames these for Europe's declining competitiveness. Labour costs rose by four times as fast during the Eighties as they did in the US and Japan. And between 1974 and 1991, the US was able to create 36 million new jobs (mostly in the export sector), compared with 8 million in the EU. (Ibid.)

Some EU Member States have done better than others in creating new paid employment, but even those which have done best have still not done as well as either the United States or Japan, as acknowledged in the White Paper:

> The EU has done much less well than the United States or Japan at translating economic growth into jobs, the White paper says. Between 1970 and 1992 the Spanish economy grew by 103 per cent, by employment fell by 0.3 per cent. The British economy grew by 51 per cent but had only 3 per cent more jobs to show for it. Over the same period the US economy grew by 70 per cent and produced 49 per cent more jobs. (Carvel, 9 December 1993)

Leonard Doyle's explanation for the EU's relatively poor economic performance in terms of *the lack of labour market flexibility* appears to receive some support from Jacques Delors himself, whose solution, according to Doyle, is that of 'protecting the

European welfare model of society while making labour markets more flexible' (Doyle, November 1993). Here is an allusion to Jacques Delors's support not just for greater labour market flexibility, but also for the *welfare state*, and, moreover, for a particular model of the latter, that of the social democratic type. In this way, Jacques Delors favours a solution which is somewhat at odds with that pursued by the UK government:

> the European Commission is .... proposing a gentler version of the British model of deregulation for the rest of the EU as a way of generating growth. A white paper on growth, competitiveness and employment that is being prepared by Mr Delors aims [at] creating jobs without dismantling labour protection. (Ibid.)

For Doyle, Jacques Delors's approach can be contrasted with the trend in the UK, which 'is moving in the opposite direction, in a drive towards a low cost economy with minimal social protection for its people' (ibid.). Indeed, the UK government's strategy is presented as being at odds not only with the President of the European Commission, but also with other EU Member State governments: while the UK government 'takes steps to strip away laws that protect workers from unscrupulous employers, European leaders – whose popularity is already at rock bottom – are recoiling from publicly embracing such a confrontational approach' (ibid.).

The multi-faceted, or *hybrid*, approach to the EU's welfare-state regime signalled by Jacques Delors's White Paper is confirmed by John Carvel:

> the white paper tries to chart [a] strategy which could allow Europe to compete effectively by investing in the technologies of the future and by adapting the skills and practises of the workforce, without scrapping the principles of the welfare state. (Carvel, 9 December 1993)

The White Paper confirms and clarifies the opinion of the European Commission and its President that 'one reason for the EU's poor performance [is] inflexible labour' (ibid.). That is:

Social and employee protection systems and regulations have protected mainly those who were already active, sometimes rendering the access to jobs by new entrants more difficult.' But the paper rejects wholesale labour market deregulation. Growing inequalities of income in some member states are reason for caution in pursuing further income squeezes. Instead, firms should be encouraged to increase the number of jobs for any given level of output by ensuring that those who want to work shorter hours do not suffer loss of social protection and employment rights, and reducing incentives for the higher paid to work above-average hours, it says. The EU should encourage a shorter working week for individual employees while increasing utilisation of capital equipment. Firms should be encouraged to take on lower-skilled workers by reducing the non-wage costs of employing them (national insurance contributions etc.). Income support schemes should be restructured to allow low wages to be topped up by income support, the costs to be recouped by a switch to environmental and consumption taxes. The white paper also proposes universal access to vocational retraining, a guarantee of work or training for school leavers, and development of a 'social economy' to absorb 3 million unemployed in jobs such as caring for the young, the old and the environment.   (Ibid.)

Here, the last proposal – which, as John Carvel points out elsewhere (8 December 1993), covers 'support for working mothers and the elderly' – brings to mind again the issue of the implications of 'uncommodified care-work in the home' (Taylor-Gooby, 1991b, p. 93) within welfare-state regimes. The responsibility for such work (domestic labour) is gender-skewed to the relative disadvantages of female citizens, but the White Paper indicates that Jacques Delors and the European Commission are in favour of the socialisation (and thereby the welfare decommodification) of care-work, whereby some responsibility is transferred to the state. Such a proposal, of course, sits well with the social democratic model of welfare-state citizenship. Likewise, so does the proposal, as Leonard Doyle puts it, 'to reduce the cost of hiring workers by shifting the burden of social security away from employers to the state. The costs would be recouped by what Mr Delors calls "the rare resources of the environment": in other words an energy tax' (Doyle, 1993).

John Carvel describes these various proposals as 'far-reaching changes in employment policy, based around a new "European social pact"', the aim being that of 'creating 15 million jobs by the end of the century' (Carvel, 9 December 1993). This employment policy and social pact are, moreover, presented alongside a 'medium-term industrial strategy (for) stimulating trade and co-operation between small businesses'; and 'supplemented by speeding up the establishment of trans-European infrastructure networks – transport, telecommunications and energy links – which would improve European competitiveness and produce useful employment as a spin-off during the construction phase' (ibid.). It is for the specific purpose of helping to finance such infrastructural developments that the European Commission then proposes the introduction of 'Euro-bonds which it would use to raise 7 billion ecu' (ibid.).

However, this particular *Keynesian*, 'communitarian' and social-democratic type feature of the White Paper has attracted especially vociferous criticism, opposition and resistance. As John Carvel reported on the day the White Paper was published (Carvel, 8 December 1993), 'EU finance ministers have already signaled their opposition to ... the proposals for the Union to raise more than £30 billion over the next six years to finance investment in transport, the infrastructure and energy.' The finance ministers did this at their meeting in Brussels five days prior to the European Council summit of 10–11 December 1993, as confirmed by John Palmer:

> European Union finance ministers last night moved to block proposals from Jacques Delors ... for an investment-led economic recovery, to be funded through an extra £33 billion borrowing programme .... The negative response was predictable given the ministers' repeated insistence that the state of public finances in most EU countries will not allow more borrowing. But, inspite of this, Mr Delors intends to launch a campaign to win the backing of as many EU heads of government as possible at the Brussels summit. (Palmer, 6 December 1993)

At the subsequent European Council summit, the UK government was at the forefront of the opposition to the White Paper, at least certain aspects of it, essentially because of its preferred New Right policies and *ideological* commitment, as Michael White reports:

> London's emphasis on free market solutions to liberalise labour markets, curb non-wage costs and avoid state-interventionism in the EU's drive to prevent unemployment passing 20 million next year, puts it at ideological odds with most of its partners over the Delors white paper.... Ministers and officials are pleased, however, that their own agenda is reflected in Mr Delors's stress... on open trade systems, enhanced competitiveness, labour flexibility and help for small business. (White, 9 December 1993)

The gap over the White Paper between the UK government and most of the other Member State governments reflects the latter's *social democratic* leanings, shared of course with the Labour Party in the UK. Thus, the UK government was

> sceptical about the commission's call for EU-driven investment in European-wide road, rail, energy and information networks, designed to improve competitiveness with Asia and create jobs. The ideas are broadly acceptable, but Mr Delors wants to raise Euro-bonds. 'If they believe that borrowing will create more jobs why don't they just increase their own national deficits?' asked one [UK] government economist. Labour takes the opposite view and John Smith will endorse the broad thrust ... of the Delors paper at a pre-summit session of EU socialist leaders in Brussels today. (Ibid.)

At this meeting, John Smith's broad support for the White Paper was backed by all the delegations, and moreover was echoed at a parallel pre-summit gathering of Christian Democrats, as John Palmer and John Carvel tell us:

> At separate pre-summit meetings in Brussels, Christian Democratic and Socialist leaders agreed to back the principles

of the Commission's search for new solutions to the EU's problems of declining competitiveness and unemployment, although the finance ministers are not committed to the detail of Mr Delors' ideas. (Palmer and Carvel, 10 December 1993)

Consistent with the outcome of these meetings, Palmer and Carvel report how:

> Jacques Delors last night won the support of most of the European Union heads of government for his white paper proposals... He was subjected to a rumbustious attack by the [UK finance minister], Kenneth Clarke, but it appeared that if John Major adopts the same line in Brussels today, he will be isolated .... The Christian Democrat prime ministers of the Benelux countries called for 'concrete measures based on the white paper', and Socialist heads of government took a similar line. (Ibid.)

At the summit meeting itself, on 10–11 December 1993, the UK experienced some, but not total, isolation:

> The EU summit in Brussels yesterday backed the main aims of Jacques Delors's white paper on unemployment – but several leaders joined John Major in criticising the Commission's plan to raise money on the bond markets to fund infrastructural projects .... Mr Major adopted a conciliatory tone in the meeting, [describing] the white paper as 'intellectually impressive'. It contained many good elements, including proposals for more flexible labour markets and the rejection of protectionism and compulsory work-sharing, he said .... Helmut Kohl [suggested] that Mr Delors's plans for trans-European road, rail and telecommunications networks could better be supported through the existing facilities of the European Investment Bank. But the German chancellor left the summit in no doubt that he supported Mr Delors's plan for extra spending on infrastructure to prepare the Union for the 21st century. Against Mr Major's advice, this was expected to form part of today's final communique. (Carvel, 11 December 1993)

Accordingly, as John Carvel then went on to report:

> The final communique of the heads of governments on Saturday praised the quality of the white paper. They said it contained 'lucid analysis' of the EU's economic and social position and should form the basis of an action plan to reduce the 'unacceptable' total of 17 million without jobs. [Mr] Delors carried through his whole agenda, with the exception of two details on which the outcome was fudged. His proposal for the Commission to raise £6 billion a year in Union Bonds to finance extra infrastructure investments became a less specific commitment to provide additional funding 'as far as necessary' to ensure the survival of priority projects .... The second significant amendment to the Delors plan was that his 'target' of 15 million new jobs by the end of the century became the aspiration of 'significantly reducing' the number of unemployed. For all the British claims, the essentials of the white paper survived intact and are to form the basis of 'a short and medium-term action plan' to amplify policies to improve competitiveness and improve jobs. (Carvel, 13 December 1993)

The gap between the approach of the UK government on the one hand and the approach of Jacques Delors and the European Commission on the other towards combined economic and social reform is poignantly summarised and assessed by Will Hutton in anticipation of the summit meeting:

> Having silenced Keynesianism in the House of Commons, Mr Major does not intend it to surface in Brussels. It is one of the paradoxes of the moment that the most serious challenge to the new Right's continuing ascendency over British economic policy ideas should not have come from the official Opposition – but from the European Commission. Monsieur Delors is venturing ideas that, if canvassed in the British Labour Party, would ensure his marginalisation. For ... his White Paper on Competitiveness, Growth and Unemployment... is a serious document that carries at its heart the Keynesian proposition that in Britain still not dare speak its name. When economic activity is depressed, public agencies have an obligation to borrow and invest to create a

momentum in economic activity that the market cannot deliver. But the proposals are more sophisticated than simple Keynesianism. The exigencies of European realpolitik require that M Delors has to make concessions to right-of-centre governments and orthodox opinion ... . Thus the paper endorses the idea that too generous minimum wage legislation can cost jobs for the unskilled – and that loading social costs onto employers will deter them from hiring workers .... The British left's best contribution to its own and Europe's future would be to borrow some of the same nerve, ideas and judgement – and make some progress in contesting the prevailing ideas of Europe's most right wing state. Of that there is little sign – and meanwhile M Delors fights alone. (Will Hutton, 'A Just Case for Delors', *Guardian*, 10 December 1993)

Well, not quite alone, given the majority support Jacques Delors received for his White Paper from the EU's Member State governments at the European Council summit meeting. Such support means, of course, that the White Paper's proposals have some chance of being implemented, but only some chance. The prospects for its implementation are limited by, first of all, the decision-making process within the EU in relation to such matters. This limitation is indicated by Will Hutton:

What Delors needs most of all is political and intellectual support for the project in hand – for European initiatives now need to be fought for in a way in which British supporters [from the Labour Party] seem largely ignorant. The Commission can no longer expect support for some programme simply because it is European – even if such a climate ever existed. As a result, authors of European-wide public action are on the defensive, with a weakening political base. For, despite all the brouhaha over Maastricht, political power in Europe remains firmly with the nation states of the Union. Indeed European transport and communications 'networks' are one of the few areas where the Maastricht accords give the Commission some room for manoeuvre because they can be voted for by qualified majority vote under the Political Union Treaty. It is no accident that Delors has centred on them as the means to launch his reflation. His hope is that he can keep the paper alive long enough for circumstances to win the argument at both European and national level. (Ibid.)

This point about the political power relationship between the European Union, and in particular its Commission, and the Member States and their governments is crucial in analysing and accounting for both the content of any economic and social policy programmes issued by the Commission and, relatedly, the prospect that any programme will be implemented, or put in place. This issue is crucial to the future trajectory of the European Community and Union as a welfare-state regime: to the direction, pace and extent (judged with reference to ideal-type models of welfare-state regimes) of this trajectory. It is of paramount importance to the prospects for welfare (social and industrial) citizenship rights within the Union; and indeed to the evolution of the full range, pattern and system of citizenship rights within the Union. In particular, it will be at the forefront in determining the future of distinctively *European Community and Union citizenship*, including that which takes the form of 'new citizenship', and its place and importance in shaping 'national citizenship'. Accordingly, the issue will be explored in detail in the next chapter.

Perhaps fortunately, from the point of view of the European Commission and Jacques Delors, there does seem to be something close to unanimity of opinion among the Member States over economic and social policy, especially over the kind of pivotal matters addressed in the White Paper. At the same time, however, this near consensus is not unquestionably consistent with the policy emphases and thrust of the latter, given the way these things favour a European Community and Union welfare regime which is strongly influenced by the social democratic ideal-type model. That is, the White Paper spells out what amount to *principles* which are by no means matched by the *actual* policies and practices pursued either at the Member State level or at the Community and Union level. These actual policies and practices show considerable signs of the same neo-liberal thinking which has characterised the UK government's approach to economic and social policy since 1979.

Earlier, I referred to Taylor-Gooby's argument about the growing disillusion with the traditional model of social welfare provision (Taylor-Gooby, 1991b, p. 93), a model I equated with Maurice Roche's view of 'the dominant paradigm' of welfare citizenship. In a similar way to Taylor-Gooby, as we have noted, Roche has then suggested that this traditional dominant paradigm *has been battered by New Right ideology*. Roche adds, however, that none the less the paradigm has 'so far survived a succession of legitimacy and economic crises. In the 1990s it remains largely in place ... in most Western nations' (Roche, 1992, p. 13). He claims:

> An institutional and intellectual rethinking of the dominant paradigm of welfare [see B. Jordan, 1987] and of the welfare state [see R. Mishra, 1984] in the West has [often] (as under the Thatcher and Reagan governments in Britain and the USA) ... taken an ostensibly 'radical' New Right approach allegedly aimed at 'rolling back the state' and substituting markets for the state in the field of welfare [see C. Murray, 1984; M. Loney et al., 1987]. However, the relative failure of the New Right project to achieve longstanding reductions in states' welfare spending suggests that the dominant paradigm, although it is being undermined, has by no means been overturned.   (Roche, 1992, pp. 13–14)

Roche's assessment is somewhat ambiguous, and perhaps too optimistic (depending upon the precise interpretation). There is evidence about *welfare spending* to suggest that the traditional dominant paradigm, in so far as this is infused with the social-democratic model of the welfare state and the associated degree of de-commodification, has been effectively challenged and perhaps superseded by an alternative – by a new dominant paradigm which is instead largely shaped by neo-liberal and New Right thinking. Moreover, in so far as such a paradigm shift has been taking place, it will have been doing so in practice both at the nation-state level and, despite the possible impression given by Jacques Delors's White Paper, at the supra-national level of the European Union. Essentially, through the twin influences of, first of all – following Will Hutton – the exigencies of European *real-politik* and, second, the EU's underlying economic purpose, problems and drive –

Individualism and the European Union 217

centred as these things are on growth, revival and competitiveness – welfare provisions, rights and citizenship have been sacrificed. Thus, a few months before the publication of the White Paper, Victor Smart reported:

> Europe's leaders are to send a political signal that they can no longer afford the welfare state when they meet next week in Copenhagen. The change in post war philosophy has been forced on them by the crippling deficits from the worst recession for 60 years. Even EC Commission President Jacques Delors, one of the most ardent supporters of EC welfare provisions, has been forced into a crisis review of the implications. He will tell the summit that the burden on businesses of social costs may be a root cause of economic woes. Despite his socialist credentials, Delors now accepts that 'social security structures are an obstacle to the creation of jobs'. He believes that hard-won employment rights can rebound against workers if they lead to a rigid labour market and destroy Europe's competitive edge over Japan and the United States.   (Smart, 10–13 June 1993)

Victor Smart underlines the economic considerations by pointing out: 'With the recession worsening, forecasts suggest that unemployment in the EC will top 18 million this year and could rise to more than 20 million in 1994'; and then proceeds to claim that Jacques Delors's 'new thinking reflects the political realities across Europe where governments are saying they simply can no longer afford to run the welfare state on its present scale' (ibid.). This applies to Germany, for example, where the government is 'proposing to save Dm11 billion (Ecu 5.5bn) a year on child welfare payments, student grants and other benefits – a move described by the opposition SPD as "an orgy of knock-out blows to the welfare state"'. Similarly in France, the

> new Baladur has threatened to curb benefits to [the] three million unemployed, claiming it would not bail out the fund which has run up a deficit of Ffr31 billion (Ecu 4.7bn). Recently the Senate reported that five million jobs could be lost by companies shifting production abroad to avoid labour costs pushed up by social contributions.   (Ibid.)

Apart from further EC Member States, such as Spain – where Felipe Gonzalez, who was 're-elected on a promise to preserve the upgraded welfare system, finds himself under pressure to wield the knife' – Smart claims:

> Nordic countries are in the vanguard, beginning to dismantle their social security systems which were once the envy of the rest of Europe. In non-EC Sweden, unemployment and sickness benefits, pensions, student grants and foreign aid have all been heavily pruned. In the next 12 months an estimated 80,000 Swedish public sector jobs will be axed. (Ibid.)

Because of Sweden's renowned position as a leading welfare-state nation, exemplifying in particular (as noted by Esping-Andersen) the application of the social-democratic ideal-type model and so the traditional dominant paradigm, the stripping of the Swedish welfare system is regarded as especially significant. For instance, Hans Bergstrom (17–20 June 1993) reports how, before closing its annual session at the beginning of June 1993, the Swedish parliament 'approved a package of spending cuts and structural changes unprecedented in the history of Sweden's welfare state'. The cuts were carried through under Carl Bildt, the first non-socialist prime minister to govern for a full term, and by 1994 the first conservative leader since 1924 to face the electorate while still in office. Bergstrom claims that Bildt's 'government had the misfortune to come to power in the middle of the worst industrial decline in Sweden since 1920–21', with the result that production 'levels at the end of his three-year term will be lower than they were at the outset'. Also, unemployment 'has risen to 13 per cent, a level not seen in Sweden for 60 years. This has also caused a dramatic increase in the budget deficit. Public borrowing now totals nearly 13 per cent of gross national product, which is even higher than Italy and Greece.' It is in response to these circumstances that the Swedish government has undertaken a 'conservative and neo-liberal "revolution"' (ibid.).

The evidence from Western Europe, including from both within and beyond the European Union provides support for Taylor-Gooby's general impression of a 'trajectory of state welfare spending through the confident expansion of the 30 year boom to uncertainty and retrenchment in the chill economic climate of the last fifteen years' (Taylor-Gooby, 1991b, p. 97). Taylor-Gooby comes to the conclusion that:

> State spending continues, under altered circumstances. In the late 1980s, gloom about the future of state welfare [accompanied] new models of social policy ... under the slogans of the mixed economy of welfare, welfare pluralism, welfare consumerism and (on the left) market socialism.... The general implication is that state provision will become increasingly irrelevant to the ways in which people meet their welfare needs.... Arguments drawn from ... different writers [agree] that government will play a less significant role in welfare provision in the future than it did in the past. The implications for the future of welfare are expressed in softer and harder-nosed variants, from the advocacy of wholesale privatization to the withdrawal of government from the role of direct provider to the position of supervisor, regulator and financier of an area of state and non-state services. The role of government in welfare is diminished, and new agencies will become increasingly important in meeting social needs. A study of recent developments in nine countries concludes: 'the mixed economy of welfare, in which the state is an enabler and private participation is possible through greater individuals contribution of fees and the contractual provision of services seems to be the direction in which many welfare states are moving' (Friedman et al., 1987, p. 289. See also Taylor-Gooby 1991a; Taylor-Gooby, 1991b, pp. 98–9)

If so, then Esping-Andersen's three-model representation of welfare state regimes may be destined to become less, or at least very unevenly, applicable to actual welfare-state regimes at the national level, not to mention the supra-national level. From the evidence, it may be inferred that a process of welfare-state convergence is under way towards a common regime, which, while remaining something of a hybrid in drawing on the liberal, social-democratic and conservative-corporatist models, will be largely shaped by the first of these. Despite any continuing public declarations by 'socialist' and similarly inclined national and supra-national leaders in favour of the traditional dominant paradigm, a combination of political exigencies and economic priorities may well drive down or out welfare-state regimes which fall short of being more or less determined by the liberal model.

The new dominant paradigm would reflect the continuing ascendency of neo-liberalism, individualism and capitalism, as well as of supra-national social, economic and political arrangements, in particular that of the European Community and Union. It might also be regarded as confirmation of the kind of analyses of recent social change which have been presented by Giddens, Beck and Bauman, with their common emphasis on individuality and (societal – structural and cultural) individualisation. However, the difficulty here is that, if anything, welfare state regimes which are largely shaped by the liberal model will necessarily promote unequal distributions of citizenship rights – at least of the welfare (social and industrial) kind – and, connectedly, of enabling resources and thereby citizenship experiences. Accordingly, the new dominant welfare-state paradigm will help to perpetuate such major impediments to individuality and individualisation as social class and sex-gender structures. Although, at this point, as I mentioned in the previous chapter, we can imagine the preservation and resurgence of social class and patriarchy feeding into popular demands and movements in favour of the (re-)expansion of welfare citizenship; and therefore of a reconstruction of actual welfare state regimes largely around the social democratic model. This aside, in any case, as I also mentioned in the previous chapter, in so far as the analyses of Giddens, Beck and Bauman have credibility, the development envisaged – entailing as it does an unrelenting but unrewarding, comprehensively individualised, reflexive search for self-identity through cynically manipulated commodity-market centred consumption – may lend itself to the very same reconstruction, due to the practical (consumption) advantages of welfare citizenship rights (of de-commodification) along with the symbolic value of the status, membership and identity associated with citizenship in general.

However, there is yet a further consideration which favours the retention or revival of the traditional dominant paradigm of welfare citizenship. If the neo-liberal or New Right promotion of the new dominant 'liberal paradigm' is rationalised on the grounds that it is conducive to both enhanced individuality and economic (capitalist) progress, the campaign becomes questionable, unconvincing and unsuccessful on both counts. Not only may a paradigm determined by the liberal model be substantially inimical to individuality, but also:

> There is no firm evidence linking welfare spending with penalties on economic growth, while stable high-growth high-welfare regimes seem practicable [Esping-Andersen, 1990, pp. 223–4; A. Pfaller et al., 1991]. It is noteworthy that the rhetoric of the ineluctable challenge from these factors is loudest in the liberal regimes of the USA and the UK where ... welfare spending is relatively low. (Taylor-Gooby, 1991b, p. 99)

Recognition of the same point is demonstrated within the European Commission, in particular by 'Padraig Flynn and officials in the social policy directorate' (Carvel, 10 December 1993). In an interview with John Carvel on the first day of the European Council summit meeting in Brussels in December 1993, Padraig Flynn comes to the defence of Jacques Delors's White Paper by offering the following interpretation:

> Although it calls for greater labour market flexibility – code words in Britain and the United States for low wages and poor conditions for workers at the bottom end – its aim is to spread the benefits of worker protection, and not contract them. 'We are talking about re-regulation, not deregulation,' he said. Employers could not be expected to recruit workers whose low productivity did not produce a return. But the answer was not to cut the wages of the low-paid. It was to reduce non-wage labour costs (such as employers' national insurance contributions) and to reshape tax and social security systems to encourage the unemployed back into work. 'Look at the evidence. Wages as a proportion of GDP in the Community are at their lowest for 30 years, and they are equal to or lower than those in America or Japan. The member states with a high level of social protection are the ones which have done best economically,' Mr Flynn said. 'So our problems of competitiveness are not just a question of wages. There are other things. And one of those is

certainly the motivation of the workforce. They are not production fodder. They have the resources and skills on which our competitiveness and growth will depend.... Demotivate the workforce and you will have instability and industrial unrest. And the burden of that will fall on just two groups – the unskilled and the unemployed. We don't want a lost generation of European citizens. What we have to do now is to make it possible for them to participate. I do not want a dual society in Europe which we have a certain proportion of very high income earners and a big percentage of people who will never work and never participate. Nor do I want a dual regime of those on decent wages and those on poverty wages. That way we would end up having to supplement low wages [with income support] as happens in the American model. Let's not inject the weaknesses of other models. Let's keep the European model that has worked well and re-regulate it to make it an instrument for the 21st century,' Mr Flynn said. (Carvel, ibid.)

Padraig Flynn's interpretation of Jacques Delors's White Paper, diagnosis of European economic competitiveness, and social policy and welfare citizenship oriented prognosis raise the possibility that, within the patchwork of European Union political communities and struggles, a broad consensus of approach – if not of interests – will re-emerge between policy-makers, employers and employees, the capitalist class and the working class, in favour of the traditional dominant paradigm, or at least against the new dominant paradigm, largely determined as the latter is by the liberal ideal-type model. Perhaps the 1980s' and 1990s' ascendency of neo-liberalism is merely a phase in a continuous dialectical process whereby eventually a fresh, more evenly-balanced, hybrid welfare state regime will emerge. I wish to suggest that the chances of such an outcome are enhanced by the persistent progress of, and increasing leadership (not to mention control) from, the European Community and Union as a supra-national social, economic and political organisation, and moreover the pre-eminent instance of this type of organisation currently on the world stage.

Padraig Flynn's approach is certainly consistent with the claims which heralded the European Community's adoption of the Charter of Fundamental Social Rights for Workers for the 1990s:

> At the meeting of the European Council in Strasbourg on 8 and 9 December 1989, the Heads of State or Government of the European Community Member States, with the exception of the United Kingdom, adopted the Community Charter of the Fundamental Social Rights for Workers. The signatories intend the Charter to be at once a solemn statement of progress already made in the social field and a preparation of new advances – so that the same importance may be given to the social dimension of the Community as to its economic aspects, in the construction of the [internal] market [under the Single European Act (1986)] of 1992. In the preamble to the Charter, the Heads of State or Government also underline the priority which they attach to job creation, the importance of social consensus as a factor in economic development and their rejection of all forms of discrimination and exclusion. They also declare that, far from justifying any regression from the very diverse situations prevailing in the 12 member countries, the Charter demands a series of initiatives to develop workers' rights: responsibility for these initiatives will sometimes lie with the social partners, sometimes with the member states and sometimes with the Community itself. (Commission of the European Communities, May 1990, p. 2)

While this introduction to the *Social Charter* (as it came to be called), in a manner which echoes Padraig Flynn's summary of social or welfare policy within the general evolution of the European Union, asserts equal importance between the 'social dimension' and the *economic dimension,* the Charter overall none the less confirms the message which is made abundantly clear both by the particulars of Padraig Flynn's points and by the rest of the evidence presented in this chapter: the message that, in practice, the economic dimension has much greater importance. The evidence suggests that principally the social dimension serves the economic dimension; that the social dimension is managed and modified in accordance with the assessed needs of the economic dimension, and connectedly with the welfare state's *affordability* in terms of the economic dimension; that the social dimension is shaped with reference to the economic, and more specifically the market-capitalist, priorities of the European Community and Union; that the social dimension is constructed and re-constructed within political communities and struggles marked by distributions of interests, power and control rooted in the capitalist mode of production and its associated social class system (this is not to ignore the parts played by accompanying power distributions, such as that between men and women). At the same time (to recall a point made earlier), those with the power to best realise their interests within the political communities will take into account the interests and demands of those with less power. It serves the economic priorities of the European Union (as alluded to in the Commission's introduction to the Charter) to ensure as much 'social consensus' as possible, and, with this in mind, to treat the issues of 'job creation', 'discrimination' and 'exclusion' seriously. Once in paid employment, following Padraig Flynn, it is conducive to the realisation of the same priorities to mould people into a 'motivated workforce'; to treat them in ways which avoid 'industrial unrest' and so 'instability'. To these ends, for Padraig Flynn and the European Commission, it would seem useful to expand 'social rights'.

However, at this point, a fundamental issue arises with regard to the theme at hand, brought to mind by Flynn's reference to 'European citizens' and their 'participation' in, as opposed to, presumably, their 'exclusion' (as the Commission puts it) from *society*. The issue is: are the *social rights* involved 'citizenship rights'?

The absence of complete Member State agreement aside for the moment. *The Community Charter of Fundamental Social Rights for Workers,* as its full title indicates, goes on to specify rights which not only reflect the focused priority given to the economic dimension of the European Community and Union, but also may be too narrow in scope, judged with reference to their 'target population' – so much so that they fail to qualify as citizenship rights. Here we may recall the point made by J. M. Barbalet that *not all rights not even all legal rights are citizenship rights* (Barbalet, 1988, p. 18). For instance, following T. H. Marshall, *the provision of certain rights is precisely to compensate those who are excluded from the status of citizenship* (ibid., p. 18). I have explored this distinction around the examples of children and aliens. Just as there may be (and are, in all EU

Member States) children-specific and alien-specific legal rights, the purpose of which is to compensate children and aliens respectively for being denied full citizenship rights and thus citizenship status, so the rights listed in the Social Charter may not qualify as 'citizenship rights' because of the way they are worker-specific; or, that is, because of the way they are not *universalistic* in scope. The scope of the Social Charter's rights is narrowly limited to 'workers', or paid employees, and their assumed special requirements, rather than being extended to adults and their requirements in general. If so, of course, the further issue arises as to whether worker-specific legal rights are also 'compensatory' vis-a-vis the special location of paid employees within the system of citizenship rights, enjoyment and experience: are in recognition of the way the citizenship system *fails* paid employees, with the implications this has for social participation and inclusion; and consequently for such matters as social consensus, unrest and instability.

The Charter declares:

> Every worker of the European Community shall have the right to freedom of movement through the territory of the Community, subject to restrictions justified on the grounds of public order, public safety or public health... . The right to freedom of movement shall enable any worker to engage in any occupation or profession in the Community in accordance with the principles of equal treatment as regards access to employment, working conditions and social protection in the host country.   (Ibid., p. 3)

The further detail in the Social Charter has been neatly summarised by Pascal Fontaine:

> the ... Charter ... defined the rights that should be available to all workers throughout the Community: freedom of movement, fair pay, improved living and working conditions, social protection, freedom of association and collective bargaining, vocational training, equal treatment for men and women, worker information, consultation and participation, health protection and safety at the workplace, and the protection of children, the elderly and the disabled. (Fontaine, 1990, p. 40)

One point to emerge here is the apparent overlap between the Social Charter's list of rights and that category of citizenship rights which J. M. Barbalet has distinguished (from 'social rights') as 'industrial rights'. Earlier in this chapter I suggested that in recognition of the sectoral and practical connections between 'social rights' and 'industrial rights', in particular by way of occupational and social-insurance-linked rights, it may be sociologically appropriate and analytically useful to adopt the overarching label of 'welfare rights'. I have now added the suggestion that, in so far as industrial rights are confined to paid employees rather than being attached to adults in general, such rights may not qualify as 'citizenship rights'. Of course, this should be viewed in conjunction with the point I have made (in the context of my criticism of Barbalet's ideas) that rights which permit 'freedom of association and collective bargaining', among other industrial rights, are not necessarily exclusive to people who are actually in paid employment. Instead, industrial rights may well be universally enjoyed by all adults, and so may be more readily counted as citizenship rights. Having said this, however, the list of rights in the Social Charter would appear to be precisely of the kind which, on the basis of the 'universality test', do fail to qualify as citizenship rights because of their narrow scope.

Pascal Fontaine's summary brings out a further important point about the Social Charter's list of welfare rights. The list in not so much descriptive (of an established set of rights) as prescriptive. The rights are recommendations, ostensibly selected with the immediate aim of furthering the social dimension, with the following rationalisation in mind:

> social progress ... goes hand in hand with, or is even stimulated by, legislation guaranteeing a 'European core' of basic social rights throughout the Community. This European social area consists of principles incorporated into the Treaty [of Rome], such as equal pay for men and women, or flows from recent Directives establishing social protection for workers (health and safety at the workplace) and recognition of basic safety standards (the Directive on machinery).   (Ibid., p. 40)

Individualism and the European Union

Such employee, employment and economy oriented or biased social progress has been given an especially large boost by the creation of the European Union's 'internal market', with the assistance of the Single European Act (1986), as indicated by the following outline:

> The European internal market is due to become reality on 1 January 1993. From that date on, there should be no restrictions on movements of persons, services, goods and capital in the Community of Twelve. The grafting together of the national markets will give a new impetus to the economy.... . The Commission's 1985 White Paper gave new momentum to the movement for the creation of an internal market. The White Paper lays out 289 steps which should be taken to harmonize conditions and dismantle barriers.... . In addition, the entry into force of the Single European Act on 1 July 1987 paved the way for speedier decision-making by the Council of Ministers, while at the same time extending the fields in which the Community is competent to intervene. (European Documentation, 1990, p. 5)

As pinpointed by Pascal Fontaine, the relevance of the internal market, in conjunction with the SEA, as a piece of facilitating legislation for the social area or dimension of the European Union stems from, in particular, 'the decision enshrined in the Single European Act to eliminate all [migration] controls' (Fontaine, 1991, p. 30). That is:

> Freedom of movement without having to submit to checks is the first condition to be met if there is to be a frontier-free area. Such a right would be no more than an empty formality, however, if it did not go hand in hand with the right of establishment, the right to work and the right of abode throughout the Community, without any limits or other discriminatory conditions restricting the freedom to engage in an occupation. (Ibid., p. 33)

To this end:

Employed workers ... are now fully entitled, with the proper qualifications, to take up employment in another Member State without any restrictions on grounds of nationality. Access to employment, even on a part-time basis, automatically gives a worker right of abode for a renewable period of five years. European citizens working within the Community have the right to be joined by their spouses, their minors or dependent children and their parents. They enjoy the same social security and tax benefits as workers who are nationals of the host country under Article 51 of the EEC Treaty... . This equality extends to the right of abode in the host country after retirement, which becomes a permanent right under certain conditions.   (Ibid., p. 33)

But the rights involved, no matter how 'progressive', are still employee, employment and economy oriented and biased. They fall short of what Fontaine, following the European Commission, refers to as 'a people's Europe' (see Commission of the European Communities, *A People's Europe: Reports from the Ad Hoc Committee*, 1985; Commission of the European Communities, *A People's Europe*, 1992), which he clarifies as follows:

In 1975, at the request of the European Council ..., the Belgian Prime Minister ... produced a report on European union. The report emphasized that 'the construction of Europe is not just a form of collaboration between States. It is a rapprochement of people who wish to go forward, together adapting their actions to changing conditions in the world while preserving those values which are their common heritage... . Europe must be close to its citizens.' (Fontaine, 1991, p. 6)

With this idealisation in mind, Fontaine claims that if 'the whole concept of a people's Europe [is not to be] devoid of substance', the social (welfare) rights which underpin the internal market

must also apply to those categories of people who are neither workers, nor members of workers' families, nor those pursuing regulated professions. What about students, pensioners, the unemployed, in short, all those people not covered by separate provisions? Are they to be refused the free right of abode in any country? ... The goal of a true people's Europe ... will be achieved by making freedom of movement, the right to work and the right of abode universally and unconditionally available to every national of the Community. (Ibid., p. 36)

Certain directives were agreed by the Member States on 28 June 1990 with the intention of including 'categories which had not previously possessed the right of abode':

students, to whom host countries will grant residence permits valid for the actual duration of their course of studies and renewable annually if necessary ... ; retired workers, whether formerly employed or self-employed, who have a pension and health insurance or sufficient resources to prevent their becoming a charge on the host country during their stay; unemployed people, on condition that they and their families are covered by health insurance and have sufficient resources. (Ibid., p. 36)

But, such directives still fall short of achieving *the goal of a true people's Europe* because their target populations are 'still hampered by excessively tight restrictions' and because they do not establish 'the basic right' of all European Community citizens 'to live in the country of one's choice' (ibid., p. 36).

A year and a half after these directives, however, the foundation for taking the major leap of allowing all European Community citizens the rights to move and reside freely irrespective of Member State nationality was laid with the signing by the European Council of the Treaty on European Union at Maastricht. Title II of the Treaty states that:

Citizenship of the Union is hereby established. Every person holding the nationality of a Member State shall be a citizen of the Union... . Every citizen of the Union shall have the right to move and reside freely within the territory of the Member States, subject to the limitations and conditions laid down in this Treaty and by the measures adopted to give it effect.

As we now know, the Maastricht Treaty was finally ratified on 1 November 1993, bringing into being the European Union. But, was that enough to finally establish the *true people's Europe*, as Fontaine puts it, with its *freedom of movement, the right to work and the right of abode universally and unconditionally available to every national of the Community*? Well, while such citizenship rights may well suit the economic priorities of the European Union and, connectedly, may well be enshrined in the Treaty establishing the EU as such, this is not necessarily enough to ensure their implementation and enjoyment at the level of 'the people's Europe'. There are further and considerable hurdles to jump, the foremost one of which I have touched on already when I referred to Will Hutton's judgements on the European Commission's 1993 White Paper and subsequent European Council summit meeting. Hutton made the crucial observation that *despite all the brouhaha over Maastricht, political power in Europe remains firmly with the nation-states of the Union* (Hutton, 1993). We have yet to explore the full significance of this point for citizenship, Europe and change. This we will do in the next chapter.

6 Citizenship and the European Supra-state

> A ... positive legacy of World War II was the determination of some far-sighted statesmen to minimize further conflict by welding firm economic links between formerly combatant countries. This initiative led eventually to today's European Community, an association of states which, despite numerous problems, has evolved into one of the world's most important socio-economic groupings. But the European Community is about political as well as economic union. In 1992, the year of the so-called 'Single Market', a reform programme was initiated to expand the EC's decision-making powers, enabling the member states to act as one in many political and social as well as financial areas.
> (Beazley, 1992, p. 10)

> Created from the ruins of World War II, the European Community's goal is to bring about peace and prosperity for its citizens in the framework of an ever-closer union. This process is a gradual one with economic, political and social dimensions. (Commission of the European Communities, *Questions and Answers about the European Community*, 1993, p. 2)

These statements on the origins, purposes and progress of the European Community lend themselves to the view that, in order to make sense of citizenship within Europe towards the end of the twentieth century, it is important to examine the implications of European integration in terms of three analytically distinct societal dimensions: the social, the economic and the political. This inference is consistent with central sociological insights about basic societal structure, processes and change; the accompanying sociological task being to analyse, trace and disentangle the practical links between the three dimensions, assisted by, while in return contributing to, sociological theory (see Ian Craib, 1984; Anthony Giddens, 1982).

Although, within the European Community and Union, the economic purposes are paramount, making the economic dimension the most prominent, a widely held sociological axiom invites us to acknowledge the interdependence of all three societal dimensions at and between all societal levels; and so between, for instance, the level of the immediate, mundane experiences of the people, nationals and citizens of Europe on the one hand, and the emergent supra-national level of policies, laws, bodies, mechanisms and procedures of the European Union on the other. Applied to Europe as anywhere, the distinction between the social, economic and political dimensions of society represent the principal threads along which statutory policy, legislation and procedures are decided, pursued and implemented; legal and citizenship rights are granted, guaranteed, enforced and exercised; citizenship is realised, enjoyed and experienced; people conduct their everyday lives, relationships and activities; and the thrust of European integration takes place.

At the same time, while the social, economic and political dimensions will thread through all areas of European society, they will nevertheless surface differentially and unevenly, the result being the occurrence of distinct societal sectors and spheres. In particular, there will be those sectors which may be distinguished (and which I have elucidated earlier) as the state and the civil sectors. The state sector is constructed around the political dimension of society, while the civil sector is constructed around, or encompasses, the social and economic dimensions. Connectedly, the various categories of citizenship rights are differentially associated with the same dimensions and sectors. Political citizenship rights are exercised along the political dimension and within the state sector; civil, social and industrial (or civil and welfare) citizenship rights are exercised along the social and economic dimensions and within the civil sector. This is not to ignore the point that the full range of citizenship rights and categories are struggled over, granted, guaranteed and enforced (as distinct from exercised) along the political dimension, within political communities, and so within the state sector.

The focus of this chapter is the political dimension and state sector of the European Union; the way 'the political' operates at and between different levels of European society, especially by

Citizenship and the European Supra-state 233

virtue of the progress of the European Community and Union as a supra-state; and the implications of this particular development for the everyday lives, relationships and experiences of the people and citizens of Europe. That is, the focus of this chapter is the 'political communities' of the European Union, including the overlap, relationships and change among the political communities, especially under the impact of the European Union as a political community itself and the implications of this impact for the various levels of citizenship, including for their relative importance within the Union and in everyday life.

There are various clues as to the growing importance of the European Union within the continent of Europe and more widely. For instance, there are those signs in the evidence which indicates that the European Community and Union is 'the world's major trading power' (Fontaine, May 1992, p. 6). By the end of the 1980s, with 35 per cent of world trade, the Community had become 'the world's largest trading bloc' (Minshull, 1990, p. 336). Relatedly, in 1990 the gross domestic product (GDP) of the Community was Ecu 4 738.5 billion, compared with Ecu 4 235.1 billion for the USA and Ecu 2 319.9 billion for Japan (Eurostat, 1992, p. 39).[1]

By the end of 1990 (following the re-unification of Germany on 3 October 1990), the European Community consisted of twelve Member States: Belgium, Denmark, France, Germany, Greece, Ireland, Italy, Luxembourg, the Netherlands, Portugal, Spain and the United Kingdom. The Community occupied a total geographical area of 2 368 000 square kilometres and had a total population of 344 925 000 (ibid., p. 107). The geographical area and population of the whole of Europe were about 10 400 000 square kilometres[2] and 492 000 000 respectively (in 1985), excluding Turkey and the former Soviet Union (*Hutchinson Softback Encyclopedia*, 1992), or almost 700 000 000 if the former Soviet Union as far as the Urals is included, but not Turkey or the sub-Caucasus states (Beazley, 1992, p. 10).

At the beginning of the 1990s, the community was poised on the brink of considerable and rapid expansion as a number of countries across Europe were lining up to become new Member States. These countries included the seven former Efta countries (Austria, Finland, Iceland, Liechtenstein,[3] Norway, Sweden and Switzerland);[4] the Mediterranean countries of Cyprus, Malta and Turkey, all of which had 'association agreements with the Community, aimed at the gradual creation of a customs union' (Fontaine, May 1992, p. 29); and 'the new democracies of eastern Europe' (The European, *Maastricht Made Simple*, 1992, pp. 40–1), some of which had already acquired 'association agreements' (ibid). In particular, what were the 'Visigrad Three' – Hungary, Poland and Czechoslovakia (before that country split on 1 January 1993 into the Czech and Slovak republics) – had each signed an association agreement with the Community (Commission of the European Communities, *From Single Market to European Union*, April 1992). Other potential central and eastern European candidates for membership have been variously identified as Bulgaria, Estonia, Latvia, Lithuania, Romania, and the former Yugoslavian republic of Slovenia (see Commission of the European Communities, *Europe: World Partner – The External Relations of the European Community*, April 1991; Commission of the European Communities, *From Single Market to European Union*, April 1992; The European, *Maastricht Made Simple*, 1993, pp. 40–1; Fontaine, May 1992); and even Albania and the five former Yugoslavian republics apart from Slovenia – that is, Croatia, Serbia, Montenegro, Macedonia and Bosnia-Herzegovina; along with the former Soviet republics of Armenia, Azerbaijan, Belarus (or Byelorussia), Georgia, Moldova, and the Ukraine. The potential outcome by the year 2020, according to Dick Leonard, is an organisation of seven hundred million people 'making up a genuinely European Community' (Leonard, 10 May 1992).[5]

The first firm steps in this expansion were taken during 1992–3, when formal negotiations got under way with Austria, Finland, Norway and Sweden with a view to their joining the European Union by 1995–6. In preparation for this, on 1 January 1994, these four former members of Efta, along with Iceland, combined with the EU to create the European Economic Area (EEA). The result was the formation of the 'world's biggest trading market', outstripping

> the free trade zone created by the North American Free Trade Agreement which brought together the United States, Canada and Mexico. While Nafta covers a far bigger area than the EEA, the EEA is bigger in terms of popula-

tion, gross domestic product and share of world trade .... The UK trade minister [has] welcomed the creation of the EEA .... 'The EEA ... covers 17 countries extending from the Arctic to the Mediterranean. It removes single market non-tariff barriers, such as national standards, from businesses selling to some 370 million customers, in an area representing 40 per cent of world trade.' Though the EEA does not constitute a full customs union, ... it will provide for the free movement of goods, services, capital and people and include some 1,500 of the EU's single market measures. The EEA will have 372 million customers, against 360 million in Nafta, with a GDP of £5,068 billion against £4,574 billion in Nafta. The EEA exports £2,620 annually per person against £1,137 for Nafta .... The EEA, whose members overall, send more than half their exports to each other, will cover £1,134 billion in imports and £1,091 billion in exports against £483 billion and £421 billion respectively in Nafta. (Milner, 1 January 1994.)

Beyond Austria, Finland, Norway and Sweden, the most likely candidates for membership are certain countries of central and eastern Europe. What is referred to as 'the collapse of communism [which] has enabled the new democracies of eastern Europe to look west rather than to Moscow' (The European, *Maastricht Made Simple*, 1992, p. 41), has been held to have heralded the prospect of the Union's eventual eastward expansion as far as the Caucasus (if not the Urals[6]). This is apart from the same event having more immediate developmental implications:

the ending of the cold war, German unification and the collapse of communism in Eastern Europe (have) increased the Community's external responsibilities. Long-held aspirations to create a common foreign policy and even to give the Community a security and defence role became attainable. (Commission of the European Communities, *From Single Market to European Union*, 1992, p. 12)

Here, in effect, the point is being made that the European Union is more than just an *economic arrangement*. A prominent political dimension runs through, shapes and helps drive the

Union: shaping its characteristics, content and form; shaping its relationships with the rest of Europe and of the world, and so its place within the *new world order*. Thus, it has been proposed: 'Besides implementing its internal agenda, the Community must assume its responsibility as the leading power in Europe and as a global partner in helping fix the post-war international order' (ibid., p. 6). This view is elaborated as follows:

> The European Community is having to assume global responsibilities. This is partly the result of the EC's own aspirations and partly as a response to external factors. One of the main reasons for drawing up [the Maastricht Treaty as] a treaty on political union in parallel with EMU [European Monetary Union] was to give the Community an international voice and status in political affairs to match the additional commercial and economic weight acquired through the single market and the EMU. Otherwise the Community would risk being an economic giant but a political dwarf. The concrete expression of this new dimension is the decision to create a common foreign and security policy (CSFP) by the European Council in December 1991 and contained in that part of the Maastricht Treaty concerned with political union. The other impetus has come from the disintegration of the communist system, bringing about the unification of Germany and the end of the cold war .... The Community is now seen as the main focus of peace, democracy and growth by all of Europe .... It must consolidate this position if it is to increase its weight and influence in the creation of a more stable world order. (Ibid., p. 32)

The prospect and appeal of the Union assuming world responsibilities' (ibid., p. 32) within the *new world order* is reflected in and reinforced by the inclusion in the Maastricht Treaty (agreed in December 1991; signed in February 1992; and finally ratified in November 1993) of 'provisions on a common foreign and security policy', whereby the

> union and its Member States shall define and implement a common foreign and security policy ... [the] objectives of [which] shall be: to safeguard the common values, funda-

mental interests and independence of the Union; to strengthen the security of the Union and its Member States in all ways; to preserve peace and strengthen international security ...; to promote international co-operation; to develop and consolidate democracy and the rule of law, and respect for human rights and fundamental freedoms. (Treaty on European Union, Title V, 1992)

The Treaty provisions go on to stipulate:

The Member States shall support the Union's external and security policy actively and unreservedly in a spirit of loyalty and mutual solidarity. They shall refrain from any action which is contrary to the interests of the Union or likely to impair its effectiveness as a cohesive force in international relations. The Council shall ensure that these principles are complied with.   (Ibid.)

The Maastricht Treaty's provisions on a common foreign and security policy (CFSP) have formally established one of the three 'pillars' of the European Union: one of the other two pillars being the European Community, which, as amended by the Treaty, remains in place as a separate institutional, primarily 'economic', entity; and the third being Home Affairs and Justice. The latter has been described as follows:

Maastricht for the first time makes interior policy, specifically justice and home affairs, a matter for intergovernmental co-operation between the 12 EC countries in the European Union. It becomes one of the new pillars alongside Common Foreign and Security Policy and the existing European Community .... Impetus for the initiative came with the clear realisation that relaxing the internal Community frontiers in the drive to the 1992 single market made cross-border co-operation more imperative to tackle a possible growth in international crime. A second factor was the spectre of waves of immigrants entering the community from the south and east.   (The European, *Maastricht Made Simple*, 1992, p. 18)

The second consideration mentioned here, leading to the creation of the Home Affairs and Justice pillar of the Union (which also covers such concerns as 'asylum, drugs, fraud, terrorism, legal co-operation on civil and criminal matters and closer contacts between customs officers' (ibid., p. 19) takes us back to the issue of migration in relation to citizenship. This particular matter aside for the time being, however, the Home Affairs and Justice pillar of the Union is like the CSFP pillar in being constructed alongside, and so outside, the European Community. This has important implications for the Union as political organisation and *political community*. That is:

> foreign policy does not become a Community competence …. At the heart of the CFSP is a readiness, indeed eagerness, to develop a single foreign policy. Yet this is counterbalanced by an equally fierce desire not to be caught up in the full Euro-machine by European Commission, Parliament and Court of Justice. The compromise was to put joint policy on an inter-governmental footing rather than a supranational one. CFSP is in effect half in and half out of the Community machinery. If the litmus test for federalism is granting the Commission the right to initiate policy and overturning each nation's right to veto, then the CFSP pillar is self-evidently not federalist.   (Ibid., pp. 20–1)

This conclusion begs several questions, including: what is meant in general by 'supra-national'?; and what is meant in general by 'federal'?. Probably the approach taken by *The European* to the notion of 'supra-national' and to the application of this notion to the European Community as just one – albeit the central – pillar of the new Union is indicated by Klaus-Dieter Borchardt:

> the Community ... was created by treaties taking effect under international law. But these treaties area at the same time the foundation documents establishing independent Communities endowed with their own sovereignty rights and competence. The Member States have pooled certain parts of their own legislative powers in favour of these Communities and have placed them in the hands of Community institutions …. The Community is thus a new form of relationship between States, something between a State in the traditional sense and an international organiza-

tion. The concept of 'supranationality' has become accepted by lawyers as a means of describing their legal nature. This is intended to indicate that the Community is an association endowed with independent authority, with its own sovereign rights and legal order independent of the Member States to which both the Member States and their citizens are subject in matters for which the Community is competent. (Borchardt, 1991, p. 9)[7]

Whatever, in precise terms, *The European* means by 'supranational', the implication of its attempt to clarify the character and form of the CFSP as one of the three pillars of the new Union is that it cannot be counted as 'federalist' because it fails to meet the condition of being organised on a 'supranational' basis. The CFSP is organised instead on an intergovernmental basis. On these grounds, this pillar can be contrasted with the European Community pillar, which *is* organised on a supra-national basis. However, if so, then the further question arises: is the European Community 'federalist'?. On this point the European newspaper appears to be guilty of what it accuses the European Council of doing in deciding to have the CFSP organised on an inter-governmental basis only: the 'lopsided and inelegant architecture betrays the political fudge underneath' (ibid., p. 20). That is, the question of whether the European Community is 'federalist' is fudged by *The European*:

If the Federalists were hoping to create a United States of Europe with the Maastricht treaty, then they have suffered a setback. Any single state, however federally devolved, must have a single and coherent foreign policy, and this is still a long way off. (Ibid., p. 20)

The European's ambiguity over the meaning and application of 'federal' allows for two possibilities: either the notion of 'federal' can be applied only to the European Union as a whole; or it can be applied also to individual pillars of the Union. On balance, *The European* appears to adopt an approach according to which, because only one 'pillar' – the European Community – is 'federal', the Union overall is not 'federal'.

As such, this approach may be contrasted with that which appears to have been adopted by the European Commission. The Commission has confidently backed the claim that the Union as a whole is becoming, just as it ought to become, a *federal union*, while indicating what it understands by this process:

> The European Community has to proceed to a federal-type European Union .... [The] Community will not be able to claim to be a true union if it does not reinforce its structures and rationalize its decision-making procedures, which must be both efficient and democratic. Four decades of integration have left an indelible mark on the Continent and on the mentality of its people. They have also altered the balance of power. Member State governments of all political shades know that absolute sovereignty is no longer a realistic option. They understand that formerly sovereign nations can only continue their economic and social progress, and continue to have an influence on world affairs, if they pool their resources and accept that their fate is now intertwined. (Commission of the European Communities, *From Single Market to European Union*, 1992, p. 18)

For the Commission, being a federal union requires a redistribution of decision-making powers, and so of sovereignty, from the Member State level to the Community and Union level, which is precisely what has been happening. This process, the Commission argues, has inter-dependent internal and external consequences and advantages. Essentially, in a mutually supportive manner, the internal strengthening of the supra-national constitution of the Union feeds into its external, inter-national stature, and vice versa. Of course, this does not in itself mean that either the two non-EC pillars or the Union overall have or will become 'federal'.

However, we can be confident at least that the creation of the CFSP pillar reflects the way the Union recognises and wishes to meet its greater *political responsibilities* within the *new world order*. We can be sure that the Union will also recognises how, on the one hand, its greater external political responsibilities will come from its enhanced (especially economically rooted) political power; while on the other hand, greater integration, in particular by way of 'political union' and the CFSP pillar, will in turn enhance the Union's external political (not to say economic) power, thereby improving its chances of meeting the same responsibilities. As such, for some writers, the political ascendency of the European Union holds considerable promise:

> In a global context ..., the superpowers [both the Soviet Union and USA] no longer have the dominating superiority [once] possessed, and the European Community [is] a potential super-power in its own right .... As the 1990s begin, political developments in Eastern Europe ... look set to continue. The emergence of Europe as a world power ... may be significantly affected by developments in the Eastern European countries as the millennium draws to a close. (Minshull, 1990, p. 332)

What might be noted here is that the prospect of becoming a world super-power is essentially about developments at one end of the broad spectrum which represents the political dimension running through the European Community and Union.[8] At the other end of the political dimension are those developments which are immediately relevant to the everyday, mundane existence, circumstances and concerns of *the people of Europe*. The developments at this end of the political dimension include, most importantly, the possibility of the European Community and Union being or becoming a 'supra-power', because this possibility will have immediate implications for (apart from anything else) citizenship. As we noted in the previous chapter, the European Commission has appeared to show considerable interest in promoting a *people's Europe*. As the Commission explains:

> in June 1984, the European Council (the 12 Heads of State or Government) officially endorsed the idea of 'a people's Europe', setting up a special committee ... which produced two reports putting forward proposals to bring Europe more closely in touch with the ordinary citizen. More recently, on 7 February 1992 in Maastricht, the leaders of the Twelve took a further big step with the signing of the Treaty on European Union, which includes a chapter on European citizenship. (European Commission, A People's Europe, 1992, p. 1)

More precisely, the Maastricht Treaty contains provisions introducing the status of 'Citizenship of the Union', where the rights of *Citizens of the Union* include one relating to the participation of the people of Europe in the decision-making processes. That is, every 'citizen of the Union residing in a Member State' of which he or she 'is not a national shall have the right to vote and to stand as a candidate' both at municipal elections and at elections to the European Parliament 'in the Member State in which he [or she] resides, under the same conditions as nationals of that State'. As summed up by Pascal Fontaine:

> The process of a people's Europe began in 1985 with the publication of the Adonnino Report, commissioned by the Fontainebleau European Council. The decision taken in Maastricht to allow every citizen residing in a Member State other than his [sic] own to vote and stand in municipal and European elections marks the beginning of a new phase. This decision ... has sparked a debate on the concepts of national identity and national sovereignty.   (Fontaine, May 1992, p. 25)

The debate is about where sovereignty lies; where it should lie; and where it will lie in the future. The alternative locations for sovereignty cover not only the national and supra-national levels, but also the sub-national level, including as far down as 'the people'.[9] The debate – in that it concerns the distribution of sovereignty, or decision-making power, between the supra-national institutions of the European Community and Union, the Member States and 'the people' – has attracted the critical attention of the European Commission:

> The powers of the EC's institutions have developed over the years as the activities of the Community have expanded and deepened. This is particularly true of the European Parliament. Its rights have been extended with successive constitutional reforms of the Community. But the expansion of Parliament's powers has not always matched the pace of the transfer of authority from individual countries to the EC. As a result, a 'democratic deficit' has arisen. National parliaments have lost control over executive power

transferred by their governments to the EC, while their right of control has not been fully handed to the European Parliament. Other criticism of the degree of democracy in the EC has centred on the lack of openness in the way EC decisions[10] are taken and on the inadequate accountability of the European Commission. Some of these problems received answers in the 1987 Single European Act; others are dealt with in the Maastricht Treaty on European Union. Further reforms are foreseen when the Maastricht Treaty is reviewed in 1996. (Commission of the European Communities, *Strengthening Democracy in the EC*, 1993, p. 1)

For the Commission, the task of 'filling the democratic deficit' (ibid., p. 7) entails, in part, redistributing the control over decision-making between the Community's three 'branches of government – the legislative, executive and judiciary', where the executive and legislative branches are 'split between the European Commission, the European Parliament and [the] Council of Ministers' (ibid., p. 2). More specifically, the task mainly requires shifting the balance of power between the Parliament and the other institutions of the Community, whereby the Parliament increases its particular control over the decision-making process. The Maastricht Treaty includes provisions which ostensibly address this issue of 'rebalancing the powers' (The European, *Maastricht Made Simple*, 1992):

> For years, one of the most strident criticisms of the EC's three [main] institutions – European Commission, European Parliament and Council of Ministers – has been their lack of democratic accountability. Maastricht makes some attempt to remedy this so-called 'democratic deficit' by granting greater powers to the European Parliament ... the one body of the three that is directly elected.   (Ibid., p. 38)[11]

In the same way as before the Maastricht Treaty, European Community decision-making, in particular that involved in arriving at legislation, continues to be conducted largely as a three-way process between the Commission, the Parliament and the Council (where the Council covers the Council of Ministers and the European Council of Heads of State and Government). Roughly speaking – especially if the Maastricht

Treaty provisions are bracketed – the Commission proposes, the Parliament debates, and the Council decides (ibid., p. 30), in the process of arriving at all types of EC legislation[12]. The different types of Community legislation 'are classified and described in brief terms in Article 189 EC' (J. Shaw, 1993, p. 110), a reference by Josephine Shaw to the original European Economic Community Treaty of 1957 as amended by the Single European Act of 1987:[13]

> In order to carry out their task and in accordance with the provisions of this Treaty, the European Parliament, acting jointly with the Council, the Council and the Commission shall make regulations and issue directives, take decisions, make recommendations or deliver opinions. A regulation shall have general application. It shall be binding in its entirety and directly applicable to all Member States. A directive shall be binding, as to the result to be achieved, upon each Member State to which it is addressed, but shall leave the national authorities the choice of form and methods. A decision shall be binding in its entirety on those to whom it is addressed. Recommendations and opinions shall have no binding force.   (Quoted in Shaw, ibid., p. 110)

Josephine Shaw clarifies as follows:

> Regulations are like Community 'Acts of Parliament'. Regulations have 'general application', are binding in all respects and 'directly applicable'. Thus they are general, non-individualised legislative measures which take effect directly in the national legal order, without need for national implementing measures. Indeed national re-enactment is not permitted, unless it is required by the terms of the Regulation .... Directives amount only to obligations of result .... However, the implementation of Directives is a positive obligation for the Member States .... The Member States have a discretion as to how they implement Directives. This normally involves either adopting or changing legislation, but exceptionally nothing need be done if existing legislation is sufficient. [Decisions] are measures of an individual nature which may be addressed to individuals or undertakings, or to Member States.   (Ibid., pp. 111–13)

Citizenship and the European Supra-state 245

The distinction between regulations and directives has been otherwise outlined by Klaus-Dieter Borchardt, who usefully refers to the applicability of each type of legislation to 'citizens':

> regulations ... lay down the same law throughout the Community ..., and apply in full to all Member States; and [have] direct applicability, which means they do not have to be transformed into domestic law, but confer rights or impose duties directly on the citizens of the Community in the same way as domestic law; the Member States and their governing institutions and courts are bound directly by Community law and have to comply with it as they have to comply with domestic law .... Unlike the regulation, [the directive] does not create new uniform Community law binding throughout the whole Community: it requires the addresses to take such measures as may be necessary in order to achieve an aim desired by the Community .... The reasoning behind this form of legislation is that it allows intervention in domestic legal and economic structures to take a milder form, and in particular enables Member States implementing the Community rules to take account of special domestic circumstances [thereby] preserving the multiplicity of national characteristics. [Unlike regulations,] directives do not confer direct rights and duties on Community citizens, as they are addressed solely to the Member States. Citizens acquire the relevant rights and duties only when the directive ... is incorporated into domestic law by the responsible authorities in the Member State. (Borchardt, 1991, pp. 26–7)

One of the most important examples of the use of directives in the history and development of the European Community is that of the 282 legislative items (The European, *Maastricht Made Simple*, 1992, p. 42) designed to facilitate the completion of the single internal market. That is, as Josephine Shaw says, 'the effective implementation of Directives is one of the keys to the realisation of the Community's objectives in the internal market sphere' (Shaw, 1993, p. 112), with its implications (as discussed in the previous chapter) for the welfare rights of

Member State citizens, albeit selectively and unevenly. As reported by the Commission during March 1993:

> Nearly 95% of the measure set out in the White Paper on the completion of the single European market had been agreed by 5 February 1993. Of a total of 282 measures, 261 had been definitively adopted and 3, adopted by ministers, had yet to come before the European Parliament before being definitively adopted, making a total of 264. Among these measures and 'European laws', 257 are already in force in principle, while 213 of them require to be transposed into the national laws of the Twelve. Of course only 95 of these 'laws' have been transposed in all 12 EC countries without exception; but 80% of national transposition measures have already been taken – a substantial advance over 1992. Denmark continues to lead its EC partners when it comes to transposing EC legislation with 92%; it is ahead of Italy (87%), the United Kingdom (86%) and Belgium (85%). Greece is the laggard, with 72%, while the other countries range between 74 and 82%. As for the four freedoms of movement promised by the single market, three are almost complete: they are the freedom of movement for goods, services and capital. The fourth, freedom of movement of people, is still awaited. Such is the balance sheet the European Commission presented to EC ministers on 8 February. (Commission of the European Communities, *Frontier-free Europe*, March 1993, p. 2)

In other words, those measures which were designed to realise that 'freedom' which is most directly and immediately pertinent to the everyday lives of the people, citizens and nationals of Europe were precisely the ones that more than any others had still to be implemented at the Member State level. The significance of this delay with regard to the background issue of the empirical links between citizenship, migration and race-ethnicity has been examined already (especially in Chapter 3); but its significance specifically in relation to citizenship and the European Community and Union as a *political community* has to be more fully explored.

The Maastricht Treaty has made a difference to the procedures or methods by which each type of Community legislation is decided. Whereas before the Treaty there were just two procedures in place, since the Treaty there have been three. The two pre-Treaty methods were the *consultation procedure* (the rules of which were laid down in the Treaty of Rome, 1957) and the *co-operation procedure* (which was introduced by the Single European Act, 1987); the additional post-Treaty method is the *co-decision procedure* (the European, *Maastricht Made Simple*, 1993, pp. 28–9).[14] The consultation procedure is 'the oldest and least complicated way' in which European Community law is decided:

> After consultation throughout the EC, the Commission makes a draft proposal, which is then sent to be debated in the European Parliament ..., in consultation with [the Economic and Social Committee].[15] The Commission then reacts to what parliament and the economic and social committee have to say, and may amend their proposal. The proposal is then sent to the Council of Ministers, who, after discussion and compromise, must agree unanimously on it before it becomes law. The unanimous voting system, spelled out in Article 100 of the Treaty of Rome, [however, meant that] as the Community expanded ... unanimity on proposals became rarer and rarer. Eventually the member states could agree on almost nothing at all. The system had to change. (Ibid., p. 30)

The Council's inability to agree and to make decisions resulted in a plan for change, which Jacques Delors, the President of the European Commission, presented to the European Parliament, for the 'revival of Europe' (Commission of the European Communities, *From Single Market to European Union*, 1992, p. 42). More precisely, what Jaques Delors presented to the Parliament on 12 March 1985 was the '1992 single market programme' (ibid., p. 42). As Gordon Minshull summarises:

> The painful economic adjustments of 1975–1986[16] were associated with a period of 'Eurosclerosis' during which few important decisions were taken and the Community was damaged by acrimonious discussions about the budget contributions of the UK and the increasing problems of agriculture

surpluses. The survival of the Community through this period seemed to focus thoughts, and to concentrate minds, upon possibilities for the future, and has formed the basis for a great psychological, economic and political 'leap forward'. The European Council, at Summit meetings in 1984 and 1985 drew up the Single European Act, which came into force in July 1987. Its principal objective was the creation by 1992 of the Single European Market. (Minshull, 1990, p. 332)

Moreover, the Single European Act introduced the cooperation procedure, the method by which the bulk of all European Community law soon came to be made (The European, *Maastricht Made Simple*, 1992, p. 30). According to this method, if 'the Council fails to agree unanimously on a proposal (almost always), they agree a "common position" by qualified majority vote (QMV), a system laid down in Article 100a of the Single European Act'. The QMV aspect of the co-operation procedure allows a *common position* to be achieved when at least 54 out of the total of 76 votes on the Council are cast in favour of a proposal – the total being distributed among the twelve Member States as follows: France, Germany, Italy and the United Kingdom, ten votes each; Spain, eight votes, Greece, Portugal, the Netherlands and Belgium, five votes each; Denmark and Ireland, three votes each; and Luxembourg, two votes. It has been claimed that 'without Article 100a, the 300 odd measures of the Single European [Act] would not have been possible' (ibid., p. 31).

Using the co-operation procedure, with its QMV system,

A common position must be agreed within three months. The proposal is then passed back to Parliament for a second reading. If Parliament approves, the Council will act and turn it into law. Parliament may also reject and amend the proposal by an absolute majority (i.e. more than half the Parliament's 518 members). If it amends the proposal, the Commission may add its opinion before it is passed back to the Council. If the Commission accepts Parliament's amendments, Council may ratify by QMV. If the Commission rejects Parliament's amendments, Council may only act unanimously.   (Ibid., p. 31)

However, under this method, whereas 'the Commission, an unelected body, clearly has a lot of weight in what becomes law and what does not', the Parliament, the only elected body, has relatively little weight. This method, in other words, preserve the unaccountability of the EC's institutions; the democratic deficit within the EC; and so, the lack of control which the people of Europe have over the decision and law-making processes – processes which, after all, have major consequences for the everyday lives, relationships and experiences of the citizens of Europe, such as, by way of the creation of the single internal market. This feature of the European Union as a *political community* provides the backcloth and rationale behind the introduction in the Maastricht Treaty of the 'co-decision procedure' for arriving at Community legislation, a method which allows 'Parliament to reject certain key issues by an absolute majority vote, thus overriding the Council for the first time – the so-called "negative assent"' (ibid., p. 28). The co-decision procedure has been summarised as follows:

> Co-decision, laid down in Article 189 of Maastricht, is the Treaty's most significant institutional innovation, tilting the balance of power away from the Commission and towards Parliament. If, within the [co-decisional] procedure the Council does not approve a proposal, the proposal will pass to a new 'conciliation committee', whereas it used to be dropped. Council and Parliament will be equally represented on this committee – for the first time. They may agree to a joint text, which must then be approved by QMV in Council and by a simple majority in Parliament. If the conciliation committee cannot agree on a text, Parliament will have the ultimate right to reject the proposal by absolute majority .... The parliamentary right to veto [is] extended to major sectors that include internal market legislation, consumer protection, health, education and environmental programmes. (Ibid., p. 31)

The full range of fields to which co-decision applies under the EC Treaty, as amended by the Maastrich Treaty, is: the free movement of workers; the freedom of establishment and mutual recognition of diplomas: the internal market; incentive measures in the educational field; incentive measures in the cultural field; incentive measures in the health field; consumer protection; trans-European networks; research and development in the multi-annual framework programme; and general action programmes in the environmental field (Shaw, 1993, pp. 83–4). It might be borne in mind that the Maastricht Treaty has merely extended 'the Parliament's right of co-decision' (Commission of the European Communities, *Strengthening Democracy in the EC*, 1993, p. 8), in that the Parliament already possessed this right in relation to certain areas: 'The founding Treaties gave the Parliament the right to dismiss the European Commission through a vote of censure. In 1975, the Parliament acquired the right to co-decision alongside the Council of Ministers over the Community's annual budget' (ibid., p. 8).

The upshot of the changes stretching all the way to the Maastricht Treaty may be seen as a gradual but substantial rebalancing of decision and law-making powers between the Parliament and the Council, on the one hand, and the Parliament and the Commission, on the other hand. Thus, 'under the old co-operation procedure, the Commission is entitled to "add its opinion" after a proposal's second reading in parliament, and before it is passed to the council. Under co-decision, the Commission's "opinion" stage may be by-passed altogether' (The European, *Maastricht Made Simple*, 1992, p. 31). Therefore, according to *The European*:

> The Commission and its opinions are largely excluded from the co-decision procedure. There are other ways that Maastricht favours the Parliament at the expense of the Commission .... Both the Commission and its president will be subjected to parliamentary approval.... In addition, parliament will be able to 'request' the Commission to submit any proposal where it decides, by absolute majority vote, that new legislation is required.   (Ibid., pp. 28–9)

But, as *The European* then points out, 'whether or not Parliament will have the right to initiate legislation (and thus whether or not Maastricht properly addresses the problem of "democratic deficit") depends entirely on the interpretation of the word "request"'. In this regard, *The European* raises the possibility of the democratic deficit remaining in place 'because the Commission may not interpret ["request"] as an "obligation", whereas the Parliament obviously would' (ibid., p. 29). Despite this caveat, *The European* stands convinced that the outcome of the Community's new decision and law-making procedure means that 'Parliament will ... gain power', bringing 'the workings of the EC closer to its citizens' (ibid., p. 29)[17]. Not all observers, however, are as convinced. Josephine Shaw, for instance, argues:

> It must be concluded that while the legislative process of the European Community is now vastly different and more complex than that established in the original Treaties, it is still strongly inter-governmental in nature. This contributes to the generally high level of secrecy which surrounds the law-making process, and to the absence of transparency. The increase in complexity has not overcome the lack of accountability on the part of the Council for the manner and type of decisions it takes. Community legal acts are bargained for and negotiated, rather than debated openly .... Significant areas of Community competence are still excluded from the new procedures, including agricultural policy, indirect taxation and the system of Community own resources, as well as the general legislative powers in Articles 100 and 235 EC ....The democratic deficit is only very partially offset by alternative mechanisms whereby different interests can ensure input into the legislative process. Although the intensity and effectiveness of lobbying in the Community has increased dramatically since the early 1980s, it remains only a partial substitute for a 'genuinely' democratic and legitimate legislative process. (Shaw, 1993, pp. 84–5)

This reference to the players and their power within the actual political process and political community through which decision and law-making takes place brings us back to the issue, in assessing the democratic deficit, of the part which is played by and available to the people and citizens of the new Union. The extent to which the attempt (however successful) to remould the *power profile* of the Parliament will contribute to filling the democratic deficit is dependent upon the degree of control that is exercised over the decision and law-making processes, and so over Parliament itself, by *the people and citizens* of the Union. The Commission has acknowledged this:

> The ordinary citizen is at the basis of the democratic process within the European Community. He or she has two direct votes. One is at national level when voters elect their national parliament and government. Ministers of this government then represent the country concerned in the EC Council of Ministers. The second comes when the electorates in all Member States choose the Members of the European Parliament. These European elections take places every five years. (Commission of the European Communities, *Strengthening Democracy in the EC,* 1993, p. 4)

In a footnote in the same document, the Commission alludes to a further way in which the participation of 'ordinary citizens' in *democratic process* through his or her voting rights in Parliamentary elections may be seen to have been boosted by the Maastricht Treaty: 'The Treaty ... gives all European citizens the same right to vote and stand for election in local and European elections in the country where they live as if they had been born in that country' (ibid., p. 8).

Thus, according to *The European*, following the final ratification of the Maastricht Treaty on 1 November 1993:

> every one of the 345 million individuals in the community will, in addition to their own nationalities, be citizens of the Union. The new concept is not intended to weaken existing national identities. It will bring new rights and benefits. Three of these are provided for in the Treaty. Firstly, as far as local and European elections are concerned, an EC citizen living in another EC country will be treated as a national of that country. This means that community citizens will be able to stand as candidates and vote in these elections (but not general elections) even if they live in an EC country other than their own .... Secondly, citizens of the Union will be able to raise any cases of alleged maladministration by an EC institution in the course of its activities with a Community ombudsman – a new post created by the Maastricht Treaty .... Finally, citizens of the Union will be able to enjoy wider diplomatic protection outside the com-

munity. The Maastricht Treaty provides that any EC citizen will be able to use the diplomatic and consular facilities of another EC country if travelling, working or living in a part of the world where his [sic] own country is not represented. (The European, *Maastricht Made Simple*, 1992, p. 10)

Several points and issues arise from this passage. First, the summary is confusing in its use of the terms 'citizenship' and 'nationality', appearing to apply the terms interchangeably. As we know, the two notions and statuses of 'citizenship' and 'nationality' are not necessarily identical. I have argued in favour of using the terms 'nationality' to refer to an individual's externally-oriented relationship with the state (apparatus) which lies at the core of that nation-state which accepts him or her as its 'national': that is, of his or her membership nation-state.[18] This approach allows us to reserve the term 'citizenship' for an individual's internally-oriented relationship with the same state. An individual's nationality status comes into play in his or her relations with those nation-states of which he or she is not a national – relations which thereby, in turn, bring nation-states into relationships with each other. Nationality does this by virtue of the rights, and so expectations, it brings to the individual in his or her dealings with nation-states; or, that is, by virtue of the obligations it brings to the state at the core of his or her membership nation-state. One such right is likely to be the kind of 'diplomatic protection' mentioned in the Maastricht Treaty's provisions on *Citizenship of the Union*. Under the Maastricht Treaty, all the nationals of all the Member States of the European Union have acquired the (universal) right to receive from all the Member States (equal) diplomatic protection in their (external) dealings with those nation-states of which they are not nationals.

However, being a national of a Member State does not necessarily mean being a citizen also. All the citizens of a Member State will be nationals of that Member State simply because being a national will be a preliminary condition (a pre-requisite) for citizenship. But the obverse does not follow. Being a national will be necessary for citizenship, but it will not be sufficient. Being a national will mean enjoying 'nationality rights' (including the right to diplomatic protection); and it will also mean enjoying various 'citizenship rights', such as to social benefits and services. But merely being a national will not by itself qualify an individual for the full range of citizenship rights within a Member State; and only when an individual (a national) enjoys the full range of citizenship rights granted and guaranteed by the state within his or her membership nation-state will that individual be a citizen. The further conditions which a national will be required to meet before he or she can enjoy the full range of citizenship rights, and so the status of citizenship, will be one concerning age. While nationals will enjoy certain citizenship rights during childhood and adolescence, they will not enjoy the full range of such rights until they have attained adulthood. Among the more important instances of citizenship rights is the right to vote. Not all nationals will have the right to vote, but all citizens will. What the Maastricht Treaty provisions on *Citizenship of the Union* do is to embellish the right to vote in local and European Parliament elections, as enjoyed by all the citizens (along with many nationals who have yet to reach full adulthood) of the Member States of the Union, with the right to vote in the same elections wherever they are residing within the Union.

While *The European*'s summary of the Maastricht Treaty's provisions under *Citizenship of the Union* lists what are referred to as three new rights and benefits, a second point or query about the summary is the way it fails to include that entitlement whereby 'Every citizen of the Union [is permitted] to move and reside freely within the territory of the Member States'. This is a major innovation of the Treaty, with important implications for the everyday lives, relationships and experiences of the people, citizens and nationals of the Member States of the European Union. It represents an expansion of the right which the citizens and many of the nationals of each Member State will already enjoy within the boundaries of that Member State; and a new right, which is extended not only to citizens but also to many people who are merely nationals – those people who are nationals but have not yet achieved citizenship. The right to move and reside freely can be counted as a 'citizenship right' on the grounds that it has been universally awarded to all adults, so that it is possessed equally (formally speaking) by all Member States citizens. In effect, the right to move and reside freely within the territory of the

Member States of the Union amounts to an extension of the same right as previously enjoyed by various *target populations* under the Single European Act and other Community legislation.

Here a third point about the summary by *The European* arises. The Maastricht Treaty's provisions include the right to move and reside freely irrespective of national boundaries; the right being awarded to all citizens and many nationals of the Member States; and awarded, moreover, to these people by virtue of the introduction of a new legal status, that of Citizenship of the Union. *The European* emphasises that Citizenship of the Union, or Euro-citizenship, has been established in addition to what we have distinguished as (following J. P. Gardner) 'national citizenship'. The Treaty's innovation is not merely to establish, expand or extend 'new citizenship' (along the lines of the United Nations' Universal Declaration of Human Rights, or the Council of Europe's Convention on Human Rights), but to begin the process of establishing a fresh set of citizenship rights attached to a novel, distinct and – crucially – supra-national citizenship status. The novelty of Citizenship of the Union, with its rights – and concomitant obligations on Member States – whereby 'national citizens' are permitted to move and reside freely without hindrance from nation-states, reflects the supra-national standing of the status. Accordingly, the status may be taken to reflect and reinforce the occurrence within the Union of a 'supra-national authority', or 'supra-national state': of a 'supra-state'. It may even be taken as confirmation and consolidation of the existence of the European Union as a *federal state.*

These possibilities invite clarification of the general meanings of, and relationships among, the notions of 'supra-national', 'federal' and 'state'. For Josephine Shaw, 'a supranational body' occurs when 'Power is transferred to a central authority which exists at a level above the nation state, and which exercises powers independently of the Member States' involved (Shaw, 1993, p. 11). Shaw further elucidates the meaning of the term 'supranational' by applying it specifically to the development of the European Community and Union. She tells us that 'supranationalism' (ibid., p. 12) can be associated with what she refers to as 'neo-functionalists', who 'advocate a more incremental and piecemeal approach to European integration' than do 'federalists' (ibid., p. 10). Shaw argues:

> Neo-functionalism underlay the decision of the founding fathers of the Community such as Jean Monnet and Robert Schuman to abandon grand federalist projects and to promote instead the adoption of the ECSC [European Coal and Steel Community] Treaty [of 1951], which concentrated simply on putting two strategically important commodities – coal and steel – into the hands of a central authority outside national control. Subsequently they supported the EEC [European Economic Community) Treaty [of 1957] which, in particular in its original form, had a remit limited to economic integration .... The idea behind neo-functionalism is that sovereign states may be persuaded in the interests of economic welfare to relinquish control over certain areas of policy .... However, [each] transfer of powers is viewed [by neo-functionalists] as just part of a continuing process. One level of integration will lead on to the next; a sectoral Treaty dealing with coal and steel leads on to a general Treaty covering all economic sectors .... This process is called 'spill-over' by neo-functionalists .... Spillover has also operated in the extension of the powers of the Community out of the purely 'economic' field into other related areas such as environmental and social policy. It has also fueled the debate about political union in the Community .... If the functionalist logic is followed to its conclusion the supranational authority will ... merge into [sic] a federal authority as more and more powers become increasingly separated from the nation state level. In this scenario the sovereign powers of the nation state are shared between the centre and its component parts, and power is exercised a the federal level not by the Member States, but by autonomous organs of the federation. (Shaw, 1993, pp. 10–11)

The sovereignty, or control over decision-taking and law-making of the Member States would be redistributed in accordance with the general principles of a 'federation' or 'federal union', this being the type of 'sovereign state where power is divided between a central authority and a number of regional authorities' (ibid., p. 10). The place and power of the Member States in a European Union organised as a federation would be reduced to that of a 'regional authority', at the most.[19] Examples of current federal states include those of Australia, Canada, Germany and the United States, as well as the former Soviet Union and Yugoslavia; and there are signs of others emerging, perhaps the principal examples in Europe being Belgium and Italy.

When it comes to the European Union, federalists advocate a

> transition to a sovereign United States of Europe. A single central body would ... assume responsibility for the core activities typically pursued by a federal authority: foreign policy, defence and security, external trade and representation in international organisations, management of the currency, macro-economic policy, and matters concerned with citizenship. Such a federal authority would incorporate the key features of the modern [Western, liberal] democratic state, including in particular a legislature elected on the basis of universal suffrage. A judicial authority would mediate conflicts within the federal authority and between the federal authority and the constituent states. (Ibid., p. 10)

Judged with reference to its participation in Shaw's *typical core activities*, there are impressive signs of the European Community and Union becoming, if not already being, a federal union. For instance, a Commission document published in April 1991 (Commission of the European Communities, *Europe: World Partner – The External Relations of the European Community*, April 1991) tells us :

> In some policy areas, like trade and agriculture, [the Community] has exclusive authority to act in place of and on behalf of its Member States. Other areas such as transport or the environment are spheres of 'mixed' responsibility, with the Community able to take decisions on some aspects while national governments retain – at least for the time being – responsibility for others. Certain areas of policy, such as defence, have hitherto lay outside the competence of the community altogether. (Ibid., p. 7)

A few months after the publication of this document, in December 1991, the Maastricht Treaty was agreed, thereby establishing 'new areas of Community "competence"' (The European, *Maastricht Made Simple*, 1992, p. 32), covering matters to do with education, 'culture', public health, trans-European networks, and the environment (ibid., pp. 32–3). These areas of competence are, of course, primarily of the internally-oriented type. Nevertheless, the Community's *internal competences*, perhaps especially those concerning economic matters, have considerable external relevance, and in turn (following Shaw) have major implications for the prospective supra-national and federal character of the Community. For instance, as claimed by the Commission with regard to the Community's connection with the General Agreement on Tariffs and Trade (GATT):

> Since its entry came into force in 1948, the GATT has become the principal instrument governing the conduct of world trade. It is both a code of rules and a forum in which negotiations and other trade discussions take place.... The Community has a special position in GATT. It is the Member States and not the Community as such which are contracting parties to the GATT agreement. But the Community is signatory to a number of international agreements concluded under the auspices of GATT. Because the Treaty of Rome gives the Community exclusive competence in the external trade matters of the Member States, it has established itself as a de factor contracting party, with the Commission as the sole negotiator and spokesman on behalf of its members. (Commission of the European Communities, *Europe: World Partner – The External Relations of the European Community*, April 1991, pp. 19–20)

However, the same document then alludes to the spill-over effect (as described by Shaw) of gradualist, supra-nationalism into the political field, and not only in an internally-oriented manner. Thus, by April 1991, almost 150 countries maintained 'diplomatic missions in Brussels accredited to the European Community. On its side, the Community has set up its own network of diplomatic missions abroad, currently consisting of 90 delegations and offices' (ibid., p. 33). Presumably, these missions will assist with the diplomatic protection granted to Citizens of the Union, following the Maastricht Treaty, in these citizens' dealings with nation-states beyond the boundaries of the new European Union.

The Commission's April 1991 document summarises by referring to the 'unique nature of the Community – more than an intergovernmental organization but less than a sovereign State – makes it specific international role more difficult. So does its basic constitution, the Treaty of Rome, which gives the Community wide economic powers but few political ones' (ibid., p. 6). On the other hand, the Maastricht Treaty, apart from extending the internal competences, as listed above, and establishing Citizenship of the Union, first of all contains provisions which have implications for the 'economic powers' of the Community, and thereby both for its external *de facto* responsibilities on behalf of the Community and for its supranational and federal qualifications (keeping in mind Shaw's list of 'typical core activities'):

> The Maastricht Treaty comes in two distinct parts. Political union is the first and most wide-ranging. Yet it is the second, covering economic and monetary union [EMU], which comes closest to meeting the federalist impulse. Whereas only hesitant, intergovernmental steps towards a common policy [and pillar] on such matters as foreign affairs and defence were eventually agreed, creation of a single currency becomes inevitable .... There are to be three stages .... At the heart of the strategy is the technical process of convergence .... At the centre [of the drive towards EMU] is an independent central bank much like the Bundesbank in its role. Called the European Central Bank, this will sit in a European System of Central Banks alongside the central banks of each member state. (The European, *Maastricht Made Simple*, 1992, p. 12)

As touched on by *The European*, the provisions of the Maastricht Treaty demonstrate a hesitancy on the part of the Member States to move as far or as fast – compared with what they have put in place with regard to economic matters – in the direction of greater 'federation' in the areas of foreign and security policy and home affairs and justice. The result being that the Treaty establishes these two areas as separate pillars of the Union, to be handled through the mechanism of inter-governmental co-operation, rather than through the kind of supra-national arrangements whereby the 'economic' (European Community) pillar is handled. None the less, these are, as *The European* also mentions, in a manner which is consistent with what Shaw identifies as the incremental and spill-over drift of European integration towards ever-greater, more inclusive, supra-national integration: 'Modest advances, perhaps, but leaving the door ajar for greater changes later on' (ibid., p. 21).

Furthermore – in line with Shaw's point about how a federal European Union would, if it were to be consistent with 'the traditions of Western liberal democracy' (Shaw, 1993, p. 11), incorporate a legislature elected on the basis of universal suffrage together with an *autonomous*, supra-national judicial authority – Shaw tells us:

> Within the Community, the European Parliament is in fact now a democratically elected body, but its legislative powers are minimal. Power in truth is exercised by the representatives of the governments of the Member States, meeting as the Council of Ministers [and the European Council]. Pressure to alter this situation in order to remedy a democratic deficit within the Community is understandable and logical from a functionalist perspective. (Ibid., p. 12)

Hence, the incremental provisions of the Maastricht Treaty vis-à-vis decision and law-making procedures, Parliamentary power, and (in particular, assisted by the rights attached to Citizenship of the Union) Parliamentary accountability. None the less, we might recall Shaw's conviction that even the Maastricht Treaty has only 'very partially offset' the democratic deficit; and that, overall, the European Community remains 'strongly inter-governmental' (ibid., pp. 84–5), as opposed to being supra-national and federal. Accordingly, the Community largely restricts itself to 'the types of activities more commonly undertaken by international organisations founded on Treaties ... characterised by co-operation between states rather than by the independent action of an autonomous body' (ibid., p. 12). Shaw summarises the applicability of the notion of 'supra-national' to the European Community and Union in the following way:

> the essence of supranationalism is found in a ... transfer of competences to the higher level, and in ... a distinctive form of decision-making at the higher level where ... decisions are taken on a majoritarian basis, rather than by consensus. This form (or aspect) of supranationalism has been termed 'decisional supranationalism'..., and has generally been an area in which the Community has been quite weak, at least until the changes in the decision-making process introduced by the Single European Act and more recently the Treaty of Maastricht. It can be distinguished from a specifically legal facet to the supranational nature of the Community, ... termed 'normative supranationalism'. This concerns the authority of the Court of Justice to give binding and authoritative rulings on the nature and effects of Community law, and to fashion a legal system in which Community law takes precedence over national law. In that respect, the Community has evolved more rapidly. (Ibid., p. 12)

Inter-governmentalism favours the retention of decision-making powers, and so if 'national sovereignty' (ibid., p. 12), at the Member State level; and accordingly favours 'a Community of states, or at the most a confederal union of states, in which [nation] state sovereignty is preserved' (ibid., p. 12). For Shaw, although the European Community and Union remains strongly inter-governmental overall, it has gone furthest along the path to becoming a supra-national and federal organisation specifically in its legal system, centred on the European Court of Justice. That is, although the Community is not 'explicitly termed a federation, ... its legal system now displays certain of the characteristics of a federal system' (ibid., p. 13). In this context, we might note first of all that there is 'little clear indication in the Treaties as to the exact relationship between Community law and national law and of the effect of Community law within the domestic legal systems of the Member States' (ibid., p. 14). This omission has, however, permitted the Court of Justice to play 'a pivotal role in the legal system' through the mechanism of its 'judicial pronouncements' (ibid., p. 13). Consequently, an important factor in determining the impact the Community's legal system within the Community overall has been the Court's commitment to the pursuit of integration through law'. Thus, the Court

> has consistently given a maximalist interpretation of the authority and effect of Community law, of the regulatory competence of the institutions and of its power to control both the institutions and the Member States to ensure that 'the law is observed' (Article 164 EC). (Ibid., pp. 13–14)

The Court has asserted that 'by accession to the Community the Member States have transferred sovereign rights to the Community, creating an autonomous legal system in which the subjects are not just states, but also individuals' (ibid., p. 14). The implication here, of course, is that the Community's legislation, including that concerning the single internal market and that contained in the provisions of the Maastricht Treaty (with regard to Citizenship of the Union, for instance), is directly applicable to, and binding upon, Member State citizens and nationals, notwithstanding how directives (as opposed to regulations) have to be transposed by Member States into national law. Shaw mentions how the Court of Justice's view about the transfer of Member State sovereignty to the Community is reflected in its articulation of four key legal principles (ibid., p. 14):

> Community law penetrates into the national legal systems, and can and must be applied by the national courts, subject to authoritative rulings on the interpretation, effect and validity of Community law by the Court of Justice; [second,] individuals may rely upon rules of Community law in national courts, as giving rise to rights which national courts are bound to protect (the principle of 'direct effect'); [third,] in order to guarantee the effectiveness of this structure, Community law takes precedence over conflicting national law, including national constitutional provisions (the principle of 'supremacy' or 'primacy'); [and fourth,] the organs and constituent bodies of the Member States, including the legislative, executive and judiciary, are fully respons-

ible for reversing the effects of violations of EC law which affect individuals. This may, for example, involve the courts ordering the government to pay damages for loss caused by breach of Community law.   (Ibid., pp. 14–15)

Member States, with the help of their constituent bodies, including in particular their national courts, are responsible not only for implementing Community legislation, but also for ensuring that any violation is corrected and that anyone suffering from a violation is compensated. Member States and their national courts exercise this responsibility at the insistence of the Court of Justice on behalf of the Community, and thereby act as a legal and judicial bridge between the Community (its legislation) and the individual (the national; the citizen) and his or her rights. In accordance with this principle, national courts are responsible for the 'indirect enforcement' of all Community legislation:

> The Court has given an extensive task to the national courts which are responsible for ensuring what is often termed 'indirect enforcement' of Community law at the instance of individuals. It has stressed the binding nature of Community law, including not only the Treaties themselves, but also those acts of the institutions (Regulations, Directives and Decisions), to which binding effects are ascribed in Article 189 EC. These can where appropriate be enforced by individuals in national courts.   (Ibid., p. 15)

The upshot is that whereas The Community makes laws – whereby, for instance, rights may be granted to people, nationals and citizens – Member States and their institutions, most notably national courts, are held to be responsible for implementing, guaranteeing and enforcing the legislation and rights, including those rights which distinguish the new status of Citizenship of the Union. While the Community and its institutions grant rights to people, it is the Member States which have incurred the obligation to ensure that those rights are honoured, guaranteed or enforced. If a Member State fails in this regard, individual nationals and citizens can seek correction and compensation through the Court of Justice. As reported by Shaw, according to 'Article 5 EC':

> Member States shall take all appropriate measures, whether general or particular, to ensure fulfilment of the obligations arising out of this Treaty or resulting from action taken by the institutions of the Community. They shall facilitate the achievement of the Community's tasks. They shall abstain from any measure which could jeopardize the attainment of the objectives of this Treaty.   (Ibid., p. 14)

Shaw is led to comment:

> This provision has been described ... as the key to the whole system of remedies which exist for the enforcement of Community law. In terms of specific enforcement procedures, Articles 169 and 170 EC make it possible for the Commission and other Member States to bring infringing Member States before the Court of Justice, and Article 171 EC gives the Court the power to make a declaration that there has been an infringement and requiring the Member State to take measures to put an end to the infringement. Financial penalties for non-compliance have been introduced by the Treaty of Maastricht. These measures allow for the 'direct enforcement' of Community law.   (Ibid., p. 15)

That is, these measures allow the Community, through its Court of Justice, to *directly* enforce Community legislation and rights, on behalf of individuals in general or in particular, by finding Member States at fault over their responsibilities for implementation and 'indirect enforcement', and perhaps by penalising or punishing such Member States. In sum, Shaw adds, the 'key to the structure of indirect enforcement lies in the organic connection between the Court of Justice and the national courts' (ibid., p. 15), whereby the enforcement of all Community law and rights, and with it the part these things play in people's everyday lives, 'depends for its effectiveness on cooperation between national courts and the Court of Justice' (ibid., p. 16).

For me, the question which arises, however, is 'can this key process of co-operation be guaranteed, given the pattern of interests, principles and power which characterises the overlapping political communities within the European Community at the national and supra-national levels?' Shaw alludes to the possibility that it cannot. For instance, the way the Court of Justice, in accordance with *the principle of supremacy or primacy*, expects national courts to apply Community law in preference to national law 'gives rise to some difficulty in the context of the UK where the principle of [national] parlimentary sovereignty leads judges conventionally to regard themselves as subordinate to the will of Parliament' (ibid., p. 16). Nevertheless, Shaw asserts that:

> the Court [of justice] has constructed a system which comes close to power conventionally held by the supreme court in a federal system, namely the power to invalidate state legislation which contravenes the federal constitution. (Ibid., p. 16)

Despite this, Shaw's opinion on whether the Community is therefore already 'federal' along with supra-national is left unclear and ambiguous. On the one hand, the Court of Justice has been behind the construction of a legal and judicial system which is not only supra-national but also federal in character. This might be taken to be enough to warrant the application of the label 'federal' to the Community as a whole, in view of (a) they way in which its ('federal') Court plays a determining, even *deciding*, role in constructing the Community-wide legal and judicial system; combined with (b) the degree to which the overall shape of the Community is determined by its legislation, and accordingly its Court. But, on the other hand, as we have noted, for Shaw, 'decisional supranationalism', judged with reference to the decision and law-making processes which operates by way of the Council, Commission and Parliament, is weak, at least relatively speaking. Shaw implies that decisional supra-nationalism may have been given a boost by the provisions of the Single European Act and the Maastricht Treaty (ibid., p. 12). None the less, Shaw argues, the Community beyond its legal system remains characterised not so much by federalism, or even supra-nationalism, as by inter-governmentalism. For Shaw, we might recall again, despite the SEA and Maastricht, the European Community overall 'is still strongly inter-governmental' (ibid., p. 84) – an assertion with resounding echoes of Will Hutton's claim that 'political power in Europe remains firmly with the nation states of the Union' (Hutton, 10 December 1993).

This conclusion takes us back, also, to Shaw's point about how the system of enforcing the laws and rights decided by the Community, and thereby the legal system per se, hinges on national courts co-operating with the principles and requirements set out by the Court of Justice. In so far as the overlapping political communities within the European Community are characterised not just by competing principles and interests, but also by a distribution of power which remains firmly tipped towards the nation-state, then a considerable question mark hangs over the federal credentials even of the Community's legal system – something which therefore underscores a similar doubt about the Community as a whole. This has important implications for citizenship, including by way of Citizenship of the Union, and so, for people's everyday lives within the European Community and Union, not only at present but for the foreseeable future.

The occurrence of 'supra-national citizenship' as a distinct legal status within the European Union will depend upon the accompanying, and moreover the prior, occurrence of a 'supra-national body' which exists at a level above the Member State level, and which has the 'authority' – the legitimate, autonomous power – to establish this status, and accordingly to grant, and in some way or another to guarantee or enforce, distinct (supra-national) rights. These supra-national rights or entitlements will be awarded universally (to all Member State national citizens or adults) on a formally equal basis, albeit by way of any necessary and obligatory transposition (of the directives involved) at the Member State level. The rights will reflect, symbolise and confirm the authority of the supra-national body which grants them, and they will be exercised by individuals without prevention from the Member States. The occurrence of supra-national citizenship within the Union will mean that any individual who enjoys the citizenship rights entailed will have a direct, internally-oriented relationship with the supra-national, granting (and ultimately guaranteeing or enforcing) body; and therefore a relationship which by-passes and supersedes the authority and sovereignty of the Member States. Connectedly, it will mean that the individual will enjoy rights which will not merely supplement, but will also take precedence over, his or her national citizenship rights. This latter feature will be important to people's everyday lives in the event of any inconsistency, clash or conflict between their national citizenship rights, and their supra-national citizenship rights.

In the case of the European Community and Union, the most likely candidates for supra-national citizenship rights are those granted in conjunction with the introduction of Citizenship of the Union under the Maastricht Treaty itself. Of course, as we have considered, the issue arises as to whether even the Community represents, or at least foreshadows, the kind of supra-national body and authority which are necessary for supra-national citizenship and its associated rights to be both established and secured. There is the possibility that the Community lacks, and will continue to lack, the necessary supra-national authority because of the way decision and law-making power, and so sovereignty, are held firmly in the grip of the Member States due to the preferences, policies and practices pursued at this level.

Having said this, however, for me, (a) there is a strong chance of the European Union gradually becoming more of a supra-national and federal organisation; and (b) in any case, even the slimmest prospect of a European supra-national federation – or, of a European supra-state – invites speculation as to the most appropriate citizenship model for accommodating, analysing and making sense of the actual patterns and trends of citizenship within the European Union.

For me, the Maastricht Treaty's introduction of Citizenship of the Union lends itself to the evolution of three distinct, inter-related and shifting tiers – 'horizontal dimensions' – of the European Union's scheme or system of citizenship. Accordingly, I wish to outline a model of citizenship for the purpose of representing, analysing and interpreting European Union citizenship which stresses the pervasive and dynamic importance not just of struggle and conflict within the prevailing (decision and law-making) political communities, but also of contradictions between the different tiers which constitute the system itself. The model bears some resemblance to, and overlaps with, another tripartite model of European citizenship – that recently presented by Maurice Roche (Roche, 1992). Roche argues that, in modern Europe, citizenship in general, and social citizenship in particular, operates at and between three (what I will refer to as) *geo-political levels*:

Europeans in the 1990s will continue to be simultaneously both united and divided in their political loyalties and identities ... according to the three factors of locality (the ethnicity and 'nationhood' of city and region), nationality and Europeanness. But post-1992, economic, social and possibly political integration and federalism, a United States of Europe, will give historically unprecedented form to this traditional complexity of political experience .... In the EC context [there] has been ... the simultaneous growth in size and importance of the transnational EC level itself and also of EC regions at the subnational level. Both levels offer people forms of general citizenship and of social citizenship in addition to their national citizenship. Circuits of citizenship capable of bypassing the nation-state were created with the Treaty of Rome – circuits on the one hand between EC citizens ... and the EC political and legal institutions, and on the other hand between the latter and local (urban and regional) governments. These circuits and relationships have often been filtered and detoured through the national government level. But there is every probability that increasingly in the post-1992 [Single European Act] era they will become relatively independent of the national level and will grow in scale, complexity and importance. These political and social changes will require a rethinking not only of traditional national citizenship but also of the nature and balance of rights and duties of individuals and collectivities within and between all three of the political levels: local, national and European .... This new complexity in the circuits of citizenship has implications for the future of social citizenship in Europe.   (Ibid., pp. 218–19)

The three-level, geo-political perspective on European development has received support from elsewhere. Thus, Chistopher Harvie reports how, in June 1991, the United States Secretary of State, James Baker, noted:

Perhaps the most striking phenomenon across all of Europe today ... is 'the combined and simultaneous evolution and devolution of the nation-state.' While the nation-state remains the most significant political unit ... 'its political role is being increasingly supplemented by both supra-national and sub-national units.' Some of the nation-state's functions are being delegated 'upward' ... and others 'downward'. (Harvie, February 1993)

The most likely repository of any upward redistribution of political power away from the 'nation-state' within Europe is, of course, the European Community and Union. Certainly, the Community is what John Palmer has in mind when he asserts that 'the odds are getting shorter on the emergence of a federal-style European union by the end of the decade' (Palmer, 25 February 1993). Palmer elaborates by arguing that 'while the shape of European politics for the rest of the decade is unclear, there are unmistakable and synergetic trends to both greater regional self-government and greater European union'. There is a *synergetic* process under way entailing a 'combination of more European (and global) supra-nationalism and greater devolution of power to the regions and local communities'. For instance:

Belgium may break up into two self-governing regional mini-estates before long, and Italy seems headed in the same direction. France and Spain are moving in their own ways more and more to the German federal model in which the political bonds between the regions and the future European union will be as important as those between the EC and the existing nation states at present. It is a trend which has not gone unnoticed in Edinburgh and Cardiff. (Palmer, ibid.)

The views of James Baker and John Palmer are consistent with the expectation, and for some the fear, that the EU Member States are involved in a process whereby their sovereignty is being *synergetically* diverted in favour of both sub-national (regional, local) political communities and a supra-national political organisation or community; where the latter is, moreover, a federal union or state.

I wish to argue that while this kind of synergetic process may well be taking place, it does not follow that it is therefore appropriate to adopt the kind of three-level geo-political model of European citizenship suggested by Roche; or, for that matter, to adopt any kind of geo-political model of European citizenship. This is not to say that Roche's model does not contain certain important clues as to a sociologically more appropriate and useful model. Thus, Roche fleetingly touches on the possibility that the relationships and circuits among what he sees as the three geo-political levels of European citizenship will become increasingly characterised by not just complexity, but also 'contradiction and ... conflict (which calls for political management and reconciliation)' (Roche, 1992, p. 5). In this regard, Roche's view of the development and future of citizenship is similar to that of another prominent writer on citizenship patterns and trends, although in this case within a frame of reference which is much broader than the European Community and Union. Thus, according to Bryan Turner:

> The contemporary world is structured by two contradictory social processes. On the one hand, there are powerful pressures towards regional autonomy and localism and, on the other, there is a stronger notion of globalism and global political responsibilities. The notion of citizenship is therefore still in a process of change and development. We do not possess the conceptual apparatus to express the idea of global membership, and in this context a specifically national identity appears anachronistic. (Turner, 1990, pp. 211–12)

Turner adds:

> We may in conclusion indicate two possible lines of the theoretical development of the (western) notion of citizenship. The first would be the conditions under which citizenship can be formed in societies which are ... constituted by the problems of ethnic complexity (such as Brazil), and the second would be an analysis of the problems which face the development of global citizenship as the political counterpart of the world economy. (Ibid., p. 213)

The view taken by both Turner and Roche of recent and continuing citizenship trends assumes (a) a shift away from a simple, uni-dimensional, national pattern of citizenship towards a more complex, multi-dimensional – national, sub-national and trans-national, even global – system; and (b) the presence of societally and historically important, and so sociologically (theoretically) significant, contradictions among the emergent dimensions or levels of citizenship: contradictions which feed into and drive the continuing progress of the multi-dimensional system of what might be described as the 'post-national' phase of citizenship.

The view taken by Turner and Roche of the development of citizenship through its late-twentieth-century post-national phase shows considerable similarities with an earlier account of the previous phase, during which national citizenship was established, expanded and extended in a gradual manner covering several stages. This earlier account similarly focuses on how a simple, uni-dimensional stage of citizenship gave way to subsequent, increasingly complex, multi-dimensional stages; and furthermore stresses the pivotal part played in the transitions by contradictions. The account I have in mind here is, of course, T. H. Marshall's. As we can recall, Marshall's analysis of the long-term historical emergence, expansion and extension of the system of national citizenship hinges on the identification of three separate dimensions of citizenship (rights) – namely the civil, the political and the social dimensions. Marshall argued that during the eighteenth century there was the advent of modern (national) citizenship in conjunction with the emergence of civil citizenship rights. This stage was followed in the nineteenth century by a second stage, distinguished by the growth of political rights; and finally, in the twentieth century, by a third stage, marked by the expansion of social rights. As we know, J. M. Barbalet, among others, has since argued that the third stage has seen, also, an expansion of industrial rights; and I have proposed that social rights and industrial rights be collectively referred to as 'welfare rights'.

Therefore, Marshall, like Barbalet (not to mention Giddens), focuses on the empirical distinctions between, and historical unfolding of, what I will call the three or four 'vertical dimensions' of modern citizenship. But what Roche and Turner have gone on to pay attention to are the distinctions between and development of a further set of dimensions of citizenship – that is, the 'horizontal dimensions'; and so, that set which is a prominent and distinguishing feature of the patterns and trends of citizenship in its post-national phase. This difference in approaches aside, however, the way in which Roche and Turner emphasise the part played by contradictions in the post-national phase of citizenship closely resembles the way in which Marshall portrays and accounts for the patterns and trends of the national phase. Thus:

> At the heart of Marshall's account of citizenship lies the contradiction between the formal political equality of the franchise and the persistence of extensive social and economic inequality, ultimately rooted in the character of the capitalist market place and the existence of private property. Marshall proposed the extension of citizenship as the principal political means for resolving, or at least containing, those contradictions. (Ibid., p. 191)

As we have already noted, Marshall was concerned with how the

> issue of who can practise citizenship and on what terms is not only a matter of the legal scope of citizenship and the formal nature of the rights entailed in it. It is also a matter of the non-political capacities of citizens which derive from the social resources they command and to which they have access. A political system of equal citizenship is in reality less equal if it is part of a society divided by unequal conditions. (Barbalet, 1988, p. 1)[20]

Or, as Marshall himself puts it, it is 'reasonable to expect that the impact of citizenship on social class should take the form of a conflict between opposing principles' (quoted in Barbalet, ibid., p. 8). Such 'conflict' – or, following Turner, 'contradictions' (see also Barbalet, pp. 919) – then acts as the impetus behind societal change, apparently towards a reconciliation of the 'conflict', or a resolution of the 'contradictions', perhaps in something of a *politically managed* fashion (Roche, 1992, p. 5), through the expansion and extension of citizenship (rights).[21] If so, presumably, for the time being we can expect the continued extension and expansion of citizenship rights, in a way which is driven and motivated by the persistence of contradictions between (i) formally equal citizenship rights and (ii) unequal distributions of conditions, opportunities and capacities (rooted in what I have referred to as 'enabling resources') among citizens. The result of such contradictions is that citizens are unequally able to realise, enjoy and experience their formally equal citizenship rights; which thereby helps to sustain and shape the struggles and conflicts within political communities over both citizenship rights and enabling resources; and which in turn contributes to the resolution of the contradictions. However, guided again by Turner and Roche, the possibility arises that, because of the particular pattern of citizenship within the post-national phase, there will be not merely the persistence but also the exacerbation and augmentation of contradictions. This follows from the way in which the transition from the national phase to the post-national phase is marked by the onset of a more complex, multi-level system of citizenship.

At this point, however, a further difference between the approach of Marshall and that of Turner and Roche emerges. As Barbalet points out, 'in *Citizenship and Social Class* Marshall is concerned with the antagonisms between citizenship and social class rather than with the contradictions within citizenship itself' (Barbalet, 1988, p. 19). Marshall was interested in what might be described as 'the vertical contradictions' – or 'antagonisms' or 'conflicts of principles' – between (i) the universal distribution of formally equal citizenship rights and (ii) the unequal distribution of enabling resources. These 'contradictions' will variously impinge upon the everyday lives, relationships and experiences of citizens in accordance with the way enabling resources are unequally distributed by not just social class, but also race-ethnicity, sex-gender, age-generation and so on.

The alternative as implied by Barbalet, is to pay attention to the presence and importance of contradictions within the system of citizenship itself, and so between the various dimensions of which the system is composed. Thus, there is the issue of the contradictions among the vertical dimensions (such as between civil rights and social rights); but there is also the issue of the contradictions among what, in the post-national phase of the historical development of citizenship, have emerged as the horizontal dimensions or levels or tiers of citizenship. In a sense, Roche and Turner have brought Marshall's analysis up to date by addressing *the realm of emergent, perhaps gathering, horizontal contradictions within citizenship itself*; the contradictions among the separate horizontal dimensions of citizenship rights, which for Roche translates as the contradictions between geo-political levels. The possibility arises of such 'horizontal contradictions' compounding and invigorating the drive behind the further progression of post-national citizenship.

However, I contend that Roche's particular three-level model, especially by virtue of its geo-political orientation, is afflicted by certain analytical difficulties which invite a basic modification leading to an alternative, tripartite model of post-national European citizenship: a model which is not so much geo-politically as socio-politically oriented. The difficulties with Roche's model concern the political sources of citizenship rights and status, and the locations of this sources within Europe – issues which have to be satisfactorily addressed by any model. The difficulties stem from the conceptual, institutional and historical links between 'citizenship' and 'the state'. In a similar way to Roche's model, the model I have in mind is informed by the observation that late-twentieth-century European society is undergoing a process of integration around the progress of the European Community and Union, which in turn is being increasingly organised along supra-national and federal lines. In effects, the EU is moving inexorably towards the consolidation of a European suprastate. But the model I wish to recommend is equally informed by the observation that there is no parallel or equivalent (and so competing, antagonistic or contradictory) development under way at the sub-national level of European society. Essentially, in so far as Roche's geo-politically oriented three-level model of European citizenship rests on evidence for the existence or emergence of a European-wide, separate sub-national level of 'the state' as the source of a distinctive set of citizenship rights, then the necessary evidence is lacking. While Roche's model has itself a major socio-political aspect; while Roche implies the conceptual, institutional and historical dependency of 'citizenship' on 'the state'; while 'the state' has a presence in various way and forms at the sub-national level within Europe; none the less, there is no convincing evidence that what is emerging or in the offing is a sub-national level of 'the state' which is of the form and the extent required for the occurrence of a distinct level or tier of

European-wide citizenship (as opposed to merely legal) rights which are accordingly universally possessed by all the adults or national citizens of all the Member States. What exists, and is likely to persist, at the sub-national level is a highly varied, uneven patchwork of political bodies, communities and forms which are both variously similar (but not identical) to, and variously empirically or institutionally related to, 'the sate' as it exists at the national level throughout Europe, on the one hand, and as it is emerging at the supra-national level by virtue of the European Community and Union, on the other hand. This patchwork is not the location of a European-wide level or tier of citizenship alongside (or underneath) national and the supra-national levels or tiers, and there is no evidence which convincingly leads to the conclusion that it is in the process of becoming such a source.

An examination of the meaning and presence of 'the state', together with clarification of the conceptual, institutional and historical links between 'the state' and 'citizenship', invites us to abandon Roche's three-level geo-political model of late-twentieth-century European citizenship (especially in that it assumes a sub-national level of European Citizenship), in favour of a socio-politically (socio-legally or institutionally) oriented three-tier or track model. The model I have in mind is constructed around the proposition that during the late-twentieth-century, post-national phase of citizenship, there are across the European Union three politically distinct, Union-wide tiers of European Citizenship, two of which occur at the level of the European Community and Union as a political community itself.

Tier I European Citizenship occurs at the Member State level of the European Union and corresponds to 'national citizenship'. Within the context of the Union, it is appropriate to refer to this tier of citizenship as Member State Citizenship. It entails a spectrum of citizenship rights which are clustered within the three or four vertical dimensions – civil, political and welfare (or social and industrial). At the same time, following J. P. Gardner (1991), Tier I European Citizenship is being increasingly shaped by 'new citizenship' through such international agreements as the United Nations, Universal Declaration of Human Rights (1948) and the European Convention on Human Rights (1950), and such supporting organisation as the International Court of Justice (the Hague) and the European Court of Human Rights (Strasbourg). Furthermore, this tier of European Citizenship is being increasingly infused with that 'new citizenship' which is embodied in the Treaties, legislation and rights arrived at and supported by the European Community and Union. In other words, Tier I European Citizenship is being increasingly determined by Tier II European Citizenship.

Tier II European Citizenship, in contrast with Member State Citizenship, takes the form of a category, status and set of rights which are awarded 'universally' across the European Union; and accordingly occurs at the level of the European Union, within which it represents 'new citizenship'. Tier II European Citizenship may be referred to as 'European Union New Citizenship', or simply 'European New Citizenship'. It exists in so far as the European Union creates citizenship rights which are, in the first instance, distinct from Tier I European Citizenship rights; and which at the same time are in place without, before or beyond the establishment of a distinct category and status of European Citizenship, as exemplified by the Maastricht Treaty's Citizenship of the Union. In other words, Tier II European Citizenship rights are not attached to a distinct citizenship category and status above Member State Citizenship. European New Citizenship rights include those granted under the heading of 'equal opportunities' by sex-gender (although the legislation involved may refer specially to women). Thus:

> EC ministers [have] agreed directives – laws transposed into Member States' legislation – on equal pay in 1975, and on equal treatment in access to employment, training, promotion and working conditions in 1976. Equal treatment in social security, as well as for the self-employed, complements this legislation. Rights to maternity leave and pay, and a guarantee to adequate health and safety at work for pregnant women and nursing mothers were agreed in 1992. Ministers have agreed recommendations and resolutions intended to encourage good practice on: positive action, vocational training, childcare, combating unemployment, equal opportunities in schools, integrating women into working life, combating unwanted sexual behaviour at work, educa-

tion, and updating protective legislation affecting women. The European Court of Justice ... has played an important part in developing the jurisprudence in which equality policies are carried out through its contribution to case law. (Commission of the European Communities, *Equal Opportunities for Women in the Community*, 1993, p. 3)

An example of where the Tier II European Citizenship rights contained within the Union's directives on sex-gender equality are transposed into Tier I European Citizenship is touched on by Stephen Castle and Robert Chote in their reference to the UK:

The retirement age for women will be raised to 65 .... The equalisation of male and female pension ages [is] due to be announced this week .... The move will be unpopular with women, who currently have the right to retire at 60, but fits in with government attempts to reduce welfare spending. Harmonisation of retirement age is required under European law. (Castle and Chote, November 1993)

Another possible instance of a range of Tier II European Citizenship rights is that contained in the legislation leading to the single internal market, and in particular that which is designed to facilitate 'the freedom of movement of people' within this market. However, as I have mentioned previously, in so far as these rights are targeted on selected sections only of the adult population, rather than being granted universally to all adults, a question mark hangs over whether to count them as 'citizenship' rights.

Recalling Josephine Shaw's argument about the intergovernmental character of European Community decision and law-making, especially that which takes place outside the legal system centred on the Court of Justice, Tier II European Citizenship, being 'new citizenship', may be developed through inter-governmental institutions. But its foundation will be enhanced in so far as it is developed through supranational institutions, authority and decisions such as (following Shaw) those which already characterise the legal system. Tier III European Citizenship, however, is categorically dependent for its existence on the presence of supra-national institutions. Again, this tier occurs at the European Union level, but in a way which is separate from not only 'national citizenship', but also 'new citizenship'. It occurs by virtue of the establishment of a distinct category and status of European citizenship, the Maastricht Treaty's Citizenship of the Union, attached to which are specific universal citizenship rights, such as the right to live and move anywhere within the territory of the Union, irrespective of national boundaries and unhindered by national institutions. This level of citizenship may be referred to as European Union Supra-citizenship.

The three-tier or track model of European Citizenship I am proposing allows for the possibility not only of the pattern of citizenship rights at each tier being constantly in flux, but also of the patterns changing at different speeds, in different directions and perhaps contradictorily. A possible example here concerns the relationship between Member State Citizenship and European New Citizenship by way of sex-gender legislation and rights. Whereas throughout Europe, over several decades, women have been making advances in their legal rights relative to men,[22] Tier II European Citizenship legislation concerned with, for instance, equalising retirement ages and pensions, has entailed somewhat contradictory development by virtue of the way it is being transposed at Member State level by raising the age at which women have the right to retire and receive 'state' pensions.

In the light of my earlier discussion, such contradictions will provide a 'self-resolving' dynamic impetus. However, if so, this will occur within the context of, or mediated by, the struggles and conflicts of overlapping political communities which, for me, favour the ascendency of, in particular, the political community, struggles and conflicts which occur specifically at the European Union level, and so, which favour the redistribution of sovereignty away from the Member State level to the EU level; and which thereby favour the consolidation and importance of the two European Union tiers of citizenship as opposed to Member State Citizenship. For me, in the long term, the contradictory relationships between the three tiers of European Citizenship will be driven towards a resolution which – by virtue of the pattern and elevation of the power, principles and interests which characterise the specifically European Union political community – favours European Union Supra-citizenship at the expense of the other two tiers of European Citizenship. This view implies and anticipates the unstoppable progress of the European Union towards a supra-national organisation; towards a federal union or United States of Europe (see Roche, 1992, ch. 8; and Wistrich, 1989, 1994); towards the establishment of state apparatus at the level of the European Union, and so, above the state, at Member State level; towards the Union's consolidation as a 'supra-state'.

Here we can recall that for Maurice Roche, in a contradictory fashion, Europeans will continue to be simultaneously both united and divided in their political loyalties and identities according to three factors of locality (Roche, 1992, pp. 218–19); and similarly for Turner the modern world is structured by two contradictory social processes: powerful pressures towards regionalism and localism; countered by even stronger pressures towards globalism. Even though these propositions may well be valid, I have suggested abandoning a geo-political model of modern, European (if not 'world') citizenship, to be substituted with a socio-political, or institutional, model; while nevertheless retaining Roche's and Turner's emphasis on the part played by contradictions in the overall scheme and evolution of European citizenship.

My view has some similarities with Allan Williams's, which stresses the pivotal part played in the development of the European Community and Union by economic considerations, reflecting the way these considerations have priority over – and so, consequently, have major shaping implications for – social and political ones (Williams, 1991). Thus, after pointing out that 'the central logic behind much of the long term evolution of the Community has been the requirements of capital accumulation', Williams asserts that therefore it 'was inevitable that the largely capital-driven process of integration would engender serious contradictions' (ibid., p. 112). Williams distinguishes two sets of contradictions, the first of which brings to mind what T. H. Marshall regarded as the basic vertical contradiction associated with the development of the nation-state pattern of citizenship. That is, for Williams, one 'set of contradictions [is] centred on the balance between growth and the distributional aims of the EC' (ibid., p. 12).

Williams lists for such contradictions: (i) the 'creation of a single market tends to favour large-scale capital ... contrary

to the EC's avowed aims of fostering competition';
(ii) 'Economic growth has been accompanied by the continuance or deepening of social inequalities within the EC. As these are endemic to capitalist societies, there are limitations to the extent to which the EC ... can modify such inequalities';
(iii) 'Regional inequalities have been widespread within the EC ... largely because [they] are endemic to capitalist economies. Indeed they are an essential prerequisite of continued capital accumulation', the 'single minded pursuit of economic goals has inevitably brought the policies of the EC into conflict with environmental objectives' (ibid., p. 12). Williams argues that these contradictions 'will be deepened by the 1992 Single Market programme with its emphasis on large markets, productivity and competitiveness' (ibid., pp. 12–13). Essentially, while the EC remains 'a champion of private capital, and while it is locked into a system of global interdependence, the scope for redistributional policies or for constraints on the actions of capital will be limited' (ibid., p. 13).

Williams's summary of what he identifies as the contradictions centred on the relationship between (a) the European Community's capitalist priorities, purposes, demands and constraints, and (b) its distributional policies (by social class, for instance), contains clear echoes of Marshall's concern with the 'vertical contradictions' associated with the development of national citizenship. But what Williams distinguishes as the second set of contradictions generated by the economic, or more precisely the capitalistic, priorities of the Community is regarded by him as being the 'most important' (ibid., p. 11). This second set may be contrasted with the first in that it is composed of what I have labelled 'horizontal contradictions' of the kind which pervade the relationships between the institutional (political, economic) levels of the European Community and Union. That is, this

> set of contradictions centre[s] on the institutions of the EC and its system of governance. The political organisation of the EC is unique although, in essence, it is a form of intergovernmentalism. Power is divided between three bodies: the European Commission, the Council of Ministers (Heads of national governments)[23] and the European Parliament. The balance of power has shifted over time but, ultimately,

has largely rested with the Council of Ministers, with the
Commission having a secondary role. (Ibid., p. 11)

This view of decision-making within the Community confirms
Shaw's similar point about the predominance of inter-
governmentalism, rather than supra-nationalism or federalism.
According to Williams, the institutional contradictions involved stem from 'the limitations of intergovernmentalism,
that is of joint decision-making by the member states rather
than a single federal body. By the early 1980s decision-making
in the EC was characterised by minimalism' (ibid., p. 11). This
is because the decisions made on behalf of the EC, in particular by 'the Council', were constantly and considerably constrained by 'the requirement of satisfying the national
aspirations of *all* its member states' (ibid., p. 11). Here, we can
recall the similar point made by *The European* about how the
'unanimous voting system' laid down under Article 100 of the
Treaty of Rome meant that, eventually, the Member States *could
agree on almost nothing at all*; how, as a result, the 'co-operation
procedure', entailing the qualified majority voting system, was
introduced by the Single European Act of 1987; how subsequently this method of Council decision-making has been the
one whereby *the great majority of EC law has come to be made*; and
how the use of this method has been extended under the
terms of the Maastricht Treaty of 1991 (The European,
Maastricht Made Simple, 1992, pp. 30–1). Perhaps here is an
example of the way in which horizontal, institutional contradictions within the European Union and Community act as a
driving force behind their own resolution through appropriate
changes at and between the different socio-political levels.

Williams touches on the way the institutional contradictions
he identifies (vis-à-vis political decision-making) determine
both (a) the (changing) relationships among the institutional,
or socio-political, levels themselves, as well as (b) the changing
and expanding relationships between the various areas of
European Community (now Union) activity and competence,
in particular the political, economic and 'social' (or social
policy and welfare) areas. Thus:

> The political contradictions of integration for the EC stem
> from the ambiguities of its decision-making process in the

face of an expanding range of ... economic and social policies, especially in consequences of the 1992 [single internal market] programme. There [have] been growing pressures for greater political integration ... [leading to the] provision of majority voting in the Single European Act .... However, ... many social, environmental and taxation matters are still subject to unanimous voting .... Any shift to greater monetary integration and or [sic] a European Central Bank will also require some transfer of powers from individual states to the centre of the EC. There is therefore pressure, resulting from the 1992 programme and the Single European Act, for greater political union in order to provide more rapid and effective decision making at the centre of the EC. (Ibid., p. 152)

On the one hand, there is the pressure of the economic priorities of the Community in favour of increasing political union, and so, supra-nationalism and even 'federalism' (ibid., p. 152). On the other hand, 'Against this, there are still strongly entrenched national interests and a reluctance to countenance further losses of national sovereignty' (ibid., p. 152). Essentially, therefore, the 'contradiction for the EC is how to reconcile an increasingly-harmonized economic space and integrated economic policy-making with a still largely fragmented political space' (ibid., p. 152).

However, at this point, Williams might have mentioned the possibility of this fundamental contradiction within the European Community, between (a) its economically driven supra-nationalism and federalism and (b) its 'politically' driven nationalism (and perhaps to some extent sub-nationalism), being – because it is a contradiction – self-resolving. Perhaps what is already under way is a process of reconciliation, mediated by the ever-increasing prominence of the political community which is specific to the Community and Union, and entailing the ascendency of supra-nationalism and federalism. Again, this possibility is given some credibility – with an eye to Williams's point about the implications of *growing pressures for greater political integration and the provision of majority voting* – by the introduction of qualified majority voting through the Single European Act; and of the co-decision procedure through the Maastricht Treaty.[24]

The prospect of a supra-national, federal European Union implies the development of 'the state' at the European Union level, and so, above 'the state' at the Member State level. It implies, in other words, the emergence of a European supra-state. The issue of whether the European Union is – or at least is becoming – a supra-state is of crucial importance to the further issue of whether, at the same time, the Union is creating supra-national citizenship. This follows from an examination of the conceptual, institutional and historical relationship between 'citizenship' and 'the state'. Citizenship rights are not only arrived at by way of struggle and conflict within political communities; they also facilitate membership of such communities; or, as Maurice Roche puts it: 'Citizenship refers to membership in a political–legal community' (Roche, 1992, p. 3). In a similar way, Barbalet tells us that 'Citizenship ... defines those who are, and who are not, members of a common society. Citizenship is a manifestly political enterprise' (Barbalet, 1988, p. 1). Barbalet acknowledges how, in this regard, his notion of citizenship is similar to T. H. Marshall's conceptualisation, in that both are 'entirely conventional. [Marshall says, firstly, that citizenship is a status attached to full membership of a community, and secondly, that those who possess this status are equal with respect to the rights and duties associated with it' (ibid., p. 5); or, for Marshall:

> Citizenship is a status bestowed on those who are full members of a national community, and citizens rights, therefore, are those which derive from and facilitate participation in this 'common possession', as Marshall [Marshall, 1950, p. 92] calls it.   (Ibid., p. 18)

Roche similarly acknowledges how his notion of citizenship is consistent with Marshall's, and in doing so touches on an aspect of Marshall's approach which rounds out and firms up the political character and basis of citizenship:

> For Marshall, citizenship in general involves an equality of membership status and of ability to participate in a society, and it refers to what the society collectively acknowledges as legitimate and enforceable citizens' rights in respect of the various elements of the concept.   (Roche, 1992, p. 19)

The point here is that for Marshall, Roche and Barbalet, citizenship is 'political' in that it is a status attached to which there are rights (a) which are arrived at through struggles and conflicts within political communities; (b) which, while covering more than political rights, generally facilitate membership of a 'political community'; and (c) which, furthermore, are granted, guaranteed or enforced within the same 'political community' by that political apparatus which is otherwise known as 'the state'. As Barbalet expressed it, citizenship rights are 'Legally constituted rights ... enforced by public authorities' (Barbalet, 1988, p. 16), which means that

> Citizenship rights, as the rights of persons in the community of a nation-state, will ultimately be secured by the state ... Citizenship rights impose certain limitations on the state's sovereign authority. In this vein H. R. G. Greaves [1966, p. 185] says that citizenship rights 'may be better called the duties of the state to its members'. [Citizenship] rights ... constrain the state. (Ibid., p. 18)

In other words, empirically, politically, institutionally or structurally, 'the different component rights of modern citizenship are ... guaranteed by the state' (ibid., p. 21); and historically, 'the emergence of citizenship' is linked to and dependent upon the accompanying and prior emergence of 'the modern nation-state' (ibid., p. 5). Historically the existence and development of citizenship is dependent upon the antecedent existence and development of the state; or the existence of citizenship, either at any historical moment or at any level, is politically, institutionally or structurally dependent upon and determined by the state at the very same moment or level. Citizenship's existence is subject to the existence of the state simply because citizenship rights are necessarily granted, guaranteed or enforced by the state – by state apparatuses and agencies. Of course, it does not follow that the existence of the state is equally tied to the existence of citizenship. As we have noted, citizenship is a '(western) notion' (Turner, 1990, p. 213); and, as Turner discusses, there are plenty of examples from before or beyond modern Western society to illustrate the way the state exists without citizenship rights being granted (ibid., pp. 195–213). This is not to ignore the argument that the state's security may be enhanced by, and may even rest upon, its provision of citizenship rights (as Giddens has argued; see also Held, 1989).

For Marshall, Western citizenship helps distinguish modern society from 'pre-modern society', as Roche tells us:

> Marshall's picture of citizenship is a picture almost exclusively of rights rather than duties. ... [In] comparing pre-modern tradition-based society with modern citizenship-based society he observes that 'the old morality stressed obligations more than rights; in the new it is the opposite. It is in the nature of the polity and of the economy to foster this change' [Marshall, 1981, p. 175]. (Roche, 1992, p. 20)

In a similar way, while not ignoring pre-modern instances of the state-citizenship nexus, Turner comments that the 'development of the concept of the political citizen was an important adjunct to the historical development of the nation-state as the principal political unit of the contemporary political life' (Turner, 1990, p. 211). Accordingly, Turner asserts, 'Any theory of citizenship must also produce a theory of the state' (ibid., p. 193). On these grounds, Turner criticises Marshall:

> In Marshall's scheme it is implicitly the state which provides the principle element in the maintenance and development of social rights, being the political instrument through which various political movements seek to redress their circumstances through the legitimisation of their claims against society. (Ibid., p. 193)

However, when it came to incorporating an explicit theory of the state into his analysis, 'Marshall's work was ... underdeveloped' (ibid., p. 193). But equally, it is difficult to find in the work not only of Marshall, but also of Turner himself, not to mention of both Roche and Barbalet, any clear and consistent notion of 'the state' of the kind that is invited by the acknowledged conceptual, political, institutional, structural and historical tie between 'the state' and 'citizenship'. There is no unambiguous indication from any of these writers of what is meant and counted, in general, by *the state*. Presumably, they would concur with a definition of 'the state' along the lines of (as I have mentioned previously) the best known and most influential sociological notion: 'The most usual definition [of the state] is that of Weber: an organization which successfully upholds a claim to binding rule-making over a territory, by virtue of commanding a monopoly of the legitimate use of force' (Mann, 1983, p. 373).

Weber's definition has found its way into numerous other formulations. Thus, again as I have previously mentioned, according to Patrick Dunleavy and Brendan O'Leary:

> The state is a recognizably separate institution or set of institutions, so differentiated from the rest of society as to create identifiable public and private spheres. The state is sovereign, or supreme power, within its territory, and by definition the ultimate authority for all law i.e. binding rules supported by coercive sanctions. Public law is made by state officials backed by a formal monopoly of force.   (Dunleavy and O'Leary, 1987, p. 2)

Similarly, according to Adam and Jessica Kuper, 'State refers to ... any self-governing set of people organised so that they deal with others as a unit. It is a territorial unit ordered by a sovereign power' (Kuper and Kuper, 1989, p. 818).

However, this particular definition of 'the state' seems to come close to actually defining what for others is 'the nation-state', and so to equating and confusing the two notions. Here we might refer to, for example, the definition of 'the nation-state' provided by Anthony Giddens and summarised by David Held and John Thompson:

> Giddens [has] argued that 'the nation-state, which exists in a complex of other nation-states, is a set of institutional forms of governance maintaining an administrative monopoly over a territory with demarcated boundaries, its rule being sanctioned by law and direct control of the means of internal and external violence' [Giddens, 1981, p. 190]. (Held and Thompson, 1989, pp. 106–7)

In effect, we can think of 'the state' as being that political apparatus which lies at the core of those geo-political entities we recognise as modern 'nation-states'. Giddens's definition of

Citizenship and the European Supra-state 287

'the nation-state' resembles J. P. Gardner's definition of 'the State', which again I have previously mentioned:

> The legal analysis of citizenship derives in part of the notion of a State [sic] ... A State ... is a territory, subject to an authority which is recognised by other States.... An attribute of a State, an aspect of its sovereignty, is ... its ability to confer nationality [and national citizenship] on its population. (Gardner, 1990, p. 64)

Putting aside the terminological (if not conceptual) confusion between 'the state' and 'the nation-state', Gardner's definition specifically touches on the political, institutional or structural link between 'the state' and 'citizenship'; and thereby on the point that the occurrence of the latter is dependent upon the prior existence of the former. As such, the presence of citizenship within the European Community and Union at any level other than the nation-state level is questionable if Pascal Fontaine's argument is anything to go by:

> As a body founded by international treaties, the Community is a creation of law, and is itself the source of a body of autonomous law that applies directly to the Member States and to individual citizens. In ... 1964 ... the Court said that 'by contrast with ordinary international treaties, the EEC [Rome] Treaty has created its own legal system which, on entry into force of the Treaty, became an integral part of the legal systems of the Member States and which their courts are bound to apply. By creating a Community of unlimited duration, having its own institutions, its own personality, its own legal capacity and capacity for representation on the international plane and, more particularly, real powers stemming from a limitation of sovereignty or transfer or powers from States to the Community, the Member States have thus created a body of law which binds both their nationals and themselves.' (Fontaine, 1991, pp. 9–10)

On the other hand, Fontaine adds

> The Communities, of course, stem from the Treaty of Paris and the Treaty of Rome and only exercise competence by

attribution (conferred powers). Even though these powers are tending to expand, particularly since the Single European Act of 1986 and the establishment of the internal market, they remain far narrower than those which point to the existence of a federal state. (Ibid., p. 11)

In a similarly ambivalent manner, Klaus-Dieter Borchardt argues, first, that the Paris and Rome treaties are

> the foundation documents establishing independent Communities endowed with their own sovereign rights and competence. The Member States have pooled parts of their own legislative powers in favour of these Communities and have placed them in the hands of Community institutions. (Borchardt, 1991, pp. 7–8)

On the other hand, Borchardt argues

> the points of resemblance between the Community order and the national order of a State do not ... suffice to confer on the Community the legal character of a (federal) State. Sovereign powers have been conferred on the Community institutions only in ... limited spheres ..., and those institutions have not been given any power to increase their competence merely by their own decisions. (Ibid., p. 9)

For Borchardt, this last restriction on the power of the Community is crucial in judging whether or not the Community has become or is becoming a (federal) state. Whatever power has so far been conferred on the Community, it falls short of enabling it to add to its competence, control and power independently of the decisions, control and sovereignty which remain at Member State level. That is, 'it depends on [the] will [and decisions of the Member States] whether the Community develops further in the direction of a European federal State or of European Union' (ibid., p. 9). For Borchardt, while the European Community has acquired 'sovereign powers' (ibid., p. 9), it does not qualify as a 'federal supra-state' simply because, in the first place, 'the Community is not yet a State' (ibid., p. 9). Essentially, 'the Community lacks both the universal jurisdiction characteristic of a State and the power to create its own field of competence' (ibid., p. 9).

On the second of this two considerations, perhaps signs of the necessary inclination and will on the part of the Community's Member States to move towards a federal state are to be found in the Maastricht Treaty on European Union, as well as in the provisions of the Single European Act, along with the various associated single internal market directives. When it comes to the second of Borchardt's considerations, there are signs also of this being gradually realised by way of the same legislation, in combination with the role of the European Court of Justice in interpreting Community law and in determining the relationship between the legal and political system of the Community and those at Member State level. In this context, however, it may be argued that the realisation of 'universal jurisdiction' depends, in the end, on acquiring and exercising, following Weber, 'the legitimate use of force', and that in this regard the European Community and Union fall short of incorporating 'the state' – at least for the time being. Only if, or when, 'the state', and thereby a 'supra-state', exists at the level of the European Community and Union will Tier III European Citizenship occur and so play a part in the everyday lives, relationships and experiences of the people of Europe. But the Maastricht Treaty's introduction of the status of Citizenship of the Union, along with its provisions allowing for the 'direct enforcement' of Community law (Shaw, 1993, p. 14), are clear pointers towards the consolidation of a European Community and Union supra-state along with European Union Supra-citizenship.

Certainly, there are convincing clues as to the current existence of a nascent EU supra-state if Weber's notion of 'the state' is treated as an *ideal type*: that is, as 'an "exaggeration" of certain features which tend to be present in reality; once the type is constructed, a concrete situation can be understood by means of comparison with the ideal type' (Mann, 1983, p. 164). Judged with reference to Weber's ideal-type notion of 'the state', the evidence suggests that the European Union has embarked upon a process of gradually acquiring *for itself* even those ideal-type attributes which involve *the legitimate use of force*, although it may have a long way to go before it acquires a monopoly of such force. We are probably witnessing the building of the foundations on which European Union Supra-citizenship will be more and more soundly placed, and concomitantly the demise of national citizenship within Europe.

The increase in the European Union's coercive capabilities by way of the progressive, spill-over introduction of the 'direct enforcement' of its legislation brings the ever-greater prospect of supra-citizenship for the people of Europe: of the implementation, enjoyment and experience of supra-national citizenship rights by Citizens of the Union. It brings the ever-greater prospect of Level III European Citizenship playing a major part in shaping the everyday lives, relationships and experiences of the people of Europe, and doing so instead of Member State Citizenship. This is because any increase in the Union's access to legitimately based *direct force* for the purpose of guaranteeing, rather than merely granting, supra-citizenship rights will enhance the likelihood of Member States co-operating more fully and uniformly in the process of implementing, applying and defending such rights. It may well mean a decline in the tardiness, not to say reluctance, shown by Member State in their commitment to this process, as exemplified in the case of the requirement of Member States to implement those Community directives which are designed to facilitate the 'freedom of movement of people' within the territory of the Union in accordance with the single internal market programme; and which are consistent with the Maastricht Treaty provisions on Citizenship of the Union. This case reflects clearly the pattern of interests, struggle and power within the European Community and Union as a 'political community'; and in particular the way in which Member State have been prepared, and have had the ability, to adopt self-interested, somewhat maverick and occasionally conflictual approaches to the issue of citizenship rights.

The intention was to complete the '1992' single internal market programme by the first day of 1993. However, this goal was not achieved, and even several months later there was quite a long way to go, noted earlier in this chapter and as confirmed by Lucky Walker:

> The European Commission is to relaunch the Single Market for four months after the deadline. ... [While] more than

95% of the 282 measures proposed in the 1985 White Paper have been adopted by ministers ... [there remains] the political dispute over passport controls. Continued controls on travellers have prompted a storm of complaints and the threat of legal action by the European Parliament against the Commission. ... [The hope is] that by the end of the year [1993] passport inspections at more than 200 airports in nine countries will have been replaced by the 'blue wave' where travellers simply flash their passports as they walk past. Ireland, Denmark and Britain, the only EC members not to have signed the Schengen agreement ending passport controls in 1993, may introduce the blue wave at ports. Although a split between Schengen and non-Schengen countries would be a 'terrible problem', [Commissioner] Vanni d'Archirafi insist security considerations remain paramount. 'There can be no trade-off between free movement and security. You have to realise that the Community today is not the same as it was in 1985,' he said. 'We need flanking measures to make the system work in the present political, as well as juridical, framework. The splitting of the Soviet empire has increased the pressure of immigration from the East and we cannot ignore this.' Neither legal action by the European Parliament nor proceedings by the Commission against member states for failing to end passport controls is a good idea, he says, warning that legal action could paralyse negotiations. But he insists that the Commission has not gone soft on member states who flout the rules. 'We will maintain a constant pressure to make sure they keep their side of the bargain.'   (Walker, 22–25 April 1993)[25]

Commissioner Vanni d'Archirafi's statement is intriguing because, despite his reassurance, it does signal a softening of the Commission's approach to Member State implementation of the Community's directives concerning passport controls, even though this is rationalised and made intelligible by his claim that *the pressure of immigration from the East cannot be ignored*. Until a short time earlier, the European Commission had been signalling an uncompromising and threatening stance on recalcitrant Member States. As John Carvel reported in late February 1993:

The European Commission is about to re-open its offensive against British passport controls on travellers from elsewhere in the community. Padraig Flynn, the EC commissioner for social affairs and immigration ... would ... insist on further action by the UK to allow the free movement of people across the EC's internal borders. Mr Flynn warned that the commission would have to take 'the ultimate sanctions' against any country which fails to honour its commitment under the Single European Act. This would involve action against Britain in the European Court of Justice. Mr Flynn [is] coming under intense pressure from the European Parliament, which has described continued passport controls inside the supposedly frontier-free Europe as 'intolerable'. It is threatening to take the commission to the European Court in an unprecedented action for dereliction of duty if nothing is done by early April. None of the 12 EC governments are [sic] yet allowing full free movement and so if the commission were to take legal action now it would have to act against all 12. [The] nine member states which have signed the Schengen agreement ... are preparing to complete the elimination of passport checks at ports in June and airports by December. [Last] December ... Mr Clarke withdrew his offer to relax passport controls by allowing the so-called Bangemann wave, named after the former internal commissioner Martin Bangemann. This would have allowed EC citizens to march past immigration officials waving their unopened passports. Mr Flynn said the commission always viewed the Bangemann wave as a transitional solution. (Carvel, 25 February 1993)

The European Parliament's and Commissioner Flynn's strident promotion of the Community's policy of removing internal passport controls, although wholly consistent with and necessary for the process of completing the single internal market, has come up against contrary preferences, policies and practices at the Member State Level. At the same time, Member State resistance to joint Parliamentary and Commission demands in this regard may be seen as not unambiguously at odds with Community policy, including that in relation to the single internal market, given the Community's concern over *immigration pressure,* as expressed by Vanni D'Archifari and others on behalf of the Commission. We have already noted the way in which a Commission publication of 1993 set out to reassure those people who were already safely installed as citizens or nationals behind the walls of 'fortress Europe' on the implications of the single internal market for immigration:

> Community citizens have new opportunities and new freedoms. The EC enables them to live and work in the country of their choice [by the] removal of internal frontiers.... The Maastricht Treaty creates a common European citizenship in addition to national citizenship.... Mobility is enhanced with the disappearance of border controls at land frontiers and soon – for flights within the EC – at airports too. Some exceptions have been requested by the United Kingdom, Ireland and Denmark.... The removal of internal frontiers within the Community is being matched by a corresponding strengthening of controls at the EC's external frontiers. These are aimed at preventing terrorists, drug smugglers and other criminals as well as illegal immigrants from entering the Community. In addition, spot identity checks will still be possible inside the territory of the Member States. Community countries have drawn up a common list of States whose nationals will need visas to enter the Community.[26] In addition, the conditions for granting asylum to political refugees will be tightened to make it more difficult for so-called 'economic' migrants to settle in the EC. National police forces will cooperate through a new body called Europol. (Commission of the European Communities, *Questions and Answers about the European Community,* 1993, pp. 2–8)

This is the Commission's answer to the question it poses itself of 'will open frontiers increase immigration pressures?' The concern not only of the Commission, but of the Community overall with this question has been manifested in various ways, including in its decisions on applications for new membership, at least if Nigel Dudley's claims are accepted:

there are still political and economic barriers to Turkey's full membership [of the EC]. There are ... worries about its economy. ... [But also, some] in Brussels fear that Turkey would become a drain on EC funds and that its rapidly growing population would flood into richer parts of the Community once free movement of people was introduced. (Dudley, 12–16 May 1993)

As far as the current Member States are concerned, when it comes to implementing the directives relating to the single internal market, to persist with passport checks at internal, national borders is consistent with the policies of resisting immigration pressures, thwarting illegal immigration and, therefore, conducting *spot identity checks.* This is the case even if, at the same time, the European Union's policy of permitting and facilitating the freedom of movement of people – or more precisely of Member State citizens and nationals – within the total territory of the Union is also being thwarted. As such, the simultaneous affirmation and negation of *the freedom of movement of the people of Europe* represents a contradiction – a contradiction which in the first place is a feature of institutional or socio-political patterns, circuits (to use Roche's notion) and trends; but which will be – often acutely – registered at the level of people's everyday lives, relationships and experiences.

The concern over immigration and asylum-seekers, commonly shared by both the Commission and the Member States, has even undermined progress towards the final implementation of the Schengen agreement. Thus, Hilary Clarke tells us about

doubts over whether EC member states will ever agree to end passport controls .... The nine countries which have signed the Schengen agreement – creating a single market without passport controls – are due to end passport inspections at all ports by July [1993] and at more than 200 airports by December. However, passport controls will continue to be applied at Amsterdam's Schipol, Milan, Rome, and two Greek island airports because of the volume of international traffic and the difficulty of reorganising ground services. (Clarke, 29 April 1993)

As we noted earlier, some Member States and even Schengen signatories have not only moved slowly in removing the barriers to the free movement of people within the territory of the Community and Union, but have also proceeded in the opposite direction. In France in particular, the police have been given powers 'to crack down on illegal immigrants' by making 'preventive' identity checks, a move which has been strongly condemned within France itself on the grounds that it will 'lead to arbitrary and discriminatory checks based on a person's appearance' (*The European*, 29 April 1993). The French right-wing government's decision to tighten its internal checks in order to track down illegal immigrants, with its racially-biased overtones, has been accompanied by a similar policy applied at the nation's external frontiers, including those with other Schengen signatories. As Victor Smart reports:

> The timetable for a frontier-free Europe has been derailed by France's sudden refusal to lift border checks on EC nationals despite its commitments under the Schengen Treaty.... France is openly accusing the Netherlands of lax enforcement of drug laws thereby encouraging a flood of drugs into France via Belgium.... The nine were due to sweep away passport controls at land frontiers on 1 July and at airports on 1 December this year, creating a huge frontier-free zone within the EC. Both deadlines will now be missed, as was the previous symbolic date of 1 January when Europe was meant to become a single market.... The new conservative government of Edouard Balladur, fearful that the single market will prove a bonanza for drug traffickers and illegal immigrants, says it will not proceed with Schengen for the forseeable future. (Smart, 6 May 1993)

A frontier-free Europe had still not been completed by the beginning of 1994, and, in the face of the prevarication, obstruction and resistance from Member States, Vanni D'Archirafi appeared to have been persuaded to ignore his own earlier warning (as reported by Lucy Walker) that *neither legal action by the European Parliament nor proceedings by the Commission against Member States for failing to end passport controls is a good idea.* That is, by January 1994, Vanni D'Archirafi seemed to have reverted to making threats to use *force* in order to get *all* the Member States to participate equally and fully in the process of achieving the frontier-free goal, as John Carvel reports:

> The European Commission plans a directive later this year to force Britain to abandon passport checks on travellers from other parts of the EU, which ministers claim are vital.... Ranerio Vanni D'Archirafi, the commissioner responsible for completing the frontier-free Single Market, said yesterday he would act to ensure complete free movement of people throughout once arrangements for removing border controls between nine of the European countries were in place. The directive would be brought forward as a Single Market measure which could be carried by a qualified majority vote in the Council of Ministers. This would mean that Britain, Ireland and Denmark, which have rejected abolition of internal frontier controls, could be obliged to comply.... The [UK] Governments has rejected the Commission's interpretation of the provision for free movement of people in the 1987 Single European Act. It would probably take a case to the European Court in Luxembourg to challenge Mr Vanni D'Archirafi's approach.... Mr Vanni D'Archirafi has in mind a 'paradigmatic directive' to extend the arrangement to all 12 members of the EU. The Schengen treaty, signed by all the EU except Britain, Denmark and Ireland, seeks to abolish internal borders. Martin Bangemann, his predecessor as Single Market commissioner, promised in 1991 that he and his colleagues would 'fight like lions' to end frontier checks and would encourage community citizens to sue governments which did not lift controls.... The directive to lift passport controls at internal borders will come towards the end of the year when the nine Schengen countries show that the arrangement can work. (Carvel, 14 January 1994)

If Vanni D'Archirafi and the Commission do proceed to use the European Community and Union's acquired decision-making procedures and legal system to successfully *force*[27] all the Member States to fully and finally implement the frontier-free programme, it will represents a landmark event in the history and development of the European Community and Union. It will reflect a major shift in the distribution of political power and sovereignty away from the nation-state level to the supra-national level. It may be taken to signify the kind of redistribution of sovereignty to the supra-national level which (judged in terms of Borchardt's criteria, for instance) confirms the existence of 'the state' at the level of the Union. In turn, therefore, it would lend itself to the conclusion that European Union Supra-citizenship had arrived, with its associated legally granted and guaranteed right to move *freely* throughout the territory of the Union, irrespective of national borders, preferences and power; not to mention irrespective of nationality, race-ethnicity, sex-gender, social class, and so on. Of course, as I have emphasised, the process by which formal citizenship rights are awarded and enforced is only part of the story from the point of view of the people of Europe. Thus, I have examined the issue of how unequal distributions of *enabling resources* – or material possessions – mean that the people of Europe will realise, enjoy and experience citizenship in highly disparate, uneven and unequal ways. Despite the universal provision of citizenship rights to adults, the experience of citizenship by the poor, the working class, women, immigrants and non-whites will be quantitatively and qualitatively less than the experience of citizenship by, respectively, the rich, the middle class, men, nationals and whites. It might be added, however, that even taking into account how enabling resources intervene between the provision and experience of citizenship rights still falls far short of completing the story for the people of Europe. People's experience of the right to move *freely* within the Union will depend not only on their enabling resources, but also on other factors. In the case of sex-gender, for instance, women's citizenship experience will be quantitatively and qualitatively impaired relative to men's, not just by virtue of any discrepancies between women and men in their material resources, but also by virtue of the operation of prevailing sex-gender systems in so far as these are centred on patriarchal distributions of power, are rooted in sexist ideology, and are characterised by sex discrimination, harassment, containment and control.[28] It remains to be seen if the advent of the European supra-state and of European

Supra-citizenship heralds the progressive elimination of such sex-gender systems in favour of equality among European citizens, not just in law, but, more importantly, in the quality of the mundane activities, routines and experiences by which in the end both European citizenship and European integration are to be judged.

Notes

Notes to Chapter 1: Towards a Framework for Analysing Modern European Citizenship

1. See, for instance, B. S. Turner, *Citizenship and Capitalism* (1986a), *Equality* (1986b), *Status* (1988), 'Outline of Theory of Citizenship' (1990); and J. M. Barbalet (1988).
2. See, for instance, the Commission on Citizenship, *Encouraging Citizenship: Report of the Commission on Citizenship*, 1990; and P. Johnstone Conover, I. Crewe and D. Searing, 'The Nature of Citizenship in the United States and Great Britain; Empirical Comments on Theoretical Themes', *Journal of Politics*, November 1990.
3. Here the Report is quoting from an unpublished paper given by R. Henderson to *The Commission on Citizenship Seminar*, April 1980, p. 2.
4. J. P. Gardner, 'What Lawyers Mean by Citizenship', Appendix D to the Report of the Commission on Citizenship, *Encouraging Citizenship*, 1990, pp. 63–78.
5. The page numbering referred to here is taken from a copy of the article sent to me by the author as a personal communication.
6. Here, Wallace has in mind the particular notion of citizenship developed by T. H. Marshall, and to which we will turn shortly.
7. R. Lister, 'Women, Economic Dependency and Citizenship', *Journal of Social Policy*, 1990, pp. 445–67; Y. Summers, 'Women and Citizenship: the Insane, the Insolvent and the Inanimate', in P. Abbott and C. Wallace (eds), *Gender, Sexuality and Power* (1991).
8. See Chapter 6.
9. Here, Barbalet appears to come close to distinguishing 'a person' and 'a group', and to using the term 'a person' in the sense of 'an individual man or woman'. That is, he may be alluding to an individualistic notion of citizenship, given that he refers to 'persons as citizens'. However, this inference is not certain, in that it is countered by what he goes on to argue are, in effect, the (transferred or assumed) citizenship rights of certain collectivities, in particular of trade unions.
10. 'Every year, about 10 to 15 young people aged under 18 are convicted and given custodial sentences for murder in England and Wales. In 1990, the latest figures, eight teenagers aged between 14 and 16 were found guilty of murder' (Tyrell and Langdon-Down, 'The Law and How it Works for Children aged 10', 1993).
11. Gerison Lansdown is the Director of the Children's Rights Development Centre in London.
12. 'A 14-year-old girl who wanted to live with her 18-year-old boyfriend's parents in Surrey was made a ward last November by the President of

the High Court's family division .... She was later reconciled with her parents' (Clare Dyer, 'Girl, 13, Tests Legal Right to "Divorce" Adoptive Parents', *Guardian*, 26 April 1993).

13. Although we can note that Lansdown acknowledges how it 'is extremely difficult for any adult to determine the best interests of the child' (Lansdown, 'Participation or Protection', 1993, p. 11).
14. See P. Dunleavy and B. O'Leary, *Theories of the State: The Politics of Liberal Democracy*, (1987), pp. 4–5.
15. Ireland decriminalised homosexual acts between men on 24 June 1993.
16. The UK is one of four European countries where men acquire the right to engage in homosexual acts at a later age than females (apart from Cyprus where homosexual acts among men, but not women, are illegal at any age). Until the beginning of 1994, the gender gap in this regard in the UK was five years – taking, that is, the heterosexual age of consent of 16 years as the age at which women gain the right freely to engage in either heterosexual or homosexual acts. One other European country had a greater gender gap. That is, Liechtenstein the gender gap was six years.

    During the first few weeks of 1994 a bill went before the UK's Parliament which proposed to even out the ages for heterosexual consent and homosexual consent of 16 years. The prior expectation on the part of many commentators was summed up by Martin Wroe when he asserted that 'MPs are set to refuse gay men's demands for sexual equality before the law' (Wroe, 'Vexed Question of Gay Consent', *The Observer*, 9 January 1994). Accordingly, on 21 February 1994, the House of Commons rejected the proposal to lower the age of homosexual consent for men to 16 years. Instead, it accepted an alternative proposal to lower the age to 18 years. Of course, this compromise decision left Britain as one of the minority of European nations with a gap between the heterosexual age of consent and the homosexual age or ages; as well as one of the even smaller number of nations with a gap between the right of men to engage in homosexual acts and the right of women to do the same.

    However, it has been anticipated that the UK will be obliged to equalise its ages of consent by the Court of Human Rights. As pointed out by Chris Smith, a 'case has been brought by three young gay men, arguing that a discriminatory age of consent breaches the Convention on Human Rights, of which Britain is a founder signatory' (Smith, 'Inequality at 18 is No Answer', *The Independent*, 23 February 1994).
17. Among the most personally and societally important citizenship rights acquired in all modern societies are those concerned with schooling and paid employment.

    In the UK, schooling (which may be conducted at home) is compulsory for young people aged between 5 and 16. But this is longer than in many other European countries. For instance, in Sweden education is compulsory between 7 and 15; in Holland, from 5 to 15; in Italy from 6 to 14; in Greece, from 5 1/2 to 14 1/2; and in Finland, from 7 to 16. The school-leaving age is usually linked to the age at which a

Notes 301

person is allowed to take up full-time employment. This is 15 in most countries – such as Austria, Denmark, Ireland, Luxembourg, the Netherlands and Switzerland. In finland, although schooling is compulsory until 16, there are ways for young people to take up full-time work at 15. In Austria, Denmark, finland, the Netherlands and Switzerland, there are restrictions on 16- to 19-year olds working in jobs considered to be dangerous. In Ireland, Luxembourg and Germany, a person must have reached the age of 18 for this type of employment. The school-leaving age in Portugal is 14, although 'dangerous' employment is limited to those 18 and over. France and Britain place restrictions on the employment of 16- to 18-year-olds (*Guardian*, 'Rights: Young at Heart', 5 January 1993). See Paul Close, 'Children's Rights, Labour and Citizenship', paper to the *ESRC Seminar Series 1993–4 on Childhood and Society*, University of Keele, July 1993.

18. I am aware of the way this particular notion of *enabling resources* may be regarded as too narrow in scope, in that in any thoroughgoing assessment of people's opportunities to realise their citizenship rights we need to take into account various possessions which are not so cleary 'material' as financial ones. For instance, people's educational resources play a major intervening part in the transposition of formal citizenship into *real citizenship*. See Paul Close, 'State Care, Control and Contradictions: Theorizing Resistance, Change and Progress in Modern Society', in P. Close (ed.), *The State and Caring* (1992). However, my focus on 'enabling resources' is meant to be for illustrative purposes.

19. The report being referred to here is not specified, but would appear to be the Commission's Final Report of the European Parliament and Council on the Second European Poverty Programme (1985–1989) [COM (91) 29 final]' (Commission of the European Communities, *Background Report: the European Poverty Programme*, 1991, p. 1). The Eurostat figures probably have the same source.

20. 'The poverty threshold applied is 50 per cent of national average expenditure', rather than of average national income (Brindle, 'Britain Moves to Top of EC's Poverty League', April 1991).

21. See Chapter 6 for a more detailed examination of this issue.

22. 'Whereas a household is defined as a person living alone or a group of people living together, a family is a married couple with or without children, or a lone parent. People living alone are not families' (*Social Trends 23*, 1993, p. 28).

23. Unicef, *Progress of Nations* (1993).

24. At the end of the week beginning 22 November 1993, one ecu was worth 0.761 British pounds; 1.920 German marks; 6.668 French francs; and 1.131 US dollars (*The European*, 19–25 November 1993).

25. See also, Lydia Morris and Sarah Irwin, 'Employment Histories and the Concept of the Underclass', *Sociology*, August 1992, pp. 401–20.

26. Melanie Phillips tells us about how 'the Policy Studies Institute [brought] together a group of policy analysts at a conference [in 1991] on the subject of the underclass ... [at which] Nick Buck ...

made a stab at defining [the underclass] as people who [are] permanently removed from the labour market excluding those not of working age, those who [have] retired early, students and people with long-term illnesses' ('Encounters with the Underclass', *Guardian*, 13 March 1992).

27. In an interview in the *Independent* newspaper on 14 September 1987, shortly after the 1987 General Election, the Prime Minister, Margaret Thatcher, announced her determination to end the 'dependency culture'.

28. The 'culture of poverty' approach to accounting for the plight of the poor has a long history. The notion was introduced during the 1950s by the American anthropologist Oscar Lewis (*Five Families*, 1959; *The Children of Sanchez*, 1961; *La Vida*, 1966), who argued that the culture of poverty is a 'design for living', by way of which the poor keep themselves in poverty intra- and inter-generationally. Likewise, Michael Harrington (*The Other America: Poverty in the United States*, 1963) argued that there is 'a language of the poor, a psychology of the poor, a world view of the poor. To be impoverished is to be an internal alien, to grow up in a culture that is radically different from the one that dominates society.' But, in turn, the approach has a long history of being heavily criticised and rejected: see, for instance, Charles Valentine, *Culture and Poverty* (1968); Ken Coates and Richard Silburn, *Poverty: The Forgotten Englishmen* (1970).

29. See also C. Murray, 'The Emerging British Underclass', *Choice in Welfare Series No. 2* (1990).

30. Nick Buck – who, as we have noted (see Note 26), defines the 'underclass' as those people 'who [are] permanently removed from the labour market excluding those not of working age, those who [have] retired early, students and people with long-term illness' (Melanie Phillips, 'Encounters with the Underclass', *Guardian*, 13 March 1992) – has 'worked out that in 1979 the underclass amounted to 1.96 million people or 4.2 per cent of the population, a figure that had grown by 1986 to 4.58 million people or 9.9 percent of the population. In that period, single parent families belonging to the underclass grew more slowly than other groups, although they were still a large proportion: in 1986 they accounted for 29 per cent of such households compared with 56 per cent seven years earlier. Groups more likely than average to belong were council tenants, people with no educational qualifications, youngest and oldest age groups, families of West Indian origin and families with large numbers of children' (ibid.).

31. This is not to deny that the government imposes various conditions on who gets what and how much, as far as social benefits are concerned. However, these conditions currently fall short of those conditions imposed under the United States' workfare programme.

32. Hence the emphasis of John Major's *Citizen's Charter* launched in April 1991. According to Patrick Wintour: 'The Prime Minister yesterday moved to give teeth to his Citizen's Charter by promising consumers additional powers to obtain redress from recalcitrant public services, in-

cluding the individual right to sue unofficial strikers .... In what amounted to a relaunch of a becalmed policy, he set out seven yardsticks. They are: published standards by which performance can be measured; consulting users and customers when improving services; increased openness such as staff name tags; more and better information for consumers; more and better choice of services; greater accessibility; better response to claims when things go wrong .... 15 individual charters [have] already [been] published and more – including the Court and Traveller's Charters – [are] to come' ('Major Offer Right to Sue Strikers', *Guardian*, 28 January 1992). For example, the Patient's Charter, first of all, 'confirmed the seven rights [a patient has] in the National Health Service from the day it started ... [but has added] three rights' (Southern Derbyshire Health Authority, *Achieving the Patient's Charter*, 1993). The first seven are: 'to receive health care on the basis of clinical need, regardless of ability to pay; to be registered with a GP (General Practitioner) – that is [a] family doctor; to receive emergency medical care at any time ...; to be referred to a consultant ...; to be given a clear explanation of any treatment proposed ...; to have access to [one's] health records ...; to choose whether or not ... to take part in medical research or medical student training' (ibid.). The additional three are: 'to be given detailed information on local authority services, including quality standards and maximum waiting times'; to be 'guaranteed admission for virtually all treatments by a specific date not later than two years from the day when [a] Consultant places [one] on a waiting list'; 'to have any complaint about NHS services ... investigated and to receive a full and prompt written reply from the Chief Executive of [the] health authority or ... hospital' (ibid.).

33. For detailed examinations of the ideological ramifications of social citizenship rights, see P. Close (ed.), *The State and Caring* (1992); V. George and P. Wilding, *Ideology and Social Welfare* (1985); I. Gough, *The Political Economy of the Welfare State* (1979); R. Lowe, *The Welfare State in Britain since 1945* (1993); F. Pampel and J. Williamson, *Age, Class, Politics and the Welfare State* (1989); P. Spicker, *Principles of Social Welfare* (1988).

34. For an impressive, but much neglected, account of poverty in terms of social inclusion and exclusion and which hinges centrally on people's contribution or lack of contribution to society, see G. Simmel, 'The Poor', *Social Problems*, 1966 (originally published in 1908).

35. For discussions, see Coates and Silburn, *Poverty: The Forgotten Englishmen* (1970); and Townsend, *Poverty in the United Kingdom* (1979).

Notes to Chapter 2: Citizenship, the State, the Nation-State and Nationality

1. It is precisely because social/welfare rights give people entitlements to automatically have the benefits and services involved that the New Right object to them.

2. This is not to ignore the point that due to various factors welfare benefits are often not taken up.
3. More accurately still, property rights define relationships between the owners and others, where the non-owners include, for instance, merely 'managers' of property. See P. Close, 'Towards a Framework for the Analysis of Family Divisions and Inequalities in Modern Society', in P. Close (ed.), *Family Divisions and Inequalities in Modern Society* (1989).
4. Barker and Padfield make this point in the following way: 'we must be careful to distinguish the thing itself from the rights which attach to it. A cheque, for example, is in common experience merely a piece of paper on which appear words and figures. That is, it is a physical manifestation. However, *in law* it represents certain rights, the most important of which is the right (enforceable in action) to payment of a sum of money' (Barker and Padfield, *Law Made Simple*, 1992, p. 265).
5. For much fuller accounts of the long-term trends, see A. B. Atkinson, *Unequal Shares: Wealth in Britain* (1972); A. B. Atkinson (ed.), *Wealth, Income and Inequality* (1980); A. B. Atkinson, *Economics of Inequality* (1983); A. B. Atkinson and A. J. Harrison, *The Distribution of Personal Wealth in Britain* (1978); Chris Pond, 'The Changing Distribution of Income, Wealth and Poverty', in C. Hamnett et al. (eds), *Restructuring Britain: The Changing Social Structure* (1989). See also, N. Abercrombie, *Contemporary British Society* (1988), especially Parts 2 and 3; and J. Scott, *The Upper Classes* (1982).
6. Full membership *in the fullest sense* is still dependent upon the possession and use of, perhaps highly unequally distributed, 'enabling resources', and so, of income and wealth.
7. Barbalet fails to provide any examples to illustrate the provision of compensatory rights.
8. Since the coming into force of the Maastricht Treaty on 1 November 1993, the European Community has been complemented by the establishment of the European Union. I will return to this event.
9. Here, perhaps Barker and Padfield should use the term 'nationals' instead of 'citizens'.
10. Under *British Constitution* many non-citizens have not been treated as aliens, and thereby enjoy certain basic citizenship rights within the United Kingdom. Thus, in the United Kingdom, in 'order to qualify for voting, a person must be aged eighteen, be a United Kingdom (or Commonwealth or Irish) citizen and have his [sic] name on the electoral register' (Padfield and Byrne, 1987, p. 30).
11. This distinction, and in particular the appropriateness of the term 'new citizenship', is problematic. The question arises as to who, or what, not only grants but also guarantees or enforces the 'rights' covered by 'new citizenship' in the same kind of way that 'national citizenship' rights are both granted and guaranteed by 'the state' at the level (and at the core) of 'the nation-state'. If 'new citizenship' is rooted in extra-national agreements (such as the Council of Europe's founding 1950 Convention, or the European Community's Maastricht Treaty), what, if any, institutional arrangement or agency guarantees

them at the extra-national level? Or, that is, what, if any, 'supra-national' institutions enforce them? If the answer is 'none', in that the only coercive support exists at the nation-state level, then the question arises of whether 'new citizenship' can be regarded as 'citizenship' in any sociologically appropriate, consistent or useful sense. This issue is taken up later in some detail (see Chapter 6).
12. See the Commission on Citizenship, *Encouraging Citizenship* (1990) p. 49 onwards.
13. The Commission investigates violations of human rights. In addition, there is a Committee of the foreign ministers of the member countries.
14. The European Court of Human Rights should not be confused with the European Community's European Court of Justice, which is based in Luxembourg (but occasionally sits in Strasbourg), the 'task of [which] is to ensure that [Community] law is observed in the interpretation and application of the Treaties establishing the Community and the legal instruments adopted by the Council [of Ministers] and the Commission' (Klaus-Dieter Borchardt, *The ABC of Community Law*, 1991 p. 21). Nor should the European Court of Human Rights be confused with the United Nations' International Court of Justice, which sits in the Hague. This Court administers the UN's Declaration of Human Rights (1948), as well as the UN's Convention on the Rights of the Child, first approved in 1989, ratified by 20 countries by 2 September 1990, by the United Kingdom in 1991, and by 126 countries by the end of 1992.
15. See, for instance, Anatol Lieven, *The Baltic Revolution* (1993).
16. The term 'supra-national' and related terms, such as 'supra-state', are examined more fully in Chapter 6.
17. 'The Single Act describes the internal market as "an area without internal frontiers in which the free movement of goods, persons, services and capital is ensured in accordance with the provisions of this Treaty"' (*Europe's Parliament and the Single Act*, May 1989, p. 3).
18. 'The Twelve' may well become 'The Sixteen' during 1995–6, with the entry into the European Union of Austria, Finland, Norway and Sweden.
19. The relative weakness of the Council of Europe's founding agreements is reflected in David Rose's comment that 'Our failure to "incorporate" the Convention into UK law means that individuals whose rights are breached have no alternative but to endure the long wait for justice at Strasbourg' (Rose, 'UK Blocks Key Reform of Human Rights Court', May 1993). John Palmer adds that 'Britain and Ireland are virtually the only council members which have still not formally incorporated the European Convention on Human Rights into domestic law. Both cite the lack of a written constitution as the reason for this' (Palmer, 'Human Rights Court to Expand', October 1993). According to Ferdinand Mount: 'Until recently there were two other civilised countries [other than Britain] which didn't [sic] possess some kind of entrenched document setting out the rules of the game – New Zealand and Israel; in recent years, though, the passing of the

constitutional semi-entrenched law in New Zealand has given that country something resembling a single written constitution. In Israel, similar basic laws have been passed in recent years. So we are now more or less on our own' (Mount, 'A Constitution Unwritten and Unbound', May 1992). For more guidance, see C. Padfield and A. Byrne, *British Constitution* (1987).

Notes to Chapter 3: Citizenship, Migration, Asylum and Race-ethnicity

1. Gardner's use of 'State' rather than 'state' appears to reflect that by 'State' he means 'nation-state'.
2. An alternative definition of 'nation-state', presented by Anthony Giddens, differs in an important way from Gardner's in that it does not clearly imply that a nation-state's existence is conditional upon *recognition or acceptance* by other nation-states. This omission makes Giddens's definition even closer than Gardner's to Weber's notion of 'the state'. Thus, Giddens has argued that 'the nation-state, which exists in a complex of other nation-states, is a set of institutional forms of governance maintaining an administrative monopoly over a territory with demarcated boundaries, its rule being sanctioned by law and direct control of the means of internal and external violence' (Giddens, *Historical Materialism*, Vol. 1, 1981, p. 190; of Giddens, *Historical Materialism*, Vol.3, 1985, p. 125–quoted in Held and Thompson, *Social Theory and Modern Societies*, 1989, pp. 107–8).

    As we will see, a definition of 'the state' along Weberian lines brings into question the occurrence of new citizenship or any instance of supra-national citizenship within Europe, as well as anywhere else. This is because of the possible absence of 'the state', in the Weberian sense, higher than the nation-state level, and therefore of that which grants and (coercively, violently) guarantees citizenship rights at any such higher level. If the state is a pre-requisite for *citizenship*, then (by definition) *citizenship* may not occur over and above the level of the nation-state.
3. It might be argued, therefore, that in a sense nationality is not just about *individual rights*, but is at the same time about *collective rights*: about those rights enjoyed and exercised among nation-states and governed by extra-national agreements and codes. This is a reflection of the way nationality is a relationship which is conducted wholly within the network of external relations among nation-states. In contrast, citizenship is always an internal relationship, and connectedly always 'an attribute of individuals' (Gardner, 'What Lawyers Mean by Citizenship', 1990, p. 63).
4. Perhaps a crucial limitation of these provisions in the Universal Declaration of Human Rights for the individual is the absence of any reference to a particular nationality and nation-state. They give rise to

Notes 307

the question: to which particular nationality does a person have a right?
5. The newspaper report mentions that not only Mrs Ejaz, but also her 'children' – aged 16 months to eight years – are liable to deportation'. In which case, the children will be deported despite being born and living all their lives in Britain. Like their mother, the children will be deprived of the UK nationality, but unlike their mother, they will not be deprived of their UK *national citizenship*, simply because, like all those under eighteen years, not having reached the *age of majority*, they do not enjoy this status.
6. See Chapter 6.
7. For the sake of discussion, in what follows, the term 'citizen' is used in the limited sense of *national citizen*, except when otherwise indicated.
8. Here, what is being recognised is the way race-ethnicity, social class, sex-gender and age-generation operate as intervening factors between being a 'national' and being a 'national citizen'. This is apart from the way the same factors intervene further between, on the one hand, the acquisition of legal or formal citizenship rights and status and, on the other hand, the realisation of citizenship rights by people in their everyday lives and relationships. The way in which these factors intervene between the acquisition and realisation of citizenship is a major thread running through this book.
9. Elsewhere, it has been suggested that as a result of the 1981 Act ' The UK has five different categories of citizenship, with varying rights.' That is: 'Under the British Nationality Act 1981, amended by the British National (Falkland Island) Act 1983 and the Hong Kong Act 1985, only a person designated as a British Citizen has a right of abode in the UK; basically anyone born in the UK to a parent who is a British Citizen, or to a parent who is lawfully settled in the UK. Four other categories of citizenship are defined: British Dependent Territories citizenship, British overseas citizenship, British subject, and Commonwealth citizen. Rights of abode differ widely for each' (*Hutchinson Softback Encyclopedia*, 1992, p. 188). Here, in effect, Padfield and Byrne's third *class* of British Overseas Citizenship has been split into three *categories*.
10. The British Nationality Act 1981 has been amended by the British National (Falkland Island) Act 1983 and by the Hong Kong Act 1985 *Hutchinson Softback Encyclopedia*, 1992, p. 188).
11. 'These are members of those territories described as Protectorates, Protected States or Mandated or Trust Territories and declared as such by an Order of Council' (Barker and Padfield, *Law Made Simple*, 1992, p. 90).
12. Barker and Padfield also list the ways in which the 'loss of nationality' may occur: '(i) *Renunciation*. This is effected by a person of full age and capacity making a declaration of renunciation, which must be registered with the Home Secretary. Any person who is married is deemed to be of full age. A person who has renounced British citizenship in order to retain or acquire some other citizenship or nationality may resume it but this right can only be exercised once.

(ii) *Deprivation.* This applies only to citizens who [have] acquired citizenship by naturalization or by registration, and may be ordered by the Home Secretary for serious misconduct, e.g. criminal acts' (Barker and Padfield, *Law Made Simple*, 1992, p. 90).
13. Portugal is another Member State which did not, at the time, permit its nationals to have dual nationality.
14. See also: E. Gellner, *Culture, Identity and Politics*, (1987).
15. Nationalism, according to Michael Mann, is the 'belief among a people that is comprises a distinctive community, with special characteristics that mark it off from others, and the desire to protect and promote that distinctiveness within an autonomous state' (Mann, 1983, pp. 256–7). For Anthony Giddens, the 'formation of modern nation-states [in post-mediaeval Europe] was closely related to the rise of nationalist sentiments. Nationalism can be defined as the shared feelings of attachment to symbols which identify the members of a population as belonging to the same overall community. The development of nationalism in Europe was more or less convergent with the formation of nation-states' (Giddens, *Sociology*, 1986, p. 155). That is, according 'to Giddens, modern nation-states face a problem of social reproduction – creating the necessary conceptual community for effective co-ordination – which has to be solved in one way or another. "Nationalism" – a common symbolic historicity – is the pre-eminent solution. It is a dispositional fact of nation-states that nationalism will contribute to social reproduction. Through the process of historical learning, leaders come to understand this, and thus the functional solution becomes generalized' (Held and Thompson, *Social Theory and Modern Societies*, 1989, p. 81).
16. Described by Bryant as a 'draft article in progress' (Bryant, 'Europe and the European Community 1992', 1991, p. 207).
17. See also (*a*) P. Schmitter and W. Streeck, 'Organized Interests and the Europe of 1992' (paper presented at a conference on *The United States and Europe in the 1980s*, American Enterprise Institute, Washington D.C., March 1990), which is referred to by Christopher Bryant (1991, p. 201), and which draws on the work of Lash and Urry on 'disorganized capitalism' (S. Lash and J. Urry, *The End of Organized Capitalism*, 1987) in arguing that 'in the European Community of 1992, [the] trend towards supra-national pluralism in both the structures of authority and the associations of interest can advance unchecked by powerful mechanisms of territorial representation and electoral accountability' (Schmitter and Streek, 1990, p. 30); and (*b*) the work of Immanuel Wallerstein in, for instance, *Geopolitics and Geoculture* (1991) (especially Ch. 4 on 'European Unity and its Implications for the Interstate System'), and *The Politics of the World Economy* (1984).
18. See Chapter 6. What I have in mind by 'direct implications' covers those which stem from the possibility of *the state* being a pre-requisite (conceptually, institutionally, structurally, historically) for *citizenship*, in that it is the state which grants, guarantees or enforces *citizenship rights* in accordance with, following Weber, its *monopoly of the legitimate use of force.*

19. R. Robertson and F. Lechner, 'Modernisation, Globalisation and the Problem of Culture in World-systems Theory', *Theory, Culture and Society*, (1985) pp. 103–18; R. Robertson, 'Globalisation and Societal Modernisation: A Note on Japan and Japanese Religion', *Sociological Analysis* (1987) pp. 35–42.
20. Turner's use of the term 'contradictory' is questionable. It might have been more appropriate to have used the term 'conflict', in so far as he is referring to opposing supra-national and sub-national tendencies. While these tendencies may be in conflict with each other, they are mutually supporting the same intermediary trend – that of the demise of the nation-state. On these grounds, it is inappropriate to regard the two trends as 'contradictory'. However, Turner's usage is consistent with the catch-all approach which unfortunately reduces the potential sociological value of the notion. See P. Close, 'State Care, Control and Contradictions: Theorizing Resistance, Change and Progress in Modern Society', in P. Close (ed.), *The State and Caring* (1992).
21. According to Andrew Gumbel, the 'European Convention on Human Rights, to which France is a signatory, stipulates a person's right to marry and live with anyone, regardless of nationality. But a French law introduced on August 24 [1993] states that foreigners are entitled to full residency papers only after the first year of wedlock. The rule is intended to deter marriages of convenience' (Gumbel, Where French Law is No More than a Mirage', October 1993).
22. As reported by Paul Webster, the 'constitutional council ... acts as a supreme court' (Webster, 16 August 1993). Webster also points out that the chairman of the council was Robert Badinter, 'a former Socialist Justice minister and a close friend of President Francois Mitterrand'. In fact, of the *nine council members, six were appointed either by Mr Mitterrand or by the previous socialist parliament.*
23. The number of *Socialist and allies* seats in the General Assembly was reduced from 282 to only 67; the Centre Right (UDF) increased its seat from 129 to 206; the Gaullists (RPR) increased their share from 127 to 242 seats; and the 'other Right' grouping increased its seat from 11 to 37.
24. The total number of asylum-seekers to EC countries crossed the 100 000 mark for the first time in 1986; 200 000 in 1989; 300 000 in 1990; and 400 000 in 1991.
25. Charles Pasqua declared this on 2 June 1993. Thus: 'France no longer welcomes immigrants and intends to pursue a policy of "zero immigration", the interior minister, Charles Pasqua said yesterday, on the eve of presenting legislation to legalise random identity checks and hasten expulsions. "France has been a country of immigration and no longer wants to be," he said' (Webster, Pasqua Aims for "Zero Immigration", June 1993).
26. As John Carvel has put it, in Germany 'the government is amending the constitution to restrict the liberal regime which was its inheritance from the anti-Fascist imperative after the Hitler era' (Carvel, 'Changing Face of EC Refugees', June 1993).

Notes to Chapter 4: Citizenship, Social Change and the Individual

1. Put at its simplest, 'the state' refers to the political apparatus which lies at the core or hub of the social structure of each modern nation-state, understood as a geo-political entity.
2. In a manner which is consistent with the *liberal-democracy* approach to political rights, citizenship and participation, the *Commission on Citizenship* tells us that in the United Kingdom: 'Rights are residual entitlements. There is no accessible, comprehensive statement of the rights of citizens in the UK, such as is found in the constitution of other countries. The foundation of government in the UK is the notion that Parliament is the supreme authority, and that the validity of its legislation cannot therefore be challenged in the UK courts. As a result, the individual's freedoms are residual: that is, they exist to the extent that Parliament has not enacted restrictions, and they are vulnerable to any subsequent enactment of Parliament' (Commission on Citizenship, *Encouraging Citizenship*, 1990, p. 7).
3. David Lockwood, 'Social Integration and System Integration', in G. K. Zollschan and W. Hirsch (eds), *Explorations in Social Change* (1964).
4. Anthony Giddens, *Central Problems in Social Theory* (1979).
5. See R. A. Dahl, *Polyarchy* (1971); and Charles E. Lindblom, *Politics and Markets* (1977).
6. See also Eli Zaretsky, *Capitalism, the Family and Personal Life* (1975).
7. See Giddens, *Historical Materialism*, vol. 2 (1985) pp. 205ff.
8. In 'some writings social rights are themselves referred to as economic rights' (Held, 1989, p. 169).
9. Held claims that 'Giddens's lack of attention to reproductive rights is symbolic of his disregard for the whole question of the social organization of reproduction, and of women and gender relations more generally' (Held, 'Citizenship and Autonomy', 1989, p. 176).
10. See Ann Oakley, *Women Confined: Towards a Sociology of Childbirth* (1980).
11. Marshall treats industrial rights as a distinct type of citizenship right, but he does not regard them as a separate category.
12. See, for instance, N. Abercrombie and A. Warde (eds), *Social Change in Contemporary Britain* (1992) Chs. 1, 2 and 9.
13. An issue raised here is whether this definition of 'industrial rights' is too narrow in that, first of all, it appears to exclude individuals other than employees. The question arises: is it only employees who have industrial rights? But second, the definition may exclude the rights *not* to form or join trade unions, *not* to strike, and so on. The inclusion of this latter range of rights would have important implications for whether industrial rights are necessarily exercised collectively, and thereby are necessarily 'collectivistic'. This point is followed up in the ensuing discussion.

14. Legally speaking, 'persons' include entities other then individuals, as we will see.
15. On trade union rights and obligations, see, for instance: John Dearlove and Peter Saunders, *Introduction to British Politics* (1984).
16. To recap, for Barbalet, unions exercise 'collective' rights, but instead of collective *civil* rights, they exercise collective *industrial* ones.
17. See Chapter 1.
18. An argument first presented by J. H. Goldthorpe and D. Lockwood, in 'Affluence and the British Class Structure', *Sociological Review* (1963).
19. Such evidence and arguments relating to individuality at (rather than just through) the work-place bring to mind, of course, the discourse surrounding the issue of Fordism and post-Fordism. See, for instance, John Allen and Doreen Masey (eds), *Restructuring Britain: The Economy in Question* (1988).
20. See also R. Burrows and B. Loader (eds), *Towards a Post-Fordist Welfare Strate?* (1994).
21. See also Alan Warde, 'Consumers, Consumption and Post-Fordism', in R. Burrows and B. Loader (eds), *Towards a Post-Fordist Welfare State?* (1994).
22. See D. Marquand (*The Unprincipled Society*, 1983), who, among other writers, argues 'for an expansion in the bundle of rights to which individuals are entitled ... to defend individual liberties' (Taylor-Gooby, 1991b, p. 94).
23. Although, by way of a parting shot, as Irwin reminds us, 'One is left wondering whether these problems of identity and choice relate more to certain angst-ridden, mobile and relatively-affluent sections of society than others' (Irwin, *Review of Anthony Giddens* (1993) p. 339). At the same time, of course, this point takes us back to the issue of the persistence, influence and importance of social class; while also bringing to mind the possibility that the principal beneficiaries of the extension and expansion of citizenship rights, perhaps especially social and industrial ones, are those with the (social-class) power to manipulate the consumer market

Notes to Chapter 5: Individualism, Citizenship and the European Union

1. See also Bruce Jesson et al., *Revival of the Right: New Zealand Politics in the 1980s* (1988).
2. A tendency which has occurred alongside the impact of 'government responses to economic pressures, [and of] changes in demography, employment and popular expectations ... on the state' (Taylor-Gooby, 1991b, p. 93).
3. Roche tells us that 'the "welfare state" and "social citizenship" can be argued to have their origins in the effectively pre-democratic context

of Bismarck's Germany (e.g. Rimlinger 1971), nonetheless the modern assumption is that their context is typically the liberal democratic state' (Roche, *Rethinking Citizenship*, 1992, p. 11). See G. Rimlinger, *Welfare Policy and Industrialisation in Europe, America and Russia* (1971).

4. Although Esping-Andersen does acknowledge the issue involved (see, for instance, Esping-Andersen, *The Three Worlds of Welfare Capitalism*, 1990, pp. 26–9).

5. The alternative comes to mind of defining and distinguishing welfare-state regimes in terms of 'type and degree of the decommodification of goods and services', that is, of those items which as commodities would (have to) be purchased on the market in (wage) goods and services. See Esping-Andersen, *The Three Worlds of Welfare Capitalism* (1990), pp. 18–21.

6. But how far can the analogy be taken, in view of Esping-Andersen's follow-up comment that it 'is for exactly this reason that employers have always opposed de-commodification' (Esping-Andersen, *The Three Worlds of Welfare Capitalism*, 1990, p. 22).

7. Here, Roche's reference to 'new social rights' reminds us of J. P. Gardner's notion of 'new citizenship' as distinct from 'national citizenship' (Gardner, 'What Lawyers Mean by Citizenship', 1990). Gardner notes that 'many new citizenship rights are protected by the European Convention on Human Rights'; and therefore by the European Commission of Human Rights and 'the European Court of Human Rights in Strasbourg (ibid., p. 72). Gardner also alludes to 'the development of the European Communities' for 'new citizenship' (ibid., pp. 73–4), especially by way of the EC's 'main competence ... in economic matters' (ibid., p. 69). Thus, the EC has established Community-wide rights whereby people 'enjoy freedom of movement to seek jobs or to establish businesses' (ibid., p. 69); although, as Gardner points out, those who enjoy such rights 'are essentially the economically active rather than the whole citizenry' (ibid., p. 69).

8. In fact, Carvel describes the White Paper as Jacques Delors's 'swansong' given Delors's expected retirement as President of the Commission within the year.

Notes to Chapter 6: Citizenship and the European Supra-state

1. That is, 'at market prices', which 'do not reflect the relationships between the domestic purchasing powers of the currencies' (Eurostat, 1992a, p. 39). The exchange rate of the Ecu at the end of November 1993 was 1.134 to the GB£; 0.521 to the GerDM; 0.150 to the FRFr; and 0.885 to the US$ (Beazley, *The European*, 19–25 November 1993).

2. Although, because 'Europe's eastern frontier lacks a clearly defined physical boundary' (*The New Europe: An Encyclopedic Atlas*, 1992, p. 8), estimates of its total area vary. According to Mitchell Beazley, for instance, Europe's land area covers 4 066 000 square miles or 10 532 000 square kilometres (ibid., p. 8).

3. Liechtenstein joined Efta on 1 September 1991.
4. In 1990, the GDP in billions of EC PPS – 'value expressed in constant purchasing power based on the ecu in 1975 and annually updated in line with average EC price indices for GDP' (Eurostat, 1992b, p. 31) – of 'the Twelve' was ecu 5 752.1 billion; and of the Efta countries was ecu 688.7 billion (ibid., pp. 12–13). The countries of the Community plus those of Efta (with the exception of Switzerland, following a referendum in December 1992) created the European Economic Area (EEA) on 1 January 1994.
5. This makes prospectively 45 Member States by 2020. Of course, this is a highly optimistic forecast, especially in view of the ethnic struggles and conflicts in the Balkan and Caucasus regions.
6. Although, a '"greater Europe" stretching from the Atlantic to the Urals' is a possibility for some. See Pascal Fontaine, *Europe in Ten Lessons* (May 1992) p. 6.
7. It is of interest to note that, while Klaus-Dieter Borchardt argues that in 'its structure the Community order resembles the constitutional order of a State', none the less the 'points of resemblance between the Community order and the national order of a State do not ... suffice to confer on the Community the legal character of a (federal) State' (Borchardt, *The ABC of Community Law*, 1991, pp. 7–9).
8. For further discussion, see B. Laffan, *Integration and Co-operation in Europe* (1992) especially ch. 6.
9. The issue of 'subsidiarity' arises here. See The European, *Maastricht Made Simple* (1992) pp. 34–5; and P. Spicker, 'The Principle of Subsidiarity and the Social Policy of the European Community', *Journal of European Social Policy* (1991).
10. Here the term 'decision' is being used in its loose, everyday sense, rather than in its technical, EC-specific sense. In the latter sense a 'decision' is one of several types of European Community law. The term will be used in its loose sense, unless otherwise indicated.
11. For a fuller exposition of the European Community's institutions, see Klaus-Dieter Borchardt, *The ABC of Community Law* (1991); Commission of the European Communities, *The Institutions of the European Community* (November 1993); J. Harrop, *The Political Economy of the Integration of the European Community* (1992) Ch. 2; J. Shaw, *European Community Law* (1993) Chs. 3 and 4.

According to the Commission, the 'Community is managed by common institutions: a democratically elected Parliament, a Council representing the Member States and composed of government ministers or, more rarely, heads of State or government, a Commission which acts as guardian of the Treaties and has the power to initiate and implement legislation, a Court of Justice which ensures that Community law is observed and a Court of Auditors which monitors the financial arrangements of the Community. In addition, there are a number of advisory bodies which represent economic, social and regional interests.' The Commission goes on to describe 'the European Council' as that which is made up of 'the Heads of Government (or in France's case, the Head of State) and the President of the

Commission. The European Council, which meets twice a year in theory, acts as a guide and driving force.' On the other hand, the 'Council of the European Union ... comprises Ministers from each Member State. Meetings are attended by different Ministers according to the agenda' (Commission of the European Communities, *The Institutions of the European Community*, November 1993, pp. 1–4).

12. This has been expressed otherwise as follows: 'the Commission proposes and the Council disposes', although the 'treaties give the European Parliament the right to be consulted' (Borchardt, *The ABC of Community Law*, 1991, pp. 28–9).
13. There are some variations between the scheme of the different founding Treaties. See Borchardt, *The ABC of Community Law* (1991) pp. 24–8; Shaw, *European Community Law* (1993) p. 111.
14. For a fuller examination of the three procedures, see J. Shaw, *European Community Law* (1993) ch. 4.
15. 'The Economic and Social Committee (or Ecosoc) is a 189-member assembly, consulted by both parliament and the commission, with representatives from industry, the unions and all sectors of society' (The European, *Maastricht Made Simple*, 1992, p. 29).
16. What Minshull has in mind here is the EC's response to the 'increase in the price of oil and other commodities in 1973–74 [which] completely altered the terms of trade, and were the major causes of inflation, loss of confidence, economic stagnation, and recession of the period 1974–1982. Growth in all the European Community countries was severely curtailed, and their economies began to diverge seriously' (Minshull, *The New Europe: Into the 1990s*, 1990, p. 330). The event is otherwise summarily referred to as 'the Oil Crisis'.
17. In support of the view that there has been a marked redistribution of control over decision-making in favour of the Parliament, John Palmer reports: 'The European Commission last night conceded the European Parliament's right to have the last word on whether to approve the Gatt Uruguay round agreement. Although the Parliament is most unlikely to veto the General Agreement on Tariffs and Trade deal, its success in winning the right to approve it will be seen as a milestone in its power struggle with national governments. The European trade commissioner, Sir Leon Brittan, told MEPs in Strasbourg yesterday that he would recommend to the Commission that the Parliament should use the new Maastricht treaty to approve the Gatt agreement' (Palmer, '*MEPs Win Right to Veto GATT*', 20 January 1994).
18. See the reference by Josephine Shaw to the 'core activities typically pursued by' the State (Shaw, *European Community Law*, 1993, p. 10), and the discussion below.
19. A federal union made up of sub-national, regional authorities presents itself as an, at least partial, alternative.
20. This follows from Marshall's point that '"A property right [for instance] is not a right to possess property, but a right to acquire it, if you can, and to protect it, if you can get it". Thus paupers and millionaires possess the same capacities through property rights without the

distribution of property being in the least degree affected' (Barbalet, *Citizenship: Rights, Struggle and Class Inequality*, 1988, p. 17).
21. Turner, in common with many writers, uses the term 'contradiction' in a loose, ill-defined manner, so that it appears to be interchangeable with several other terms and notions, such as 'conflict', 'antagonism', 'inconsistency' and 'ambiguity'. It seems to me, however, that there is some sociological advantage to be had from defining the term in a precise and distinctive way, and subsequently to be had from using the notion in a reasonably consistent manner. To this end, I have elsewhere defined 'contradiction' as *the simultaneous affirmation and negation of an item or issue* (Paul Close (ed.), *The State and Caring*, 1992, ch. 1.
22. See, for instance, G. Kaplan, *Contemporary Western European Feminism* (1992).
23. This is a misrepresentation; a confusion. Williams should have said either the Council of Ministers or the European Council (made up of the heads of state or government of the Member States). On the distinction and relationship between the European Council and the Council of Ministers (within what may be collectively referred to as 'The Council'), see David Allen, 'European Union', in Dennis Swann (ed.), *The Single European Market and Beyond* (1992) p. 41. See also, Note 126.
24. In the last few pages of his book, Williams speculates on 'the possibility of a two-speed Europe' as far as the move towards 'economic and monetary union' is concerned (Williams, *The European Community*, 1991, p. 165). The same possibility is addressed by *The European*, summarised as the 'idea that some countries in the EC should press ahead towards unity, while others take things more slowly'. At the same time, this idea is 'actually as old as the Community itself. There is a vast lexicon of expressions, ranging from "differentiation" and "variable geometry" to "à la carte Europe" and "concentric circles". Generally, Brussels insiders have disapproved of any structure that seemed to involve second-class status, and in any way reduced the obligations of membership of the Community' (The European, *Maastricht Made Simple*, 1992, p. 45).

Alongside this, similarly, there has been speculation about the possibility of a two-tier, two-track or two-speed European Community and Union with regard to social policy, and so, to the Union's social space or dimension. This is taken to be illustrated by the UK's opting out of the proposed 'social chapter' of the Maastricht Treaty, based as it was on the Community Charter of Fundamental Social Rights for Workers. With this kind of development in mind, my model of European Citizenship employs similar figurative devices for distinguishing between the tiers, rates and directions of post-national citizenship patterns and trends. My argument is that within the EU, by virtue of the inter-tier contradictions and the attendant overlapping political communities, the speediest track is that designated as Tier III European Citizenship.

Bibliography

Abbott, P. and C. Wallace (eds), *Gender, Sexuality and Power* (London: Macmillan, 1991).
Abercrombie, N., *Contemporary British Society* (Cambridge: Polity Press, 1988).
Abercrombie, N. and A. Warde (eds), *Social Change in Contemporary Britain* (Cambridge: Polity Press, 1992).
Allen, D., 'European Union', in Dennis Swann (ed.), *The Single European Market and Beyond* (London: Routledge, 1992).
Allen, J. and Doreen Masey (eds), *Restructuring Britain: The Economy in Question* (London: Sage, 1988).
Almond, M., 'Cruel Reality of a Future Without any Work', *The European*, 16–19 September 1993.
Archer, C., *Organising Western Europe* (London: Routledge, 1990).
Arrow, K. J., 'Problems Mount in Application of Free Market Economic Theory', *Guardian*, 4 January 1994.
Atkinson, A. B., *Unequal Shares: Wealth in Britain* (London: Allen Lane, 1972).
Atkinson, A. B. (ed.), *Wealth, Income and Inequality* (Oxford: Oxford University Press, 2nd edn, 1980).
Atkinson, A. B., *Economics of Inequality* (Oxford: Oxford University Press, 2nd edn, 1983).
Atkinson, A. B. and A. J. Harrison, *The Distribution of Personal Wealth in Britain* (Cambridge: Cambridge University Press, 1978).
Barbalet, J. M., *Citizenship Rights, Struggle and Class Inequality* (Milton Keynes: Open University Press, 1988).
Barker, D. and C. Padfield, *Law Made Simple* (Oxford: Butterworth-Heinemann, 8th edn, 1992).
Baubock, R., 'Migration and Citizenship', *New Community*, 18 (1 October 1991) pp. 27–48.
Bauman, Z., *Freedom* (Milton Keynes: Open University Press, 1988).
Bauman, Z., *Thinking Sociologically* (Oxford: Blackwell, 1990).
Bauman, Z., *Modernity and Ambivalence* (Cambridge: Polity, 1991).
Beazley, M., *The New Europe: An Encyclopedic Atlas* (London: Mitchell Beazley International, 1992).
Beck, U., *Risk Society: Towards a New Modernity* (London: Sage, 1992).
Bell, A., 'France Moves to Restrict Nationality', *Guardian*, 12 May 1993.
Bergstrom, H., 'Sweden Learns to be Less Stable, More Normal', *The European*, 17–20 June 1993.
Berry, L., 'Poverty, Is it a Crime or a Social Malady?', *The European*, June 1993.
Bobbio, N., 'Clash of Freedom and Power', *Guardian*, 6 March 1992.
Borchardt, K-D., *The ABC of Community Law* (Luxembourg: Office for Official Publications of the European Communities, 3rd edn, 1991).
Bornat, J., C. Pereira, D. Pilgrim and F. Williams (eds), *Community Care: A Reader* (London Macmillan, 1993).

Bibliography

Boyle, N., 'The End of Individualism?', *Guardian*, 15 October 1991.
Brindle, D., 'Britain Moves to Top of EC's Poverty League', *Guardian*, April 1991.
Brindle, D., 'Rich get Richer as VAT Soaks the Poor', *Guardian*, 23 January 1992.
Bryant, C., 'Europe and the European Community 1992', *Sociology*, 25, 2 (May 1991) pp. 189–207.
Burrows, R. and B. Loader, *Towards a Post-Fordist Welfare State?* (London: Routledge, 1994).
Campbell, D., 'No Charges in Under-age Gay Case', *Guardian*, 14 September 1993.
Carvel, J., 'EC Commission Turns up Heat on Clarke over Border Controls', *Guardian*, 25 February 1993.
Carvel, J., 'Changing Face of EC Refugees', *Guardian*, 1 June 1993.
Carvel, J., 'Ministers Agree Moves to Reinforce Fortress Europe', *Guardian*, 2 July 1993.
Carvel, J., 'EC to Investigate Matthews Expulsion', *Guardian*, 15 July 1993.
Carvel, J., 'Child Poverty Blamed on Welfare Cuts', *Guardian*, 23 September 1993.
Carvel, J., 'Tales of the Newsboy, Crisps and Sausage', *Guardian*, 16 October 1993.
Carvel J., 'Delors Plans New Workforce of 3m', *Guardian*, 8 December 1993.
Carvel, J., 'European "Social Pact" is at Heart of New Strategy', *Guardian*, 9 December 1993.
Carvel, J., '"Caveman" with a Modern View', *Guardian*, 10 December 1993.
Carvel, J., 'Europe to Force Visa Laws on UK', *Guardian*, 8 January 1994.
Carvel, J., 'British Passport Checks "May Go"', *Guardian*, 14 January 1994.
Castle, S. and R. Chote, 'Pension Age for Women will Rise to 65', *Independent on Sunday*, 28 November 1993.
Clarke, H., 'Airports Muddled by Open Frontiers', *The European*, 29 April 1993.
Close, P., 'Family Form and Economic Production', in P. Close and R. Collins (eds), *Family and Economy in Modern Society* (London: Macmillan, 1985).
Close, P. (ed), *Family Divisions and Inequalities in Modern Society* (London: Macmillan, 1989).
Close, P., 'Toward a Framework for the Analysis of Family Divisions and Inequalities in Modern Society', in P. Close (ed.), *Family Divisions and Inequalities in Modern Society* (London: Macmillan, 1989).
Close, P., 'State Care, Control and Contradictions: Theorizing Resistance, Change and Progress in Modern Society', in P. Close (ed.), *The State and Caring* (London: Macmillan, 1992).
Close, P. (ed.), *The State and Caring* (London: Macmillan, 1992).
Close, P., 'Children's Rights, Labour and Citizenship', *ESRC Seminar Series 1993–4 on Childhood and Society*, University of Keele, July 1993.
Close, P. and R. Collins (eds), *Family and Economy in Modern Society* (London: Macmillan, 1985).
Coates, K. and R. Silburn, *Poverty: The Forgotten Englishmen* (Harmondsworth: Penguin, 1970).
Commission on Citizenship, *Encouraging Citizenship: Report of the Commission on Citizenship* (London: HMSO, 1990).

Commission of the European Communities, *A People's Europe: Reports from the Ad Hoc Committee* (Luxembourg: Bulletin of the EC, Supplement no. 7, 1985).

Commission of the European Communities, *The Community Charter of Fundamental Social Rights for Workers* (Luxembourg: Office for Official Publications of the European Communities, May 1990a).

Commission of the European Communities, *European File: The Community Charter of Fundamental Social Rights for Workers* (Luxembourg: Office for Official Publications of the European Communities, May 1990b).

Commission of the European Communities, *Europe: World Partner – the External Relations of the European Community* (Luxembourg: Office for Official Publications of the European Communities, April 1991).

Commission of the European Communities, *Background Report: The European Poverty Programme* (Luxembourg: Office for Official Publications of the European Communities, August 1991).

Commission of the European Communities, *Background Report: First Report on the Application of the European Community's Social Charter* (London: Jean Monnet House, January 1992).

Commission of the European Communities, *From Single Market to European Union* (Luxembourg: Office for Official Publications of the European Communities, April 1992).

Commission of the European Communities, *A People's Europe* (Luxembourg: Office for Official Publications of the European Communities, 1992).

Commission of the European Communities, *Questions and Answers About the European Community* (Luxembourg: Office for Official Publications of the European Communities, March 1993b).

Commission of the European Communities, *Frontier-free Europe* (Luxembourg: Office for Official Publications of the European Communities, March 1993a).

Commission of the European Communities, *The Institutions of the European Community* (Luxembourg: Office for Official Publications of the European Communities, November 1993).

Commission of the European Communities, *Equal Opportunities for Women in the Community* (Luxembourg: Office for Official Publications of the European Communities, 1993a).

Commission of the European Communities, *Strengthening Democracy in the EC* (Luxembourg: Office for Official Publications of the European Communities, 1993b).

Coote A. and T. Gill, *Women's Rights: A Practical Guide* (Harmondsworth: Penguin, 3rd edn, 1988).

Corrigan, P., 'Deviance and Deprivation', in P. Abrams (ed.), *Work, Urbanism and Inequality* (London: Weidenfeld, 1978).

Craib, I., *Modern Social Theory* (Brighton: Wheatsheaf, 1984).

Crompton, R., *Class and Stratification: An Introduction to Current Debates* (Cambridge: Polity, 1993a).

Crompton, R., 'Social Citizenship and the Underclass', in her *Class and Stratification: An Introduction to Current Debates* (Cambridge: Polity, 1993b).

Dahl, R. A., *Polyarchy* (New Haven: Yale University Press, 1971).

Bibliography

Dahredorf, R., 'The Erosion of Citizenship and its Consequences for us All', *New Statesman and Society*, 12 June 1987.
Dalley, G., *Ideologies of Caring* (London: Macmillan, 1988).
Dean, H., 'In Search of the Underclass', in P. Brown and R. Scase (eds), *Poor Work: Disadvantage and the Division of Labour* (Milton Keynes: Open University Press, 1991).
Dean, M., 'Setting Europe to Rights', *Guardian*, 29 December 1992.
Dean, M., 'Isolated Britain Delays Reform on Human Rights', *Guardian*, 15 May 1993.
Dearlove, J. and P. Saunders, *Introduction to British Politics* (Cambridge: Polity Press, 1984).
Doyle, L., 'UK Isolated over Four-day Week Option', *Independent on Sunday*, 28 November 1993.
Dudley, N., 'Path to Brussels Clears', *The European*, 12–16 May 1993.
Dunleavy, P. and B. O'Leary, *Theories of the State: The Politics of Liberal Democracy* (London: Macmillan, 1987).
Duplain, J., 'No Baulking in the Baltic', *Observer*, 4 July 1993.
Dyer, C., 'Girl, 13, Tests Legal Right to "Divorce" Adoptive Parents', *Guardian*, 26 April 1993.
The Economist, 'Citizenship: What is a European?', 17 August 1991.
Elliot, L., 'Jobless Rise Jolts Hope of Recovery', *Guardian*, 17 September 1993.
Esping-Andersen, G., *The Three Worlds of Welfare Capitalism* (Oxford: Polity, 1990).
The European, *Maastricht Made Simple* (1992).
The European, 'Immigrants Face Checks on Identity', 29 April 1993.
The European, 'Focus on Forgotten who Live in Poverty', 3–6 June 1993.
The European, 'Russians Stripped of Rights', 24–7 June 1993.
European Documentation, *1992 – The Social Dimension* (Luxembourg: Office for Official Publications of the European Communities, 1990).
European Parliament, *Europe's Parliament and the Single Act* (London: UK Office of the European Parliament, May 1989).
European Parliament News, 'Bringing the New Poor in from "Social Exclusion"', 21–5 June 1993.
European Parliament and Council, *Final Report on the Second European Poverty Programme (1985–1989)*, COM (19) 29 Final, February 1991.
Eurostat, *A Social Portrait of Europe* (Luxembourg: Office for Official Publications of the European Communities, 1988).
Eurostat, *Basic Statistics of the Community* (Luxembourg: Office for Official Publications of the European Communities, 29th edn, 1992a).
Eurostat, *Facts Through Figures: A Statistical Portrait of the European Community in the European Economic Area* (Luxembourg: Office for Official Publications of the European Communities, 1992b).
Eurostat, *A Social Portrait of Europe* (Luxembourg: Office for Official Publications of the European Communities, 1992c).
Fontaine, P., *A Citizen's Europe* (Luxembourg: Office for Official Publications of the European Communities, June 1991).
Fontaine, P., *Europe in Ten Lesson* (Luxembourg: Office for Official Publications of the European Communities, May 1992).

Friedman, R., N. Gilbert and M. Sherer (eds), *Modern Welfare States* (Hemel Hempstead: Wheatsheaf, 1987).
Gamarnikow, E., et al. (eds), *The Public and the Private* (London: Heinemann, 1983).
Gardner, J. P., 'What Lawyers Mean by Citizenship', Appendix D in Commission on Citizenship, *Encouraging Citizenship: Report of the Commission on Citizenship* (London: HMSO, 1990).
Gellner, E., *Culture, Identity and Politics* (Cambridge: Cambridge University Press, 1987).
Gellner, E., 'Nationalism Reconsidered', *Review of International Studies*, 18 (1992) pp. 285–93.
George, V. and P. Wilding, *Ideology and Social Welfare* (London: Routledge and Kegan Paul, 1985).
Giddens, A., *Central Problems in Social Theory* (London: Macmillan, 1979).
Giddens, A., *A Contemporary Critique of Historical Materialism*, vol. 1, *Power, Property and the State* (London: Macmillan, 1981).
Giddens, A., 'Class Division, Class Conflict and Citizenship Rights', in his *Profiles and Critiques in Social Theory* (London: Macmillan, 1982a).
Giddens, A., *Profiles and Critiques in Social Theory* (London: Macmillan, 1982b).
Giddens, A., *Sociology: A Brief but Critical Introduction* (London: Macmillan, 1982c).
Giddens, A., *A Contemporary Critique of Historical Materialism*, vol. 2, *The National State and Violence* (Cambridge: Polity, 1985).
Giddens, A., *Sociology: A Brief but Critical Introduction* (London: Macmillan, 2nd edn, 1986).
Giddens, A., *Social Theory and Modern Sociology* (Cambridge: Polity, 1987).
Giddens, A., *Modernity and Self-identity: Self and Society in the Late Modern Age* (Cambridge: Polity, 1991.
Gittings, J., 'Britain Condemns Chinese Brutality', *Guardian*, 30 June 1993.
Glyn, A., 'Decade that Made Rich More Equal', *Guardian*, 8 June 1992.
Goldthorpe, J. H. and D. Lockwood, 'Affluence and the British Class Structure', *Sociological Review*, 11, 2 (1963).
Goldthorpe, J. H., D. Lockwood, F. Bechhofer and J. Platt, *The Affluent Worker in the Class Structure* (Cambridge: Cambridge University Press, 1969).
Goodway, N., 'The 35 Billion Bequest to Britain's Children', *Observer*, 25 July 1993.
Gough, I., *The Political Economy of the Welfare State* (London: Macmillan, 1979).
Gow, D., 'Transit Terminal gives Foretaste of Fortress Europe', *Guardian*, 27 May 1993.
Gray, J., 'It's Time to Challenge the New Right's Love Affair with the Wonders of the Global Market', *Guardian*, 4 January 1994.
Graz, L., 'Two Cheers for Human Rights Better than None', *Observer*, 27 June 1993.
Greaves, H. R. G., *The Foundations of Political Theory* (London: Bell and Sons, 2nd edn, 1966).
Guardian, 'Rights: Young at Heart', 5 January 1993.
Guardian, 'Citizenship Act Angers Russia', 24 June 1993.

Guardian, 'Estonians are Told to Change Controversial Law', 7 July 1993.
Guardian, 'Estonian Leader Halts Aliens Law', 8 July 1993.
Guardian, 'Estonian Leader Signs Aliens law', 13 July 1993.
Guardian, 'Plan to Widen Choice of Birth', 2 August 1993.
Gumbel, A., 'Where French Law is No More than a Mirage', *Guardian*, 28 October 1993.
Halsey, A. H., 'Class Ridden Prosperity', *The Listener*, 19 January 1978.
Halsey, A. H., 'T. H. Marshall: Past and Present', *Sociology*, 18, 1 (1984).
Harbury, C. and G. Hitchins, 'The Myth of the Self-made Man', *New Statesman*, 15 February 1980.
Harrington, M., *The Other American: Poverty in the United States* (Harmondsworth: Penguin, 1963).
Harris, C. C., *The Family and Industrial Society* (London: Allen and Unwin, 1983).
Harrop, J., *The Political Economy of the Integration of the European Community* (Aldershort: Edward Elgar, 2nd edn, 1992).
Harvie, C., 'Review of Paul Stares, *The New Germany and the New Europe*', *Guardian*, 16 February 1993.
Hattersley, R., 'Stand Up for Europe', *Guardian*, 10 November 1993.
Held, D., 'Citizenship and Autonomy', in D. Held and J. Thompson (eds), *Social Theory of Modern Societies: Anthony Giddens and his Critics* (Cambridge: Cambridge University Press, 1989).
Held, D. and J. Thompson (eds), *Social Theory and Modern Societies: Anthony Giddens and his Critics* (Cambridge: Cambridge University Press, 1989).
Helgadottir, B., 'A Helping Hand for the One in Seven', *The European*, June 1993.
Henderson, R., '*The Commission on Citizenship Seminar*', unpublished paper, April 1980.
Herbert, S., 'Court Clears UK on Terrorism Law', *Guardian*, 19 May 1993.
Holman, B., 'Poor Lore', *Guardian*, 15 September 1993.
Hurd, D., 'Freedom will Flourish where Citizens Accept Responsibilities', *Independent*, 13 September 1989.
Hutchinson Softback Encyclopedia (Oxford: Helicon Publishing, revised edn, 1992).
Hutton, W., 'A Just Cause for Delors', *Guardian*, 10 December 1993.
Irwin, A., Review of Anthony Giddens, *Modernity and Self-Identity: Self and Society in the Late Modern Age*, *Sociology*, 27: 2 (May 1993) pp. 338–9.
Jeffries, I., *Socialist Economies and the Transition to the Market* (London: Routledge, 1993).
Jensen, A-M., 'Reproduction in Norway: An Area of Non-responsibility?' in P. Close (ed.), *Family Divisions and Inequalities in Modern Society* (London: Macmillan, 1989).
Jesson, B., A. Ryan and P. Spoonley, *Revival of the Right: New Zealand Politics in the 1980s* (Auckland: Heinemann Reed, 1988).
Johnstone Conover, P., I. Crewe and D. Searing, 'The Nature of Citizenship in the United States and Great Britain; Empirical Comments on Theoretical Themes', *Journal of Politics*, 52, 4 (November 1990).
Jones, G. and C. Wallace, *Youth, Family and Citizenship* (Buckingham: Open University Press, 1992).

Jordan, B., *Rethinking Welfare* (Oxford: Blackwell, 1987).
Kaplan, G., *Contemporary Western European Feminism* (London: Allen and Unwin, 1992).
Kelly, R., 'Gap between Rich and Poor Widens', *Guardian*, May 1993.
Kingston, P., 'Homosexuality: The Freedom to Choose', *Guardian*, 29 June 1993a.
Kingston, P., 'Homosexuality: Loosening the Straitjacket', *Guardian*, 29 June 1993b.
Komatsu, R., 'The State and Social Welfare in Japan: Patterns and Developments', in P. Close (ed.), *The State and Caring* (London: Macmillan, 1992).
Korpi, W., *The Democratic Class Struggle* (London: Routledge and Kegan Paul, 1983).
Kuper, A. and J. Kuper, *The Social Science Encyclopedia* (London: Routledge, 1989).
Laffan, B., *Integration and Co-operation in Europe* (London: Routledge, 1992).
Landsdown, G., 'Participation or Protection: Are Children's Rights Compatible with Parental Rights?', *ESRC Seminar Series 1993–4 Childhood and Society*, University of Keele, July 1993.
Lane, R., 'Why Riches Don't Always Buy Happiness', *Guardian*, 9 August 1993.
Lash, S. and J. Urry, *The End of Organized Capitalism* (Oxford: Polity, 1987).
Leonard, D., 'Mapping Out a Europe of 42 Countries', *Observer*, 10 May 1992.
Lewis, O., *Five Families* (New York: Basic Books, 1959).
Lewis, O., *The Children of Sanchez* (New York: Random House, 1961).
Lewis, O., *La Vida* (New York: Random House, 1966).
Lieven, A., *The Baltic Revolution* (New York: Yale University Press, 1993).
Lindblom, C. E., *Politics and Markets* (New York: Basic Books, 1977).
Lipset, S. M., 'Introduction', in T. H. Marshall, *Class, Citizenship and Social Development* (Westport, Connecticut: Greenwood Press, 1973, first published in 1964).
Lister, R., *The Exclusive Society: Citizenship and the Poor* (London: Child Poverty Action Group, 1987).
Lister, R., 'Women, Economic Dependency and Citizenship', *Journal of Social Policy*, 14, 4 (1990) pp. 445–67.
Lockwood, D., 'Social Integration and System Integration', in G. K. Zollschan and W. Hirsch (eds), *Explorations in Social Change* (Boston: Houghton-Mufflin, 1964).
Loney, M., et al. (eds), *The State or the Market* (London: Sage, 1987).
Lowe, R., *The Welfare State in Britain since 1945* (London: Macmillan, 1993).
McIntosh, M., 'Family, Regulation, and the Public Sphere', in G. McLellan et al. (eds), *State and Society in Contemporary Britain* (Oxford: Blackwell, 1984).
McIvor, G., 'Refugees Influx Reveals Sweden's Hidden Racism', *Guardian*, 31 July 1993.
McIvor, G., 'Sweden to Deport Victims of Russian Anti-semitism', *Guardian*, 11 November 1993.

Bibliography

Mann, M., *The Macmillan Student Encyclopedia of Sociology* (London: Macmillan, 1983).
Marquand, D., *The Unprincipled Society* (London: Cape, 1988).
Marret, M. and M. Bond, 'Hungarians in Romania are Fighting Back', *The European*, 14–17 October 1993.
Marshall, G. et al., *Social Class in Modern Britain* (London: Hutchinson, 1988).
Marshall, T. H., *Citizenship and Social Class and Other Essays* (Cambridge: Cambridge University Press, 1950, 1952).
Marshall, T. H., 'Citizenship and Social Class' (first published in 1950), in *Class, Citizenship and Social Development* (Westport, Connecticut: Greenwood Press, 1973, first published in 1964).
Marshall, T. H., *Class, Citizenship and Social Development* (Westport, Connecticut: Greenwood Press, 1973, first published in 1964).
Marshall, T. H., 'Reflection on Power' (first published in 1969), in his *The Right to Welfare and Other Essays* (London: Heinemann, 1981a).
Marshall, T. H., *The Rights to Welfare and Other Essays* (London: Heinemann, 1981b).
Mead, L., *Beyond Entitlement: The Social Obligations of Citizenship* (New York: Free Press, 1986).
Meyer, H., 'Frontier of Hate', *Guardian*, 17 August 1993.
Millar, F., 'A Law that Cares at Last', *Guardian*, 5 January 1993.
Milner, M., 'Bloc Bigger than Nafta "From Many Points of View"', *Guardian*, 1 January 1994.
Minshull, G. N., *The New Europe: Into the 1990s* (London: Hodder and Stoughton, 4th edn, 1990).
Mishra, R., *The Welfare State in Crisis* (Hemel Hempstead: Wheatsheaf, 1984).
Mishra, R., *The Welfare State in Capitalist Society* (Hemel Hempstead: Wheatsheaf, 1990).
Morris, L., and S. Irwin, 'Employment Histories and the Concept of the Underclass', *Sociology*, 26, 3 (August 1992) pp. 401–20.
Mount, F., *The Subversive Family* (London: Cape, 1982).
Mount, F., 'A Constitution Unwritten and Unloved', *Guardian*, 12 May 1992.
Murray, C., *Losing Ground* (New York: Basic Books, 1984).
Murray, C., 'Underclass', *Sunday Times Magazine* 26 November 1989.
Murray, C., 'The Emerging Britain Underclass', *Choice in Welfare Series*, no. 2 (1990).
Nereth, P. and Julie Reid, 'Mothers Pay Price of Being Single', *The European*, 15–25 November 1993.
Oakley, A., *Women Confined: Towards a Sociology of Childbirth*, (Oxford: Martin Robertson, 1980).
Padfield, C. and A. Byrne, *British Constitution* (Oxford: Heinemann, 7th edn, 1987).
Palmer, J., 'The Fast Road to Europe', *Guardian*, 25 February 1993.
Palmer, J., 'Human Rights Court to Expand', *Guardian*, 1 October 1993.
Palmer, J., 'A Shift in Common Ground as European Union Comes of Age', *Guardian*, 1 November 1993.
Palmer, J., 'Ministers Spurn £33 billion EU Recovery Plan', *Guardian*, 6 December 1993.

Palmer, J., 'MEPs Win Right to Veto GATT', *Guardian*, 20 January 1994.
Palmer, J. and J. Carvel, 'Delors has Backing for Jobs Boost', *Guardian*, 10 December 1993.
Pampel, F., and J. Williamson, *Age, Class, Politics and the Welfare State* (Cambridge: Cambridge University Press, 1989).
Pfaller, A., I. Gough and G. Theorborn (eds), *Can the Welfare State Compete? A Comparative Study of Five Advanced Capitalist Countries* (London: Macmillan, 1991).
Phillips, M., 'Encounters with the Underclass', *Guardian*, 13 March 1992.
Phillips, M., 'Human Rights Going Down the Euro-drain', *Observer*, 8 August 1993.
Pilkington, E., 'UK Heads Europe Bias Against Gays', *Guardian*, 20 August 1993.
Pilkington, E., 'Silent Birth of European Era', *Guardian*, 7 November 1993.
Pond, C., 'The Changing Distribution of Income, Wealth and Poverty', in C. Hamnett, L. McDowell and P. Sarre (eds), *Restructuring Britain: The Changing Social Structure* (Milton Keynes: Open University Press, 1989a).
Pond, C., 'Wealth and the Two Nation', in L. McDowell, P. Sarre and C. Hamnett (eds), *Divided Nation: Social and Cultural Change in Britain* (London: Hodder and Stoughton, 1989b).
Rex, J., and S. Tomlinson, *Colonial Immigrants in a British City* (London: Routledge, 1979).
Rimlinger, G., *Welfare Policy and Industrialisation in Europe, America and Russia* (New York: John Wiley, 1971).
Robertson, R., 'Globalisation and Societal Modernisation: A Note on Japan and Japanese Religion', *Sociological Analysis*, 47 (1987) pp. 35–42.
Robertson, R. and F. Lechner, 'Modernisation, Globalisation and the Problem of Culture in World-systems Theory', *Theory, Culture and Society*, 2 (1985) pp. 103–18.
Roche, M., *Rethinking Citizenship: Welfare, Ideology and Change in Modern Society* (Cambridge: Polity Press, 1992).
Rogaly, J., 'The Active Citizen for All Parties', *Financial Times*, 5 October 1988.
Rose, D., 'UK Blocks Key Reforms of Human Rights Court', *Observer*, 16 May 1993.
Saunders, P., *Social Theory and the Urban Question* (London: Unwin Hyman, 1987).
Schmitter, P., 'The European Community as an Emergent and Novel Form of Political Domination', draft article in progress, 1990.
Schmitter, P. and W. Streeck, 'Organised Interests and the Europe of 1992', paper presented at a conference on *The United States and Europe in the 1980s*, American Enterprise Institute, Washington, D. C., March 1990.
Scott, J., *The Upper Classes* (London: Macmiillan, 1982).
Sharrock, D., 'Terror Act "Does Not Usurp Rights"', *Guardian*, 27 May 1993.
Sharrock, D., 'Nightmare of Life Under Banning Order', *Guardian*, 17 July 1993.
Shaw, J., *European Community Law* (London: Macmillan, 1993).
Showstack Sassoon, A. (ed.), *Women and the State* (London: Hutchinson, 1987).

Simmel, G., 'The Poor', *Social Problems*, (1966, first published in 1908).
Simmons, M., 'Mother Wrongly Naturalised can be Deported', *Guardian*, 17 July 1993.
Smart, V., 'Schengen Express Derailed by France', *The European*, 6 May 1993.
Smart, V., 'Delors Faces "Social" Crisis', *The European*, 10–13 June 1993.
Smith, C, 'Inequality at 18 is No Answer', *The Independent*, 23 February 1994.
Social Trends 22 (London: HMSO, 1992).
Social Trends 23 (London: HMSO, 1993).
Southern Derbyshire Health Authority, *Achieving the Patient's Charter* (1993).
Spicker, P., *Principles of Social Welfare* (London: Routledge, 1988).
Spicker, P., 'The Principle of Subsidiarity and the Social Policy of the European Community', *Journal of European Social Policy*, 1, 1 (1991) pp. 3–14.
Summers, Y., 'Women and Citizenship: The Insane, the Insolvent and the Inanimate', in P. Abbott and C. Wallace (eds), *Gender, Sexuality and Power* (London: Macmillan, 1991).
Swann, D., 'The Single Market and Beyond – an Overview', in D. Swann (ed.), *The Single European Market and Beyond* (London: Routledge, 1992).
Taylor-Gooby, P., *Social Change, Social Welfare and Social Science* (Hemel Hempstead: Wheatsheaf, 1991a).
Taylor-Gooby, P., 'Welfare State Regimes and Welfare Citizenship', *Journal of European Social Policy*, 1, 2 (1991b).
Thatcher, M., interview in *Woman's Own*, 31 October 1987.
Thatcher, M., *Britain and Europe* (London: Conservative Political Centre, 1988).
Toffler, A. and H. Toffler, 'Societies Running at Hyper-speed', *Guardian*, 3 November 1993.
Tomforde, A., 'Bonn Defies Protesters to Curb Asylum Rights', *Guardian*, 27 May 1993.
Townsend, P., *Poverty in the United Kingdom* (Harmondsworth: Penguin, 1979).
Travis, A., '"New" British Citizens at 10-year Low as Nationality Act Bites', *Guardian*, 26 June 1993.
Travis, A., 'Asylum Act "to Play Pass the Refugee"', *Guardian*, 26 July 1993.
Traynor, I., 'Rights Meeting Ends in Split', *Guardian*, 26 June 1993.
Turner, B. S., *Citizenship and Capitalism* (London: Allen & Unwin, 1986a).
Turner, B. S., *Equality* (London: Tavistock, 1986b).
Turner, B. S., *Status* (Milton Keynes: Open University Press, 1988).
Turner, B. S., 'Outline of a Theory of Citizenship', *Sociology*, 24, 2 (May 1990) pp. 189–217.
Tyrell, H. and G. Langdon-Down, 'The Law and How it Works for Children Aged 10', *Observer*, 21 February 1993.
Ungerson, C., 'Paid Work and Unpaid Caring: A Problem for Women or the State?', in P. Close and R. Collins (eds), *Family and Economy in Modern Society* (London: Macmillan, 1985).
Unicef, *Progress of Nations* (London: UK Committee of Unicef, 1993).
Valentine, C., *Culture and Poverty* (Chicago: University of Chicago Press, 1968).
Verity, C., 'An Ethnic Powder Keg in the Baltic?', *The European*, 24–7 June 1993.
Vitaliev, V., 'Luxembourg is Friendly ... but Don't Ask to Vote', *The European*, 5–11 November 1993.

Walker, L., 'Many Measures but Single Goal', *The European*, 22–25 April 1993.
Walker, L., 'Workers Squeezed in Jobs Crisis', *The European*, 14–17 October 1993.
Walker, L., 'Know Your Rights, Citizens', *The European*, 5–11 November 1993.
Wallace, C., 'The Concept of Citizenship: An Overview', *Slovak Sociological Review*, March 1993.
Wallerstein, I., *The Politics of the World Economy* (Cambridge: Cambridge University Press, 1984).
Wallerstein, I., *Geopolitics and Geoculture* (Cambridge: Cambridge University Press, 1991).
Warde, A., 'Consumption, Identity Formation and Uncertainty', *The Fourth Symposium on the Sociology of Consumption*, University of Helsinki, June 1993.
Warde, A., *Consumers, Consumption and a Post-Fordist Welfare State?* (London: Routledge, 1994).
Watson, R., 'Hidden Misery of the Have-nots', *The European*, 14–17 October 1993.
Webster, P., 'Pasqua Aims for "Zero" Immigration', *Guardian*, 3 June 1993.
Webster, P., 'Random Police Identity Checks Come into Force in France', *Guardian*, 8 August 1993.
Webster, P., 'Curbs on Aliens Rule Unlawful', *Guardian*, 16 August 1993.
Webster, P., 'France to Restrict Political Asylum', *Guardian*, 26 August 1993.
Westergaard, J., 'The Rediscovery of the Cash Nexus: Some Recent Interpretations of Trends in the British Class Structure', *Socialist Register*, 1970.
Weston, C., 'Tories "Add 1m to Lowest Paid"', *Guardian*, 26 August 1992.
White, M., 'Britain Attacks "Cynical" Commission Ploy', *Guardian*, 9 December 1993.
White, M. and K. Harper, 'Two-thirds "Below Family Income Norm"', *Guardian*, 19 July 1993.
Wickham, G., 'Citizenship, Governance and the Consumption of Sport', *The Fourth Symposium on the Sociology of Consumption*, University of Helsinki, June 1993.
Williams, A., *The European Community* (Oxford: Blackwell, 1991).
Williams, F., *Social Policy: A Critical Introduction* (Cambridge: Polity, 1989).
Wintour, P., 'Major Offers Right to Sue Strikers', *Guardian*, 28 January 1992.
Wistrich, E., *After 1992* (London: Routledge, 1989).
Wistrich, E., *The United States of Europe* (London: Routledge, 1994).
Wroe, M., 'Vexed Question of Gay Consent', *Observer*, 9 January 1994.
Zaretsky, E., *Capitalism, the Family and Personal Life* (London: Pluto Press, 1975).

Index

Abercrombie, N.; Abercrombie, N. and Warde, A., 304, 310
adolescence, 9, 11–30, 36, 189–92, 200, 254, 299, 300, 301
adulthood, 8–30, 37–8, 53–4, 67, 254, 297, 299, 300, 301
age; generation; life-cycle, 8–29, 34, 36–9, 42, 53–4, 67, 70, 75, 107, 114, 124, 142, 144, 146, 171, 189–92, 200, 209, 217–18, 224–5, 228–9, 254, 273, 277–8, 297, 299, 300, 301, 302, 307
Albania, 76, 234
aliens, 69–72, 77–81, 94–5, 99, 102, 109–13, 124–6, 169, 224–5, 304; *see also* migrants
Allen, D., 315
Allen, J. and D. Masey, 311
Almond, M., 35
Archer, C., 75
Armenia, 234
Association of South-East Asian Nations (Asean), 118
asylum, 97–137, 238, 293–4, 309; *see also* migrants
Atkinson, A.B.; Atkinson, A.B. and A. Harrison, 304
Australia, 39, 109, 202, 257
Austria, 22, 25, 26, 28, 29, 75, 135, 202–3, 233–5, 301, 305
Azerbaijan, 234

Baker, J., 268–70
Balkan region, 130–1; *see also* Albania; Bulgaria; Bosnia-Herzegovena; Croatia; Greece; Macedonia; Montenegro; Romania; Serbia; Slovenia; Turkey; Yugoslavia
Baltic region, 76–81; *see also* Estonia, Latvia, Lithuania

Barbalet, J. M., 7–11, 28, 55–6, 68–9, 108, 141–6, 148–52, 157–66, 168–9, 171–2, 175, 206, 224, 226, 271–3, 283–5, 299, 304, 310, 315
Barker, D. and Padfield, C., 10–14, 57, 66–8, 70–1, 104, 106, 111, 169, 304, 307, 308
Baubock, R., 5–6, 69, 81, 141
Bauman, Z., 184–6, 199–200, 220
Beazley, M., 231, 233, 312
Beck, U., 181–6, 220
Belarus, *see* Byelorussia
Belgium, 26–7, 29, 32–3, 38, 75–81, 129–30, 201–2, 228, 233, 246, 248, 257, 269, 295
Bell, A., 123–4
Benelux countries, 212; *see also* Belgium, Luxembourg, Netherlands
Bergstrom, H., 218
Berry, L., 43–4
Bobbio, N., 138–9, 146
Borchardt, H. D., 238–9, 245, 288–9, 297, 305, 313, 314
Bornat, J. *et al.*, 6
Bosnia-Herzegovena, 234
Boyle, N., 187–8, 193, 203
Brindle, D., 32–3, 60, 301
Britain, 7, 9, 13, 24–5, 35, 37–9, 42–4, 46–51, 65–71, 77, 81–8, 90, 93, 97, 100, 102–5, 108–12, 114, 122–3, 127–8, 132–3, 137, 141–52, 155, 160–3, 171–86, 187, 189, 207, 213–14, 216, 221, 291–2, 296, 300, 301, 304, 305, 307, 308; *see also* England & Wales; Scotland; United Kingdom
Bryant, C., 118–20, 308
Buck, N., 301, 302
Bulgaria, 26, 76, 129–30, 234
Byelorussia, 76–7, 79, 234

Index

Campbell, D., 24
Canada, 39, 109, 123, 202, 234, 247
capitalism; capitalist society; market capitalism, x, 64–5, 145–52, 155, 166–3, 171–86, 187–9, 192–4, 196–204, 207–14, 216–22, 224, 227–8, 230, 272, 279–80
Carvel, J., 36, 39–40, 44, 87, 128–31, 206–10, 212–13, 221–2, 291-2, 296, 309, 312
Castle, S. and Chote, R., 277
Catholicism, 187–8, 193, 202–3
childhood; children, 4, 9–23, 28–30, 37–9, 45, 48, 53–4, 67–9, 75, 112, 140, 142, 217, 224–5, 228, 254, 299, 300, 301, 307
Children Act 1989, 15–21
China, People's Republic of, x, 102–3, 110–11, 123
citizenship, active, 50–2; civil, 5–8, 12, 19–21, 46, 55–6, 65–8, 71–4, 105, 141–2, 144, 147–15, 154–63, 168, 170–1, 180, 184, 232, 271, 273, 275–6, 311, 314, 315; concept of, 1–13, 18–20, 23, 26–30, 45–54, 55–7, 68–9, 74–5, 97–110, 113–15, 120–2, 138–43, 164–75, 227–30, 232, 253–4, 270–1, 274–5, 283–90, 299, 308; economic, 151, 154–9, 164–75; geo-political model of, 267–75, 279; industrial, 7, 41–2, 49, 51, 73, 93, 151, 154–9, 162–75, 180, 184–5, 200, 206, 215, 220, 223–6, 232, 245–6, 271, 275–7, 310, 311; national, 3, 8, 72–3, 77–81, 89–90, 95–6, 97–117, 120–2, 127–8, 132, 135–7, 138, 140–2, 215, 255, 266–8, 270–1, 275–80, 287, 290, 293, 304, 305, 307, 308, 312; new, 3, 72–90, 95–6, 97–104, 120, 132, 139–40, 142, 215, 237, 275–9, 304, 305, 306, 312; political, 6–9, 14, 19–20, 46, 55, 71, 73–4, 94, 141–4, 147, 153–5, 158, 162, 170–1, 232, 242, 271–2, 275, 284, 310; social, 4, 6–7, 35–6, 39–54, 55, 71, 73–5, 93, 141–2, 144, 151, 154–63, 170–1, 175, 180–1, 184–5, 190–230, 232, 245–6, 267–8, 271, 273, 275–7, 311, 312, 315; socio-political model of, 274–83, 289–90, 294, 315; welfare, 56, 156, 195–6, 206–7, 215, 217, 220, 226, 232, 245–6, 271, 275, 277
Citizenship of the (European) Union, x–xi, 93–6, 113, 120, 127, 135–7, 215, 229–30, 252–6, 259–60, 262–3, 266–7, 276, 278–9, 289–90, 293, 297–8
Citizen's Charter, 302, 303
civil society, 7–8, 147–51, 154, 156, 189, 193
Clarke, H., 294
Close, P.; Close, P. and R. Collins, 6, 175, 301, 303, 304, 309, 315
Coates, K. and R. Silburn, 302, 303
Commission on Citizenship, 2–3, 74, 192, 299, 305, 310
Commonwealth, 70, 109–12, 123, 141, 170
Commission of the European Communities, *see* European Commission
commodification; de-commodification, *see* commodity market
commodity market; consumption, 177–86, 196–204, 206, 209, 216, 220
Community Charter for the Fundamental Social Rights of Workers, *see* social charter
compensatory rights, *see* non-citizenship rights
conflict, resistance and struggle, x, 85–9, 91, 97, 103, 115–17, 122, 132, 136, 144–63, 165, 175, 180, 184–6, 224–5, 267, 270, 272–3, 278, 280, 283, 290, 309, 315
contradictions, 90, 120–2, 137, 145–7, 160–3, 175, 181–3, 199, 206, 267, 270–4, 278–82, 284, 294, 309, 315
Coote, A. and Gill, T., 68
Corrigan, P., 31
Council of Europe, 36, 69, 73–86, 90–1, 95, 97–8, 102–4, 255, 304, 305, 312

Council of Europe's Convention of Human Rights, *see* European Convention on Human Rights
Craib, I., 231
Croatia, 76, 234
Crompton, R., 45–7, 173
Cyprus, 25–6, 75, 234, 300
Czechoslovakia; Czech Republic; Slovakia, 26–7, 75–6, 116, 234

Dahl, R., 310
Dahrendorf, R., 48
Dalley, G., 6
Dean, H., 47
Dean, M., 74–5, 77, 79, 81–3, 98
Dearlove, J. and P. Saunders, 310
democratic deficit, 242–4, 249–52, 260
Denmark, 22, 26, 29, 32–3, 37–8, 75, 82, 112, 129–30, 137, 202, 233, 246, 248, 291, 293, 296, 301
dependency; dependency culture, 4–6, 17–22, 37, 43–54, 160–1, 189–92, 200–1, 203, 302
domestic labour, *see* gender
Doyle, L., 207–10
Dudley, N., 293–4
Dunleavy, P. and B. O'Leary, 99, 142–3, 147–8, 192–3, 196, 286, 300
Duplain, J., 77
Dyer, C., 16–17, 300

East Germany, *see* Germany
Economic and Monetary Union (EMU), 93, 259
education, 7, 9, 10, 12, 20–1, 53, 71, 73, 82, 93, 118, 139, 141, 162, 188–9, 194, 300, 301
Elliot, L., 35
enabling resources, 4–5, 30–1, 51–4, 56–68, 75, 142, 161, 171, 178–9, 185, 198, 200, 220, 272–3, 280, 297, 301, 304
England; England and Wales, 4, 10, 15–18, 20–2, 25, 28–9, 36, 67, 105, 111, 169, 299; *see also* Britain; United Kingdom

Esping-Andersen, G., 196–206, 218–19, 221, 312
Estonia, 25, 76–81, 90, 102–3, 234
ethnicity, *see* race-ethnicity
European Citizenship, models of, 267–83, 289, 294, 315
European Commission, 31–6, 38–43, 53, 87, 92, 119, 128, 206–15, 217, 221–4, 227–8, 230, 231, 238, 240–4, 246–52, 257–9, 265, 277, 280–1, 291–6, 301, 305, 312, 313, 314
European Community (EC); European Union (EU), x–xi, 1, 31–6, 38–43, 53, 69–70, 87–8, 91–6, 103–4, 112–13, 117–20, 122, 125, 127–37, 187–230, 231, 298, 304, 305, 308, 312, 313, 314, 315; as a super-power, x, 119, 236–7, 240–1; as a supra-state, x–xi, 92–6, 118–20, 136, 195, 205–6, 216, 219–23, 231–98, 308; as a welfare-citizenship regime, 189, 205–6, 208–10, 215, 219–24
European Community's Charter for the Fundamental Social Rights of Workers, *see* social chapter
European Community's Commission, *see* European Commission
European Community's Council of Ministers, 31, 92–3, 119, 128–9, 131, 237, 243–50, 252, 260, 280, 296, 305, 313, 314, 315
European Community's Court of Auditors, 92–3
European Community's Court of Justice, *see* European Court of Justice
European Community's Economics and Social Committee, 247, 314
European Community's Parliament, *see* European Parliament
European Convention on Human Rights, 72–86, 90–1, 97–8, 138–9, 275
European Council, 41, 187, 210–14, 217, 221, 223, 228, 230, 236–7, 239, 241–4, 248, 260, 280–1, 313, 314, 315

European Court of Human Rights, 24–5, 74, 81–6, 90–1, 97–8, 276, 300, 305, 309, 312
European Court of Justice, 89, 92–3, 238, 261–6, 277, 289, 292, 296, 305, 313
European Economic Area (EEA), 234–5, 313
European Free Trade Area (Efta), 233, 313
European Parliament, 42, 69, 87, 92–4, 113, 119, 238, 242–4, 246–52, 254, 260, 265, 280–1, 291–2, 295, 313
European supra-citizenship, see Citizenship of the (European) Union
Eurostat, 32–3, 69–71, 301, 312

Federal Republic of Germany, see Germany
federalism; federation, x, 91–2, 118, 120, 238–41, 255–61, 265–9, 274, 279, 281–3, 288–9, 297, 313, 314
feminism, 3–6; see also gender
Finland, 21, 25–6, 75, 135, 202, 233–5, 300, 305
Fontaine, P., 225–30, 233–4, 242, 287–8, 313
Ford, G., 69–70
Fortress Europe, 124–37, 293–5
France, 22, 26–9, 32–3, 35, 37–8, 43–4, 70–1, 75, 112, 117, 123–9, 131–2, 134–5, 137, 139, 202–3, 217, 233, 248, 269, 295, 301, 309, 313
Friedman, R. *et al.*, 204, 219

Galbraith, J. K., 59
Gamarnikow, R., 149
Gardner, J.P., 2–3, 6, 71–3, 76, 97–102, 107–9, 138, 255, 275, 287, 299, 306, 312
gender; sex-gender, 4–6, 9, 13–14, 21, 23–7, 36–8, 47–8, 68, 75, 107, 114, 140, 142, 146, 149, 156–7, 197–200, 203, 209, 220, 224–6, 273, 276–8, 297–8, 300, 307, 310; see also sexuality
Gellner, E., 115–17, 122, 136, 308

General Agreement on Tariffs and Trade (GATT), 258, 314
George, V. and P. Wilding, 303
Georgia, 234
German Democratic Republic, see Germany
Germany, 21–2, 25–7, 32–3, 35, 38, 43–4, 70–1, 75, 112, 114, 116–17, 119, 123, 129–30, 132–3, 137, 139, 187–8, 201–3, 212, 217, 233, 235–6, 248, 257, 269, 301, 309, 312
Gibraltar, 111
Giddens, A., 118–20, 144–7, 149–58, 162, 165–6, 175–81, 184–6, 199–200, 206, 220, 231, 271, 285–7, 306, 308, 310, 311
Gittings, J., 102
global systems, 117–23; see also new world order
Glyn, A., 58–60
Goldthorpe, J. and D. Lockwood; Goldthorpe, J. *et al.*, 172–3, 311
Goodway, N., 61–4
Gough, I., 303
Gow, D., 135
Graz, L., 139–40
Greaves, H. R. G., 284
Greece, 8, 22, 26, 28–9, 32–3, 37–8, 43, 75, 129–30, 218, 233, 246, 248, 300
Gumbel, A., 126–7, 309

Halsey, A. H., 62–3, 145
Hamnet, C. *et al.*, 304
Harbury, C., and G. Hitchins, 61–2
Harrington, M., 302
Harris, C. C., 175
Harrop, J., 313
Harvie, C., 268–9
Hattersley, R., 118
health; medical, 21, 43, 53, 71, 75, 93, 118, 156–7, 194, 218, 225–6, 229, 303
Hegel, G., 149–51
Held, D.; Held, D. and Thompson, J., 144–7, 151, 153–7, 162, 165–6, 285–6, 306, 308, 310
Helgadottir, B., 42–3

Index

Helsinki Watch, 76
Henderson, R., 299
Herbert, S., 84–5
Holland, *see* Netherlands
Holman, B., 30
homosexuality, 23–8, 300
human rights, *see* new citizenship
Hungary, 26, 76, 234
Hurd, D., 50–1
Hutton, W., 213–14, 216, 265

Iceland, 75, 233
ideal type, 203–5, 215, 218, 222, 289
ideology, 2, 3, 51, 97–8, 138–40, 142, 146, 149, 172, 188, 192, 211, 297
immigrants; immigration, *see* migrants
individual; individualisation; individualism; individuality, 1–7, 31–2, 44–54, 72–3. 82–3, 97–101, 106–7, 138–86, 187–230, 266, 268, 287, 299, 306, 310, 311
industrial rights, *see* industrial citizenship
internal market, *see* Single European Act
Ireland, Republic of, 22, 25–6, 28, 32, 35, 38, 43, 70, 75, 82, 112, 202, 233, 248, 291, 293, 296, 300, 301, 311; *see also* Northern Ireland
Irwin, A., 176–7, 181, 311
Israel, 305, 306
Italy, 22, 26–7, 29, 32, 38, 43, 75, 82, 112, 116–17, 129–30, 202–3, 218, 233, 246, 248, 257, 269, 300

Japan, x, 35, 117, 187, 202, 204, 207, 217, 221, 233
Jeffries, I., 205
Jensen, A. M., 204
Jesson, B. *et al.*, 311
Johnstone Conover, P. *et al.*, 299
Jones, G. and C. Wallace, 189–92, 200
Jordan, B., 216

Kaplan, G., 315
Kelly, R., 58–9

Kingston, P., 24–7
Komatsu, R., 204
Korpi, W., 196
Kuper, A. and Kuper, J., 286
Kurth, J., 187

Laffan, B., 313
Lane, R., 174
Lansdown, G., 15–21, 299, 300
Lash, S. and Urry, J., 308
Latvia, 25, 76–8, 116, 234
law; legal systems, institutions and processes, 1–54, 55, 65–72, 78–82, 85–90, 92–3, 95, 98, 101, 103, 105–7, 109, 111–14, 124–8, 132–3, 141–3, 149–51, 154, 163–73, 188, 192, 197, 205, 214, 226, 232, 237–9, 243–52, 260–7, 272, 275–8, 284, 286–92, 295–8, 300, 304, 305, 306, 309, 310, 311, 313, 314
Leonard, D., 234
Lewis, O., 302
liberalism; liberal democracy, x, 97–8, 138–40, 142–4, 146–9, 168, 171, 174, 176, 187, 191–4, 196–206, 211, 214–16, 218–22, 257, 260, 310, 311
Liechtenstein, 26, 75, 233, 300, 313
Lieven, A., 307
Lindblom, C., 310
Lipset, S. M., 145
Lister, R., 4, 49–52, 299
Lithuania, 25, 76–9, 234
Lockwood, D., 146, 310
Loney M. *et al.*, 216
Lowe, R., 303
Luxembourg, 26–7, 29, 36, 38, 92–4, 13, 129–30, 233, 248, 301

Maastricht Treaty, *see* Treaty on European Union
Macedonia, 234
McIntosh, M., 191
McIvor, G., 134–5
Malta, 26, 75, 234
Mann, M., 99, 149–50, 286, 289, 308
Marcuand, D., 311
Marrett, M. and M. Bond, 76
Marshall, G. *et al.*, 173

Marshall, T. H., 6–7, 11, 28, 49, 55–6, 66, 108, 114–16, 141, 144–6, 148–51, 155–8, 160–3, 165–6, 168, 175, 206, 224, 271–3, 279–80, 283, 285, 299, 310, 314, 315
Marx, K.; Marxism, 150–1, 193–4
Mead, L., 49
Mediterranean Rim region, 204
men, *see* gender
Meyer, H., 125
migrants; migration; movement of people, 34, 42, 44–5, 69–74, 81–2, 86–8, 94–5, 97–137, 225, 227–30, 237–8, 246, 249, 254–5, 277–8, 290–8, 305, 309
Millar, F., 15–16
Milner, M., 235
Minshull, G. N., 233, 241, 247–8, 314
Mishra, R., 196, 216
modernity; post-modernity, 176–86, 199–200
Moldova, 76, 234
Montenegro, 234
Moore, J., 49
Morris, L. and S. Irwin, 301, 302
Mount, F., 191, 305, 306
Murray, C., 47–9, 216, 302

nation, nationalism, nationality, nation-state, x, 2–3, 8–9, 11, 25, 32–3, 39, 68–73, 75–8, 81, 85, 88–91, 94–5, 97–128, 132, 135–7, 138, 140–2, 188, 192–5, 200–1, 203–6, 214–16, 218–19, 227–30, 232, 238, 240, 242, 244–6, 252–71, 275–97, 304, 305, 306, 307, 308, 309, 310, 313, 315; *see also* national citizenship
Nereth, P. and J. Reid, 37–8
Netherlands, 22, 26–7, 32, 38, 43, 75, 129, 201–2, 233, 248, 295, 300, 301
New Right, 39, 44–54, 58–62, 66, 160–3, 174, 180–1, 189–96, 198–203, 206–8, 211, 213–14, 216–19, 221–2, 303
new world order, x, 117–24, 137, 236, 240–1
New Zealand, 109, 202, 305, 306

non-citizenship rights, 11–13, 15–22, 28, 68–9, 72, 224, 304
North American Free Trade Association (Nafta), 118 , 234–5
Northern Ireland, 15, 82, 84–8, 90–95, 97, 103–4; *see also* United Kingdom
Norway, 21, 26, 28–9, 38, 75, 135, 202, 233–5, 305

Oakley, A., 310
Organisation of Economic Cooperation and Development (OECD), 207

Pacific Rim region, 207
Padfield, C. and A. Byrne, 107, 109–10, 304, 306, 307
paid employment; paid labour, 13, 19–20, 49–54, 68, 71, 73, 75, 77–9, 93, 101, 107, 112, 138, 151, 154–6, 158–60, 165–7, 171–5, 182, 189–90, 194, 196–8, 200–3, 206–15, 217, 221–30, 300, 301, 302, 310
Palmer, J.; Palmer, J. and J. Carvel, 76, 82–4, 91–2, 210, 212, 269–70, 305, 314
Pampel, F. and J. Williamson 303
patriarchy, *see* gender
people's Europe, x, 95, 228–30, 232–3, 238–40, 242–3, 246, 249, 251–2, 254, 264, 266–7, 289–90, 294, 297–8
Pfaller, A. *et al.*, 221
Phillips, M., 47–8, 131–2, 301, 302
Pilkington, E., 25–7, 93
Poland, 26, 38, 75–6, 234
political rights, *see* political citizenship
political systems, institutions and processes, x, 1–9, 14, 19–20, 43, 46–8, 55–6, 65, 72, 77, 81, 89–92, 102, 105–6, 116–21, 126, 128, 133–4, 139–44, 147–8, 150, 152–6, 158, 160–1, 163, 172, 174–5, 180–1, 184–5, 187–90, 193–6, 205, 214–15, 217–20, 222, 224, 227, 230, 231–3, 235–6, 238–41, 246, 248–52,

256–61, 264–70, 272–5, 278–86, 290–1, 293–4, 296–7, 310, 314
Pond, C., 60–5, 304
Portugal, 26–7, 32–3, 38, 40, 75, 93–4, 129, 233, 248, 301, 308
poverty, 30–54, 58–61, 132–3, 171, 174, 222, 297, 301, 302, 303
power, 1, 4–8, 15, 17–18, 21–2, 31, 52, 55–8, 62–6, 72, 80, 84, 89–91, 93, 95, 99, 101–4, 117–18, 134, 141–4, 147–9, 152–3, 155–6, 160–1, 163, 174, 184–5, 188, 193, 200, 214–15, 224, 230, 231, 236, 238–40, 242–5, 249–51, 255–8, 260–2, 264–5, 269, 278, 280–2, 286–90, 297, 311, 313, 315
property, 4, 7, 14–15, 56–68, 77, 101, 107, 112, 144, 148–50, 159–61, 171, 192, 272, 304, 314, 315
protective rights, *see* non-citizenship rights
Protestantism, 187–8
public–private, 147–51, 154, 175, 193, 196, 198, 286

race, race-ethnicity, 9, 69–70, 75–81, 94–5, 97–137, 144, 146, 268, 270, 273, 295, 297, 307, 313; *see also* migrants
racialism; racism; *see* race
reproductive rights, 156–7
Rex, J.; Rex, J. and S. Tomlinson, 45–6
Rimlinger, G., 312
risk society, 176–86
Robertson, R.; Robertson, R. and Lechner, F., 121, 309
Roche, M., 74, 150, 267–75, 279, 283, 285, 294, 311, 312
Rogaly, J., 50
Romania, 25, 76, 90, 129–30, 234
Rose, D., 82–3, 305
Rowntree, S., 52
Russia; Russian Federation, 26, 76–81, 88, 90, 102, 116, 134, 235,

San Marino, 75
Saunders, P., 46–7
Scandinavian region, 112, 201, 208

Schengen Agreement, 291–7
Schmitter, P.; Schmitter, P. and W. Streeck, 120, 308
Scotland, 10, 14–15, 22, 25, 28–8, 111, 269; *see also* Britain; United Kingdom
Scott, J., 304
Serbia, 234
sex-gender, *see* gender
sexuality, 13–14, 21, 23–8, 68, 276, 300; *see also* homosexuality
Sharrock, D., 84–6, 90
Shaw, J., 87, 244–6, 250–1, 255–67, 277, 281, 289, 313, 314
Showstack Sassoon, A., 6
Simmel, G., 303
Simmons, M., 100
Single European Act (SEA); single internal market, 35–6, 41–2, 87–8, 95, 119, 128, 136–7, 223, 227–9, 231, 235–7, 243–9, 255, 261–2, 265, 268, 277, 279–82, 288–9, 305
Slovakia, *see* Czechoslovakia
Slovenia, 76, 234
Smart, V., 217–18, 295
Smith, C., 300
social benefits, services and welfare, 4, 6–7, 12, 15–18, 21–2, 39, 44–54, 58–9, 63, 71, 73–5, 93, 115, 118, 125, 134, 141, 154–5, 160–1, 171, 189–230, 232, 245–6, 277, 281–2, 302, 303, 304, 311, 312; *see also* social charter, social citizenship, welfare citizenship, welfare dependency, welfare state
social charter (Community Charter for Fundamental Social Rights of Workers); social chapter, 35–6, 41, 93, 195, 223–4, 225–6, 315
social class, 8, 9, 43–54, 56–8, 107, 142, 144–8, 150–8, 161, 163, 171–4, 178–85, 193–4, 197, 199, 203–4, 206, 209, 214, 220, 222, 224, 272–3, 280, 297, 307, 311
social democracy; socialism, 138–9, 146, 187–8, 192–3, 196–8, 200–6, 208–13, 215–20
social exclusion, 9, 39–54, 151, 2, 185, 223–5

social rights, *see* social citizenship
socio-christianity, 138–9, 146
sociology, xi, 1–6, 55, 69, 98–9, 104, 107–8, 114, 138–9, 226, 231–2, 270–1, 286, 305, 309, 315
sovereignty, 22, 91, 95–6, 98–9, 101, 104, 119–20, 143, 153, 205, 214, 230, 238–45, 251, 256–9, 261–2, 265–7, 269, 278, 282, 284, 286–8, 297, 310
Soviet Union, 75–7, 233, 241, 257, 291; *see also* Russia
Spain, 22, 27–8, 32–3, 35, 38, 40, 75, 112, 129, 207, 218, 233, 248, 269
Spicker, P., 303, 313
state, 1–4, 6–9, 28, 46–54, 55, 72–3, 85, 97–102, 104–7, 114–17, 120–2, 138, 141–4, 147–50, 152–6, 160–1, 163, 166, 171, 183, 187–230, 232, 238–9, 253–5, 274–5, 283–9, 297, 304, 306, 308, 310, 313
subsidiarity, 313
Summers, Y., 4, 299
supra-citizenship, x–xi, 93–6, 97–8, 104, 120–2, 136–7, 215, 255–7, 266–7, 270–1, 274–5, 277–8, 283, 289–90, 293, 297–8, 304, 305, 306, 308, 309, 315
supra-national organisations; supra-state, x–xi, 90–6, 97–8, 103–4, 117–21, 136–7, 140, 187, 195, 205–6, 216, 219–20, 222, 231–98
Swann, D., 87–8, 315
Sweden, 21, 27, 29, 37, 75, 134–5, 202, 204, 218, 233–5, 300, 305
Switzerland, 22, 27, 75, 202, 233, 301, 131

Taylor-Gooby, P., 194–8, 200, 203–6, 209, 216, 218, 219, 221, 311
Thatcher, M.; Thatcherism, 50, 88, 163, 187–8, 190, 206, 216, 302
Toffler, A. and H. Toffler, 117–18
Tomforde, A., 133
Townsend, P., 30–1, 53, 303
trade unions; trade union rights, 141, 148, 151, 154–6, 158–60, 163–75, 188, 207, 225–6, 310–11; *see also* industrial citizenship

Travis, A., 123, 133
Traynor, I., 140
Treaty on European Union (Maastricht Treaty), x, 35–6, 42, 91–5, 113, 127, 136–7, 187, 214–15, 229–30, 236–9, 241–4, 246–7, 249–50, 252–5, 258–62, 264–5, 267, 276, 278, 281, 289–90, 293, 304, 314, 315
Treaty of Rome, 87, 95, 188, 226, 228, 238, 247, 249–51, 256, 258–9, 264, 281, 287–8, 314
Turkey, 27, 70, 75–6, 112, 233–4, 294
Turner, B. S., 120–2, 137, 145, 162, 270–3, 279, 284–5, 299, 309, 315
Tyrell, H. and Langdon-Down, G., 10–12, 299

Ukraine, 25, 76–7, 79, 234
underclass, 43–54, 132, 301, 302
unemployment, 34–6, 42, 206–15, 217–18, 221–4, 229
Ungerson, C., 6
Unicef, 39, 301
Union of Soviet Socialist Republics (USSR), *see* Soviet Union
United Kingdom, 2, 11, 15, 18–23, 26–7, 32–3, 36–8, 40, 41–2, 49–50, 57–72, 75, 84–9, 90–5, 97, 104–5, 107–12, 122–3, 128–30, 163, 168–70, 202, 204–6, 208, 211–12, 215–16, 221, 223, 233–4, 246–8, 265, 277, 296, 300, 302, 305, 307, 310, 315
United Nations, 20–1, 39, 72–3, 86–9, 100, 102–3, 129, 138–40, 255, 275, 292–3, 305, 306, 307
United Nations' Conference on Human Rights (1993), 139–40
United Nations' International Court of Justice, 89, 276
United Nations' Universal Declaration of Human Rights, 72–3, 86–7, 100–4, 138–9; *see also* new citizenship
United States of America, x, 35, 39, 43–4, 47–50, 117, 187, 192, 194, 207, 216–17, 221–2, 233–4, 241, 257, 268, 302

United States of Europe, 91, 239, 257, 279
universal rights, *see* new citizenship

Valentine, C., 302
Verity, C., 77–8
Visigrad countries, 234; *see also* Czech Republic; Slovakia; Hungary; Poland
Vitaliev, V., 94
voting rights, 7, 8, 14, 20, 68, 70, 77–8, 93–5, 101, 107, 109, 113, 141, 143, 154, 171, 242, 252, 254, 272, 304; *see also* political citizenship

Walker, L., 35, 92–4, 290–1, 295
Wallace, C.; Wallace, C. and P. Abbott, 3–6, 114–17, 198, 299
Wallerstein, I., 308
Warde, A., 176, 179–86, 199, 311
Watson, R., 69–70, 76
Weber, M., 99, 286, 289, 306, 308, 309
Webster, P., 126, 133–4
welfare citizenship regimes, *see* welfare state regimes

Welfare dependency, *see* dependency
welfare rights, *see* welfare citizenship
welfare state; welfare state regimes, 4, 39, 45–7, 54, 120, 154–5, 160–1, 171–2, 188–230, 311, 312; *see also* social benefits; social charter
West Germany, *see* Germany
Westergaard, J., 173
Weston, C., 36
White, M.; White, M. and K. Harper, 59, 211
Wickham, G., 3
Williams, A., 279–82, 315
Williams, F., 6
Wintour, P., 302–3
Wistrich, E., 91, 279
women, *see* gender
Wroe, M., 300

Yugoslavia, 70, 75, 116, 129–30, 134, 234, 257

xenophobia, 69–70, 132–7

Zaretsky, E., 310

GPSR Compliance
The European Union's (EU) General Product Safety Regulation (GPSR) is a set of rules that requires consumer products to be safe and our obligations to ensure this.

If you have any concerns about our products, you can contact us on

ProductSafety@springernature.com

In case Publisher is established outside the EU, the EU authorized representative is:

Springer Nature Customer Service Center GmbH
Europaplatz 3
69115 Heidelberg, Germany

www.ingramcontent.com/pod-product-compliance
Ingram Content Group UK Ltd.
Pitfield, Milton Keynes, MK11 3LW, UK
UKHW041415180426
11947UKWH00007B/151